W9-DDA-830

Backroad Mapbooks

Kootenays BC

Table of Contents

www.backroadmapbooks.com

Backroad Mapbooks

DIRECTORS
Russell Mussio
Wesley Mussio
Penny Stainton-Mussio

VICE PRESIDENT
Chris Taylor

COVER DESIGN & LAYOUT
Farnaz Faghihi

COVER PHOTO
"Meadow Mountain north of Kootenay Lake"
by Dennis Dunn

PRODUCTION MANAGER
Brett Firth

PRODUCTION
Andrew Allen
Shaan Desai
Farnaz Faghihi
Colin Holdener
Jason Marleau
Grace Teo
Dale Tober

SALES /MARKETING
Jason Marleau
Chris Taylor

WRITERS
Russell Mussio
Wesley Mussio
Trent Ernst

National Library of Canada Cataloguing in Publication Data

Mussio, Russell, 1969-

Mussio Ventures presents Backroad mapbook with relief maps.

Prepared by Russell Mussio, Wesley Mussio and Trent Ernst.

Cover title.

Includes indexes.

Contents: v. 1. Southwestern B.C. – v. 3. Kamloops/Okanagan – v. 4. Kootenays – v. 7. Chilcotin

ISBN 1-894556-20-8 (v. 1).—ISBN 1-894556-21-6 (v. 3). —ISBN 1-894556-27-5 (v. 4).—ISBN 1-894556-19-4 (v. 7)

1. Recreation areas--British Columbia--Maps. 2. British Columbia--Maps. I. Mussio, Wesley, 1964- II. Ernst, Trent III. Title. IV. Title: Backroad mapbook.

G1170.B23 2003   912.711   C2003-900142-3

Published by:

Backroad Mapbooks

5811 Beresford Street
Burnaby, BC, V5J 1K1, Canada
P. (604) 438-3474   F. (604) 438-3470
E-mail: info@backroadmapbooks.com
www.backroadmapbooks.com
Copyright © 2004 Mussio Ventures Ltd.
Updated 2005

Acknowledgements

This book could not have been compiled without the help of a tremendous team of individuals working for Mussio Ventures Ltd. This is a hat's off to Trent Ernst for digging up countless new recreational opportunities. To Jason Marleau and his first hand knowledge of the Kootenays and to Stuart Kenn the man behind the relief cartography. Combined with the talented people at Mussio Ventures Ltd., Andrew Allen, Shawn Caswell, Shaan Desai, Farnaz Faghihi, Brett Firth, Chris Taylor, Grace Teo, Dale Tober , we were able to produce the most comprehensive guidebook for our home away from home, the Kootenays!

In our efforts to update this book we have come across a number of people who have contributed invaluable knowledge. Our father, Sergio Mussio, has been keeping his eyes and ears peeled for new information. Stacy Donald and Lance Mitchell who helped us explore the West Kootenays over the years. A big thank you to Kim Kratky from the Kootenay Mountaineering Club who went over our maps and trails with a fine toothcomb. Our book is much better for it. Walter Volovsek from Friends of Trails also provided a lot of information about trails in the Castlegar area. And he should know about trails in the Castlegar area. He built, or helped build, many of them. Irene Teske and Larry Wells helped out with the Wildlife Watch Section, and Peter Frew, Dan Reibin, Neil Shuttleworth and Marylou Nesbitt helped us sort through the confusion that still surrounds the Forestry Service Recreational Site program. We spoke to a number of snowmobile associations who confirmed or updated our information. People like Mike Bobak at the Elkford Snowmobile Association and Dwayne Paynton with the Slocan Valley Snowmobile Association. Our book also represents the growing ATV crowd thanks to people like Ron LaRoy with the Revelstoke ATV Club.

We would like to express our gratitude to the helpful map providers such as Walter Hayashi of the former Boundary Forest District, Valerie Beard at the Columbia Forest District, Richard Logan with the Kootenay Lake Forest District as well as Steve Wood with the Arrow Forest District. Thank you also to all the people who sent us emails to tell us updated information on their favourite areas, be it road deactivations, new trails, or species of fish that can't be found in certain lakes. We could not have done this without you all, and your help is appreciated. And to all of you who we may have forgotten to mention, but who have provided input into making this the best mapbook on the market, we are grateful for your help and support.

Finally we would like to thank Allison, Devon, Jasper, Nancy, Madison and Penny Mussio for their continued support of the Backroad Mapbook Series. As our family grows, it is becoming more and more challenging to break away from it all to explore our beautiful country.

Sincerely,

Russell & Wesley Mussio

Help Us Help You

A comprehensive resource such as **Backroad Mapbooks** for Kootenays could not be put together without a great deal of help and support. Despite our best efforts to ensure that everything is accurate, errors do occur. If you see any errors or omissions, please continue to let us know.

Please contact us at:
Mussio Ventures Ltd.
5811 Beresford St
Burnaby, B.C. V5J 1K1

Email: updates@backroadmapbooks.com

Call (604) 438-3474 or toll free 1-877-520-5670
Fax 1-604-438-3470

Disclaimer

Distributed by **Gordon Soules Book Publishers Ltd.**
1359 Ambleside Lane, West Vancouver, BC Canada V7T 2Y9
PMB 620, 1916 Pike Place #12, Seattle, WA 98101-1097, US
Web site: www.gordonsoules.com E-mail: books@gordonsoules.com
604-922-6588 Fax: 604-688-5442

Backroad Mapbooks

Kootenays Mapkey

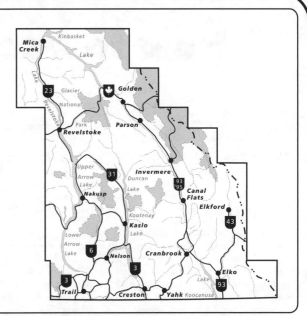

Welcome to t h e third edition of the Backroad Mapbook for the Kootenays.Found in the Southeastern corner of British Columbia, this is a beautiful area that is dominated by spectacular mountain peaks and broad valleys that are home to large rivers and even bigger lakes. Mountain parks, natural hot springs, world-class snowmobiling, cascading waterfalls, and great fishing are a few of the highlights of the area.

The Backroad Mapbooks have had a history of doing substantial changes and updates to the book and we are very confident you will be astounded by the improvements found within this book. The first part of the book is devoted solely to the reference section. It is easy to see that this section has been expanded. People will find more lakes and streams to fish, more parks to visit, more areas to paddle and even places to look for wildlife.

Despite the additions to the writing, followers of the Backroad Mapbooks will be more impressed with the new look maps. The first thing that will jump out at you is the relief shading. This amazing feature will help people understand the dramatic topography found in Southeastern BC. Another prominent feature is the clarification of paved roads. Now people with RV's and cars will know which roads they will find much smoother to travel on. We have also spent countless hours updating the road and trail systems as well as adding new recreational features such as new provincial parks and wildlife viewing areas.

In the Kootenay edition of the Backroad Mapbook Series we cover a large portion of southeastern BC. Geographically, it is an area that stretches from Christina Lake and Revelstoke in the west to the Flathead and the Alberta border in the east and from the USA border in the south to Kinbasket Lake in the north. The bigger cities include Castlegar, Cranbrook, Golden, Nelson, Revelstoke and of course Trail, which is the birthplace of the authors Wesley and Russell Mussio. Within these boundaries it is easy to see why the Kootenays will always remain dear to the hearts of the authors and people who visit this gorgeous area.

The Backroad Mapbook is much more than a set of maps. It is an explorer's guide. The maps and writing will let you dream of places not so far away. So sit back and enjoy what we have to offer.

How to Use this Mapbook

The Backroad Mapbook is a truly unique product. No other source covers Kootenays BC with as much detail for information on outdoor recreation activities as this book.

The mapbook is simple to use. There are two main sections in the book, a reference section and the maps. If you know the activity you are planning, you simply turn to that section and find the activity you are interested in. We cover a broad range of outdoor activities that can be enjoyed year round when spending time outdoors.

Reference Section Features
The writing found in the guide includes information on lake and stream fishing, paddling routes, parks and conservation areas, multi-use trails (hiking/biking, and ATV trails) and winter recreation. Countless hours have been spent in researching this book, making it the most complete compilation of outdoor recreation information you will find on the region anywhere. This information can be enjoyed by anyone who spends time in the great outdoors.

Index and Map Key
If you are planning a trip to a specific area or site, you should consult the **index** at the back of the book to find the appropriate reference page or map. You can also use the **map key** to find a general area you want to explore. Individual write-ups on paddling routes, parks, trails, etc. can be found through the index or by searching the appropriate reference section. Please note that National Park fishing and trail information have been grouped together separately from other listings in those sections.

Map Features
Looking at our maps you will notice they highlight all sorts of recreational opportunities as well as the backroad/logging road and trail systems in the area.

Recreational Features
You will find the maps mark points of interest, paddling routes, parks and conservation areas, trail systems and even wildlife viewing opportunities. Both **snowmobile trails** and **long distance trails** are highlighted with a background colour to aid users in tracking these systems. Hunters and anglers will also be happy to see that we have included the **Management Units** on the maps. The big green number notes the zones while the boundaries are marked with a faint green border.

Road Features & Map Legend
By combining city and rural roads with current forestry and logging road maps our maps are designed for people wishing to get outdoors. However, they very detailed and the myriad of logging roads in addition to the various trail systems can be confusing. We provide a **map legend** at the start of each section of the maps to illustrate the region we cover as well as how to decipher the various grades of roads and symbols used on the maps.

UTM Grids & Longitude and Latitude
Another interesting feature on our maps is the small numbers provided around our map borders. The blue numbers and thin blue line represent UTM Grids (datum NAD 1983; projection Transverse Mercator), while the black numbers represent Longitude and Latitude reference points. Although both can be used by GPS users, the UTM Grids are more accurate for land-based travel. We must emphasize that these are for reference only. This generality is because of the scale of the maps and we have to consult several different sources to create the maps.

Area Covered
The Kootenays BC mapbook has been laid out in a manner most accessible to the average user. All maps run north to south parallel to the side borders and east to west parallel to the top and bottom borders. The maps start at the southwest corner of the region and end at the northeast corner. The scale of this mapbook is 1:200 000, this means that 1 centimetre is equal to 2 kilometres. Each page represents approximately 38 kilometres east to west and 50 kilometres north to south for a total area of 1,900 km².

Special Note On Backroad Travel
Generally, Kootenays BC has a sparse, but established secondary road system that provides access to many outdoor activities. With such a vast area of pristine wilderness, most of the region is not accessible by vehicle. Of the roads that do lead to desired destinations, some farming and logging roads are restricted to public access. Be sure to pay attention to road signs and please do not trespass. The roads marked by thinner black lines and the deactivated roads/trails shown by thin dashed lines on our maps can be explored by off-highway enthusiasts (4x4 and ATV's) as well as trail users. However, people who do venture off the main roads should have good navigational skills and a way to track where they came from.

Updates
Although the Backroad Mapbook Series is the most detailed and up-to-date resource available for backcountry travel, it must be noted that it is only a planning and access guide. We have gone to great lengths to ensure the accuracy of this book. However, over time, the road and trail conditions change. If you do notice a discrepancy, please let us know by calling 1-877-520-5670 or emailing us at updates@backroadmapbooks.com. All updates are posted on our website under the individual book page information.

If you are a GPS user, we welcome you to submit us your tracks and waypoints. These tracks will be used to help put together a Digital Edition of the maps in this book. Finally, backcountry travellers will have a reliable and up to date map set to use in association with a GPS unit.

We invite you to let us help you explore this vast area of British Columbia. But we ask that you go prepared to deal with emergencies and always respect private property.

Russell and Wesley Mussio: Founders of Backroad Mapbook Series

Backroad Attractions
(Hot Springs)

While hot springs are sparse across most of the province, the Kootenays are blessed with numerous hot springs ranging from commercial sites to undeveloped backcountry pools. The commercial springs are a great way to sample hot mineral pools in a luxurious setting. Ainsworth Hot Springs is probably the most interesting to explore as it has a horseshoe shaped cave in which to soak. Other commercial springs are Fairmont (Canada's largest odourless mineral pools), Canyon, Halcyon (a rediscovered hot spring from the gold rush era), Nakusp and Radium Hot Springs.

Our descriptions concentrate on the backcountry hot springs. These pools are often difficult to find and very rustic in nature. The remote setting and the free admission is our favourite part about exploring natural hot springs.

Remember that au natural individuals often visit natural hot springs. Because these hot springs are not commercialized, anything goes, and one of the first things to go is clothing. We're not complaining, mind you, just giving you fair warning. Hot springs etiquette dictates that, if there are naked people there before you, don't stare or glare. You knew the risks before heading out. Likewise, if there are folks with suits on, courtesy dictates that you ask if it is okay before jumping in starkers.

Some natural hot springs have suffered from abuse at the hands of stupid people. Broken bottles, garbage, and other crap can make the experience less-than-pleasant. (Sometimes literally crap). Elsewhere in the province, hot springs have been shut down because of high fecal coliform count in the water. If you gotta go, go elsewhere. We recommend reading How to Shit in the Woods to learn the proper protocol.

Last but not least, remember: a hot spring is not a bathtub. Don't lather up with soap or shampoo in the spring. It's offensive, unsanitary, disrespectful, and it could get you in trouble.

Buhl Creek Hot Springs (Map 20/B7)
These small, creek side hot springs are found off the Skookumchuck Road, near the confluence of Buhl Creek and Skookumchuck Creek. The springs are best in late summer or fall as the pools are flooded by the creek in spring run-off and are too cool to soak in. The water temperature is 40°C (104°F) and the area is relatively undeveloped with only boulder edged pools.

Dewar Creek Hot Springs (Map 19/D7)
The Dewar Creek Hot Springs can be visited year round and are one of the largest in BC. To find the hot springs, drive to the end of the Dewar Creek Road and hike the Dewar Creek Trail about 9 km (5.4 miles/3 hours) one-way. The area is undeveloped and found in the sub-alpine west of St. Mary's Alpine Park. The springs are truly spectacular, cascading over a large bedrock area towards the creek below. The main bathing pools are built out of rocks with some piping and plastic sheets.

Halfway River Hot Springs (Map 24/B6)
Driving up the Halfway River Road and taking a left at the 11 km sign reach these hot springs. Follow this old road 70 m (300 feet) to the parking area. From there, a well-developed trail leads steeply downhill to the springs located in a forested setting near the river. The main pool is a wooden structure about 2 m (6 feet) wide and 1 m (3 feet) deep. There is also a smaller wooden pool next to the main pool and another pool next to the river. The later pool is very hot and is lined with plastic and boulders. The Upper Halfway River Hot Springs are found further up the valley and are undeveloped and seldom visited, as the water temperature is only 28°C (82°F).

Lussier Hot Springs (Map 21/A4)
Located in Whiteswan Lake Provincial Park, these popular hot springs are accessed off the Whiteswan Lake Road. There is a main soaking pool made of wood as well as several creek side soaking pools made out of boulders. A wooden stairway leads down to the springs from the road offering easy access to the area. On the weekends in the summer, the hot springs are very busy. During spring run-off, the water temperature of the pools is reduced dramatically from its normal 44°C (111°F) making them too cool to soak in.

Octopus Creek Hot Springs (Map 9/F3)
This secluded, hot spring is found on the western slopes of the Lower Arrow Lake and is not considered one of the better hot springs to visit. To reach the site, hike to the end of the old road north of Octopus Creek (allow about an hour). From the end of the road, you must bushwhack up the creek draw for another hour. Keep your eyes open for a pool dug out of gravel and lined with boulders. The hot springs are difficult to find and see few visitors.

Ram Creek Hot Springs (Map 21/A5)
The Ram Creek Hot Springs are not very popular because they are a cooler 37°C (99°F) and a long drive from the highway. They are located south of Lussier Hot Springs on the Ram Creek Road. The two main pools are damned by boulders and are set on the edge of an open hillside. Although the hot springs are an easy walk from the road, the hill is covered with poison ivy. Please be careful not to rub against this pretty plant. There is room in the pools to hold up to 20 people.

St. Leon Hot Springs (Map 24/A7)
Unfortunately, this natural hot spring has been closed to the public due to excessive garbage. The access road is gated and the pools have been covered. Please help keep British Columbia beautiful and pack out any garbage you come across.

Freshwater Fishing

(Lake, River and Stream Fishing)

Anglers come from around the globe to experience the world-class fishing that the Kootenays have to offer. The region is home to the legendary Gerrard Rainbow Trout and is known for it's superb fishing, spectacular scenery and abundance of wildlife. Despite the good fishing, it is not hard to find yourself a secluded spot to soak in the natural beauty of the area. The many mountain lakes and remote streams are teeming with trout, landlocked sockeye salmon or kokanee are common in the large lakes and the warm water lakes offer some of the best bass fishing in the province.

In the following section we have provided the most comprehensive listing of lakes and streams of the Kootenay area available anywhere. We have also included a few helpful tips to help you catch the many different sportfish available. Whether you are looking to land a trophy trout or you are just looking for a place to lay your line in peace and solitude, the Kootenays has it all.

Please note that we have listed the National Parks Lakes under a separate section. This is because fishing in National Parks is a different beast than fishing elsewhere in the province. The regulations governing fishing in National Parks are different, the lakes are not stocked, meaning that all the fish you'll find in the parks are native, and you'll need a special license to fish there. Check with Parks Canada for more information. Regulations can be downloaded from **www.parkscanada.gc.ca**. The fish symbol beside the lake name indicates that the lake is included in the **FISHING BC: Kootenays** book.

Lake Fishing

Most lake write-ups include a reference to the size of the lake and the elevation. As a general rule, the smaller the lake, the smaller the fish. Elevation is important to note, as ice melts off lower lakes sooner than high elevation lakes. In the summer however, the high elevation lakes remain cool, while the lower elevations warm up, making the fish lethargic, and fairly unresponsive to lures. They also tend to stay in deeper water, making them harder to find, especially for shoreline anglers. We have occasionally made reference to the depth of a lake, which affects things like winterkill, water temperature, and where the fish will congregate. For more detailed information, depth charts, recent stocking information and specific hints and tips to over 100 of the best lakes in the region, be sure to pick up a copy of our **Fishing BC: Kootenays** book.

Aid Lake (Map 37/G1)

This small (13.2 hectare) lake is found north of Golden, alongside the Bush River FSR. It offers some good fishing, at times, for small rainbow and cutthroat. The lake is found at (956 metres/3,107 feet) and offers a place to launch small boats. In cooler weather, you can catch fish most anywhere, but in the heart of summer, they tend to congregate in the southern portion of the lake, which is deeper than the north. The lake is stocked annually with 1,500 rainbow, and is subject to winterkill.

Alces (Moose) Lake (Map 21/B4)

Found in Whiteswan Provincial Park, this is an artificial fly fishing only lake. The lake is often overlooked, due to its proximity to the much more popular Whiteswan Lake, but rainbow to 5 kg (10 lbs) are sometimes found here, although the average size is 30–35 cm (12–14 inches). The best time to fish the 30.1 hectare lake (found at 1,201m/3,903 feet) is in the early spring or late fall. Fishing is closed from December 1 to April 30. Try trolling a wet fly along the drop-off or cast a dry fly into the shallows for best results. There is a boat launch at the lake but note that there is an electric motor only restriction. The lake is stocked annually with 2,000 rainbow.

Aosta Lakes, Upper and Lower (Map 29A A/5)

The Aosta Lakes are a pair of very small lakes found near Upper Elk Lake. Access to these lakes is along the Carol Pass Route in Elk Lakes Provincial Park. Both lakes are small, totaling less than 10 hectares combined, and both are high elevation lakes (over 1,700 m/5,525 feet). This means that the fishing season is short, but the stocked cutthroat will voraciously attack anything that looks edible.

Arkansas Lake (Map 3/E5)

Off the rough Bayonne Road, Arkansas Lake has cutthroat to 30 cm (12 inches). Good fishing is offered even in the summer. There is a large forest service site with deteriorating picnic tables and an outhouse on the lake. The road in is rough, and doubly so when wet.

Armstrong Lake (Map 24/C2)

This shallow little (18 hectare) lake located off Highway 31 offers good fly fishing for small bull and brook trout. There is a rustic campground and boat launch available. The lake is 686m (2,230 feet) above sea level.

Arrow Lake, Lower (Maps 1–2, 9, 16–17)

This man-made lake on the Columbia River stretches from the Hugh Keenlyside Dam west of Castlegar to the narrows near East Arrow Park south of Nakusp, where it turns into the Upper Arrow Lake. Both lakes are quite similar. They are both narrow, low elevation (477 m/1,388 feet) lakes, are subject to significant drawdown in the summer months, have lots of debris and can get quite windy. The Lower Arrow Lake covers 20,032 hectares and is less developed with only a few access points. It does offer some beautiful boat access forest service sites. Over the last decade, fishing has improved dramatically thanks to extensive rainbow and bull trout stocking. There are now plenty of trout, whitefish and burbot. Gerrard trout were stocked in the lake and are now growing up to (and over) 8 kg (20 lbs). The most productive method of fishing for trout is a fast troll at 12–30 m (40–100 feet). Any plug that looks like a minnow or even a silver or bronze coloured wobbler stands a good chance of success, particularly in the early spring or late fall. Kokanee can be caught by slowly trolling until early September, when the larger fish begin spawning in the creeks. The kokanee tend to be quite small with the larger ones growing to 30 cm (12 inches) in size.

Arrow Lake, Upper (Maps 17, 23, 30)

This man-made lake on the Columbia River is a continuation of Lower Arrow Lake. It starts at the narrows near East Arrow Park, south of Nakusp, and stretches north to Revelstoke. There is highway access along its entire length, and several resorts, campsites and boat launches to choose from. Fishing here is similar to that in the Lower Lake (see above). One of the best stretches for fishing on the lake is between Nakusp and Shelter Bay.

Baird Lake (Map 32/B2)

This small lake is found off of the Spillimacheen FSR, west of Parson. It's a long, rough drive to the lake, with the last section recommended for 4wd vehicles only. The lake is home to a healthy population of trout, most of which are small. The larger trout are best found at the southeast corner of the lake (where the lake is deepest) by fly fishing or spincasting. This is a high elevation lake (1,509m/4,904 feet), and fishing remains good throughout the ice-free season.

Baker Lake (Map 12/B7)

It is a long hike or drive and hike into Baker Lake, but when you get there you will be rewarded with good fishing for small rainbow and bull trout to 1 kg (2 lbs) using most mountain lake fishing methods. There is also a small population of stocked cutthroat in the lake.

Barbour Lake (Map 27/A6)

This small lake offers good fishing for brook trout (average 20–25 cm) since the access to the lake is limited by private property.

Barrett Lake (Map 2/G2)

Located off an old deteriorating mining road/trail west of Porto Rico, this lake offers fairly good fishing for small rainbow. The lake is stocked every even year.

Baynes Lake (Map 6/G4)

Baynes Lake is stocked annually with rainbow, which can grow up to 1 kg (2 lbs). In addition to the rainbow, eastern brook trout and largemouth bass are found in this 28.2 hectare lake lower elevation lake. Try trolling a Willow Leaf and worm, or spincasting the weeds with a top plug, plastic worm, spoon or spinner. Fly fishermen should try an attractor type pattern such as a leech or Woolly Bugger for both the brook trout and bass. There is an electric motor only restriction.

Bayonne Lake (Map 3/D5)
Located right next to the rough Bayonne Road (4wd recommended), the lake has small but plentiful cutthroat. There is a rustic trail that anglers have made to access the lake.

Bear Lake (Map 2/C5)
This lake is one of those secret fishing holes that few people are willing to talk about. It is found 12 km along the Bear Creek FSR along a rough side road that becomes overgrown. This small, marshy lake can yield stocked brook trout up to 1.5 kg (3 lbs) on a fly in the spring or fall. A floatation device will help to get away from the weedy shoreline.

Bear Lake (Map 18/C6)
Off Highway 31A near New Denver, this small lake can be fairly good for small rainbow in the spring. Found at an elevation of 1,067 m (3,500 feet), beneath the alpine peaks of Goat Range Provincial Park, this lake is a fantastic place to spend the afternoon. The lake is small (10.8 hectares), but deep (up to 8 m/26 feet), and fishing remains good year round. The best time to go is during the big caddis fly hatch in spring. The lake is stocked annually with rainbow and ice fishing is popular in winter.

Bear Lake (Map 23/E7)
Of all the Bear Lakes, this is the most difficult to get to. The small (11 hectare) lake requires a 4 km hike off a logging road leading to the base of Mount Baldur. The lake has a good population of rainbow trout, which come readily to a fly, spinners or bait. Dry flies presented from a float tube are very productive.

Beatrice Lake (Map 10/D1)
Located in the heart of Valhalla Provincial Park, this gorgeous mountain lake is accessed by a 12 km (7.2 mile) trail from Slocan Lake. It is a deep (up to 95 metres/310 feet) high elevation (1,448 m/4,751 feet) lake that sees very little fishing pressure. As a result, angling is quite good for smaller trout, although the bigger fish (up to 2 kg/4 lbs) are harder to catch.

Beaver Lake (Map 17/F3)
Found along the East Wilson Creek Road, this small (11.2 hectare) lake offers some good fishing for small kokanee and stocked rainbow. A lucky few have been known to catch one of the lakes few bull trout to 2 kg (4 lbs). Fly fishers should try matching the spring chironomid hatch. Fishing slows down in the heart of summer in this mid elevation (957 m/3,110 feet) lake.

Bednorski Lake (Map 6/B1)
Found on the Ha Ha Creek Road, this tiny (9.6 hectare) lake offers fair fishing for eastern brook trout by spincasting or bait fishing. The lake is stocked with brook trout annually.

Ben Abel Lake (Map 19/G1)
Located in the heart of the Purcell Wilderness Conservancy (East) Provincial Park, this small (18.2 hectare) high elevation lake is stocked every couple years with cutthroat. This is a gorgeous wilderness destination with good fishing, but few anglers make the long trek in. Watch out for bears.

Bergilen (Parachute) Lake (Map 12/D2)
This walk-in lake off St Mary's-White FSR offers cutthroat to 1 kg (2 lbs) and bull trout to 4 kg (9 lbs).

Big Fish Lake (Map 26/F1)
There are a fair number of picky cutthroat in this 21.2 hectare lake, but folks return again and again, as the fussy fish grow up to 2.5 kg (5.5 lbs). This lake is best fished by boat or off the dam below the lake inlet. There is a powerboat restriction (less than 10 hp) on the scenic lake that is 1,087 m (3,533 feet) above sea level.

Bittern Lake (Map 33/C5)
Bittern Lake looks like a big, deep lake, but much of it is less than 2 m (6 feet) deep. There are a pair of holes, including one 12 m (39 feet) deep just out from the forest service site that people in boats or float tubes can work. The 19.5 hectare lake is located south of the small town of Parson, and is 1,087 m (3,533 feet) above sea level. Bittern offers decent fishing for rainbow as it is stocked with rainbow annually.

Blackwater Lake (Map 37/G2)
This small (19.2 hectare) lake is long and narrow, and runs generally north and south. It is paralleled on both sides by roads. The best access onto the lake is from the Blackwater Lake Recreation Site, which in turn is found off the Bush River FSR. The lake offers some good fishing for small, but feisty rainbow (which are stocked annually) and cutthroat. The best place to try your luck is near the drop-offs in the middle of the lake. Try anytime from ice break-up (May) to September-October.

Blue Lake (Map 20/C3)
Accessed off the Whitetail Lake Road, this tiny (2 hectare) lake offers small rainbow (average 25–35 cm/10–14 inches) on a fly, bait or by trolling.

Botts Lake (Map 26/F1)
This lake contains a fair number of cutthroat to 1 kg (2 lbs) with the average size being 20–35 cm. Spincasting or fly fishing from a boat is your best bet due to the heavy reed cover near the shore. A forest service site is on the lake and there is an electric motor only restriction. The lake is 1,097 m (3,565 feet) above sea level.

Boulder Lake (Map 4/C3)
A fire in 2003 has affected the cutthroat population in this small mountain lake. Luckily the lake is part of a stocking program and small trout will be ready for the taking again in 2004. The lake is 1,219 m (3,962 feet) above sea level.

Boundary Lake (Map 3/F7)
This is a high elevation (1,219m/3,999 feet) lake located on the sometimes rough logging road. Ice doesn't usually leave the 28.1 hectare lake until June, after which the lake offers fly fishing and trolling (no powerboats) for cutthroat and stocked rainbow averaging 30 cm (12 inches). There are also a few bull trout and brook trout. A forestry forest service site is found on the north side of the lake and shore fishing is possible from there. Getting off shore and casting towards the drop-off works even better.

Box Lake (Map 17/B2)
One of the best small Kootenay Lakes (it covers 70.8 hectares) is found right next to Highway 6, near Nakusp. This lake can produce non-stop action throughout the ice-free season, which can start as early as mid-March due to its low elevation (305 m/991 feet). The best place for brook trout, which average 20–30 cm (8–12 inches), is the southeast side of the lake near the weed beds. The fatter rainbow are usually found further away from the weeds. Use chironomids in the spring, while trolling works best in the summer. The popular forest service site has a small dock and a primitive boat launch. An electric motor only restriction applies. The lake is stocked annually with rainbow.

Bridal Lake (Map 3/C7)
At 1,774 m (5,820 ft), the Kootenay Summit is the highest highway pass in the country. Resting on the summit is a lovely roadside lake with good shore access. Evening fishing is particularly good between June 15 and August 15. The lake is stocked annually with rainbow to help alleviate some of the heavy fishing pressure it gets. No powerboats are allowed.

Bronze (Weatherhead) Lake (Map 6/D1)
A tiny (6.1 hectare) lake located east of where the Kootenay River becomes Lake Koocanusa, Bronze Lake is stocked annually with brook trout. It is found off the Pickering Hills Road, which is designated as part of the Trans Canada Trail. The lake is 930 m (3,023 feet) above sea level.

Burton Lake (Map 6/G2)
This tiny (2 hectare) lake, just northwest of Elko is actually pretty deep, with a maximum depth of 14.9 m (48 feet). The popular ice fishing lake is stocked annually with brook trout.

Cadorna Lake (Map 29A/A6)
A beautiful, remote 13.7 hectare lake found in the Elk Lakes Provincial Park, Cadorna offers good fishing for cutthroat that average 25–35 cm (10–14 inches). Because of its remoteness, the lake sees little fishing pressure. Shore fishing produces well, which is good, because hauling in a float tube along the 15 km (9.3 mile), rugged trail is difficult, to say the least. Spring is the best time to fish here, especially during the chironomid hatches, but the ice stays pretty late on the high elevation (1,905 m/6,191 ft) lake.

Cahill Lake (Map 10/E1)
Found along the Beatrice Lake Trail in Valhalla Provincial Park, this mountain lake makes a fine camping destination with some good fly fishing and spincasting. The small rainbow and kokanee are best caught in the early summer at this 72.1 hectare, high elevation (1,234m/ 4,010 feet) lake.

Cameron Lake (Map 16/G1)◁
In the past, Cameron was stocked with brook trout (which now grow up to 1 kg/2 lbs). More recently, the lake is stocked with rainbow, which can reach some nice sizes (up to 2 kg/4.5 lbs). The 35.4 hectare lake is found in the hills west of Upper Arrow Lake, at 1,000 m (3,250 feet) in elevation. There is a forest service site and cartop boat launch at the lake.

Campbell Lake (Map 13/A5)
Campbell Lake is not a big lake, at 5.6 hectares, but it offers fair fishing for stocked rainbow. The marshy low elevation lake also contains brook trout, which are best caught in the early spring or fall. The lake is right beside Highway 93/95 (there is a rest area on the shores of the lake), just north of Fort Steele.

Canuck & Yankee Lakes (Map 21/A7)
From the campground on Premier Lake, a one hour one-way trail leads to Yankee and Canuck Lakes. Both lakes contain good numbers of rainbow trout, due to an annual stocking program. Fishing from a flotation device in the spring or fall is your best bet. The lakes are found around the 860 m (2,795 ft) elevation level.

Canyon Lake (Map 32/F1)
Accessed off 12 Mile Forest Service Road, there is a short hike into this 5 hectare lake. In addition to the odd cutthroat to 2 kg (4 lbs), the lake is stocked annually with rainbow.

Caribou Lakes (North and South) (Map 16/F3)
These lakes, totaling 22.5 hectares in size, offer good small rainbow fishing caught primarily on the fly. The lakes are stocked annually. There is a forest service site with a cartop boat launch for electric motor only boats.

Cartwright Lake (Map 26/E1)◁
Stocked annually with rainbow, this 42.7 hectare lake is the largest of the lakes in the area. The clear lake can offer good fishing for rainbow to 35 cm (14 in). Try trolling a wet fly along the drop-off or cast a dry fly into the

shallows. There is a popular forest service site at the lake as well as a powerboat restriction (less than 10 hp). The lake is 1,189 m (3,864 feet) above sea level.

Catherine Lake (Map 23/G7)
The often-rough Shelter Bay FSR provides fair access to 29 hectare Catherine Lake. The deep lake (42 m/137 feet) contains good numbers of stocked rainbow that can grow to 2 kg (4.5 lbs). Fly fishing (a black ant pattern or pheasant-tail nymphs) is the preferred method throughout the ice-free season, which lasts from April to November. The lake does not receive a great deal of pressure and is 866 m (2,815 feet) above sea level.

Cat's Eye Lake (Map 14/A1)
Cat's Eye Lake is reached by an easy, 15 minute (one-way) walk from the campground on Premier Lake. It offers good fishing for stocked rainbow trout primarily by fly fishing or spincasting.

Cedar Lake (Map 32/E1)◁
Cedar Lake covers only 5.1 hectares, but is 25 m (81 feet) deep. You may have to fish deeper than you would expect to find some of the stocked rainbow. The lake is found just outside of Golden, and sees heavy pressure, but still offers fair fishing for rainbow and cutthroat to 1 kg (2 lbs). There is a cartop boat launch, beach and forest service site at the lake, which is 1,018 m (3,308 feet) above sea level. A powerboat restriction applies.

Centaur Lakes (Map 20/E4)
Located on the bench south of Columbia Lake, these three small lakes offer slow fishing for a small population of brook trout. The trout are stocked on occasion and rumoured to reach 40 cm (15 inches) in size.

Cerulean Lake (Map 29B/A2)
A spectacular setting and big fish makes the long, tough 20 km (12 mile) hike in worth it. The high elevation (2,213 m/7,192 foot), 25.3 hectare lake is catch and release only. You will find cutthroat and rainbow up to 2.5 kg (6 lbs) with some as large as 7 kg (15 lbs). Shore fishing is tough so you should use a flootation device to cast towards the drop-off and shallows.

Chain Lake (Map 6/E4)
Situated an even kilometre above sea level (3,280 feet), this 12.4 hectare lake is located west of Lake Koocanusa, just off the Caven Creek Road. The shallow lake is occasionally stocked with brook trout.

Champion Lakes (Map 2/C5)○
This trio of lakes are called, originally enough, first, second and third Champion Lakes. You will reach the lakes in reverse order coming into the park from Highway 3B. The third lake offers the slowest fishing of the three, and sees heavy pressure, as there is a popular campground and beach area on the lake. Fishing is marginal for pan sized, stocked trout. The Second Lake receives slightly less pressure than the third lake. It is also stocked annually with rainbow that can get to 1.5 kg (3 lbs). Angling can be spotty, especially in the summer. The first lake offers the best fishing. Much of that is owing to the fact that the lake is only accessible by a trail. It too is stocked annually. The best place to focus your effort is near the south end using a fly. There are powerboat restrictions on all lakes, catch and release restrictions on the first and second lake, and ice fishing is only allowed on the third lake. The lakes are all around 1,050 metres (3,412 feet) in elevation and should be ice-free in May.

Cherry Lake (Map 6/B5)◁
While this isn't a really high elevation lake (it is 1,227 m/4,026 feet above sea level), the mountainous terrain keeps the lake from getting hot in the summer. The fishing remains good throughout the ice-free season and the 38.4 hectare lake holds a good number of small rainbow and cutthroat (average 20–30 cm/10–12 inches). There is a forest service site and boat launch at the east end of the lake.

Christina Lake (Map 1/A6)
On Highway 3, east of Grand Forks, this large (2,509 hectare) recreation lake is very popular for water sports given its warm waters. (The lake is only 450 m/1463 feet above sea level.) Trolling for large rainbow to 9 kg (20 lbs), small kokanee and whitefish can be productive particularly in the spring or fall. Spincasting or fly fishing for smallmouth bass and rainbow in the shallow bays and at the creek mouths, especially at the north end of the lake

is excellent. The southern end of the lake is well developed and has several resorts and campgrounds to accommodate visitors.

Clanwilliam Lake (Map 30/A5)

Clanwilliam Lake is a 7.3 hectare widening of the Eagle River. The lake contains stocked rainbow and cutthroat trout. This is a low elevation lake that opens up sooner than others in the area but it is subject to summer doldrums.

Cleland Lake (Map 33/F7)

The 23.5 hectare Cleland Lake offers fair fishing for stocked rainbow in the 30–35 cm (12–14 inches) range. Due to the nice shoal, it is best to fish by boat/floatation device by casting near the drop-offs. Using a dry fly in summer evenings can be a lot of fun. There is a small forest service site with a rustic boat launch and dock at the northeast tip of the lake. A powerboat restriction applies on the lake, which is 1,158 m (3.969 feet) above sea level.

Cliff Lake (Map 14/D5)

A difficult hike, which requires a scramble around a waterfall, is required to access this lake from the Bull-Van FSR. The lake contains cutthroat that can be taken on a fly or by spincasting.

Clute (Murphy) Lakes (Map 18/G7)

From the mouth of Murphy Creek, there is a 4 km (2.4 mile) one-way hike leading to these two lakes, which cover a total of 28 hectares between the two of them. Small rainbow are readily caught on almost any lure or fly.

Columbia Lake (Map 20/E2)

This large (2,574 hectare) lake is the headwaters for the famed Columbia River, which flows through parts of British Columbia and Washington State before finding its way to the Pacific Ocean. There is good access to the lake off Highway 93/95, and the small towns of Fairmont Hot Springs and Canal Flats provide full amenities. Columbia Lake is not generally recognized as a great fishing lake but it can produce modest numbers of rainbow and cutthroat to 1 kg (2 lbs) and the occasional bull trout to 7 kg (15 lbs). An extensive stocking program has been a place for the last decade or so, which has had a positive effect on fishing in the lake. The best methods of fishing are trolling or fly fishing around Dutch Creek. If trolling, be careful of the depth, as the lake is only 5 m (15 feet) deep. Ling cod and whitefish (to 40 cm/14 inches) are also caught in the fall and winter.

Comfort Lake (Map 37/G2)

This 9.1 hectare lake is found north of Golden, and offers some fair fishing for small, stocked rainbow. Spincasting or fly fishing will yield the best results. Try anytime from break-up (May) to September-October. Comfort Lake is 978 m (3,209 feet) above sea level.

Connor Lakes (Map 22/A1)

The lakes, which are actually a chain of three water bodies, can be accessed by trail and there is a campsite and cabin on the main lake. The fishing for cutthroat, which reach 4 kg (9 lbs) but average 30–40 cm (12–15 inches), can be unbelievable at times. In recent years, however, fishing success has declined as rumor of these large, easy to catch fish has increased pressure on the lake. The high alpine lake is closed to fishing from May 1–June 30 to protect the spawning area.

Cooley Lake (Map 10/D7)

This tiny lake offers spectacular views of Perry Ridge, Mount Peters, Mount Hoover, Mount Drummond and the Slocan Valley. The rough road in leads to a short (400 m) trail to the lake. The muddy shoreline and bugs make a floatation device a necessity. The fishing can be slow but the fish are fat and can reach 30 cm (12 inches).

Cooper Lake (Map 5/A2)

Accessed by a 3 km (1.8 mile) hike, this 49.2 hectare lake was heavily stocked with cutthroat trout back in the mid 1970s. A healthy population of small cuts (up to 0.5 kg/1 lb) still remains and fishing is good throughout the open water season. The lake is 1,601 m (5,203 feet) above sea level.

Copper Lake (Map 20/E6)

After about an hours walk along an old road, you will be rewarded with some good fishing for small cutthroat to 40 cm (15 inches) but averaging 20–30 cm in size. Fly fishing or spincasting have proven effective.

Cottonwood Lake (Map 3/A1)

Located south of Nelson alongside Highway 6, this 6 hectare lake contains small rainbow and kokanee. Ease of access and small but feisty trout make this an exciting lake to take the kids out fishing. There are trails around the lake for shore fishing and it is also possible to launch a canoe (there is an electric motor only restriction). Parking is available at the regional park at the north end of the lake. The lake is 884 m (2,900 feet) above sea level, and is stocked annually with rainbow.

Coursier Lake (Map 23/E2)

West of Shelter Bay, this popular off-roading area is well known for its scenic value. Many people test their luck in Coursier for trout but the lake is not well known for its fishing. There is a place to launch small boats.

Cranberry Lake (Map 23/E1)

Located alongside Highway 23, this small lake has fair fishing for small rainbow and cutthroat trout.

Cub Lake (Map 33/G7)

This small, surprisingly deep lake (it is over 12 m/39 feet deep, but is only 1.4 hectares in size) contains good numbers of rainbow that average 20–30 cm (10–12 inches). Shore fishing is limited so your best bet is to cast or troll from a boat. There is an electric motor only restriction on the lake, which is stocked annually with rainbow. The lake is 1,189m (3,500 feet) above sea level.

Curtis Lake (Map 3/C6)

Since the bridge at Sheep Creek is often washed out, it could be a long walk into the lake. Further, a rockslide at the north end of the lake limits access. The reward is good cutthroat fishing for small but feisty fish.

Dainard Lake (Map 33/G3)

After a long difficult hike, you can expect some great fishing for cutthroat averaging 25–35 cm. The lake is rarely fished, except by guide outfitters, since it is difficult to find. The lake is stocked every even year with western slope cutthroat.

Deep Lake (Map 6/C2)

Stocked annually with 1000 rainbow, this tiny (1.9 hectare) lake is found just north of Caven Creek Road.

Devils Hole Lake (Map 3/D5)

This fishing lake is reached by way of a 4 km (one-way) hike/bushwhack off Batanee Road. Fishing can be rewarding for small cutthroat.

Diamond Lake (Map 21/A7)

Diamond is a tiny lake (1.9 hectares) that is stocked every couple of years with rainbow. The lake is located just north of Premier Lake and is accessed by a short walk along an angler's trail.

Diana Lake (Map 34/A7)

This remote lake is accessed by a trail from Pinnacle Creek or from the Kootenay River. It contains numerous cutthroat averaging 25–35 cm (10–14 inches) in size. Spincasting and fly fishing can be rewarding since the lake receives little fishing pressure due to the difficult access.

Dog Leg Lake (Map 27/A3)

There are actually two dog legs on this small (9.3 hectare) lake found west of Radium Hot Springs. Although the lake hasn't been stocked for over a decade, it once was stocked with rainbow and brook trout. Rumours have it that these fish still survive and are thriving in the lake. There is a day-use forest service site on the eastern shores of the lake. The northern leg of the lake has a deep holding hole, which should provide good fishing in early summer

Dorothy Lake (Map 27/C6)

Located in Invermere, on a point that juts out into Windermere Lake, this tiny (1.5 hectare) lake isn't marked on our maps. There is good fishing to be had at Dorothy Lake, but only if you are under 15 or over 65. The lake contains stocked rainbow and brook trout in fair numbers.

Duck Lake and Sloughs (Map 4/B4)

Despite holding largemouth bass that can reach 4.5 kg (10 lbs), this lake receives relatively little fishing pressure. Fishing can be slow for bass but sunfish and other pan fish will keep the action steady. In the spring, bass are caught with a rubber worm, surface plug, slim-minnow lures or a fly (bass pattern). You should stick to the main lake rather than the channels, as the fishing is much better. In the summer, try casting near the weeds at dawn and dusk. Ice fishing can also be very good. Launching a boat can be very difficult. Please note that there are slot size restrictions and no powerboats are allowed.

Duncan Lake (Maps 18/F2-25/D4)
This large (7,140 hectare) lake has some fair fishing for rainbow and bull trout to 4 kg (9 lbs) and small kokanee. The preferred method of fishing is trolling in the early spring or late fall, as the fish go deep in summer. The low elevation lake is 118 metres (382 feet) deep.

Echo Lake (Map 30/F7)
Southeast of Revelstoke, this small lake offers fair numbers of small rainbow. The lake, which is at 884 m (2,900 ft) in elevation, is stocked every year. There is no ice or bait fishing allowed as well as an electric motor only restriction.

Echo Lakes One and Two (Map 13/F1)
Stocked annually with rainbow trout, this pair of lakes offer good fishing for fish that can get up to 0.5 kg (1 lb) in size. Lake Two is about twice the size of Lake One, at 12.1 hectares, and is usually accessed by portaging a small craft/tube from Lake One (although an old road system runs near the lake from the south). Lake One, in turn, is accessed via a short trail off a secondary road off of Farstad Road. There are a number of restrictions, including a one trout (over 40 cm/16 in) per day limit, and single baitless hooks.

Edith Lake (Map 6/B1)
Brook trout were stocked in the 1980s in this 14.8 hectare lake, but the main sportfish here are rainbow trout. The lake is 884 m (2,900 feet) above sea level, and is accessed off the Ha Ha Lake Road. Expect to find fair fishing for rainbow to 1 kg (2 lbs). Try fly fishing, trolling or spincasting towards the end of the lake, where it is deeper.

Edwards Lake (Map 7/A6)
Located just off Highway 93, this 33.2 hectare lake contains rainbow to 2 kg (4 lbs) and offers good fishing in the early spring and late fall. The shallow lake is subject to winterkill but the fish grow to large sizes (45 cm+/18 inches) due to an annual stocking program. For fly fishermen trying the lake in the early spring (at 802 m/2,607 feet, the lake is usually ice-free by early May), a chironomid imitation is effective. As the summer nears, try a hopper or mosquito pattern on the surface. Towards the middle of August, a black ant imitation can be quite effective. Leech patterns work year-round as the bottom of the lake is rather muddy. Camping is available at the lake, which has an electric motor only restriction.

Elk Lakes, Lower and Upper (Map 29/A5)
These beautiful alpine lakes are a popular Rocky Mountain hiking destination. These lakes offer good fishing for whitefish (average 20 cm), cutthroat (to 25 cm) and bull trout. Although ice-free from mid-June to November, fishing is best towards the end of the summer after the water has begun to clear. The Upper Lake is 100 m (325 feet) higher than the Lower, which is at 1,700 m (5,525 feet) in elevation. It is also bigger, at 67.5 hectares, compared to 25 ha, and deeper at 52.3 m (170 feet), compared to 6.8 m (22.1 feet).

Elmo Lake (Map 3/D5)
This tiny mountain lake produces small trout on a fly or by spincasting. The tough access limits visitors to the lake.

Englishman Lake (Map 6/E5)
A small (10.4 hectare) lake just west of Lake Koocanusa, Englishman Lake is stocked annually with rainbow trout. While there is no camping at the lake, the Englishman Creek Recreation Site is nearby.

Erie (Beaver) Lake (Map 2/G5)
This swampy and weedy lake is found just off Highway 3, west of Salmo. Shore fishing for brook trout is difficult, except maybe in early spring, when the fish may come close to shore. As a general rule, they stick to the deeper water, located near the west end of the 32.4 hectare lake. Largemouth bass have been introduced into this lake and take well to jigs, spinners, and top water flies or lures. Bass to 1 kg (2 lbs) can be found most anywhere in the lake, and the best time to catch them is at dusk. Parking and a nice picnic area are available at the rest area but please access the lake via the railway to avoid private property. Fishing is slow throughout the year but improves dramatically during ice fishing season and in the spring.

Evans Lake (Map 10/C1)
Rumours abound of monster trout that inhabit the depths of this lake. The remote 267 hectare lake is found in Valhalla Provincial Park, and offers plenty of average sized rainbow trout. Fly fishing is the preferred method although small spinners and bait work too. This is a very deep, cold high elevation lake with a maximum depth of 155 metres (508 feet) that sits at the 1,530 m (4,973 ft) level. Although the odd person bashes their way up Evans Creek, most visitors fly in. Because of the difficult access, this lake sees very little fishing pressure. There is a cabin with space for four at the lake.

Fenwick Lake (Map 28/A6)
Found off the Kootenay River Road along a rough 4wd road, this small (3.5 hectare) lake is not the easiest to get to. As a result, fishing can be good for stocked rainbow and cutthroat trout. This is a high elevation lake at 1,450 m (4,713 feet), and fishing remains good throughout the ice-free season.

Fish Lake (Map 14/C1)
Found in Top of the World Provincial Park (the lake itself is not at the top of the world, but at 1,722 m/5,597 feet it's pretty high), this crystal clear, blue-green lake requires a two hour hike to access. There is a cabin available (for a fee) and designated campsites for those wishing to camp. The lake produces good number of cutthroat that average 20–35 cm but can reach 1 kg (2 lbs) as well as the odd bull trout to 3.5 kg (8 lbs). Fly fishing or spincasting (no bait allowed) from a boat in the spring is your best bet as shore fishing is difficult. For fly fishermen, the best bet is to bring a sinking line since dry fly fishing isn't that effective. The flies of choice include leech patterns, any small nymph or a shrimp pattern.

Fish Lake (Map 18/C6)
Located on the Kaslo-New Denver Highway (Highway 31A), this small (7 hectare) lake has many small, stocked rainbow. You can fly fish or spincast from a boat or shore. Ice fishing is also popular. There is a rest area and boat launch next to this scenic lake, which is found at 999 m (3,247 feet) in elevation, beneath the towering peaks of the Goat Range.

Fishermaiden Lake (Map 11/B1)
This small pond is accessed by trail and provides good fishing for small, stocked rainbow (to 25 cm). There is an age restriction to fish this lake.

Fletcher Lakes (Map 11/E1)
A challenging trail leads up to these beautiful mountain lakes found high above Kootenay Lake. Fishing in the lower lake can be good in the late summer for small rainbow (average 20–30 cm/8–12 inches) but once reached 9 kg (20 lbs). The upper lake also produces small rainbow with a fly or by spincasting. Due to the thick vegetation and logs and debris around the 10 hectare lakes, a floatation device is helpful.

Flint Lakes (Map 18/D7)
These tiny mountain lakes are found on an old mining road west of Kaslo. Small rainbow (to 30cm/12 inches) take readily to most dry flies and spinners.

Floe Lake (Map 34/B4)
Despite the grueling 10 km hike, the lake receives constant fishing pressure throughout the summer. Fishing for nice sized cutthroat (average 35–40 cm/ 14-16 in) remains fair at this beautiful mountain lake.

Frozen Lake (Map 29A/A5)

Yes, the name is a pretty good description of this high elevation (2,226 m/ 7,235 feet) lake that has a very short ice-free season. As a result, the small stocked cutthroat trout are voracious eaters and most tackle will work. The 6.9 hectare lake is found on an easy trail leading north from Lower Elk Lake. The lake is set at the base of a sheer rock wall, and there are a few trees around the edge of the lake.

Fusee Lake (Map 6/G4)

Fusee Lake is located on a logging road to the west of Highway 93 and east of Baynes Lake. The 3.6 hectare lake offers fair fishing for stocked eastern brook trout.

Garlund Lake (Map 11/B3)

Found south of Kaslo Lake in Kokanee Glacier Park, this high elevation (1,981 m/6,438 feet) lake offers good fishing for small cutthroat.

Gavia Lakes (Map 33/C5)

Found just south of Bittern Lake, this trio of lakes ranges in size from 4.2 to 12.2 hectares. The smallest of the three (the farthest southeast of the lakes) is stocked annually with rainbow. The lakes are not that far apart, and it is conceivable that some trout may migrate from one lake to another. Currently, there is no report of any fish in either of the other two Gavia Lakes.

Gibson Lake (Map 11/C3)

This 11 hectare lake is easily accessed via Kokanee Glacier Park Road, so unlike the other walk-in lakes in the park, it receives more fishing pressure. The high elevation (1,524 m/4,953 feet) lake offers good numbers of cut-throat to 35 cm (14 inches) using a fly or by spincasting.

Gog Lake (Map 29B/A2)

A much smaller counterpart to Lake Magog, this high elevation lake offers hungry cutthroat trout to 1 kg (2 lbs).

Gorman Lake (Map 38/C7)

After a pleasant hike, this popular high elevation (2,109m/6,854 feet) lake can be quite productive for small rainbow caught on a fly or with a spinner (try a Blue Fox or Panther Martin). Bring a floatation device and fish on the south side of the lake to improve success. The 27.7 hectare lake is stocked with rainbow.

Grave Lake (Map 15/D1)

Over the last few years, the 120 hectare Grave Lake has been the subject of a fairly intensive stocking program, with 10,000 rainbow released annually. Of course, the lake sees a fair bit of angling pressure, due to its close proximity to Sparwood. The two forces tend to even out, and the lake is a moderate pro-ducer for small kokanee and rainbow to 1 kg (2 lbs). One of the best places to try your luck is off the large point near the north end of the lake. There are also a number of inflowing creeks on the eastern shore of the lake, which should also produce well. The Sparwood Fish & Game Club maintains a camping area and rough boat launch on the lake, which is 1,268 m (4,121 feet) above sea level.

Greenbush Lake (Map 23/B1)

After a rough drive on the North Shuswap Forest Service Road, this 172 hect-are lake offers fairly good fishing for bull trout to 3 kg (7 lbs) and rainbow to 1 kg (2 lbs). Trolling, spincasting and fly fishing all seem to be equally effec-tive. The lake is 1,030 m (3348 feet) above sea level.

Hahas Lake (Map 13/F3)

Hahas Lake is found beside a secondary road off Highway 95A northeast of Kimberley. A 4wd may be necessary when the road is wet. The 43 hectare lake is heavily stocked with rainbow trout (nearly 100,000 in the last four years), and provides fair fishing in the spring and fall by trolling, spincasting or fly fishing. The lake was once stocked with brook trout, but information is sketchy as to the current population levels. Stick to the main body of the lake since the arms can be quite shallow. The lake is 909 m (2,954 feet) above sea level.

Hahas Pothole (Map 13/F3)

Just over a kilometre south of Hahas Lake is a trio of small lakes. The centre lake, which covers an area of just 1.9 hectares, is stocked annually with rainbow and provides a fine small lake fishery.

Haiseldean Lake (Map 11/D4)

Hidden in the hills above Balfour, this high elevation (2,119 m/6,887 feet up), 4.4 hectare lake offers good fishing for rainbow. Trout were stocked back in the 1930s and are rumoured to grow up to 4 kg (9 lbs). You are more likely to find them in the 0.75 kg (1.5 lb) range using flies, bait or lures. A trail off Redfish Creek Road leads you to the lake.

Halfway Lake (Map 26/F1)

You should experience some good fishing for cutthroat to 1 kg (average 20–25 cm/8–10 inches) on a fly, by trolling or by spincasting this 5.5 hectare lake. Shore fishing is possible although a boat is preferred. Try trolling a wet fly on a sinking line for best results. There is a forest service site and cartop boat launch at the lake, which is stocked annually with rainbow. The lake is at a relatively high elevation (1,128 m/3,666 feet), and fishing should remain good throughout the summer.

Halgrave Lakes (Map 26/G2)

Located off Steamboat Lake Road, these two lakes have small cutthroat (aver-age 30–35 cm). Lower Halgrave Lake is about 50 metres below Upper Hal-grave, at an elevation of 1,080 m/3,510 feet. It is also bigger, at 8.8 hectares, compared to 6.5 hectares. The lower lake is accessed via a short trail from the north end of the upper lake, which has a recreation site. There is limited shore fishing at either lake because of the shallows around the shores. The lakes are occasionally stocked: cutthroat in the upper lake, rainbow in the lower. Please note that Lower Halgrave Lake is closed from December 1 to April 30 and both lakes have an electric motor only restriction.

Hall Lakes, Lower and Upper (Map 26/G1)

These are actually the first two in a trio of lakes (the third lake does not hold any fish). These shallow (the lower lake is almost 3 m/9.8 feet deep, while the upper lake is only 1.8 m/5.9 feet deep) lakes are subject to winterkill, and fishing from the shore is difficult. The lakes have not been stocked for over a decade but the cutthroat remain small and tend to congregate in the deeper waters.

Hamling Lakes (Map 17/E2)

At the headwaters of Hamling Creek east of Wilson Lake are a series of 8 small hike-in lakes. The lakes offer good fishing for rainbow trout since the lake system is stocked with rainbow each year. Fly fishing and spincasting are the preferred methods of fishing at these remote lakes.

Hartley Lake (Map 15/A5)

Found on the Hartley Lake Road north of Fernie, this lake offers decent fishing for western slope cutthroat by spincasting or fly fishing. The lake is stocked every even year and the Fernie Rod and Gun Club maintain a forest service site on the lake.

Heather Lake (Map 11/A2)

A 2 km (one-way) hike from Enterprise Creek Road provides access to this good fishing lake. Small cutthroat to 0.5 kg (1 lb) are caught on a fly, with bait or by spincasting. Fishing remains strong through the summer at this high elevation (1,960 m/6,370 feet) lake.

Helen Deane Lake (Map 11/C3)

This is a small (1.8 hectare) lake located in Kokanee Glacier Provincial Park, near the Slocan Chief Cabin. Like most of the lakes in the area, it is hike-in access, high elevation (1,997 m/6,490 feet) containing small, voracious cutthroat that will take to almost anything you offer during the open water season.

Help Lake (Map 37/G1)

Off the Big Bend Road, this small (12.4 hectare), shallow lake offers some good fishing, at times, for small stocked rainbow and wild cutthroat. Spin-casting or fly fishing offer the best results. Try anytime from break-up (May) to September–October. The lake is 974 m (3199 feet) above sea level, with a maximum depth of only 2.4 metres (7.9 feet).

Hiawatha (Ward's) Lake (Map 5/E1)

Although rainbow trout are stocked annually in this 4.3 hectare lake north of Moyie Lake, it is becoming better known for its largemouth bass fishing. A small population of kokanee can also be found in the lake. The largemouth bass like the lake because it is shallow and marshy. As a result, trout anglers should go in early spring or late fall and cast towards the weeds. Bass fishing

picks up when the water warms in the summer. The lake is 914 m (2,971 feet) above sea level.

High Lake (Map 33/G3)
After a long difficult hike, you can expect some great fishing for small cutthroat (average 25–35 cm). The lake is rarely fished except by guide outfitters, and can be difficult to find.

Holmes Lake (Map 16/B5)
This 36 hectare lake is a 20 minute hike from the Keefer Lake Resort, which will provide boat rentals. The lake is also accessed by road and offers good fishing for rainbow to 1 kg (2 lbs). Fly fishing, spincasting and trolling all seem to be effective.

Horseshoe Lake (Map 14/B6)
This is a small (12 hectare), pretty spring-fed lake that is home to a popular forest service site. Fishing can get quite crowded on this lake as there are rumours of rainbow that reach 2 kg (4 lbs) in size due to the abundance of shrimp for feed. However, the lake is stocked annually and most of the trout tend to be quite small. The lake is 853 m (2,772 feet) above sea level.

Horseshoe Lake (Map 17/C2)
Found on a 4wd road north of Wilson Lake, this 10.7 hectare lake has rainbow to 2 kg (4 lbs). Both fly fishing and trolling (there is a powerboat restriction) can be effective. The lake sits 853 m (2,772 feet) above sea level.

Idlewild Lake (Map 13/G7)
Located on the south edge of Cranbrook on 9th Street, this small lake is an age-restricted lake. It is only open to folks under 15 or over 65 and contains rainbow and cutthroat trout.

Island Lake (Map 14/G7)
Near Fernie, this mountain lake has a nice resort and some cutthroat to 2 kg (4 lbs). The lake is occasionally stocked with western slope cutthroat.

Jade Lake (Maps 26/F1, 33/F7)
This small (14 hectare) fly fishing only lake produces some good numbers of stocked rainbow to 1 kg (average 35–45 cm). Shore fishing is limited so try trolling a wet fly in the middle of the lake or try casting a dry fly from a boat near the shoals at each end of the lake. There is a forest service site and a

dock available but the access road is steep and bumpy. An electric motor only restriction is on the lake, which sits at 1,110 m (3,608 feet).

Jeb Lake (Map 37/G3)
This small (10 hectare) lake is found on a 4wd road off the Susan Lake Road. It can produce good fishing for brook trout to 2 kg (4 lbs), especially in the spring. In the summer, the fishing slows and the mosquitoes are unbearable. There is a forest service site and small wharf at the lake, which is annually stocked with eastern brook trout.

Jeffery Lakes (Map 20/D6)
This trio of lakes are found about 7.5 km (4.6 miles) from the furthest drivable point along the Lavington Creek Road. As a result, few anglers are willing to make the trip to the small lakes. In the spring and the fall, you will find good fly fishing (bait works, too) for cutthroat trout to 0.5 kg (1 lb).

Jim Smith Lake (Map 13/F7)
Jim Smith Lake Provincial Park is found outside of Cranbrook. At the heart of the park is the popular recreation lake itself, which was once a good trout fishing lake, but is being overrun by largemouth bass. The bass can reach 1 kg (2 lbs). The lake still offers fair fishing for stocked rainbow and wild brook trout to 1.5 kg (3 lbs). A powerboat restriction applies on the 21.2 hectare lake, which is 1,067 m (3,468 feet) above sea level.

Johnianne Lake (Map 10/F6)
This small hike-in lake is reached off of the Pedro Creek FSR east of Passmore. The lake offers good fishing for stocked eastern brook trout by bait fishing or spincasting.

Johnson Lake (Map 20/G7)
Located off Highway 93/95 north of Skookumchuck, this 13.5 hectare lake has good numbers of kokanee and rainbow, both of which are stocked in the lake. (The rainbow are stocked annually, the kokanee are stocked every few years.) The lake has also been stocked in the past with brook trout, which still remain in good numbers. A good place to focus your effort is at the southern end of the lake. There is a forest service site on the eastern side of the lake.

Joker Lake (Upper) (Map 11/C3)
After a long hike beginning off Keen Creek Road, this high elevation (2,012 m/6,539 feet) lake rewards the visitor with good numbers of small cutthroat caught on a fly or lure.

Kaslo Lake (Map 11/B3)
This picturesque, high alpine lake is 80 m (260 feet) long and surrounded by rockslides, grassy meadows and alpine timber. It holds good numbers of small cutthroat caught on a spinner or with a fly. The lake is 1,981 m (6,438 feet) above sea level.

Kate Lake (Map 23/A6)
It is a 3 km (1.8 mile) hike into Kate Lake from the end of a rough 4wd accessible road. The lake contains rainbow to 1 kg (2 lbs), which take well to flies, lures or bait.

Kearns Lake (Map 2/C5)
Found within Champion Lakes Provincial Park, this small (5.5 hectare), mid-elevation (1,263 m/ 4,144 feet) lake is accessed via a steep 2 km (1.2 mile) one-way trail, which splits off from the Champion Lake Loop Trail. The lake contains small rainbow trout (average under 25 cm/10 inches) and the fishing can be slow, especially in the summer. The lake does have its moments, usually in early spring or fall, when the action can get pretty fast and furious. Try using flies, bait or spinners from a floatation device.

Keefer Lake (Map 16/B4)
Home to the popular Keefer Lake Resort, this 502 hectare lake is also home to good fishing for rainbow that can get up to 1 kg (2 lbs). There is a boat launch at the resort, as well as boat rentals. The lake is 1,300 m (4,000 feet) above sea level and fishing remains good throughout summer.

Keen Lake (Map 11/B3)
Keen Lake is another hike-in lake in Kokanee Glacier Park containing good numbers of cutthroat trout. The high elevation lake (2,010 m/6,533 feet) lake is only 3.1 m (10 feet) deep.

Kiakho Lakes (Map 13/E7)

This is a trio of lakes west of Cranbrook. The middle of the three lakes is occasionally stocked with cutthroat trout, but all three lakes can produce on occasion.

Kimbol Lake (Map 17/D2)

Found near the Nakusp Hot Springs, a trail leads south to this 1,318 m (4,324 ft) high lake. The 9.2 hectare lake offers good fishing for rainbow to 1 kg (2 lbs). Rainbow were stocked in the 1980s.

Kinbasket (McNaughton) Lake (Maps 37–38 & 40–42)

This glacier fed lake is actually a large man-made reservoir of the Columbia River drainage that was created by the Mica Dam in 1973. Access to the many arms of the lake can be found off of a number of good forestry roads. Boat launches and campsites are well spaced along the lake. The pretty waters also offer some good bull trout fishing in addition to some ling cod, rainbow, kokanee and whitefish fishing. Try casting a Kamlooper, Red Devil or Krokodile for bull trout. Watch for the closure in Bush Arm near the bridge on the Bush-Sullivan Road. The low elevation (674 m/2,191 feet) lake covers 43,200 hectares, and gets to a depth of 99 m (322 feet).

Kokanee Lake (Map 11/B3)

Found at the foot of the Kokanee Glacier, at an elevation of 1,981 m (6,438 feet) this is a pretty hike-in lake. The small (16 hectare) lake has feisty cutthroat that average 20–30 cm (8-12 in) in size.

Kootenay Lake (Map 3–4, 11–12, 18)

The world famous Kootenay Lake forms the hub of the Kootenays and is known for its large Gerrard Rainbow Trout. Fully mature, these renowned fish average 9 kg (20 lbs) in size and have tipped the scales at 15.9 kg (35 lbs). Other sportfish in the lake include kokanee, bull trout, and to a lesser extent whitefish, burbot (catch and release only), largemouth bass and cutthroat. Resorts, campsites and boat launches are easily found along the many arms of this long lake, which is so big (41,700 hectares) that it does not freeze over in the winter. You will need a special Kootenay Lake Rainbow Trout license to fish for trout. Read the regulations for gear and fishing closures before heading out.

The best time to fish the large rainbow is between October and May when the lake is cooler and the big fish are near the surface. Try trolling with Polarbear flies, bucktails, apex lures or plugs. During the summer months the big fish go deep and trolling or working creek mouths more often catches smaller rainbow and bull trout. Kokanee are easily caught on a Willow Leaf and Wedding Ring with a maggot on a slow troll at 5–25 m (15–90 feet).

North Arm (Maps 11/F5-18/F3) The real hotspot of Kootenay Lake these days is the north arm. Highway 31 runs along the lake's western shores, providing good access in a couple of places. There are a number of forest service sites, campgrounds and launches on the east side of the lake, too. Fish seem to congregate in the bays and creek mouths in this area.

South Arm (Maps 3, 4, 11, 12) Access to the southern arm of Kootenay Lake is mainly from Highway 3A between Crawford Bay and Creston. Crawford Bay is one of the best places to fish along this big, long section of lake, as the deep water and sheltered inlet are one of the favourite places for the monster Gerrard Trout to hang out. It is also a good place to find big bull trout, and, in the shallower sections you will find largemouth bass. You will also find lots of bass around Kuskonook, in the shallow Coot Bay. The southern portion of the lake is the only place you will find cutthroat trout, which like to hang around some of the creek inflows.

West Arm (Map 11/A7–E5) The West Arm is more like a big, slow moving river than a lake, running from Balfour to Nelson. This 35 km (21.4 mile) long stretch is the most developed stretch of the lake, with Highway 3A running along its northern banks for its entire length. This section of the lake is much shallower than the main body of the lake, with a maximum depth of only 34 m (111 feet). Between Nelson and Balfour are a number of small towns offering various services, and a couple campgrounds, including Kokanee Creek Provincial Park. As a result of an extensive stocking and fertilization program, fishing for kokanee and big trout, especially around Balfour is very good. Whitefish fishing can be very good, particularly in the shallows of the West Arm.

Krao Lake (Map 11/E3)

After a long hike off Cedar Creek Road, you can expect some good fishing for small cutthroat. Try a lure or fly in this remote 5 hectare lake.

Lake Enid (Map 27/B5)

Lake Enid is home to good populations of both rainbow and brook trout, and is a popular year round fishing destination. During the ice-free season, it is possible to hook a brookie from the dock at the Lake Enid Recreation Site on a fly or by spincasting, but as the weather gets warmer, the fish head deeper, and you will need a tube or boat to get out onto the lake. During winter, the brookies are still fairly aggressive and the fishing can be good. The 22.3 hectare lake is 975 m (3,199 feet) above sea level.

Lake Koocanusa (Map 6/E3-G7)

Lake Koocanusa, which was created by the Libby Dam, is large and picturesque when the reservoir is full. Despite the silty water, the lake still produces some large bull trout to 4 kg (9 lbs). Spincasting a Red Devil lure is particularly effective at the creek mouths. Other sportfish include small kokanee and cutthroat up to 1.5 kg (3 lbs) or larger. The best fishing is between mid June and August when the reservoir level is up. The main access point is the paved boat launch at Kikomun Creek Park.

Lake Magog (Map 29B/A2)

Lake Magog is the most popular destination in Mount Assiniboine Park. The gorgeous wilderness lake is framed by snow-capped peaks, including the 3,561m (11,573 foot) high Mount Assiniboine, and offers fair numbers of cutthroat to 3 kg (7 lbs) that average 35–40 cm (13–15 inches). Access to the lake is along any one of a number of long, tough trails, which keep all but the most avid anglers from this lake. This is a high elevation lake (2,149 m/7,050 feet), and usually isn't free of ice until late spring or early summer. Shore fishing is possible even during the heart of summer, with the best time to fish being at dawn and dusk. There is a campground, four cabins and the Mount Assiniboine Lodge in the area.

Lake Revelstoke (Maps 30, 35, 36, 40)

This large, narrow Columbia River reservoir (stretching 130 km/79 miles north from the Revelstoke Dam to the Mica Dam) was created when the 175 m (569 foot) high Revelstoke Dam was completed in 1985. The lake offers fair to good fishing for rainbow to 4 kg (10 lbs), lingcod, bull trout to 8 kg (20 lbs), and whitefish and kokanee to 1 kg (2 lbs). The preferred method of fishing is trolling but if you try fishing at a creek mouth or along the rocky shoreline with a float and bait you may get good results. A fast troll at 12–30 m (40–100 feet) with any plug that looks like a minnow usually meets with success, particularly in the early spring or late fall. The lake produced a 12.7 kg (32 lb) bull trout a number of years back, and there is always a chance you may land a monster. There are a number of access points and camping spots along Highway 23. Watch for closures around the Mica Dam and be aware of wind and debris on the lake.

Lang Lake (Map 33/E7)

This 5.1 hectare lake off the Cartwright Road contains a fair number of rainbow and brook trout to 1 kg (2 lbs). The best access is to float a boat down Templeman River to avoid the private property that surrounds the lake. Spincasting and fly fishing are the proven methods at 1,080 m (3,510 ft) high.

Larchwood Lake (Map 20/F7)

Known as a consistent producer of small, feisty rainbow (although some reach 2 kg/5 lbs), the 15.2 hectare Larchwood Lake is just off a good 2wd backroad west of Skookumchuck. There is a boat launch and forest service site at the lake, which is closed for fishing from December 31 to March 31. The lake is stocked annually and sits at an elevation of only 853 m (2,772 feet).

Larson Lake (Map 16/F2)

This small (4.5 hectare) lake is accessed by the Mosquito Creek Road and has rainbow to 0.5 kg (1 lb). There is a recreation site and boat launch at the lake, which is 701 m (2,278 feet) above sea level.

Lazy (Rock) Lake (Map 14/A1)

Lazy Lake has been the subject of a rather aggressive stocking campaign in recent years. The 32 hectare lake is located on the Wolf-Lewis FSR northeast of Wasa, and holds good numbers of rainbow. There is a forest service site at the north end of the lake offering camping and a cartop boat launch. The lake is at an elevation of 914 m (2,999 feet), and there is a powerboat restriction in place.

Leach Lake (Map 4/B5)

This swampy lake near Creston has some of the best bass fishing in the province. The bass grow to 3 kg (7 lbs) and are caught in the spring with rubber worms and in the fall with surface plugs. Casting near the weeds at dawn and dusk in the summer can also produce. There is also a healthy population of perch and black crappies. There is no road access to the lake so boats must be portaged in.

Leadqueen Lake (Map 26/F1)

Accessed off the Frances Creek Road, this small (4.8 hectare) shallow (1.8 m/6 feet) lake has fair numbers of cutthroat to 35 cm (14 in). Try off the dam or use a (electric motor only) boat. The shallow nature of the lake makes it tough fishing because the fish are easily spooked.

Leadville Lake (Map 5/A3)

Leadville is a tiny (3.8 hectare) lake at the end of 4wd branching of the Goat River FSR. It holds cutthroat to 0.5 kg (1 lb), which were last stocked in 1990. These fish take well to flies, spincasting, or trolling.

Leviathan Lake (Map 18/G7)

A 6 km return hike from the eastern shores of Kootenay Lake accesses this small lake. The lake holds good numbers of small cutthroat, easily caught on a fly or with a lure.

Lewis Slough (Map 13/G3)

Found just south of Wasa Lake, this 17 hectare body of water is very shallow, but you may find largemouth bass on occasion. Bass often migrate from nearby Wasa Lake.

Lillian Lake (Map 27/B6)

This popular lake is found on the paved Toby Creek Road, west of Invermere. An aggressive stocking program offsets the heavy fishing pressure and there is still a good chance of pulling out a 2 kg (4 lb) rainbow in the spring or fall. The 27 hectare lake also contains small brook trout. In the summer, the fish go deep and are affected by an algae bloom. Shore fishing is limited so use a boat (there is a boat launch at the day-use site at the south end of the lake) to cast near the drop-off or troll a wet fly on a sinking line in the deeper water. There is an electric motor only restriction on the lake, which is 945 m (3,100 feet) above sea level.

Lisbon Lake (Map 13/C6)

To reach Lisbon Lake, follow the Perry Creek FSR and then a spur road up Antwep Creek to the trailhead. From there, a short hike leads to this good fishing lake. The lake is stocked with eastern brook trout, which are best caught by spincasting or bait fishing from either a floatation device or shore.

Little Slocan Lakes (Map 10/C5)

There are some good-sized brook trout (to 2 kg/4 lbs) and smaller rainbow caught in these two lakes. The brook trout fishing is fair and slows considerably during the spring run-off, when the lake gets muddy. The preferred method of fishing is trolling or fly fishing (if you can match the hatch). The Upper Lake sees more activity thanks in part to the beautiful forest service site at its northern end. Despite the close proximity to the road, running the

river from the Upper Lake best accesses the Lower Lake. The Upper Lake is stocked annually with rainbow, and at 651 m (2,116 feet) in elevation is only 3 m (10 feet) higher than the Lower. It is also the smaller of the two lakes, at 83 hectares, as compared to 111 hectares for the Lower Lake.

Logus Lake (Map 25/E6)

A trek along the Lake Creek Trail from Popular Creek leads to a remote mountain lake west of Duncan Lake. The 10 hectare Logus Lake is known to produce bull trout to 40 cm (16 inches) using a lure or spinner.

Loon Lake (Map 7/A6)

This Loon Lake (there are two other Loon Lakes in the Kootenays) covers 33 hectares and is found just south of the village of Elko. The lake is stocked annually with rainbow that reach 2 kg (4 lbs), and there have been reports of catches of brook trout in the past. The lake is a moderately low elevation lake, at 838 m (2,749 feet) above sea level, and fishing is possible as early as late March. The drawback is that by early summer, the waters have warmed up and the fish hold in the deeper waters. At this time, evening fishing can be effective since the fish will often cruise the shallows in search of food. There is a recreation site along the southwest shores of the lake, complete with launch for electric motor only boats.

Loon Lake (Map 11/F3)

This 19 hectare lake is found just off Highway 31 south of Ainsworth Hot Springs on the Hansen FSR. The lake is stocked every couple of years with rainbow, which can grow to 2 kg (4 lbs) on occasion. The lake is also home to a healthy population of brook trout that reach 35 cm (14 inches). In the spring, the 869 m (2,824 feet) high lake opens quicker than others in the area and the shoals just off shore are hot areas to find trout. Fly anglers will find that a Wooly Bugger is a good pattern to try. In the summer, you will need to work the middle of the lake and fish deeper. Ice fishing is also popular.

Loon Lake (Map 33/A4)

At 9 hectares, this is the smallest of the Loon Lakes found in the Kootenays. It is also the highest, sitting at 1,234 m (4,011 feet). The best time to fish is in the late spring (starting late May) to early fall with fly fishing and spincasting both yielding good results for stocked rainbow to 2 kg (4 lbs). The lake is accessed along the Crestbrook Mainline near Parson and there is a small forest service site on the lake.

Lost Lake (Map 22/D6)

This is a small trail access lake near Elkford that offers good fishing for small trout. The lake is stocked annually with rainbow and brook trout.

Lund Lake (Map 6/C1)

This small (9.8 hectare) lake is located west of Wardner on the Ha Ha Creek Road. The lake contains stocked eastern brook trout and rainbow, which can be caught by bait fishing, fly fishing or spincasting in the early spring and late fall. Recently, fisheries have been dropping a couple dozen adult Gerrard rainbow trout in order to produce some bigger fish and to counteract the largemouth bass that were illegally introduced. The lake sits at a low elevation (795 m/2,608 feet) and is a good early season option.

McNair Lakes (Map 13/E1)

A trio of small lakes (up to 4 hectares) called First, Second and Third McNair Lake are found west of Skookumchuck. They are situated at 1,097 m (3,599 feet) in elevation and the season here is shorter than lower elevation lakes in the area. Fishing is best right after ice-off in May. All the lakes are randomly stocked with western slope cutthroat, and you'll find that the fishing gets better as you get farther from the road. The First Lake is closest to Farstad Road, and as a result sees the heaviest angling pressure.

Marble Lake (Map 2/E2)

Depending on how far you can drive up the Erie Creek Road, it may be a 3 km (1.8 mile) hike into this small (3.1 hectare) lake. The lake was once stocked (way back in 1965) with 21,000 rainbow. Today, a healthy population of trout still remain in the lake, the largest of which can get up to 1 kg (2 lbs). The lake is 1,921 m (6,243 feet) above sea level, and fishing is good when the ice is off in late May.

Marian Lake (Map 33/F4)

This is a small (20 hectare) lake with fair fishing for rainbow and cutthroat to 1 kg (2 lbs). There is a small forest service site and a cartop boat launch at the lake, which is stocked with western slope cutthroat every even year. The lake is at a fairly high elevation (1,300 m/4,225 feet) and fishing remains good throughout the ice-free season.

Milford Lake (Map 18/F6)
This lake has stocked rainbow to 1 kg (2 lbs) that are caught by fly fishing and spincasting. The rough access limits fishing pressure despite the fact there is a forest service site on the lake.

Mineral Lake (Map 5/E2)
Found on the Lamb Creek FSR, the 7.4 hectare Mineral Lake is known for its clear water and good fishing. The lake is stocked annually with rainbow, which can grow to 2 kg (4 lbs) in size. The lake also contains cutthroat, which are even more aggressive than the rainbow. Despite easy access and heavy use, fishing remains good throughout the open water season. After ice off, use a dry fly such as a mayfly or chironomid pattern. As the season progresses, it is better to change to a sinking line and cast or troll a nymph pattern or leech as the fish tend to retreat to the depths of lake through the summer months. Other effective tactics include spincasting the drop-off or trolling a gang troll. The lake is 1,030 m (3,379 feet) above sea level and sports a nice day-use area and a boat launch.

Mirror (Murray) Lake (Map 11/F1)
Found next to the highway, this lake is better known as a swimming hole than a fishing destination. Regardless, the small (7 hectare), shallow lake is one of the few lakes in the Kootenays that contains smallmouth bass. The aggressive fish will take to anything that looks like dinner and can grow up to 2 kg (4 lbs). Try a bass fly pattern, or if you are spincasting the weeds and shallows, use a plastic worm, top plug, spinner or spoon. The lake is 543 m (1,781 feet) above sea level and is a good place to go fishing with the kids.

Mitten Lakes (Map 33/C5)
This popular lake is known more for its water sports than fishing. At least in summer it is. In the spring and fall the 65 hectare lake is a good producer for rainbow trout to 1 kg (2 lbs). The lake is heavily stocked with rainbow and fly fishing and spincasting produce well. There is a large forest service site on the lake. An alternative is to try **Little Mitten Lake**, which is stocked with rainbow annually. It offers better fishing than the main lake. Both lakes are found at about 990 m (1,073 feet) above sea level.

Monroe Lakes (Map 5/E2)
These two lakes are located west of Moyie Lake off the Lamb Creek FSR. Both lakes offer good fishing for stocked cutthroat and rainbow through the spring and fall. Recently, kokanee were introduced to the 47 hectare **Monroe Lake** and reports have yet to surface whether they have taken to their new habitat. The lake is fairly deep (30 m/98 feet), and is at a relatively high (1,067 m/ 3,506 feet) elevation. This means the water stays cooler, which in turn keeps the fish biting more aggressively. Monroe Lake is a popular trolling lake, while **Little Monroe Lake** is better suited for fly fishing and spincasting.

Moose (Baird) Lake (Map 33/E6)
This small lake is located on a secondary road west of Spillimacheen. The lake offers fair fishing for stocked rainbow by spincasting or fly fishing in the spring and fall.

Mosquito (Arrow Park) Lakes (Map 16/F1)
Located along the Mosquito Creek Road, this pair of lakes is not popular, despite good fishing for rainbow up to 1.5 kg (3 lbs). The lack of popularity may have something to do with the name, which is well earned. Trolling is best on the 158 hectare **Mosquito Lake**, and there is a boat launch at the forest service site at the north end of the lake. Shore fishing is difficult, though a good spot is a point just east of the recreation site. **Little Mosquito Lake** is found just north of the bigger lake and is custom made for fly fishing. It is possible to take a good-sized trout using a mid-sized leech pattern.

Moyie Lakes (Map 5/E3)
Although there are actually two lakes—Upper and Lower Moyie—connected by a short channel, most people just call this Moyie Lake. There is very little difference between the two bodies of water, other than the fact that the Upper Lake covers 583 hectares and has a maximum depth of 73 m (238 feet), while the Lower Lake is 312 hectares, and only 57 m (186 feet) deep. The lakes are a very popular summer destination for swimming, water skiing, and, of course, fishing. They are found next to Highway 3, and have resorts, campgrounds and boat launches, including a launch and camping at Moyie Lake Provincial Park. The lakes provide fair fishing for kokanee to 30 cm (12 inches), rainbow

and bull trout to 1.5 kg (3 lbs), brook trout and cutthroat to 0.5 kg (1 lb) and Rocky Mountain whitefish. Trolling with silver spoons is the most popular method. The lakes are heavily stocked with both rainbow and kokanee, and are 929 m (3,019 feet) above sea level.

Mud Lake (Map 5/E2)
This is a small (5.7 hectare) lake found 2 km (1.2 miles) west of Munroe Lake. It contains small, stocked cutthroat in good numbers.

Munroe Lake (Map 22/A4)
This higher elevation lake sits at the headwaters of the East White River and offers stocked cutthroat. The trout can reach 1 kg (2 lbs) but average 25–35 cm (10-14 in) in size. The season extends throughout the ice-free time of the year, which is usually limited to the summer and early fall. Trolling is the preferred method since shore fishing is difficult due to the thick vegetation.

Nancy Greene Lake (Map 1/F4)
Named after legendary downhill skier Nancy Greene, this 32 hectare lake is a high elevation lake (1,264 m/4,147 feet) that offers a hit and miss fishery throughout the ice-free season. Ice fishing is also popular at the lake, but the fish are usually lethargic. The rainbow are generally small (20–30 cm/10 inches) and when the fish are biting, this can be a great place to be. It is a good family fishing lake with easy access and good shore casting options. In late summer, your chances will improve greatly if you have a boat and can fish the hole at the southern end. Try trolling a small Willow Leaf, fly fishing in the early morning or in the evenings, spincasting a small lure or use a float and bait (worm or grasshopper). No powerboats are allowed on the lake, which is stocked every odd year with rainbow.

New Lake (Map 13/F7)
This 28 hectare, mid elevation (1,195 m/3,920 feet) lake is found on the west hill above Cranbrook. It offers good fishing for fast growing rainbow that can reach 2 kg (4 lbs). The lake has large shallow areas at its north and south ends, and fishing is best done early and late in the season around the deep hole near the north end of the lake. For fly fishermen, attractor type patterns such as a Woolly Bugger, Royal Coachman or leech patterns seem to be most effective. The lake sees fairly heavy pressure, but is stocked annually.

Nine Bay Lake (Map 33/D6)
A remote hike-in lake west of Spillimacheen, expect to have to walk about 2 km (1.2 miles) from the end of a deteriorating logging road (farther if you don't have a 4wd vehicle) to this 38 hectare lake. For your efforts, you will be rewarded with good rainbow fishing to 3 kg (7 lbs). Bring a float tube and try spincasting or fly fishing near the island. There is a single, baitless hook restriction, and the lake is closed to fishing from November 1 to April 30. You are also only allowed one fish, greater than 50 cm (20 inches) a day. The lake is 966 m (3,140 feet) above sea level and is stocked annually.

Nixon Lake (Map 32/F3)
This 5 hectare lake on the Spillimacheen FSR has been stocked since the mid 1990s with rainbow, some of which can reach 2.5 kg (6 lbs). The lake is also home to a small population of cutthroat trout. The lake does not receive much angling pressure, so your chances of coming away with a good catch are pretty good. Because this is a high elevation lake (1,326m/4,310 feet), the lake remains cool through the ice-free season (usually June to November). Shore fishing is difficult. Try an attractor fly like a Woolly Bugger or a small spinner like a Blue Fox.

Noakes Lake (Map 11/E4)

These remote, high elevation lakes (2,103 m/6,835 ft) see few visitors due to their limited season and no road or trail access. As a result, the fishing can be fast for small trout. The lake is stocked with western slope cutthroat every even year.

Norbury (Garbutt) Lake (Map 14/C7)

The popular Norbury Provincial Park is named after this 13 hectare lake. There is camping and a boat launch at Peckhams Lake but you will have to carry a canoe or float tube to Norbury, which has a powerboat restriction. Picky rainbow to 2.5 kg (6 lbs) and smaller cutthroat are caught by fly fishing or spincasting. The cutthroats tend to congregate near the creek mouth whereas the rainbow hang around the drop-off on the east side of the lake where there is a shoal area. The lake is 835 m (2,714 feet) above sea level and your best chance for success is in the spring or fall since the heat of summer drives the fish deeper and makes them lethargic.

North Star Lake (Map 6/F2)

Located just south of Jaffray, North Star Lake is a 21 hectare, shallow lake with a very muddy shoreline. Because of the shallows, the fishing areas in the lake are limited. While the fishing is slow, people still come, and rumours of Kamloops Trout to 3.5 kg (8 lbs) abound. You may find them in the deep water, just out from the forest service site. The lake is stocked annually and sits 847 m (2,753 feet) above sea level.

Nun & Monk Lakes (Map 3/D7)

These hike-in lakes off Monk Creek FSR can produce good numbers of cutthroat to 1.5 kg (3 lbs) on a fly or by spincasting. The trail into the lakes is 3 km (1.5 hour) one-way.

Og Lake (Map 29B/A2)

Found in the shadow of Mount Assiniboine, this 16.8 hectare lake is via a very long hike from the nearest road. As a result, it sees very little fishing pressure (even less than lakes closer to the core of the park) and anglers will find good fly fishing for cutthroat. The odd trout reaches 1 kg (2.5 lbs) but most average 25–30 cm (10–12 inches). There is good shore fishing potential and the fish are more than willing to bite. This is a high elevation lake (at 2,057 m/6,685 feet above sea level), and is free of ice only in the summer and early fall.

Paddy Ryan Lakes (Map 27/C6)

Of the series of five lakes that supply Invermere with water, all but the fifth and largest lake are closed to the public. The fifth lake holds fair numbers of brook trout to 30 cm (12 inches) and the occasional small rainbow. Shore casting is possible at the 4 hectare lake, which is 976 m (3,172 feet) above sea level.

Panther Lake (Map 3/C5)

This is another one of those small mountain lakes found below the Three Sisters. The lake produces a lot of small, stocked rainbow that are a lot of fun to catch on the fly. The use of a 4wd vehicle will shorten the walk.

Peckhams Lake (Map 14/C6)

This 10.4 hectare lake is found in Norbury Provincial Park and offers some fair fishing for rainbow to 1.5 kg (3 lbs) in a picturesque setting. Surrounded by aspen trees, the clear lake is set against the backdrop of the impressive Steeples. No powerboats are allowed on the lake but there is a dock and picnic area. There is an aggressive stocking program to offset the heavy fishing

pressure. Regardless, the best time to fish here is in spring and summer, as the waters warm in summer. The lake is 838 m (2,739 feet) above sea level and is rumoured to produce the odd brook trout.

Peters Lake (Map 23/C6)

Peters Lake doesn't see much fishing pressure. Most people are not willing to hike the 17 km (10.4 mile) trail from the parking lot along a sometimes steep trail. Those who do will find a beautiful lake with good fishing for rainbow to 1 kg (2 lb). The trout will usually take to most anything you offer.

Pickering Lake (Map 14/D7)

Found in the Pickering Hills, this tiny lake could actually be classified as a pond. The lake holds largemouth bass and brook trout. Finding the lake in the maze of roads off the Wardner-Fort Steele Road is a little tricky.

Placer Lake (Map 3/E5)

Located on a 3 km (one-way) trail from the Placer Creek Road, the lake produces cutthroat to 0.5 kg (1 lb) on a fly, by spincasting or with bait.

Plaid (Tom O'Shanter) Lake (Map 12/A3)

After a long hike off Crawford Creek Road, you will be rewarded with good fly fishing or spincasting for small rainbow and brook trout. The 78 hectare lake is a lot bigger than most mountain lakes in the area and sits at an elevation of 1,798 m (5,844 feet).

Porcupine Lake (Map 3/D4)

This lake is a long walk from the nearest road (due to washed out bridges or gates), but produces well for small rainbow on a lure or with a fly.

Premier Lake (Map 21/A7)

Ever caught a Premier Lake trout? Don't be too sure you haven't, as fish from here are used as brood stock for 350 lakes and streams throughout the province. This popular lake is found east of Skookumchuck, not far from Highway 93/95. Managed as a quality fishery, the lake offers good fishing for large rainbow to 4 kg (9 lbs), chunky brook trout to 2.5 kg (average 0.5 kg) and small cutthroat. For fly fishermen, the best casting area is beneath the cliffs halfway up the 230 hectare lake. Use a sinking line with a leech, Woolly Bugger, Royal Coachman or shrimp pattern or in the early evening try a dry fly (Adams, Mosquito, Grizzly King) if the fish are rising. The lake has a boat launch, dock and boat rentals. Watch for closures and other restrictions, as the lake is heavily regulated. The lake is 860 m (2,795 feet) above sea level.

Quartz (Rockbluff) Lake (Map 14/A1)

Quartz Lake is an excellent rainbow and cutthroat lake if you hit the lake when they are biting. The best time to fish the lake is in late May to early June after ice-off. At that time, the chironomid hatch is usually at full swing. Other patterns to try include a caddis fly or mayfly imitation in spring or attractor type patterns in the summer. The popular lake also holds a few brook trout and is stocked annually with rainbow.

Quartz (Cliff) Lake (Map 38/A5)

This 20 hectare lake is also known as Cliff Lake and is located a good 5 km (3.1 miles) from the nearest road. The hike in is strenuous and steep, but it keeps out all but the most hardcore angler. If this is you, you will be rewarded for your efforts with lots of action from smaller rainbow and cutthroat, especially if you haul in a canoe or float tube. Some rainbow can reach 2.5 kg (6 lbs). The lake is 2,246 m (7,300 feet) above sea level, so the fishing is good throughout the summer and early fall.

Richmond Lake (Map 5/A1)

Fair fishing for rainbow to 1 kg (2 lbs) is offered at this popular hike-in lake. Trolling, spincasting or fly fishing all work since the fish are not too picky.

Rock Lake (Map 34/G6)

Found near Ferro Pass to the west of Mount Assiniboine, it is about 11 km (6.6 miles) by foot to access the lake. The difficult access results in very little fishing pressure and the lake holds numerous small cutthroat in the 15–20 cm (6–8 inches) range.

Rockslide Lake (Map 10/E6)

Reached off the Pedro FSR by a short hike, this small (14 ha) lake holds fair numbers of brook trout to 30 cm (12 inches).

Rocky Point Lake (Map 33/A5)

Rocky Point Lake is stocked annually with rainbow, which provides good fishing through the ice-free season. This is a high elevation (1,311 m/4,301 ft) lake and the water does not open before late May. The season lasts into October, with rainbow to 2.5 kg (5 lbs) being taken on occasion. Shore fishing is limited at the 27.6 hectare lake and most anglers work a gang troll or try casting a fly or spinner from a float tube or canoe. Some days, the trout will take anything. Other days, they can be picky. There is a small forest service site and boat launch on the lake.

Rosebud Lake (Map 3/A7)

This small (13.4 hectare) lake is found just north of the border along a good road off Highway 6. The lake was once a local favourite, but recent construction has damaged the shoreline, and caused a lot of sluffing and washouts. This in turn has increased the level of silt in the lake, and adversely affected the fishing. Still, the lake is stocked annually with rainbow that grow to 1.5–2 kg (3–4 lbs). Fly anglers will find a good chironomid hatch in spring followed by caddis hatches. In the fall, try a float and worm, or in the winter, ice fishing with maggots or corn can produce. Shore fishing is limited due to the weeds. There is a parking area at the south end of the lake with a rustic boat launch. The lake is 808 m (2,651 feet) above sea level and warms significantly in the summer.

Rosen (McBaines) Lake (Map 6/F1)

This well developed 73 hectare lake offers boat rentals, a boat launch, cabins and a store. Fishing is better in the spring or fall for the small, stocked rainbow and wild cutthroat. The lake is 823 m (2,675 feet) above sea level.

Russ Baker Lake (Map 9/C6)

Found off the Tenderloin Road, west of Lower Arrow Lake, this is one of the few mountain lakes in the Boundary Area. The lake does hold rainbow to 2 kg (5 lbs) but the fish are hard to find.

Russel Lake (Map 10/A6)

Found at the headwaters of Russel Creek is a remote 12 hectare mountain lake. A rough logging road runs up the creek, but you will have to walk the last few kilometres into the lake, which is 1,890 m (6,143 feet) above sea level. The lake is stocked with rainbow every odd year.

Sam's Folly Lake (Map 26/G3)

This small (10 hectare) lake/pond is located off a 4wd road and offers fairly good fishing in the early spring for rainbow. The trout are stocked annually and there is an electric motor only restriction.

Sand Lake (Map 6/F1)

This narrow, shallow lake covers 40 hectares, but has a maximum depth of only 4.3 m (14 feet). And, the lake is only 862 m (2,892 feet) above sea level. This means the lake warms quickly in summer and suffers from winterkill. A floatation device is necessary to get out to the deepest parts of the lake (and away from the mosquitoes). Fishing can be tricky as the clear water makes for spooky fish. Both rainbow and cutthroat trout inhabit the lake, which is home to a small forest service site.

Saugum Lake (Map 14/A4)

Found about a kilometre west of the Lakit Lake Recreation Site, Saugum Lake holds rainbow and bull trout. In addition, the 29 hectare lake is stocked with brook trout annually.

Seven Mile Lake (Map 6/B6)

This tiny lake is found off the Caven Creek FSR and offers fishing for small cutthroat. There is a forest service site at the lake.

Shannon Lake (Map 17/E6)

Shannon Lake is a 25 hectare sub-alpine lake set below the majestic Mount Vingolf. To reach the lake, you will have to follow a series of progressively worse backroads up from Highway 6. Depending on how far you can drive, the hike is at least 1.6 km and involves climbing a steep, rocky trail. The lake sits at the 1,875 m (6,152 ft) level and rewards the visitor with aggressive cutthroat that can reach 1.5 kg (3 lbs). The lake is usually ice-free in June and frozen by November.

Silver Lake (Map 3/C4)

The removal of the bridge up the old road on the south side of Porcupine Creek makes an ATV an essential tool to access this small mountain lake.

Even with an ATV, some bushwhacking is required to reach the lake, which offers sporadic fishing for rainbow using bait, flies or lures. Shore fishing is limited by logs and debris and a floatation devise will improve fishing success.

Silver Spring Lakes (Map 7/A3)

These three lakes, east of Elko, offer good fly fishing and spincasting for stocked rainbow to 1.5 kg (3 lbs). The lakes are reached by trail so you are required to pack your float tube into the lake to maximize your fishing chances. The first lake receives the most fishing pressure, the second lake is the slowest and the third lake is most productive because it is infrequently visited. All three lakes are spring fed and have clear water, which allows fishing success to remain good throughout the summer months. Fly fishermen should use a sinking line with a Woolly Bugger or leech pattern, although dry fly fishing with a number 6–8 Adams, Humpy or mosquito can also be productive.

Siwash Lake (Map 2/E2)

Accessed by trail from the end of a 4wd road that leaves Highway 3A just south of Glade, this 7.4 hectare lake is stocked annually with rainbow. The lake is 1,852 m (6,019 feet) above sea level and the shortened angling season creates a flurry of action once the ice is off in June.

Six Mile Lakes (Map 11/A4)

This series of lakes has some good fishing for small rainbow, bull trout and brook trout using a fly or lure or by trolling. The lakes are accessed via the Lemon Creek Road from the Slocan side or up Duhammel Creek from the Kootenay Lake side.

Slocan Lake (Map 10,17)

Located between the snow-capped peaks of Valhalla Provincial Park and Highway 6, the 6,929 hectare Slocan Lake is a fine fishing destination. The big lake is notorious for big trout, as the stocked Gerrard Rainbow can get up to 5 kg (10 lbs) or more. You will also find bull trout to 4 kg (9 lbs) and small kokanee. Effective methods of fishing for the big trout include a deep troll (the lake averages 171 m/561 feet deep, so you will probably need downrigger gear) with lures or plugs (like green and yellow Flatfish, Kamlooper, Deadly Dick and Rapala) or fishing the mouth of the creeks with a float and bait, worm ball or fly. Full services are available at the small towns of Slocan City, Silverton and New Denver or at any of the resorts along the lake. Camping is available at a number of recreation sites and parks along the shores of the lake.

Snowshoe Lake (Map 7/C5)

As the name implies, this lake sits fairly high up in the Galton Range at 1,307 m (4,290 feet) above sea level. The small (18 hectare) lake is reached by hiking off the Wigwam FSR (4wd recommended). It contains good numbers of small cutthroat that are best caught in the early spring or fall from a floatation device. Cutthroat were stocked in the late 1990s.

Snowshoe Lake (Map 9/D1, 16/D7)

Accessed by 4wd, this 19 hectare lake has rainbow and brook trout to 1 kg (2 lbs) caught on a fly or by spincasting. The lake is often overlooked by anglers, and as a result fishing remains good. It is a low elevation lake, at 671 m/2,510 feet, and fishing is best in spring, when fly fishers will find that chironomid and other nymph patterns work well. There is a forest service site at the north end of the lake, which is subject to an electric motor only restriction.

Sowerby (Grundy) Lake (Map 14/A2)

This small lake is accessed by trail and offers fair fishing for rainbow to 1.5 kg (3 lbs) by trolling, spincasting or fly fishing. The lake is stocked annually with rainbow.

Spectrum Lake (Map 23/B6)

A hike-in lake in Monashee Provincial Park, this high elevation lake is located 12 km (7.3 miles) from the nearest parking lot. The trail is fairly easy to walk and the scenery alone is worth the trip. As an added bonus, the fishing for rainbow to 1 kg (2 lbs) can be very good. The lake is closed December to April.

Spring Lake (Map 6/E1)

Located between Tie Lake and Lake Koocanusa, this lake is fairly easy to get to on the backroads off of Highway 3/93. The 5.5 hectare lake has been heavily stocked over the last few years, with brook trout and fishing can be steady, especially in the spring.

Spur Lake (Map 20/E2)

Accessed via a rough 4wd road, this lake has an abundance of stocked rainbow in the 25–35 cm (10–14 inch) range. Casting from the shore is difficult, so bring a boat.

St. Mary Lake (Map 13/A5)

Despite the good road access, this 295 hectare lake is not as popular as the St. Mary River, which flows into, then out of it. Regardless, it can produce well for trout in the early fall, once the lake starts to cool. You will find rainbow, bull trout and cutthroat (to 1.5 kg/3 lbs) as well as the odd brook trout and good numbers of whitefish and ling cod. Ling cod fishing is most productive in February and March. Trolling is the main fishing method on the lake, which rests 960 m (3,120 feet) above sea level.

Staubert Lake (Map 24/D3)

Staubert Lake is located northeast of the Galena Bay Ferry on Highway 31. The 79 hectare lake is a deep lake that receives surprisingly little use in relation to its proximity to the highway. It holds good numbers of rainbow and kokanee, which can be caught by either fly fishing or trolling. There is also a fair population of bull trout and brook trout. The mid elevation (765 m/2,510 feet) lake is ice-free from April–November and is quite deep (26 m/84 feet at its deepest). In the spring, it is possible to shore fish around the drop-off at the north end of the lake.

Steamboat Lake (Map 26/G1)

This tiny (4.6 hectare) lake contains many small, stocked rainbow caught on a fly, by trolling or by spincasting. Shore fishing is possible but using a boat is preferred. The lake has a cartop boat launch and recreation site and has an electric motor only restriction. It sits at the 1,125 m (3,656 ft) level.

Summer Lake (Map 14/D3)

Accessed off the Bull-Galbraith FSR, this lake offers a nice camping area and good rainbow fishing. There is a boat launch at this beautiful wilderness lake.

Summit Lake (Map 15/F5)

On Highway 3 near Crowsnest, this popular fishing lake receives plenty of activity in the summer time. The 20 hectare lake contains cutthroat and rainbow, which are best caught by fly fishing or spincasting. Rainbow were stocked in the mid 1990s while western slope cutthroat were stocked in the late 1990s. The lake is 1,356 (4,407 feet) above sea level. Please note that the lake is closed to fishing from November 1 to April 30, has a single hook restriction and has a bait ban.

Summit Lake (Map 17/D4)

Despite the name, Summit Lake is only at 759 m (2,467 feet) above sea level, and fishing starts relatively early in spring. The 150 hectare lake is popular with local fly fishers, who find the lake produces well for rainbow trout, which can get up to 2.5 kg (3 lbs) but average closer to 1 kg (2 lbs). The lake is heavily stocked with rainbow and offers good chironomid and caddis hatches in the spring and early summer. There are a couple of campsites on the lake and several restrictions to note (electric motors only, single hook, no bait, no fishing from November 1 to March 31 and catch and release/fly fishing only in April).

Summit Lake (Map 33/A5)

Located near Parsons, this swampy small (12 hectare) lake can produce some large brook trout (to 2 kg/4 lbs) by trolling a lure in the early spring. A boat is necessary to get out onto the stocked lake (and away from the mosquitoes).

Sunburst Lake (Map 29B/A2)

Considered by many to be one of the premier fly fishing lakes in the Rocky Mountains, Sunburst Lake is found to the west of Lake Magog. This 8.6 hectare lake produces some very large cutthroat, reaching up to 5–7 kg (10–15 lbs). The high elevation (2,219 m/7,212 feet) lake has a relatively short ice-free period and the water remains cold even in the heart of summer. Despite the good reputation, the long, tough hike in deters all but the hard-core angler.

Sunset Lake (Map 11/D2)

This Kokanee Glacier Park hike-in lake offers some good fishing for cutthroat to 35 cm (14 inches). Due to the elevation (1,842 m/6,042 feet), the season lasts from summer to early fall. The trail into this lake is found at the end of the Woodbury FSR west of Kootenay Lake.

Surveyor's Lakes (Map 6/F4)

There is actually a series of five small lakes that are found within the popular Kikomun Creek Provincial Park, but only the main lake produces well. The 16 hectare lake holds plenty of largemouth bass and some good-sized brook trout and rainbow. The bass stay near the bottom in the early spring and then move towards the surface as the water warms into the summertime. Typical bass lures work if you want to try spincasting. For the fly fisher, try an attractor type pattern such as a Woolly Bugger, Woolly Worm or leech pattern. Shore fishing is difficult so bring a float tube and try working the area around the northwest corner of the lake. The lake, which is 777 m (2,549 feet) above sea level, has a campground with a beach for swimming.

Susan Lake (Map 37/G3)

In the early season, this murky, high elevation (1,524 m/5,000 feet) lake produces well for stocked brook trout that reach 2 kg (4 lbs). There are also unconfirmed rumours that rainbow trout inhabit this lake, a remnant of an earlier stocking program. Due to the extensive shallows, fishing from shore is not recommended. The Susan Lake Road provides good access and the lake can be busy during summer evenings. The 45.9 hectare lake does sport a small forest service site and boat launch.

Suzanne (Manistee) Lake (Map 6/F3)

This popular recreation lake is found south of Jaffray and is stocked annually with rainbow, including some of the large growing Gerrard strain. The 56.8 hectare lake also hosts a good largemouth bass fishery. Try using plastic worms or plugs and cast near the weeds at dawn or dusk. Bass can get up to 2 kg (4 lbs), as can the rainbow, which are best caught by trolling, fly fishing or spincasting towards the middle of the lake in spring and fall. The relatively low elevation of the lake (822 m/2,697 feet) allows the lake to open up as early as March.

Ta Ta Lake (Map 13/F2)

This 30 hectare lake is located on the Ta Ta FSR, east of Highway 93/95. The lake offers fair fishing for stocked eastern brook trout, particularly in the late spring and early fall.

Tamarack (Larch) Lake (Map 20/F7)

Tamarack Lake can be accessed by a series of logging roads just east of Skookumchuck. The shallow 36 hectare lake is an artificial fly only lake. It offers some good fishing for rainbow to 2 kg (4 lbs). The bigger trout in the lake survive on minnows, so try trolling a pattern such as a Muddler Minnow or Woolly Bugger. There is a dock, but no launch and the lake is closed to fishing from December 1 to March 31.

Tanal Lake (Map 11/B3)

Found off of Enterprise Creek Trail in Kokanee Glacier Park, Tanal Lake is a sub-alpine lake at 1,798 m/5,844 feet in elevation. The lake offers some good fishing for small cutthroat and a rustic campsite.

Three Island Lake (Map 33/A5)

This popular lake offers some good spring/fall fishing for stocked rainbow that grow to 2.5 kg (5 lbs). Dragging a gang troll and casting a fly or spinner near the drop-off are effective angling methods. There is a forest service site and boat launch at the lake, which is stocked annually with rainbow. Shore fishing is limited at the 24 hectare lake, which is 1,510 m (4,908 feet) above sea level.

Three Valley Lake (Map 30/A6)

This 105 hectare lake lies right alongside the Trans-Canada Highway, just west of Revelstoke. To offset the heavy fishing pressure, the lake is stocked annually with rainbow. The lake offers fair fishing for rainbow, lake trout, bull trout, kokanee and whitefish. At 447 m (1,464 feet) above sea level, it is one of the lowest elevation lakes in this region. Fishing starts early, but slows down in the summer, picking up again in the fall. Trolling is the best producer on this lake, as fish head deep early in the year and stay there.

Tie Lakes (Map 6/E1)

A popular forest service site and good road access makes this lake a busy place to fish. The shallow lake offers stocked rainbow and bass to 2 kg (4 lbs). The rainbow are best caught by trolling in the spring or fall, while the bass are more active in the summer and can be caught using plastic worms or plugs cast near the weeds or cover at dawn or dusk. The lake is 849 m (2,785 feet) above sea level, and gets quite warm in summer.

Topaz Lake (Map 33/F7)

Topaz Lake is a small (14 hectare), shallow lake that is accessed by a rough 4wd road. This lake lives up to its name, as the waters here are a gorgeous shade of blue and surrounded by a rugged mountain backdrop. As an added bonus, your chances of catching a nice rainbow (average 30–35 cm/12-14 in) are pretty good. Shore fishing is limited and there is an electric motor only restriction on the lake, which is 1,097 m (3,642 feet) above sea level.

Trout Lake (Maps 24, 25)

There are probably about a dozen Trout Lakes scattered about the province. This one is one of the biggest, at 2,874 hectares and likely produces the biggest fish with the mighty Gerrard Rainbow occasionally tipping the scales in the 9 kg (20 lb) range. It also has a healthy population of bull trout, which can get up to 4 kg (9 lbs). Both species are best caught on a deep troll using a plug or Flatfish in April–May or again in September–October. The lake is also home to smaller populations of ling cod (burbot), kokanee and whitefish. The lake is 716 m (2,349 feet) above sea level and has a maximum depth of 234 m (768 feet). The best access points are at either the north end (town of Trout Lake) or south end (Goat Range Provincial Park) of the lake. Portions of the lake are closed for spawning purposes so check the regulations before heading out.

Twin Lake (Map 6/D4)

This lake contains a fair number of cutthroat to 35 cm (14 inches). Spincasting or fly fishing from either a boat or the shore works.

Twin Lakes (Map 26/F1)

Although there are actually three small, marshy lakes in the area, they are referred to as the Twin Lakes. Regardless, these lakes offer fishing for small rainbow (20–30 cm/9–12 inches) if you have a boat. Shore fishing is next to impossible. The second lake is the deepest and holds the most fish, while the first and third lakes are best fished at the water inflow areas. There is a forest service site at the lakes.

Victor Lake (Map 30/A5)

Victor Lake is a blip on the continuum of the Eagle River. The 8 hectare, low elevation lake contains many of the same species as the Eagle River (cutthroat, lake and bull trout, kokanee and whitefish), but the prime reason most come here to fish is for the stocked rainbow.

Violin Lake & Mill Pond (Map 2/A7)

A long walk/bike from one of two gates on the rough Violin Lake Road will bring you to this small (26 hectare) lake, which holds a lot of small brook trout. A lure (Deadly Dick or Wedding Band) and worm can create a frenzy of action, especially in the spring and fall. For a shorter walk or ride, you can try your luck at the **Mill Pond**. This reservoir holds fewer numbers of brook trout but the fish are larger and can reach 2 kg (4.5 lbs) on occasion. You should focus your efforts at the far end of the reservoir by casting among the stumps from a float tube. Alternatively, try one of the many beaver ponds between the two lakes. Please note that this was the Trail Watershed and access is restricted.

Waldie (Wulf) Lake (Map 3/B6)

This small mountain lake offers good fishing for small trout in a fantastic setting. Shore fishing is possible but a floatation device is an asset. However, the steep hike and rough road access deters many from venturing in with more than just a rod. Most any dry fly will work but a caddis fly or mosquito is favoured. Spinners cast near the drop-off are also quite effective. This is bear country so be careful.

Wall Lake (Map 8/G7)

Named for the impressive rock wall at the lake's southern end, this remote, hike-in lake is best accessed from Waterton Lakes National Park, in Alberta (see Southwest Alberta Mapbook). From the end of the Akamina Parkway, it is only a 3 km (1.8 mile) hike. From the BC side, access is via a long trail from the end of the 4wd Kishena FSR. The high elevation (1,770 m/5,807 feet), 22 hectare lake remains cool throughout the ice-free season. The short season also means that the resident cutthroat are usually voracious, taking to anything that even remotely looks like food. These fish can get up to 40 cm (15 inches). There is a trail around the lake and a rustic campsite at the north end.

Wapiti Lake (Map 6/E2)

The old road on the west side of Wapiti Lake has been designated a part of the Trans Canada Trail. However, a shorter trail leads from Sherbourne Road to the Wapiti Lake Recreation Site. Fishing in the 15 hectare lake can be quite good since the lake is stocked annually with rainbow. There are also resident brook trout that are best caught during the ice fishing season as well as rumours of kokanee and lake trout. Rainbow can be caught in spring and fall with a float tube to get to the shoal area between the two deepest points of the lake. In winter, this is also a good spot to try your luck with a small white jig or small spoon. The lake is 820 m (2,690 feet) above sea level.

Wasa (Hansen) Lake (Map 13/G2)

This popular recreational lake is found off Highway 93/95 north of Cranbrook. The beaches are very popular during the summer and there is a provincial park campground and boat launch on the lake. The lake was once stocked with rainbow and brook trout, but both species have disappeared due to fishing pressure and being overrun by largemouth bass. The bass have taken to the warm waters, and now grow to 2 kg (4 lbs). Any of the usual bass gear will work. Please note that the lake sports a rare freshwater reef that is popular with divers.

Wedgewood Lake (Map 29B/A2, 34/G6)

At the headwaters of Mitchell River, to the west of Lake Magog, this hike-in lake offers good fly fishing and spincasting for cutthroat. However, shore casting is difficult due to the trees surrounding the lake. The fish can reach 1.5 kg (3 lbs) but average 30–35 cm (12–14 inches) in size. They travel in schools so if you find one, chances are you will catch a bunch. The 12 hectare, high elevation (1,905 m/6,191 feet) lake is a long, tough hike from the nearest road, and, as a result, the lake sees less angling pressure than it might otherwise experience.

Wee Sandy Lake (Map 17/E7)

This remote alpine lake is found near the western boundary of Valhalla Provincial Park. Access to this lake is via a difficult 14.8 km (9 mile) trail, which in turn is only accessible by boat across Slocan Lake. The lake is also accessible by helicopter or float plane. Either way, it is well worth the effort to get to. Not only is the 74 hectare lake beautiful, but it also has good fishing for resident cutthroat. The lake is at 1,951 m (6,400 feet), and is only free of ice for about four months. There are only a few places where shore fishing works, but carrying a float tube up the trail is not an option most would revel in.

Whatshan Lake (Map 16/E6)

A popular destination for local anglers, this relatively large (1,733 hectare) lake is found 655 m (2,149 feet) above sea level. Even though it is big and deep, the lake still produces better in spring for rainbow that grow to 1.5 kg (3 lbs). Trolling is the most effective method and can produce the odd bull trout up to 5 kg (11 lbs) and even some small kokanee. There is camping, a boat launch and cabins on the lake.

Wheeler Lake (Map 11/E3)

Found in Kokanee Glacier Park, this remote lake requires walking at least 2.5 km (1.6 miles) from an old road off the Cedar Creek Road. You can expect some good fishing for small cutthroat at this high elevation (1,615 m/5,249 ft) lake.

White Boar Lake (Map 12/F7)

This picturesque mountain lake is set below the towering ridge of Mount McKay. You will need a 4wd with high clearance to clear the cross ditches on route to the lake. At the end of the road a short trail leads to the shoreline. If you bring a floatation device and can match the hatch, you will have fun with the abundant small trout.

Whiteswan Lake (Map 21/C4)

This popular retreat offers a fabulous campground and a wide variety of rec-reational activities. Despite the heavy fishing pressure, the 376 hectare lake offers some good fishing for stocked Gerrard Rainbow to 5 kg (10 lbs) and wild brook trout in the 20–45 cm (8–17 inch) range. Despite the elevation (1,127 m (3,697 feet)), fishing is better in the early spring or late fall. Try troll-ing a gang troll or Flatfish in 5–7 m (15–25 feet) of water. Fly fisherman should troll or cast a wet fly (black leech, shrimp or chironomid pattern) on a sinking line or cast a dry fly (Adams or Humpy) in the shoals at the east end of the lake during the evenings. Check the regulations before heading out, as there are a number of special restrictions.

Whitetail (Deer) Lake (Map 20/C3)

This crystal clear lake is a very popular trophy fishing lake, despite the rav-ages of a forest fire than rushed through here in 2001. The 166 hectare lake produces well for stocked Gerrard Rainbow that grow to 4 kg (9 lbs) and average a good 50 cm (20 inches) in length. There are also a few brook trout that also grow big (to 2.5 kg/6 lbs). A boat is needed to effectively work the lake since the trout are finicky. Fly anglers will find good chironomid, mayfly and dragonfly hatches. Restrictions include a 1 trout limit and no bait fishing or ice fishing. The lake rests at 1,066 m (3,465 feet) in elevation and is home to a nice campsite.

Wilbur Lake (Map 33/B5)

Near Parsons, this lake receives a fair bit of activity even though action can be slow at times. The 15 hectare lake contains eastern brook trout and stocked rainbow to 3 kg (6.5 lbs), although the average catch is closer to 0.5 kg (1 lb). The extensive shallows and swampy areas around the lake make shore casting all but impossible, so bring a float tube or canoe and cast towards the weeds. The fish here seem to favour flies, especially larger nymphs (like dragonfly nymphs) earlier in the year, but by summer you will have to fish deeper to catch anything. The lake is 1,277m (4,190 feet) above sea level.

Wilmer (Munn) Lake (Map 27/C5)

This lake north of Invermere receives heavy fishing pressure throughout the late spring and into the summer. It is stocked with both rainbow and brook trout, and fishing can be good using a chironomid pattern or slowly trailing a leech. Ice fishing is popular during the winter months and jigging a small spoon or jig in 1–2 m (3–6 feet) of water is an effective method.

Wilson and Little Wilson Lakes (Map 17/D2)

West of Nakusp, the long, narrow, and deep **Wilson Lake** has two popular forest service sites complete with campgrounds and boat launches. Be care-ful of the bears that frequent the area. The large lake is a popular fishing hole and offers fly fishing, trolling and spincasting for rainbow to 1 kg (2 lbs). The fishing is good in the spring but slows considerably in the summer. Nearby

Little Wilson Lake offers good fishing for rainbow primarily by spincasting or fly fishing. The lake has a forest service site with a campground and cartop boat launch. Both lakes are stocked every even year with rainbow.

Windermere Lake (Map 27/D6)

This windy, well-developed lake south of Invermere is known more for its water sports than its fishing. There are several resorts, campsites and boat launches on the lake. The best fishing for trout and char is right after the ice is out and trolling or fly fishing can produce rainbow or cutthroat to 2.5 kg (6 lbs) and bull trout to 3.5 kg (8 lbs). Whitefish, small kokanee, burbot, bass, perch and char are the other species in the lake and they often provide summer fun for anglers. The bass and whitefish are found in the shallows. The lake is stocked periodically with rainbow and is 800 m (2,625 feet) above sea level.

Wiseman Lakes (Map 38/C5)

Easily accessed by the Donald Road, this shallow, marshy lake produces more mosquitoes than fish. Actually fishing the lake is difficult due to the swampy shoreline.

Wooden Shoe Lake (Map 4/C2)

The forest surrounding Wooden Shoe and Boulder Lakes was burned right to the lakeshore in 2003. Wooden Shoe Lake was the main water source for fighting fires in the area. It is so low that they predict that up to 80% of the cutthroat population in the lake probably died and they are assuming winter-kill will get the rest. So, stocking will begin again in the spring, but the lake won't be producing the big fish again for at least 3 years.

Wragge Lake (Map 17/E6)

You will need an ATV or sturdy 4wd vehicle to access this nice mountain lake since the road is overgrown and has a bridge out. For this reason, the fishing can be excellent for small trout.

Yankee Lake (Map 20/A7)

See Canuck Lake.

National Parks

Fishing in a national park is indeed a different experience than fishing anywhere else. You will need a special license and there are separate rules and regulations that govern the park (see www.parkscanada.gc.ca for more information). But the fishing can be excellent and the scenery is always impressive. Most of the lakes rest at a high elevation and have a limited ice-free season. They often do not open up until June and provide steady fishing through September. The streams also offer better fishing in the late summer once the waters have cleared from the spring run-off.

Glacier National Park

Illecillewaet River (Maps 31/F1-30/D5) is described in the Stream Fishing Section.

Incomappleux River (Maps 31/F2-24/C1) is described in the Stream Fishing Section.

Kootenay National Park

Cobb Lake (Map 27/E3) is accessed from Highway 93 along an easy trail that actually descends to the lake. This dark water lake has many brook trout averaging 20–30 cm (8-12 in). Try a wet fly cast past the drop-off or use a lure. Shore casting is difficult due to the tree line.

Dog Lake (Map 27/E1) is a popular fishing lake that is accessed by a 3 km (1.8 mile) trail from McLeod Meadows Campground. The lake holds good numbers of small brook trout (average 25–35 cm/10–14 inches). Shore fishing is difficult, as the shallows are weedy.

Kaufmann Lake (Map 34/A1) is a popular hike-in lake that is accessed via the Tokumm Creek Trail. The lake is found at 2,150 m (6,988 feet) in elevation and provides good fishing for stocked rainbow and brook trout. Some of the brookies reach 40 cm (16 inches) in size. Shore fishing is possible and a good area to try is near the inlet creek.

Ochre Creek (Map 34/A2) is a small trail access creek that offers small cutthroat, bull trout and whitefish. Fishing is better in the summer or fall (after the high water recedes) using a fly or bait.

Olive Lake (Map 27/E3) is located at Sinclair Pass on Highway 93. The small lake has fair numbers of small brook trout to 25 cm (10 inches). Try casting into the shallows from a boat for best results, as shore fishing is difficult due to the tree line.

Simpson River (Map 34/F5) is accessed by trail from Highway 93 and provides good fishing for small cutthroat that can reach 40 cm (16 inches) and bull trout to 4 kg (9 lbs). The fish are primarily found in the large pools in the first 8 km of the river and will take to flies or bait.

Verdant Creek (Map 34/E4) is a remote tributary of the Simpson River. The creek has numerous cutthroat and bull trout in the 20–25 cm (8–10 inch) range that readily take to bait or flies.

Vermillion River (Map 34/C1-C7) is the main fishing stream flowing through Kootenay National Park. Highway 93 provides good access to this river, which provides small cutthroat, rainbow and bull trout (averaging 20–30 cm/8–12 inches). The fishing is so so until the water clears in late summer and fall.

Mount Revelstoke National Park

Eva Lake (Map 30/E3) is a fairly easy two hour hike from the nearest road. The lake is a popular destination sitting at 1,784 m (5,850 feet), and is ice-free from mid-summer (July or so) to September. Small cutthroat and rainbow trout provide steady action.

Jade Lakes (Map 30/F3) are located about two hours past Eva Lake on the other side of the pass. They are not quite as high elevation as the other lakes in Mount Revelstoke (at 1,670 m/5,475 feet), but the fishing season is still limited to the summer. Small rainbow and cutthroat trout come readily to most presentations.

Miller Lake (Map 30/E3) is found before Eva Lake and offers a very similar fishery.

Yoho National Park

Amiskwi River (Map 39/B3-D6) is accessed by an old road (now open to hiking and biking) and a trail (hiking only). The further you are willing to travel, the less fishing pressure the better pools receive. This river is best fished late in the season after the muddy waters have subsided.

Small brook trout and bull trout (average 15–25 cm/8–10 inches) are common but the occasional bull trout will reach 2 kg (4 lbs). Try bait or flies.

Beaverfoot River (Map 33/F4-C2) is described in the Stream Fishing Section.

Emerald Lake (Map 39/D5) is found at the end of the paved Emerald Lake Road, making it a very popular tourist destination. There is some fair fishing for rainbow, brook and bull trout (average 25-35 cm/10–14 inches) using a fly, lure or bait. Cast near shore where the fish tend to congregate to avoid the silty, glacier-fed deeper waters.

Emerald River (Map 39/D6) is best accessed along the Emerald River Trail. Small brook trout and rainbow to 30 cm (12 inches) can be readily caught with bait or flies. The occasional bull trout is also found.

Hidden Lake (Map 39/E5) is accessed after a short hike from the Yoho Valley Road. This lake has modest numbers of rainbow and brook trout taken on a fly or by spincasting. Camping is available at the lake. No permit is required to fish this lake.

Ice River (Map 33/E2) is a small river located in the southern portion of Yoho National Park. It contains fair numbers of cutthroat, bull trout and whitefish that are easily caught on a fly or by spincasting. Most of the river will require bushwhacking to reach.

Kicking Horse River (Maps 39/E5-33/A1-38F7) is described in the Stream Fishing Section.

Lake Dushesnay (Map 39/E4) is accessed from Takakkaw Falls Campsite. Follow the trail to this lake where good fishing for brook trout to 1 kg (2 lbs) exists.

Lake O'Hara (Map 39/G6) is the hub of Yoho National Park and is accessed by trail or private bus. The lake holds fair numbers of small cutthroat in the 20–25 cm (8–10 inch) range caught with a fly or lure. Fishing from shore is your best bet as the fish stay close to shore due to the silty, glacier-fed water. There is a lodge and camping facilities at the lake.

Linda Lake (Map 39/F6) is a clear water lake with numerous cutthroat in the 20–30 cm (8–12 inch) range. Shore fishing is a possibility with spincasting and fly fishing proving effective. The lake is accessed by trail off the Lake O'Hara Fire Road.

Marpole Lake (Map 39/D3) is accessed from the Takakkaw Falls Campsite. A 9 km (5.5 mile) return hike brings you to this sub-alpine lake, which contains good numbers of small cutthroat and brook trout. A shelter and camping is available near the lake.

Nara Lakes (Map 39/G5) are found on the Cataract Brook Trail past Wapta Lake. Give yourself about an hour to walk to the lakes, which offer good fishing for small rainbow and brook trout.

Otterhead River (Map 39/B6) is a small river found off a fire access road to the west of the Trans-Canada Highway. The river has a fair number of small bull trout, whitefish and brook trout that average 15–25 cm (6–10 inches). Anglers use flies or bait.

Ottertail River (Maps 33/G1-39/D7) is found across the highway from the Otterhead River. The Ottertail also offers a fair number of small brook trout, bull trout and whitefish to 30 cm (12 inches). Fishing is better in the lower reaches, which can be reached along the fire road.

Ross Lake (Map 39/G5) is accessed by a short 1.5km (.9 mile) hike off Highway 1A. There are a fair number of small rainbow and brook trout (average 20-30cm) in the lake. Try fly fishing or spincasting.

Sherbrooke Lake (Map 39/F5) is accessed from Wapta Lake Lodge along a 3 km trail. The lake holds fair numbers of rainbow and lake trout to 1 kg (2 lbs) that average 20–35 cm (8–14 inches). The silty, glacier-fed water makes fishing tough so use bait or a streamer fly for best results. The lake is at 1,880 m (5,850 feet) in elevation.

Wapta Lake (Map 39/F5) is found next to the Trans Canada Highway. You can catch the odd rainbow or brook trout to 1 kg (2.5 lbs), although lucky anglers can be rewarded with a large lake trout as well.

Yoho Lake (Map 39/E5) is a tiny lake located 4.5 km (2.7 miles) from the road along a fairly steep trail. It contains rainbow, cutthroat and brook trout.

Stream Fishing

The main sportfish in Kootenay streams are rainbow, brook trout, cutthroat trout or bull trout. Since the streams and rivers provide an important spawning and rearing area for wild rainbow and char, strict regulations have been imposed to prevent over fishing. Most notably, there is no fishing from April 1 to June 14 in almost all streams. There is also a catch and release restriction for trout and char from November 1 to March 31 and the single, barbless hook restriction have been extended to all Kootenay streams. Many of the tributaries into the larger lake are closed to bull trout fishing. Always check the regulations for current information before you fish.

In most rivers, the spring runoff begins to peak in mid May and continues through to the end of June. Often times, during runoff, the rivers are very difficult to fish because they are murky and too high. Therefore, it is best to wait until mid to late July to allow the water level to subside and the water to clear before fishing.

Rainbow trout are often found in the faster water leading into a pool whereas cutthroat tend to hide behind obstructions such as sweepers, logs and root or on the outside bend of the river were the current slows. Bull trout and eastern brook trout are found primarily in the larger pools away from the main current. Whether you are bait fishing, spincasting or fly fishing, it is best to stay well back from the pool as the fish can see shadows and sense movements in the water.

Although most watercourses in the Kootenays hold fish, we have not written up every single stream in which you can catch fish. If you do not find the creek you are interested in mentioned in our write-ups, look for the river that it flows into or a nearby stream that we have written on. Most tributaries have similar fishing characteristics to each other. If you are fishing in one of the national parks, see the separate section at the end of the lakes.

Abruzzi Creek (Map 29A/A6)

A trail accessed creek in Elk Lakes Provincial Park, this stream does not see heavy fishing pressure. This is partly due to the difficult trail access as well as the heavy restrictions that are placed on the creek. It is closed to fishing from September 1 to October 31, there is a bait ban and it is catch and release only for all trout and char from June 15 to August 31.

Akamina Creek (Map 8/G7)

An abandoned road-cum-trail follows Akamina Creek all the way from the headwaters of the creek in Akamina Pass to its confluence with Kishinena Creek. The creek contains lots of cutthroat to 35 cm (14 inches) and the occasional bull trout to 50 cm (21 inches).

Akolkolex River (Maps 31/B5-30/G7)

This is a popular river with locals due to its small, fast flowing rapids. The upper stretches of this river hold good numbers of cutthroat caught using lures or a fly. There is a bait ban from June 15-October 31, a single barbless hook requirement and catch and release only. This river can be accessed 18 km (10.8 miles) south of Revelstoke along a good gravel road.

Albert River (Map 28/B4)

The Albert is a fast flowing river, with plenty of pools where the cutthroat and occasional bull trout like to hang out. A logging road runs along most of the river, meaning that access is good, but rough. You will find cutthroat to 40 cm (15 inches) and bull trout to 4 kg (9 lbs). There are also a few whitefish to 35 cm (13 inches). Try bait or flies after the high water subsides. A forest service site at the junction with the Palliser River provides a good base to explore this remote river.

Aldridge Creek (Map 22/D1)

Accessed by trail, Aldridge Creek contains cutthroat trout to 40 cm (16 inches), which you will find in good numbers. You may also find bull trout to 65 cm (26 inches).

Alexander Creek (Map 15/F3)

This creek runs parallel to the Alberta/BC boundary, about 3 km (1.8 miles) inside BC. It contains plenty of cutthroat trout to 35 cm (14 inches). A rough road/trail system follows the creek valley.

Beaton Creek (Map 24/C2)

This creek has good fishing for small brook trout and bull trout in the summer and fall. Bait fishing and fly fishing are both effective. The lower reaches of the creek have good access from Highway 31, while the upper reaches will require some bushwhacking.

Beaver Creek (Map 2/F5-C7)

Beaver Creek runs through Fruitvale and into the Columbia River near Trail. Access to the creek is easily gained from Highway 3B. Because of this, the creek receives heavy fishing pressure but can still be productive. Fly fishing, bait and spincasting for rainbow and brook trout that reach 2 kg (4 lbs) on occasion will all work. The mouth of the creek (where it meets the Columbia River) is a popular spot that can produce good size rainbow. Watch for closures from September 1–October 31.

Beaverfoot River (Map 33/F4-C2)

The Beaverfoot is a generally lethargic river that winds its way northwest and into the Kicking Horse River. The river holds fair numbers of bull trout, cutthroat and rainbow. Try using a lure, bait or fly. The river forms part of the southwestern border of Yoho National Park and has good road access, although the better pools will require some bushwhacking to reach.

Big Sheep Creek (Map 1/F7)

Accessed off the Old Cascade Highway west of Rossland, this creek offers some good brook trout fishing for small fish (to 0.5 kg/1 lb). Fishing the larger pools with bait or a fly is the preferred method. There is no fishing between September 1 and October 31.

Bingay Creek (Map 22/A3)

This creek contains cutthroat trout to 40 cm (16 inches), which you will find in good numbers. You may also find bull trout to 65 cm (26 inches).

Blanket Creek (Map 23/D1-30/E7)

A popular provincial park provides access to the mouth of the creek where it flows into the Upper Arrow Lake. This is a good place to try for some of the larger rainbow or bull trout. The upper reaches of the creek will require some bushwhacking to get to. The creek offers fair fishing for small rainbow and the occasional bull trout. The best time to fish the creek is in the summer.

Bloom Creek (Map 6/C6)

This small creek offers some good fishing for cutthroat to 35 cm (14 inches). A fly or bait worked near cover or in slower water can be very effective. Access is provided by a good gravel road and there are a few forest service sites in the area to camp at.

Bobbie Burns Creek (Maps 32/D5-33/D6)

This large glacier-fed creek flows into the Spillimacheen River, west of the Columbia Floodplains. The lower part of the creek has good access while the upper portion can be accessed by trail. The creek offers good fishing for small rainbow using bait or a fly.

Boivin Creek (Map 22/B6)

This is another small tributary of the Elk River that contains cutthroat and to a lesser degree bull trout. The close proximity to Elkford means the creek is fished more often and the fish are usually harder to catch and smaller in size.

Boundary Creek (Maps 3/F7-4/A7)

The upper reaches of Boundary Creek are on the BC side of the BC/US border. It contains rainbow and brook trout to 1 kg (2 lbs).

Brewer Creek (Maps 27/A7-20/C1)

This creek has a good number of cutthroat to 40 cm (16 inches) that average 20–30 cm and a few bull trout to 2.5 kg (5 lbs). Try bait or a fly anytime after high water. Whitefish to 35 cm (14 inches) are more abundant in the fall. The Brewer Creek Road provides access to most of the creek, although remote holes are not hard to find.

Brule Creek (Map 15/A1-C1)

This creek is home to plentiful, but small cutthroat. The usual catch is between 15–25 cm (8–10 inches) but lucky anglers can find 35 cm (14 inch) fish. The closer you get to the creek's confluence with the Elk River, the better the fishing. Access to the upper reaches of the creek is along the Brule Creek Trail.

Bugaboo Creek (Maps 26/A1-33/F7)

This creek flows from the famous glacier after which a beautiful alpine park is named. The high volume creek has good road access along most of its length. After the high water subsides, this creek has good fishing for small cutthroat by fly or with bait.

Bull River (Maps 22/A4-14/C7)

The Bull River is a popular East Kootenay River that has good gravel road access along most of its length. Some of these roads may have restricted access during logging periods. Rainbow, cutthroat and bull trout are all found in the river system with some of the larger pools producing trout to 1 kg (2 lbs). The upper reaches of the river provide better fishing with fewer restrictions. Some of the restrictions on the river include: a bait ban from June 15–October 31 and catch and release from Galbraith Creek to Van Creek (Map 14/F5) and from Aberfelde Dam to Tie Mill Dam (Map 14/E7).

Burrell Creek (Maps 9/A3-7)

Burrell Creek flows south and west before draining into the Granby River (west of this mapbook). There are a couple of forest service sites from which to explore the river from. The river contains small rainbow and is best fished once the water levels have normalized after spring runoff.

Burton Creek (Maps 9/G1-17/A7)

Burton Creek flows into the Lower Arrow Lake just south of Burton and can be accessed by logging road. The creek offers some decent fishing for rainbow and bull trout primarily by bait fishing. A sporadic stocking program included bull trout and rainbow in the mid 1990s. To protect the spawning grounds, the creek is closed from Woden Creek to Highway 6 (Map 17/A7) from June 15 to October 31 and from 300 meters downstream from the Highway 6 Bridge to the lake throughout the year.

Cabin Creek (Maps 7/G6-8/A6)

A tributary of the Flathead River, this creek contains smaller cutthroat (to 30 cm/12 inches), bull trout to 60 cm (24 inches) and whitefish to 30 cm (12 inches). The creek does not see much fishing pressure since it is closed to bull trout fishing. The creek is also closed to angling during the fall (September 1 to October 31) and in the summer (June 15 to August 31). Other restrictions include a one trout limit, with the minimum sized catch being 30 cm (12 inches). Many anglers find the regulations to be stacked against them, so don't bother, however, those that go will find fishing better the farther you head upstream. A logging road follows the creek up (and over) Cabin Pass.

Cadorna Creek (Map 29A/A6)

Cadorna Creek drains Cadorna Lake in Elk Lakes Provincial Park. It is accessed by the Cadorna Lake Trail and does not see much action. Rumour has it the fishing is fairly steady for cutthroat trout to 45 cm (18 inches).

Caithness Creek (Map 6/G2)

The easiest place to access this creek is where Highway 3/93 crosses it, although there are logging roads that run alongside the creek on both sides of the highway. The creek holds small rainbow and cutthroat trout that can grow to about 35 cm (14 inches) in size.

Caribou Creek (Map 17/B6)

This creek is found just north of Burton Creek on the Lower Arrow Lake. The creek offers good fishing for rainbow and bull trout thanks in part to stocking. In fact, both bull trout and rainbow were stocked as recently as 1995. To protect the spawning grounds, the creek is closed from Rodd Creek to Highway 6 from June 15 to October 31 and from 300 meters downstream from the Highway 6 Bridge to the lake throughout the year. The lower section of the creek is best accessed from the Burton Creek Road. The upper portion of the creek is better accessed from the Shannon Creek Road, to the west.

Carney Creek (Map 19/B4)

Carney Creek is a good fly fishing stream for small rainbow. The creek can only be reached by trail and is also home to bull trout. Working bait or lures in the larger pools can produce bull trout to 1 kg (2 lbs).

Caven Creek (Map 6/B5-F7)

Although most of this creek is easily accessed by logging roads, there are remote stretches that rarely see an angler. It is the pools in these sections that have good numbers of cutthroat trout to 35 cm (14 inches). Smaller trout are found throughout the creek.

Cherry (Mather) Creek (Map 13/E1-G4)

Found outside of Kimberley off of Highway 95A, there are plenty of small cutthroat and brook trout that can be caught with bait or on a fly. Bushwhacking to the more remote pools will increase your success. There is a limited season as the creek does dry up in the late summer.

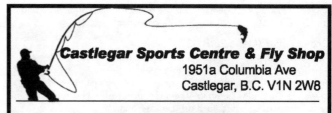
Coal Creek (Map 15/B7)

Since Coal Creek flows into the Elk River in the heart of Fernie, it sees a lot of action after the high water has receded. Regardless, the creek offers good fishing for smaller cutthroat (in the 20–30 cm/8–12 inch range). The last 7 km (4.2 miles) of the river (below the old MF&M Railway bridge) is age restricted.

Columbia River (North) (Maps 20, 27, 30, 32, 33, 38)

The Columbia is one of North America's big rivers weaving its way from deep in the heart of the Kootenays across much of southeastern BC. South of the border, it flows towards the famous Gorge, which forms the border between Oregon and Washington State. Near the headwaters of the Columbia River, the main species to catch are bull trout as well as some Rocky Mountain whitefish and rainbow. Spincasting or fly fishing from shore or boat are equally effective but do not expect great fishing. The slow fishing is partly a result of stagnant water in the endless channels that make up the river as it meanders through the Columbia Floodplains. One notable exception is the small section of river connecting Upper Arrow Lake and Lake Revelstoke (Map 30/D4). Despite its proximity to Revelstoke this section offers good fishing for bigger trout. Good highway access and full facilities are found throughout the Columbia Valley.

Columbia River (South) (Map 2/A2-C7)

The section of the Columbia between Castlegar and the US border offers some of the best river fishing in the province. However, it is a large volume river that can be frustrating to fish. The trick is to find a back eddy as the river level fluctuates often. Rainbow to 4 kg (9 lbs), ling cod (near Rivervale), and walleye to 2 kg (4 lbs) can be caught. For the rainbow, the preferred method is to fish from shore or with a boat with a 25 hp+ engine in the larger pools. Using a float and bait (salmon fly, black ant, grasshopper, etc.) or a fly that matches the predominant hatch can be fantastic. The best season for rainbow is May 15 to October 15. Fishing for walleye compares with anywhere in North America. A popular spot to catch these cruising predators is at the Waneta Dam (the mouth of the Pend D'Oreille River) from June 15 to October. Please note that there is a closure from the old Robson Ferry to the CP railway bridge from March 1 to June 3. Also, sturgeon fishing is closed throughout this entire stretch of river.

Commerce Creek (Map 8/B5)

A tributary of the Flathead River, this creek offers a similar fishery (and restrictions) as Cabin Creek described above.

Corn Creek (Maps 3/G7-4/B7)

Corn Creek is found to the west of Creston and can be broken into two different sections. The more remote upper reaches offer small cutthroat and can be accessed by trail and/or bushwhacking. The slow meandering lower section holds warm water fish such as bass and perch. This section of the creek cuts through the Creston Valley Wildlife Centre, which is a popular bird watching area.

Couldrey Creek (Maps 7/G7-8/A7)

A tributary of the Flathead River, this creek offers a similar fishery (and restrictions) as Cabin Creek described above.

Coyote Creek (Maps 14/D1-21/C5)

There are many nice pools along this creek, which is a major tributary of the Lussier River. Access into some sections is a little tricky. As a result, some nice cutthroat (to 40 cm/16 inches) and bull trout to 2 kg (4 lbs) often reward the angler. The easily accessed sections are home to trout between 20 and 30 cm (8–12 inches). You will also find the odd whitefish.

Cross River (Maps 28/B1-27/F3)
The lower reaches of the Cross are a spectacular area with a series of waterfalls and pools that impede fish migration. This section produces good numbers of cutthroat in the 20–35 cm (8–14 inch) range, the odd bull trout to 4 kg (9 lbs) and whitefish to 40 cm (16 inches). The Natural Bridge Trail system provides access to the most scenic section.

Crossing Creek (Map 22/B5)
This small tributary of the Elk River is best accessed by trail west of Round Prairie. Cutthroat trout to 40 cm (16 inches) and even bigger bull trout are found in the creek on occasion.

Cummings Creek (Map 15/C3)
This creek is home to plentiful, but small cutthroat. The usual catch is between 15–25 cm (8–10 inches) with the better action found closer you get to the creek's confluence with the Elk River.

Diorite Creek (Map 21/A7)
The Diorite Valley has seen little human activity since access into this area is poor. But the area is pretty, and the creek holds hungry cutthroat that will get up to 40 cm (16 inches).

Driftwood Creek (Map 33/D6)
Summer fishing can be good for small cutthroat using a fly or bait. Remote pools can be found by bushwhacking.

Duncan River (Maps 32/B4-25/D3; 18/F3)
The mid section of the Duncan River connects the man-made Duncan Lake with the north end of Kootenay Lake. To protect spawning channels, this section is closed to fishing except for a limited season for whitefish from March to April 15. The northern section of the river, above Duncan Lake, holds some bull trout to 2 kg (4 lbs). This section is easily accessed by a good gravel road.

Dutch Creek (Maps 19/F3-20/E1)
Dutch Creek flows 48 km (29.3 miles) from the Purcell Wilderness Conservancy to the north end of Columbia Lake. It is an excellent trout stream. After high water, this creek can produce good numbers of rainbow and cutthroat

to 2 kg (4 lbs) and the occasional bull trout to 5 kg (11 lbs). The fishing is better in the upper reaches where the fishing pressure is less and the fish tend to be larger. Watch for closures below Ben Able Creek (Map 20/A1) and a bait ban on the entire creek from June 15–October 31.

Elk River (Maps 6–7, 15, 22, 29)
The majestic Elk River is a pinnacle of the East Kootenays as it flows from high up in the Rocky Mountains to the lowlands surrounding Lake Koocanusa. Over its course, the river offers some world-class dry fly fishing for westslope cutthroat. Whitefish, and bull trout can also be caught on a spinner or fly. The cutthroat tend to be small, under 1 kg (2 lbs), and are best fished in the fall. The bull trout can reach 5 kg (11 lbs) and are mostly found in the upper reaches of the river. Many of the tributaries offer good fishing and working the pools around these creek mouths can be very rewarding. For fly fishermen, start by dry fly fishing with a size 10–14 deer hair caddis pattern (green, yellow, orange–brown color) or a size 8–12 Adams. If dry flies are not working, try a weighted stonefly or Hare's Ear nymph with a strike indicator. Sections of the river are catch and release only and the river has a bait ban from June 15–October 31.

Enterprise Creek (Maps 11/B2-10/G1)
After the high water subsides, there is good fishing for small rainbow with a fly or bait. The creek flows from Kokanee Glacier Provincial Park into Slocan Lake and has good road and trail access.

Erie Creek (Map 2/F4)
This subsidiary of the Salmo River offers good fishing for very small rainbow trout. The old standby, a worm and hook, used any time after high water will produce lots of action. Access to the lower reaches is limited.

Fairy & Hartley Creeks (Map 15/A6)
Both of these small streams flow into the Elk River near Fernie. The creeks offer good fishing for cutthroat in the 20–30 cm (8–12 inch) range as well as a few bull trout. After high water, try using a fly or bait. Your best bet is to fish just upstream of the confluence, particularly when the Elk is running dirty.

Findlay Creek (Maps 19/F7-20/G5)
Accessed via the Findlay Creek Road and trail, this creek has good numbers of cutthroat, which average 20–30 cm (8–12 inches), bull trout to 4 kg (9 lbs) and whitefish to 40 cm (16 inches). For those willing to work into remote holes, fishing can be fast and furious. Catch and release applies from Doctor Creek Bridge to Lavington Creek Bridge (Map 20/C4) and there is a bait ban on the entire creek from June 15–October 31.

Flathead River (Maps 7/E1-8/B7)
Found in the beautiful southeast corner of the province, the Flathead River offers several forest service sites from which to base camp. The river offers fair fishing for smaller cutthroat, rainbow and whitefish. The river has occasionally turned up a few monster bull trout (to 10 kg/22 lbs), but it is now catch and release only for these beauties. In addition, the river is closed to fishing during fall (September 1 to October 31), with a one trout limit (none under 30 cm/12 inches) from June 15 to August 31.

Fording River (Maps 22/D4-15/D1)
A tributary of the Elk River, this river offers a similar fishery in a spectacular setting. Watch for the catch and release restriction and enjoy the good fly fishing for cutthroat.

Forster Creek (Maps 26/E3-27/A3)
Forster Creek is another glacier-fed creek that flows down to the Columbia Valley. Summer and fall is a good time to catch the abundant small cutthroat on fly or with bait. There is good road access along most of the creek.

Forsyth Creek (Maps 29A/A7-22/B2)
Mainly a trail access creek, Forsyth Creek contains good numbers of cutthroat trout to 40 cm (16 inches. You may also find bull trout to 65 cm (26 inches). The 2 km (1.8 mile) section below Conner Lake (basically to the border of Height of the Rockies Provincial Park) is closed to angling.

Frances Creek (Maps 26/D2-27/B4)
Found to the north of Forster Creek, Frances Creek offers a similar fishing experience as most creeks in the area. After high water, there is good fishing for small cutthroat which average 20–25 cm (8–10 inches), especially in the larger pools. Try bait or flies. There are several forest service sites in the area to base camp at.

Fry Creek (Maps 19/C5-18/G5)

A trail offers access to some remote creek fishing opportunities for small rainbow and bull trout. The fish can reach 1 kg (2 lbs) on occasion and come readily to a fly, bait or small lures.

Galbraith Creek (Map 14/E2-F4)

Galbraith Creek contains plenty of cutthroat, many of which grow to an impressive 40 cm (16 inches) in size. The main creek is easily accessed by logging road, while North Galbraith Creek is accessed by trail. In the fall, bull trout and whitefish are present in the creek.

Goat River (Maps 12/F7-4/F5)

The Goat River flows into the Kootenay River near Creston and was once one of the great fishing rivers in the area. Unfortunately, the river has suffered over the years as water levels are down and the average size of catch seems to be getting smaller. As usual, the better fishing is found the further you get away from civilization. Cutthroat to 1 kg (2 lbs) can be caught on a fly or with bait above the canyon whereas rainbow to 0.5 kg (1 lb) are taken throughout the system on flies or with a spinner. The best season is during lower water (mid-June to August). There is a catch and release restriction between Leadville Creek and Cameron Creek (Map 4/F3) and a bait ban on the entire creek from June 15–October 31.

Gold Creek (Maps 5/G3-6/G7)

This large creek dissects one of the busiest logging road networks in the province before flowing into Lake Koocanusa. Several forest service sites offer camping in the area and there is no shortage of places to access the creek. In the summer, you can have good success for small cutthroat and bull trout using bait or a fly. Larger fish are found near the mouth of the creek.

Gray Creek (Map 12/A5)

The Gray Creek Pass Road is a heralded backroad route linking the West Kootenays and the East Kootenays. During the summer, this is a beautiful drive that starts by climbing steeply from Kootenay Lake to the pass. Along the way, Gray Creek offers fair numbers of rainbow and bull trout that can reach 1 kg (2 lbs) on occasion. Fishing is not possible until after the high water has receded in late June.

Ha Ha Creek (Map 6/C1)

Ha Ha Creek drains Ha Ha and Bednorski Lakes. There is good access along various backroads and a chance to catch small brook trout (to 20 cm/12 inches). The fish are more often found in the upper reaches of the creek.

Halfway River (Map 24/D5-A6)

The main attraction to the Halfway River is the two natural hot springs. As an added bonus, the river also holds fair numbers of small rainbow. The fish can be taken on a fly, lure or bait in the upper reaches of the river. Fishing is closed below the falls, 11 km (6.6 miles) from Upper Arrow Lake.

Harmer Creek (Map 15/E2)

Harmer Creek is home to plentiful, but small cutthroat. The usual catch is between 15–25 cm (8–10 inches) but the odd fish can get up to 35 cm (14 inches) in size. The closer you get to the creek's confluence with the Elk River, the better the fishing.

Harvey Creek (Maps 7/G3-8/A3)

A tributary of the Flathead River, this creek contains smaller cutthroat (to 30 cm/12 inches), bull trout to 60 cm (24 inches) and whitefish to 30 cm (12 inches). The creek does not see much fishing pressure since it is closed to bull trout fishing. The creek is also closed to angling during the fall (September 1 to October 31) and in the summer (June 15 to August 31). Other restrictions include a one trout limit, with the minimum sized catch being 30 cm (12 inches). Many anglers find the regulations to be stacked against them, and don't bother, however, those that go will find fishing better the farther you head upstream.

Horsethief Creek (Maps 26/C6-27/C4)

Another large glacier-fed stream flowing into the Columbia Valley, Horsethief Creek has some remote sections that offer good fishing for cutthroat to 40 cm (16 inches). The fishing is better later in the summer and early fall (after the high water has receded). Whitefish to 35 cm (14 inches) are also prominent in the fall and there are a few bull trout to 3.5 kg (7 lbs).

Howell Creek (Map 8/A6)

Offering a similar fishery to Harvey Creek (see above), Howell Creek has limited access beyond the forest service site near its confluence with the Flathead River.

Illecillewaet River (Map 31/F1-A3)

This river follows along the Trans Canada Highway before entering the Upper Arrow Lake at Revelstoke. The river offers fair fishing for rainbow and bull trout along most of its watercourse by spincasting, bait fishing or fly fishing. An intensive stocking program is in effect, with both bull trout and rainbow being stocked in the mid 1990s. The river is closed to fishing below Albert Canyon (Map 31/A3-30/D5) and you will need a national park permit and fishing license when in Glacier National Park.

Incomappleux River (Maps 31/F2-24/C1)

Flowing from Glacier National Park to the Upper Arrow Lake near Beaton, the Incomappleux River can be accessed by logging road as well as bush-whacking. The river has a few rainbow and bull trout to 1 kg (2 lbs) taken on fly, lure or bait. You will need a national park permit and fishing license when in Glacier National Park.

Inonoaklin Creek (Map 16/B7)

Inonoaklin Creek is a large creek, which parallels Highway 6 to the west of Lower Arrow Lake. After the high water subsides, brook trout and rainbow to 30 cm (12 inches) can be caught by fly fishing or using bait. The creek is closed to fishing below Galloping Creek (Maps 16/C7-9/D2).

Jordon River (Map 30/A2)

This river flows south into the Columbia River north of Revelstoke. The upper reaches of the river offer fair fishing for rainbow and bull trout by spincasting, bait fishing or fly fishing. An intensive stocking program has helped the fish stocks; however, the river is closed to fishing below Copeland Creek (Map 30/B2). Getting into the open stretch of river will require a long difficult bushwhack.

Kaslo River (Map 18/C6-G7)

After high water, the river has some good fly fishing for small rainbow or bull trout above Keen Creek (Map 18/E7). It is an artificial fly only stream with catch and release restrictions above Keen Creek, while fishing is closed below the creek. Highway 31A provides good access to the quick flowing but small river.

Kicking Horse River (Maps 39/E5-33/A1; 38F7)

This fast flowing river skirts the Trans-Canada Highway (Hwy 1) as it winds around the dramatic Rocky Mountains from Yoho National Park to Golden. Due to silty waters, the river offers fair to poor fishing for small brook trout that average 20–30 cm (8–10 inches). However, the odd bull trout to 60 cm (24 inches) can be caught. The section in Yoho requires a national park permit and fishing license to fish it.

Kid Creek (Maps 5/A4-4/G5)

Found to the north of Highway 3 east of Creston, this creek has some good fishing for small cutthroat, bull trout and brook trout. The fish are easily caught with bait or flies and occasionally reach 0.5 kg (1 lb) in size.

Kikomun (Rock) Creek (Map 6/G3)

This small creek drains into Lake Koocanusa just north of the Kikomun Creek Provincial Park. It is worth mentioning because the creek has good numbers of westslope cutthroat, which grow to an impressive 45 cm (18 inches) in size, as well as small rainbow. While the lower sections get more attention, the upper reaches will be more productive. In the early fall, spawning kokanee create a brilliant display near the creek mouth.

Kishinena Creek (Map 8/F7-D7)

The Kishinena flows south of our maps joining the Flathead River in Montana. Some huge bull trout make their way from Montana's Flathead Lake all the way into BC, where they spawn. In the past, these fish were heavily fished, but new regulations mean it is catch and release only for bull trout, and the river is closed to fishing during the fall. In addition to bull trout, the creek contains cutthroat to 1.5 kg (3 lbs) and whitefish to 35 cm (14 inches). The cutthroat are found in the many pools of the creek after high water has subsided in the summer, while whitefish start showing up in the fall. The creek has a one trout (over 30 cm/12 inches) per day limit and no bait is allowed.

Kitchener (Meadow) Creek (Maps 5/A5-4/F5)
This creek runs for about 16 km along Highway 3, east of Creston. From June 15 to August 31, anglers will find fair fishing for brook trout to 0.5 kg (1 lb) on a fly or small spinner.

Koch Creek (Maps 9/G3-10/B5)
One of the main tributaries of the Little Slocan River, Koch Creek has good fishing for rainbow to 0.5 kg (1 lb). Much of the length of the creek is easily accessed off the Koch Creek Road. Check the regulations for special restrictions.

Kokanee Creek (Map 11/C5)
This small glacier-fed creek does produce well for small rainbow and cutthroat by using bait or a fly. In the early fall, visitors will be astounded by the incredible display of spawning kokanee near the creek mouth.

Kootenay River (East) (Maps 13–14, 20–21, 27–28, 33–34)
The East Kootenay portion of the Kootenay River tends to have larger fish than the section south of Nelson. In the East Kootenays, the river offers two distinct sections. North of Canal Flats (Map 20/F3), it is a fast flowing, murky river. This section does offer some excellent fly fishing holes (use attractor patterns) since access is generally limited to logging road and/or bushwhacking (except where Highway 93 parallels the river in Kootenay National Park). A national park permit and fishing license is required when fishing in the park. South of Canal Flats, the river is a slower moving, warmer stream with easy access. The river flows through a more populated area and there are closures to be wary of. There is also a bait ban from June 15–October 31 on the entire river system.

Kootenay River (West) (Maps 10/G7-2/C3)
The southwestern portion of the Kootenay River lies between Nelson and Castlegar. This lake-like section is controlled by a series of dams and offers some fairly good fishing for rainbow, cutthroat, ling cod, and bull trout. Fly fishing or a float and bait using the insect in season (salmon fly, black ant, grasshopper, etc.) can be very effective for larger rainbow. Rainbow from 0.5 to 2 kg (1 to 4 lbs) are common, but the occasional 4 kg (9 lbs) fish is possible. The best time to fish is in May–June when the flying ants and locust are hatching or in August through October when the pools are more prominent. Two popular holes are found below the Brilliant Dam (Map 2/C3) or in the

Slocan Pool where the Slocan River meets the Kootenay River (Map 2/D1). Watch for closures and a bait ban from June 15–October 31.

Kuskanax Creek (Maps 24/F7-17/A2)
Before soaking in the Nakusp Hot Springs or hiking/biking one of the many trails in the area, you may wish to try your luck creek fishing. Kuskanax Creek has some good fishing for both bull trout and rainbow mainly by bait fishing. The creek was stocked in the mid 1990s. The creek is closed to fishing below the falls 1 km above Gardner Creek (Map 17/B1).

La France Creek (Map 12/A6)
This 5 km (3 mile) long creek flowing into the Kootenay Lake has rainbow and bull trout to 1 kg (2 lbs) taken in the summer or fall on fly or bait. There is good logging road access from Highway 3A.

Lavington Creek (Map 20/C5)
This is a small creek that drains into Findlay Creek. It offers fair fishing for small cutthroat (average 15–25 cm/6-10 in).

Little Bull Creek/Norbury Creek (Map 14/B4)
The Little Bull is a small stream that flows into the Big Bull near the hatchery. It is an age-restricted stream, aimed at providing kids with a nice, easy place to fish. The closer you fish to Bull River proper, the larger the rainbow are.

Lizard Creek (Maps 14/G7-15/A7)
This small creek offers good fishing for cutthroat in the 30–40 cm (12–16 inch) range as well as a few bull trout. After high water, try using a fly or bait. A beautiful campsite, cascading falls and a popular fishing hole are found at the Mount Fernie Provincial Park.

Lockhart Creek (Map 12/A7)
This 6 km long creek is accessed by a good trail heading up the north side of the creek. In the summer and fall, small rainbow are caught on bait or fly in this creek.

Lodgepole Creek (Map 7/F3-B3)
Lodgepole Creek offers some fairly good fishing for bull trout, cutthroat and whitefish on bait or a fly after the high water subsides. Good road access is found south of Morrissey, off of Highway 3.

Lussier River (Maps 13/C1; 20–21)
The Lussier is a low volume stream that looks more like a creek than a river. It sweeps north from the Top of the World Park towards Whiteswan Lake before flowing south towards Premier Lake to join the Kootenay River. When the spring run-off subsides and the pools begin to form, some decent fishing for cutthroat and rainbow to 40 cm (18 inches) is possible. There are also a few bull trout to 2.5 kg (5 lbs) and a good number of whitefish. The lower stretches of the river are difficult to fish due to a canyon but the remaining stretches of the river are fairly accessible.

Mark Creek (Map 13/C4)
Mark Creek flows through Kimberley and was abused for many years. While the stream is now producing well for smaller trout, you can still see signs of its former life as a dumping ground for all manner of chemicals and garbage; rocks are stained yellow, and old tires and drums can still be found in some corners of the stream. A lot of work has been done to restore the creek and it is now a descent place to fish.

McLatchie Creek (Map 7/F2)
A tributary of the Flathead River, this creek contains smaller cutthroat (to 30 cm/12 inches), bull trout and whitefish. The creek does not see much fishing pressure, as the creek is closed to bull trout fishing. The creek is also closed to angling during the fall (September 1 to October 31) and in the summer (June 15 to August 31). Other restrictions include a one trout limit and a minimum size catch of 30 cm (12 inches). Since fish of this size are few and far between, it may be better to try elsewhere.

McRae Creek (Map 1/C5)
McRae Creek parallels Highway 3, east of Christina Lake. In the upper reaches (above the falls), summer and fall fishing for small rainbow can be productive on bait or fly.

Michel Creek (Map 15/F7-C3)
This large creek flows from Corbin, eventually joining the Elk River at Sparwood. After high water, good fishing is offered for whitefish primarily with bait. There are also some bull trout and cutthroat to 1 kg (2 lbs).

Middlepass Creek (Map 8/B4)
Yet another tributary of the Flathead River that has been slapped with harsh restrictions (see Cabin or Harvey Creek above), Middlepass Creek is accessed by an old road cum trail.

Mitchell River (Maps 34/G7-28/A1)
Only the lower reaches below Magnesite Creek (Map 27/G1) are accessible by road. The upper reaches are accessed by pack trail. Regardless of your point of entry, the river provides many enticing pools that hold cutthroat to 35 cm (14 inches). There are also some bull trout to 4 kg (9 lbs) and whitefish.

Moyie River (Map 5/A2-E1; E4-A7)
Divided by Moyie Lake, most travellers know the Moyie as the picturesque river that meanders along Highway 3/95 as it flows south into the USA. The upper reaches are a lot more turbulent and require more effort to access as the better fishing holes require some bushwhacking to find them. The river offers fair summer fly fishing for rainbow, brook trout, and cutthroat. Also, bull trout are caught in May–June in the deeper pools. Try a Royal Coachman, nymph, Tom Thumb or dry fly (deer hair pattern). Small lures and worms also work. No powerboats are allowed below Moyie Lake.

Palliser River (Map 28/E3-A6)
The Palliser River flows through the Height of the Rockies to the Kootenay River. Along the way, good numbers of cutthroat to 45 cm (18 inches), bull trout to 4 kg (9 lbs) and whitefish to 40 cm (16 inches) can be found. Try bait or a fly in one of the many pools found in the river after high water. The lower reaches can be accessed by a good gravel road, while the upper reaches are accessed by trail.

Palmer Bar Creek (Map 5/E1)
This short 4 km long creek flows into the Moyie River north of Moyie Lake. There is fairly good fishing for cutthroat averaging 15–25 cm (6–10 inches). Bait or a fly are your best bets.

Pend D'Oreille River (Map 2/G7-C7)
Most of the river on the Canadian side of the border is dammed and provides marginal fishing for whitefish, bull trout and rainbow, however, rumours abound about sturgeon lurking in the murky waters below the Seven Mile Dam. The mouth of the river, where it flows into the Columbia River, is a very popular area for local fishermen looking for walleye and larger rainbow.

Perry Creek (Maps 5/A1-13/E6)
This large volume creek flows into the St Mary River south of Marysville. The creek is closed for fishing below Lisbon Creek (Map 13/C6) but the upper reaches offers some fair fishing for small brook trout on a fly or with bait. A logging road runs up the north side of the creek and provides good access.

Plumbob Creek (Map 6/E3)
Plumbob Creek is best known for its cutthroat, which can get up to 35 cm (14 inches). At various times in the year, rainbow, bull and brook trout and whitefish and kokanee can all be found in the lower sections of the creek.

Porcupine Creek (Map 3/B3)
For those willing to do a little bushwhacking, this small creek holds good numbers of small rainbow after the high water subsides in late June. Due to heavy bush cover, the fish are best taken with the reliable worm and hook.

Quinn Creek (Map 14/G2)
Quinn Creek flows into the Bull River at the 40 mile mark of the Bull River Road. From here, the Bull-Quinn Road follows Quinn Creek to its headwaters. The creek contains cutthroat trout to 40 cm (16 inches) and in the fall, bull trout and whitefish are also present.

Sage Creek (Map 8/E5–B7)
A major tributary of the Flathead River, fishing here is much the same as in the Flathead, as are the restrictions. There is a campsite near the Sage's confluence with the Flathead, and fishing pressure in this area is high. Anglers willing to make the drive up the Sage Road will find less pressure and more fish if they are willing to bushwhack from the road down to the creek itself.

Salmo River (Maps 3/A1-2/G7)
This river and its tributaries sport small rainbow, cutthroat and eastern brook trout caught on a fly or with spinners. In the early summer, fishing can be good north of Salmo all the way to Ymir, however, as the summer progresses, the fish seem to migrate south of Salmo. With good highway access, the river receives a lot of fishing pressure. However, the canyon, where the river enters

the Pend D'Oreille Reservoir, is a little more difficult to get to and is perhaps the best place to fish on the river. There is a bait ban June 15–October 31.

Sanca Creek (Map 4/A1)
Logging roads to the east of Kootenay Lake provide access to over 11 km of fishable waters. Rainbow and brook trout to 1 kg (2 lbs) are caught using a fly or by bait fishing.

Sand Creek (Map 6/G1-F3)
Access to this creek is gained from a number of different roads including the Big Sand Creek Road, which parallels the upper section of the creek. Rainbow and cutthroat trout, both of which can get up to about 35 cm (14 inches), inhabit the creek.

Sheep Creek (Map 3/B5)
This creek is located south of Salmo and is accessed along most of its length by the Sheep Creek Road. The creek offers fair to good fishing for small rainbow that take well to flies, bait and on occasion small lures. Camping is offered at the Sheep Creek Recreation Site near Waldie Creek.

Skookumchuck Creek (Maps 20/A7-13/G1)
This large creek is not suitable for drift fishing and the lower sections are surrounded by private property. It is a fertile stream that is best fished from August to mid October for cutthroat to 0.5 kg (1 lb) and bull trout to 5 kg (11 lbs). Please note that it is catch and release fishing and there is a bait ban from June 15 to October 31.

Spillimacheen River (Maps 32/C2-33/F6)
The Spillimacheen River flows parallel to the Columbia River floodplains and offers fishermen some good fishing for small rainbow to 0.5 kg (1 lb) caught using a spinner, bait or fly. Whitefish are also caught in the fall, primarily using bait. There is good logging road access to the upper reaches of the river where the fishing tends to be better. Several forest service campsites can be found at the small lakes near the lower section of the river.

Squaw Creek (Map 7/G1)
A tributary of the Flathead River, this creek contains smaller cutthroat (to 30 cm/12 inches), bull trout to 60 cm (24 inches) and whitefish to 30 cm (12 inches). The creek does not see much fishing pressure, as the creek is closed to bull trout fishing, which would be the main draw for anglers. The creek is

also closed to angling during the fall (September 1 to October 31) and in the summer (June 15 to August 31), there is a one trout limit, with the minimum size catch being 30 cm (12 inches). Many anglers find the regulations to be stacked against them, so don't bother with this stream.

St. Eloi Brook & Packhorse Creek (Map 8/A2)
These small tributaries of the Flathead River contain small cutthroat and whitefish (to 30 cm/12 inches) as well as larger bull trout. Unfortunately the creeks are closed to bull trout fishing and like the other creeks in the area, the creeks are closed to angling during the fall (September 1 to October 31). The restrictions and the limited access (trail or bushwhacking) mean these streams do not see many anglers.

St. Leon Creek (Map 24/B7)
St. Leon Creek is a tributary of the Upper Arrow Lake and offers travelers a scenic waterfall as well as a natural hot spring. The lower reaches of the creek, where there is good bull trout and rainbow trout fishing, can be accessed by the St. Leon Waterfall Trail. Logging road accesses the upper reaches. A stocking program helped replenish the bull trout and rainbow trout in the mid 1990s; however, the creek is closed to fishing below the barrier located 1 km above the Highway 23 Bridge.

St. Mary River (Maps 12–14)
St. Mary River is considered one the premier trout fishing streams in the Kootenays. The river contains Yellowstone cutthroat, bull trout, burbot, whitefish and suckers. Above St. Mary Lake, there is good cutthroat fishing for fish that average 20–30 cm (8–12 inches). No bait fishing is allowed. Below St. Mary Lake, the river is fly fishing only with catch and release regulations in place between Mark Creek and the McPhee Bridge. Due to limited access, the best method to fish this section of the St. Mary is to float down the river on a raft or canoe. Bushwhacking is also possible but please do not trespass on private land, which is common below the lake. The trout tend to be in the 25–30 cm range with some growing to an impressive 45 cm (18 inches) or 0.75 kg (1.5 lbs). When fishing is good, it is not uncommon to catch 15 to 20 trout in one day. Dry fly fishing with a size 10–14 deer hair or elk hair caddis pattern or a small mayfly pattern tend to work the best particularly right after spring runoff, as the weather gets warmer. The early season stonefly hatch is one of the best times to fly fish the river. If dry flies are not working, try a weighted stonefly nymph (Hare's Ear) with a strike indicator. Into the summer, try a hopper pattern as the grasshoppers arrive. The trout tend to hang around the head of the pools or at the outside curve of the river because the main pool areas contains large burbot that prey on the trout. The tributaries of the St. Mary River also contain small numbers of resident trout.

Stoddart Creek (Map 27/C5)
Fishing Stoddart is spotty for cutthroat trout to 20 cm (8 inches) and some small bull trout (to 25 cm/10 inches).

Summer Creek (Map 14/D3)
Summer Creek is a short creek that flows out of Summer Lake and into Galbraith Creek. The creek contains plenty of cutthroat, some of which grow to 40 cm (16 inches). In the fall, bull trout and whitefish are also present in the creek.

Summit Creek (Maps 3/E7-4/A5)
This fast flowing creek runs for 30 km next to Highway 3, as it descends into the beautiful Creston Valley. The upper reaches offers fair fishing for small rainbow using bait or a fly. The slow moving lower section holds bass and perch. Bull trout are catch and release only and due to high water, the creek is closed to fishing until July 15.

Sutherland Creek (Map 1/C7)
Like most creeks in the area, fishing becomes productive after high water for small rainbow on a fly or with bait. The creek is found east of Christina Lake via logging roads.

Tanglefoot Creek (Map 14/E4)
Tanglefoot Creek contains plenty of cutthroat, some of which grow to 40 cm (16 inches). It is easily accessed off of Tanglefoot Road. In the fall, bull trout and whitefish are also present in the creek.

Teepee Creek (Maps 5/G4-6/C3)
Teepee Creek holds good numbers of cutthroat trout to 35 cm (14 inches). The creek is easily accessed from the Teepee Creek Road.

Templeton River (Maps 26/D1-33/G7)
This river is best fished around Lang Lake (Map 33/E7) where there are numerous small beaver ponds that hold rainbow and cutthroat to 25 cm.

Tobermory Creek (Map 29A/B5)
There is a forest service site where Tobermory Creek flows into the Elk River. From there, a rustic angler's trail provides access to the creek that contains cutthroat trout to 45 cm (18 inches). The creek sees little fishing pressure.

Toby Creek (Maps 19/D2-27/C5)
This large glacier-fed creek flows into the Columbia River near Invermere. The paved Toby Creek Road, which leads to the Panorama Ski Village, parallels the lower portion of the creek. Below the road you will find the canyon is the best place to fish. Cutthroat to 40 cm (16 inches), bull trout to 3.5 kg (7 lbs) and whitefish to 35 cm (14 inches) are caught on a fly or with bait.

Trail Creek (Map 2/A7)
The upper stretches of this small creek hold good numbers of small rainbow and brook trout. The few larger pools that exist yield bigger fish that can tip the scales at 0.75 kg (1.5 lbs). Bait fishing is the most effective method as access is limited by heavy bush cover.

Weary Creek (Map 29A/C7)
There is a forest service site at Weary Creek, but the creek sees very little pressure upstream from the site. Although most of the fish are small, the creek does hold some big cutthroat (to 45 cm/18 inches).

White River System (Maps 28/G6-21/A1)
Sweeping around the mountains to the east of the Kootenay River, the White River system is easily accessed by a good logging road system. In low water, the White River produces well for cutthroat to 1.5 kg (3 lbs) that average 30–40 cm (12–16 inches) and bull trout to 3 kg (6 lbs). It also contains rainbow to 2.5 kg (3 lbs) and whitefish. The fish are found primarily in the larger pools and can be caught with a fly or a lure. Restrictions include a bait ban from June 15–October 31 and no bull trout fishing is allowed in September to October. The White River is also closed to fishing above North White River (Map 21/F3). The **North White River** is much the same as the upper White, but without the rainbow. The **East White River** is much like the North White, but the fish are generally smaller.

Wigwam River (Map 7/E7-A4)
This river offers some good fishing for small cutthroat and bull trout by fly fishing or spincasting (where allowed under the regulations). The river is a catch and release fishery and fly fishing only is allowed above Bighorn (Ram) Creek (Map 7/C5). Below Bighorn Creek, there is a bait ban from June 15 to October 31. Finding remote pools is not difficult.

Wild Horse River (Map 14/C2-A5)
This river is better known as a gold stream than for its fishing. Despite the human activity, the river still produces a good fishery for small cutthroat.

Wilson Creek (Maps 18/A3-17/G6)
This creek is known for its good fishing for large bull trout and rainbow caught on a fly, with bait or by spincasting. The best fishing is after high water and in the trail accessible stretches of the creek. The creek is closed to fishing below Burkitt Creek (Map 17/G4).

Windermere Creek (Map 27/E6)
A small stream that flows into Windermere Lake, the creek contains lots of small cutthroat. The odd fish reaches 35 cm (14 inches) in size.

Wolf Creek (Maps 14/A1-13/G1)
Accessed from the Wolf Creek Road, which runs northeast from Wasa Lake, this creek runs through meadows and farmland. Make sure you get permission before crossing private land. The river is home to rainbow and cutthroat trout, both of which you can find to 35 cm (14 inches).

Woodbury Creek (Map 11/E2)
Stretches of this glacier-fed creek offers some good fishing for small rainbow, bull trout and cutthroat using bait or a fly. A logging road that is found off Highway 31 accesses the creek. There is no fishing below the falls, which are 400 m above Highway 31.

Paddling Routes

(Lake and River Paddling)

The Kootenay region is renown for its natural beauty and pristine wilderness. Is there a better way to truly enjoy the surroundings then by paddling one of the small wilderness lakes or a meandering river? Whitewater enthusiasts are also blessed with spectacular runs that would rival any whitewater opportunities in the world.

Lake Paddling

There are an unlimited number of small lakes to explore. Depending on access and the quality of fishing, these lakes are seldom visited by canoeists. It is not uncommon to be able to explore a wilderness lake of the Kootenays and see more wildlife than paddlers would elsewhere in the province.

Canoeing or ocean kayaking the larger lakes is also a popular pastime. There are numerous bays, coves and sandy beaches to explore. As with all big lakes, wind and boating activity is always a concern.

Our maps show you how to access a lake and whether there are any campsites or boat launches in the area. In situations where there are no facilities at the lake, canoeists often portage their canoe into the lake. Please avoid private property and watch out for heavy bush and boggy areas.

You can also consult the other sections of our books to find out more about a given campsite or park as well as all the details on fishing a given lake.

Alces Lake (Map 21/B4)
This tiny lake is found in Whiteswan Lake Provincial Park. The lake has an electric motor-only restriction, making it a great place to beetle about in a canoe. The small lake is not subject to as much wind as the larger Whiteswan Lake, found to the northeast.

Bridal Lake (Map 3/C7)
This tiny lake is found at the summit of Highway 3 in Stagleap Provincial Park. It is a small, pretty lake that is reasonably sheltered from the wind. The area is a renowned wildlife viewing area.

Champion Lakes (Map 2/C5)
The three lakes that make up the Champion Lakes are warm, clear lakes that are extremely popular in the heart of summer. The lakes are home to many forms of wildlife, including turtles that sun themselves on driftwood. The lakes are closed to gas motors, so canoeing is a popular option for recreationists and anglers chasing after the few fish that inhabit the lakes. A 250 m (800 ft) portage is necessary to get to the first lake, the second lake has a cartop boat launch, while the busy third lake offers a paved launch.

Christina Lake (Map 1/A6)
Spend a few hours or a few days exploring the tranquil warm waters of Christina Lake. Paddlers will find the north end of the lake much more peaceful than the south. There are also several sandy beach areas and a number of great camping spots at the north end. Be sure to bring along a fishing rod for the incredible bass fishing and binoculars to better view the abundant wildlife and the Indian pictograph north of Texas Creek.

Columbia Lake (Map 20/F2)
Columbia is a big lake, which means it can get windy. Paddlers should take care when out on this lake. The east side of the lake is much more remote than the west, and a good option for canoeists might be to paddle from Canal Flats Provincial Park to Columbia Lake Provincial Park, at the north end of the lake. The lake is a prime wildlife watching area.

Duck Lake (Map 4/B4)
Found at the south end of Kootenay Lake, this lake is part of the Creston Valley Wildlife Management Area. One of the best reasons to canoe here is to see the wildlife, especially birds. You can launch a canoe from the south (Cross) dyke, or at the north end, near the pumphouse as well as from Sirdar, which requires a short walk from the parking lot to get to the lake.

Elk Lakes (Map 29A/A5)
Despite the 1 km (0.6 miles) portage to reach Lower Elk Lake (and even further to reach the larger Upper Elk Lake), you couldn't ask for a nicer place to paddle. In addition to spectacular scenery and abundant wildlife, the lakes offer good fishing and wilderness camping opportunities.

Emerald Lake (Map 39/D5)
Located in the heart of Yoho National Park, Emerald Lake lives up to its name. Soaring peaks surround this turquoise-coloured lake, and on a clear blue summer day, it is an amazing place to paddle.

Kootenay Lake (Maps 3, 4, 11, 12, 18)
Canoeists should stick close to shore on this big lake, as the wind and weather can be unpredictable. Boating traffic is also heavy on the lake. The lake is about 144 km (90 miles) long, with an average width of 4 km (2.4 miles). This lake is so big that it can take the better part of a week to circumnavigate. There are many places where a canoe or kayak can be launched from easily (including Twin Bay, Riondel, Garland Bay, Mountain Shores Resort and many, many others).

Lake Koocanusa (Map 6)
Lake Koocanusa is 148 km (90 miles) long, and stretches across the US/Canada border. The native sounding name actually comes from a combination of the first three letters of Kootenay, Canada, and USA. On the Canadian side of the border, the best places to launch a canoe is at Kikomun Creek Provincial Park on the east shore, or Englishman Creek Recreation Site on the west. It would take about a week to circumnavigate the big lake, which is subject to high winds.

Lower Arrow Lake (Maps 1, 2, 9, 16, 17)
The best time to canoe or kayak this 90 km (55 mile) long lake is July and August when the water is high. There are a number of public launches available, including Burton Provincial Park, Fauquier Provincial Park, Eagle Creek Regional Park and Syringia Provincial Park. One popular day trip is to put in at Deer Park, and canoe or kayak across to the Natural Arch trail, and hike the 1.5 km (0.9 miles) to the spectacular rock formation. There is not a boat launch at Deer Park, but this is the best place to start from if you are paddling across the lake. There is a lot of development at the south end of the lake, but as you work your way north, signs of human habitation are fewer and farther between.

Six Mile Slough (Map 4/A4)
Six Mile Slough is a series of four ponds located between the east and west branches of the Kootenay River. The shallow ponds are ideal waterfowl habitat and are part of the Creston Wildlife Management Area. To get from one pond to the next, you will have to portage up and over the dykes that separate them. At times, the middle areas of the slough may be too shallow for a canoe, but the water is deeper near the edges. Overall, you can paddle for about 10 km (6 miles). Access is from the south end of Duck Lake.

Slocan Lake (Maps 10, 17)
There are a number of trails in Valhalla Provincial Park that are only accessible by boat. Taking a canoe from the east side of the lake over to these trails is just one option for canoeing this big lake. Another is to canoe from Slocan City to the north end of the lake along the western shore of the lake. This trip can take up to five days, return.

Summit Lake (Map 17/D4)
Summit Lake Provincial Park is located at the height of land between Nakusp and New Denver. The Selkirk Mountains rise 500 m (1,625 ft) above the lake, providing a magnificent backdrop. The campground, which is on a point of land surrounded mostly by water, is the main starting point for visitors. Watch out for powerboats.

Whiteswan Lake (Map 21/C4)
Whiteswan Lake is a large, deep lake, with a large population of wildlife. Paddlers often watch mountain goats scaling the cliffs around the lake, or lay down a line in one of the finest fishing lakes in the province. The lake is subject to wind and is open to powerboats.

Windermere Lake (Map 27/D6)

As the name indicates, Windermere Lake is large enough to develop quite a chop on windy days. The lake is also a popular water sport and boating destination, so canoeists should use caution when on the water. James Chabot Provincial Park at the north end of the lake, near Invermere provides good access.

River Paddling

Below we have described the major whitewater paddling routes as well as some of the gentle river routes throughout the Kootenays. For each river, we have included the put-in and take-out locations. The length of each run, the season and general comments are also provided. To Grade the rivers, we have used a modified version of the International River Classification System, popularized by Stuart Smith. The Grade of a route describes the overall difficulty of a river, while specific features are given the designation Class. A river might be classified as a Grade II river, but there might be a waterfall that should only be run by expert kayakers. In this case, the river would be described as a Grade II run, with a Class IV waterfall.

In addition, some runs may be given two grading numbers. This is due to a couple factors. The first is that not everyone agrees on the rating of a river. More commonly, though, the difficulty of a river varies with the amount of water flowing. So a river that merrily babbles along as a Grade II paddle in late summer may be a lot harder to deal with in spring run-off.

Grade I: Novices in open canoes or kayaks. Riffles and small waves with virtually no obstruction.

Grade II: Intermediate paddlers. Maneuvering is required. Medium rapids, channels can be clearly spotted without scouting.

Grade/Class III: Advanced Paddlers. Rapids can swamp open canoes. Waves are unpredictable. Scouting should be done before approach. Skilled maneuvering is required.

Grade/Class IV: Expert paddlers; closed canoes & kayaks only. Long, challenging rapids with obstructions requiring maneuvering. Eskimo roll ability is recommended. Good swimming skills. Scouting required.

Grade/Class V: Professional Paddlers; closed canoes or kayaks only. Scouting always required. Long, violent rapids through narrow routes with obstructions. Eskimo roll ability essential. Errors can be fatal.

Please remember that river conditions are always subject to change and advanced scouting is essential. The information in this book is only intended to give you general information on the particular river you are interested in. You should always obtain more details from a local merchant or expert before heading out on your adventure. A good resource is Stuart Smith's Canadian Rockies Whitewater.

Albert River Route (Map 28/B4)

There are some tough rapids on the Albert, including Central Committee, a Class V falls that needs to be run very carefully, lest you bounce off the rocks. Give yourself up to two hours to run this 7.5 km (4.6 mile) section of the river from the put-in (accessed from a small pull-out 6.8 km/5.3 miles from the bridge over the Albert) down to the Palliser River.

Alexander Creek Route (Map 15/F3)

Alexander Creek is a low volume creek with water levels that can vary immensely day-to-day. The run is narrow, with a few Class III+/IV rapids to keep things interesting on the Grade II+/III creek. Watch for logjams and sweepers.

Blaeberry River Routes (Maps 38-39)

The Blaeberry River is a gray-blue, murky, glacier-fed river, which is found north of Golden along the Blaeberry Road. Several forestry sites and trails are found in the area. The middle and lower reaches of the river system offer some easier paddling. Here are three recommended routes for a sunny summer day:

Put-in: Cairnes Creek Forest Service Site (Map 39/A1)

Take-out: Mummery Creek Forest Service Site (Map 39/A2)

This section is an 8 km (4.9 mile) Grade II/III kayak route for experienced paddlers. It will take two or three hours to paddle.

Put-in: Mummery Creek Forest Service Site (Map 39/A2)

Take-out: Split Creek Forest Service Site (Map 38/G4)

A 15 km (9 mile) Grade I gentle paddle along the meandering river. Below Split Creek, the route is best left to experienced kayakers as there are Grade III/IV sections. Give yourself four hours to paddle this section

Put-in: Redburn Creek Bridge (Map 38/E5)

Take-out: Trans-Canada Highway Bridge (Map 38/D5)

The lower stretches of the river offer a 10 km/6 mile (2–3 hour) Grade I/II canoe route.

Bluewater Creek Route (Map 38/B4)

At high water, this large creek can be paddled from the Bluewater Bridge Forest Service Site to the K Road Branch Road. Overall, it is a short 3 km (1.8 mile) Grade II/III whitewater kayak route. Several forest service sites are in the area. Many people bring a rod and try their luck fishing as they float down this easy route.

Bull River Route (Map 14/G3-D7)

From the 40 Mile Forest Service Site, this long Grade III/IV expert kayaker route takes you to the Bull River Reservoir, near the Kootenay River junction. The Bull River Road offers restricted public access (between 6pm and 6am on weekdays) so this route is best done during the weekend.

Columbia River (Columbia Valley) Canoe Route (Maps 20, 26, 27, 32, 33, 38)

The canoe trip from Columbia Lake to Donald Station (north of Golden) takes you some 235 km/143 mile (4–6 days) along a braided, meandering river with no named rapids or portages. As you paddle down the clear water of the Columbia River, you will have a good chance of seeing some big animals (elk, moose or deer) and plenty of waterfowl. In fact, the Columbia River wetland system is the most important wetland system west of Manitoba and supports more than 260 resident and migratory species of birds. The Rocky Mountains loom in the background adding to the scenery but get ready for lots of mosquitoes. The main difficulty of the canoe trip is choosing the right channel as there are numerous side channels that lead nowhere. Fishing for rainbow or bull trout is a popular pastime as you cruise down the river.

For those not interested in a multi day adventure, you can easily break the route into shorter day trips. There are numerous places where Highway 93/95 nears the river as well as several towns along the way including Fairmont Hot Springs, Invermere, Radium Hot Springs, Parson and Golden.

Cross River Routes (Map 27/G2-G5)

The key feature to the Cross is A Mind Altering Experience, a Class V falls below the Natural Bridge that can be run by experts and portaged by people who don't mind lugging their boats up and down the gorge (tough, but not prohibitively so). Further downstream of the Natural Bridge gorge, there is a 14 metre (49 foot) waterfall that shouldn't be attempted. This 6 km (3.8 mile) section shouldn't be attempted at high, or even medium water levels. For the less adventurous, there is a 5 km (3 mile) section of Grade II whitewater above the Natural Bridge.

Dewar Creek Route (Map 12/E3)

Dewar Creek flows out of the Purcell Wilderness Conservancy and into the St. Mary's River. It is a scenic, Grade II/III paddle with a few easy rapids and one not-so-easy canyon (Class III+/IV+). The take-out is at the St. Mary's

Westfork Road Bridge, while the put-in is from a bridge on a side road off the Dewar Creek Road, 11.8 km (7.2 miles) from its junction with the Westfork Road. The run is 11 km (7 miles) long, and will take up to two hours to complete.

Elk River Routes (Maps 6, 7, 15, 22)

Like other Kootenay region rivers, run-off begins in early June making the river quite treacherous due to debris, haystacks, standing waves and hidden obstacles. After the water levels subside in mid-July through early August, canoe opportunities improve. By the early fall, water levels are low and many boulders or shallow stretches impede travel.

The beautiful river is found in the wide valley below the Rocky Mountains. There are several options for the canoeist with most of the routes being Grade I/II in nature, except for the occasional rapid. The most popular routes are noted below.

Put-in: Round Prairie Bridge (Map 22/C5)

Take-out: Bridge at Elkford (Map 22/C6)

This section of the river offers a 5.5 km/3.4 mile (1.5–2 hour) Grade I/II easy paddle. The few rapids are primarily found around the bends in the Elk River.

Put-in: Bridge on Fording Road (Map 22/C6)

Take-out: Sparwood Leisure Centre (Map 15/D3)

This stretch of the river offers an 18 km (11 mile) Grade II route that can be accessed in five locations off of the quiet Highway 43 if you wish to shorten the paddle. The full route will take about four hours. The river is braided and offers a gentle paddle, although there are some large rocks, sweepers, larger rapids (near Elk Prairie) and shallow sections to impede travel. The river between Elkford and the Line Creek Bridge can be difficult to navigate due to the debris in the river and the fact that the river is quite shallow and difficult to follow in some stretches.

Put-in: Sparwood Leisure Center (Map 15/D3)

Take-out: South Highway 3 Bridge in Fernie (Map 15/A7)

This Grade II braided route is 33 km (20.1 miles) in length with a Class II-III section below Liadnar Creek that has 1m (2–3 foot) standing waves and haystacks. There are also several shallow sections, rapids and sweepers (around the corners) that impede travel. Three different access points off of the busy Highway 3 can shorten your trip, which will take about five hours if you wish to run the full route.

Put-in: South Highway 3 Bridge in Fernie (Map 15/A7)

Take-out: Morrissey Provincial Park (Map 7/B2)

This section of the river is a 15 km/9 mile (3-4 hours) Grade I–II route with 5 access points off of Highway 3. There are few obstacles or dangerous rapids, although there are some shallow spots. In the summer, sunbathers often float from Fernie to the Fernie Snow Valley Resort Road on inner tubes.

Put-in: Morrissey Provincial Park (Map 7/B2)

Take-out: Bridge crossing the Elk River Reservoir (Map 7/A3)

This is a 14 km (8.5 mile) Grade I–II paddle that is away from the vehicle noise from Highway 3 that plagues other sections of the Elk River. A logjam near the Highway 3 tunnel and a few sweepers are the real dangers of this paddle. Make sure you don't miss the take-out, as there is a BC Hydro dam below it! At most, this section will take three hours.

Put-in: Gas Line Crossing south of Elko (Map 7/A3)

Take-out: Bridge on Highway 93 (Map 6/G5)

This is the most treacherous part of the river, a 10 km (6 mile) Grade III expert kayaker route with Class IV drops through a narrow rock face canyon where rapids and significant drops are common. Once out of the canyon, the Elk River meets the Wigwam River and the paddle to the Highway 93 Bridge is an easy Grade I float. Give yourself three hours to complete this section.

Gold Creek Route (Map 6/D5-G7)

Gold Creek is a narrow, low-volume creek with lots of tight corners, and often too many logjams to warrant the effort to explore. It is rated Grade

II, and is a good river for novices or people camping in the area. It is not a creek that most people will want to go out of their way for.

Goldstream River Canoe Route (Maps 35, 36)

Put-in: 12.75 km on Goldstream Road (Map 36/A2)

Take-out: 5.25 km on Goldstream Road (Map 35/G1)

A popular canoe route is found north of Revelstoke, off Highway 23. The meandering river travels through waterfowl and moose habitat and offers an 18 km (11 mile) 3–4 hour Grade I–II route. Due to the remote nature of the river, this route is recommended for the intermediate canoeist.

Hellroaring Creek Route (Map 13/A6)

Yeah, the name just about sums this one up, a Grade IV run with Class V+ features and that's at low water levels. Don't even think about trying this one at high water levels. The run is 5.2 km (3.2 miles) from the first bridge on the Hellroaring Road to the bridge on St. Mary's River Road.

Kettle River Route (Map 1/A7)

Most of this river is found in our Kamloops/Okanagan mapbook. The section shown in this book is popular with people on inner tubes during the summer. Earlier in the year, the river is rated as a Grade II–III river. The Kettle is one of the cleanest, warmest rivers in B.C.

Kicking Horse River Route (Maps 33, 38, 39)

East of Golden, the Kicking Horse River is a popular commercial rafting area with some of the best whitewater rafting in the world. The best place to begin the roller coaster style paddle is at the Beaver Foot Road Bridge (Map 33/B1) about half a kilometre south of the Trans-Canada Highway. From there, you quickly descend into a rugged 1.6 km (1 mile) canyon with several Class IV and V rapids (Double Trouble, Watchman's Rapids, Riptide and The Nozzle). The paddle is best left to expert kayakers and commercial rafters.

Kootenay River Canoe Route (Creston Area) (Map 4/B5-C7)

South of Kootenay Lake, the river meanders through the marshy lowlands of the Creston Valley. This area is known as the Creston Valley Wildlife Area and hosts over 265 species of birds. Fishermen also frequent this area to sample some of the best bass fishing in B.C. This gentle Grade I paddle is ideal for a leisurely afternoon float. Guided canoe trips are offered at the Wildlife Centre.

Kootenay River Canoe Route (Nelson to Castlegar) (Maps 10/G7-2/B2)

Between Castlegar and Nelson, the Kootenay River is a large, gently flowing water body that is controlled by several different dams. Canoeist can enjoy a leisurely paddle, some good river fishing and wildlife viewing, including nesting Osprey. Please be careful and do not paddle near any of the dams as they create dangerous undertows.

Kootenay River Routes (East Kootenay Area) (Maps 6, 20, 27, 28, 34)

The Kootenay River, from Kootenay Crossing in Kootenay National Park to Canal Flats, is 138 km (84.2 miles) in length and offers three different paddling routes with lots of rapids, spectacular views and plenty of wilderness camping opportunities. Continuing south past Canal Flats, the river slows as it flows through a more developed area. Water levels peak in late May to June before declining significantly in late August to September. After September, shallow sections limit travel, especially in Park Reach. The following four routes are offered.

Put-in: Kootenay Crossing (Map 34/C7)

Take-out: Settler's Road Bridge (Map 27/F3)

This section is a 57 km/34.8 mile (day+) Grade II route with the odd sweeper and logjam. To add some distance and challenge to the route, you can start on the Vermillion River. Camping is possible along the route.

Put-in: Settler's Road Bridge (Map 27/F3)

Take-out: Kootenay Bridge (Map 28/A7)

This section is a 49 km/29.9 mile (day+) Grade III route, which contains lots of rapids. The steep-walled canyons, scenery and challenging rapids make it a thrilling route. It is possible to access or camp

The Mussio Ventures' Staff

at Horseshoe Rapids, which is often portaged around due to the tight corner. Expert open canoeists and kayakers all enjoy the route.

Put-in: Kootenay Bridge (Map 28/A7)

Take-out: Canal Flats at the Highway 93/95 Bridge (Map 20/F4)

This section is a 38 km/23.2 mile (6-7 hour) Grade II paddle with some whitewater to navigate. The attraction is the spectacular sights, including Gibraltar Rock, as you travel through the heart of the Rocky Mountain Trench.

Put-in: Canal Flats at the Highway 93/95 Bridge (Map 20/F4)

Take-out: Wardner (Map 6/D1)

Beginning at the Highway 93/95 Bridge south of Canal Flats, this easy canoe route takes you 97 km/59.2 mile (3 days) to Wardner. There are several Class II rapids enroute as well as a Class III rapid at the St Mary's River estuary. The canoe route takes you through a rural setting on a silty, warm river before the river forms Lake Koocanusa. Other access points can be used to break this portion of the river into manageable day trips. In particular, the highway crosses the river near Skookumchuck, north of Wasa Lake and near Fort Steele.

Lardeau River Canoe Route (Maps 18, 25)
Beginning at Trout Lake Campsite on Highway 31 (Map 25/A5), this Grade II canoe route is 47 km/28.7 mile (1 day) long. It leads to the take-out near the river mouth south of Duncan Dam (Map 18/E2). There are a few sweepers, logjams, snags and rock obstacles to avoid so the paddle is best performed with an empty canoe. Taking out along Highway 31 can shorten the paddle since the unpaved highway follows the river for most of its length.

Lodgepole Creek Route (Map 7/C3)
The Lodgepole seems like an easy run for the first kilometre, but don't be fooled. The river features some nasty Class V+/VI rapids that will challenge experts and humble beginners. This section is only 5.2 km (3 miles) long, but it is possible to combine this with the Wigwam River for a long and varied run on three separate rivers.

Lussier River Routes (Maps 21/B5-20/G7)
If the world were perfect, the Lussier would be paddleable from where Coyote Creek flows into it (Map 21/B5) to the Sheep Creek Road Bridge (Map 20/G7), for an epic 45 km (27.5 miles). Unfortunately, there is a nearly impassible gorge just below the Lussier River Hot Springs (Map 21/B4) that splits this river into two unequal sections. The first—from Coyote Creek to the hot springs—is a 12 km/7.5 mile (2 hour) paddle through lots of boulder gardens, constrictions, and sweepers. It is rated Grade II/III, with some Class III/IV features. The lower section is rated Grade II, with some Class III rapids. This latter section is 30 km (18.3 miles) long and can be done in less than

four hours. Many people run the first section, relax at the hot springs for a while and then continue on through the next section. The put-in for the lower section is a bridge about 8 km (4.9 miles) below the hot springs.

Matthew Creek Route (Map 13/B4)
Looking for a highly technical, low volume river to play in? You could do worse than Matthew Creek. The stream peaks in June, at which time it is rated Grade IV+, with some Class V features. There are a number of long and difficult rapids on this 7.7 km (4.8 mile) stretch of creek, which are made more difficult by the presence of logs. In low flow, this river is barely passable.

Meachen Creek Route (Map 12/E6)
A good intermediate river, Meachan Creek is a continuous, short run that finishes just above a waterfall. Make sure you finish above the waterfall and not below, as the drop will probably finish you. The trail to the take-out is just past the 8 km sign on the Meachen Creek Road. Make sure you mark your take-out, as you don't want to accidentally miss it. The put-in is at a bridge on a side road, about 4 km (2.4 miles) beyond.

Michel Creek Route (Map 15/C5)
This is a 4.8 km (3 mile) paddle on a Grade II river that should take about an hour to run. It is a good training river for novices, as long as someone who knows what they're doing accompanies them.

Moyie River Canoe Route (Map 5/E3-A7)
From Moyie Lake to Kingsgate, this Grade I–II canoe route is ideal for someone who wishes to enjoy a quiet paddle through prime wildlife country. The slow, meandering river hosts a number of bird species and beaver, deer and even moose can be spotted on occasion. Highway 3 provides good access along most of the route.

Palliser River Routes (Map 28)
The Palliser is a river with deep, demanding gorges, many of them nearly unrunable, and unportagable. There are a couple sections of the river that can be run—one upstream, one down— and while they are challenging, they are not nearly as life-threatening as the middle section of the river.

Put-in: Bridge over river, found off a logging spur (Map 28/C5)

Take-out: Palliser Bridge on Albert River Road (Map 28/B5)

This section of the Palliser has some terrific, if short, sections of whitewater, up to Class III/IV+. There is some beautiful scenery that is slightly marred by logging scars. Logging has also affected the river; watch for sweepers and jams.

Put-in: 4.3 km (2.4 miles) past the bridge over the Palliser River Gorge (Map 28/A6)

Take-out: Kootenay Bridge (Map 28/A7)

Some suicidal folks might want to put-in at the bridge over the Palliser Gorge. Don't. Access down to the river is difficult, and there are a number of impossible, impassible sections between the bridge and the put-in described here. From the put-in to the Kootenay confluence, the Palliser is a spirited, but runnable Grade II/III paddle. The total length of this section is 23.1 km (14 miles), 15 km (9 miles) of which are actually on the Kootenay River.

Quinn Creek Route (Map 14/G2)
The scenery's the thing on this easy, Grade II run. There are a few small rapids or sweepers to break things up, but for the most part it is a 9 km/5.5 mile (2 hour) float down to the Bull River confluence. The put-in is difficult to see (watch for a small pull-out about 5.4 km/3.3 miles past the bridge near the 40 Mile Forest Service Site).

Redding Creek Route (Map 12/F5)
Redding Creek is all about open rapids, and great scenery. The creek is rated Grade II/III but there is one short canyon (Class IV+/V) and a few Class III+/IV+ features to worry about. Perhaps the most difficult part of this route is the take-out that features an unavoidable slog up a steep hill through alders.

Slocan River Canoe Route (Maps 2, 10)
Beginning at Slocan City (Map 10/F3), this 46 km (day) Grade II canoe route has few obstructions and no portages so it makes for an easy family oriented paddle. The river flows rapidly past numerous old homesteads, under the

snow capped peaks of Valhalla Provincial Park and past a bird sanctuary before ending at Cresent Valley north of Castlegar (Map 2/D1). Along the way, several bridge crossings can be used to shorten the paddle.

St. Mary River Route (Maps 13, 14)

Between St. Mary Lake (Map 13/A5) and the Kootenay River (Map 14/A5) the St. Mary River is a Grade III–IV paddle for experienced kayakers. It is a narrow and fast flowing water system with incredible mountain scenery and even better fishing.

Toby Creek Route (Maps 19, 26, 27)

Starting from a glacier high in the Purcell Mountains, Toby Creek quickly turns into a large, fast flowing stream. The creek is best accessed off the Toby Creek Road, past the Panorama Ski Area, where the road crosses the creek (Map 19/F1). You can take-out west of Invermere (Map 27/A6) some 2.5 hours later. Although there are Class IV roller coasters, there is plenty of opportunity to see wildlife and the scenery can be breathtaking.

Vermillion River Routes (Map 34)

Highway 93 follows the Vermillion from Vermillion Pass down to Hector Gorge, where it leaves the Vermillion and follows the Kootenay River down to the confluence of the two rivers. Such close road access means that there are lots of put-in and take-out possibilities. The paddling gets easier the farther you get downstream.

Put-in: Tokumn Creek (Map 34/B2)

Take-out: Ochre Creek (Map 34/A2)

There is a Class V+/VI gorge above the Highway 93 bridge that can be run by true experts. Most everyone else will want to put-in below the bridge. The first section is the most fun, with Class II+/III whitewater for the first little while. As the run progresses, the river gets easier. Give yourself about an hour to do this 2.5 km (1.5 mile) section of river.

Put-in: Numa Falls (Map 34/B3)

Take-out: Floe Creek (Map 34/C4)

Numa Falls are rated Class V+. As a result, most people 'seal launch' from the river right into the canyon below the falls. This 9 km (6 mile) section of river is Grade II/III, with a few ledges and one Class II+/III chute to watch out for in the upper section of the run.

Put-in: Vermillion Crossing (Map 34/D5)

Take-out: Hector Gorge (Map 34/C6)

At 13 km (8 miles), this is one of the longest runs on the Vermillion. It is also the easiest, with only a few Class II+ features to mix things up. Accordingly, canoeists and beginner kayakers favour this section, or just folks who want to look at scenery as they float downstream. It is possible to put-in 3.7 km (2.2 miles) upstream from the Crossing, which will add a Class III canyon to the proceedings. You can also add in the Hector Gorge section for a 29 km (17.8 mile), five hour float.

Put-in: near the Hector Gorge Picnic Site (map 34/C6)

Take-out: Vermillion/Kootenay confluence (Map 34/C7)

At higher water levels, this run can be quite exciting, with a major Class III rapid and lots of play waves. At lower water levels, it is an easy float through Hector Gorge, which is actually just a steep-sided valley. This section is 16 km (10 miles) long.

White River Routes (Map 21)

Northeast of Canal Flats, this semi-wilderness river offers a fast flowing waterway ideal for kayakers. There are several camping locations, trails and even hot springs in the area to help you enjoy your visit.

Put-in: 41 km mark on the White River Road ((Map 21/E3)

Take-out: 32 km mark on the White River Road (Map 21/C2)

This section is a 9 km/5.5 mile (3 hour) Grade III route for experience canoeist or kayakers. There is one Grade IV section, which may have to be portaged.

Put-in: 32 km mark on the White River Road (Map 21/C2)

Take-out: branch road of the Kootenay River Road (Map 21/B1)

A 6–8 hour Grade III route for advanced kayakers and expert canoeists.

Wigwam River Route (Map 7/A2)

The Wigwam is usually run from where Lodgepole Creek flows into it down into the Elk River. The take-out for this 23.5 km (14.4 mile) run is actually 10 km (6 miles) along the Elk River (there is no suitable take-out before this point). The route is rated Grade III/IV, and at higher water levels most of the rapids run together to form a continual run of whitewater. There are a few Class IV–V rapids to watch out for, all of which are easy to portage around. Please note that the side road to Lodgepole Creek is only open June 15 to July 15.

Wild Horse River Route (Map 14/A5)

This low-flow river is rated Grade II/III, with a number of more difficult, Class III/IV features. The section that is usually run starts from Fisherville, the first town site established in the East Kootenay, to the bridge at Fort Steele. A second, more difficult section (rated Grade III/IV+ with Class III+/V features) is located upstream, but should be left to the extremely adventurous or foolhardy.

Yoho River Routes (Map 39/E5)

The Yoho is not a river to be taken lightly. At low water levels it is rated a Grade IV+, with some features up to a Class V. At high water levels, it is even tougher. But, for expert kayakers, this is one of those epic runs that you'll talk about for the rest of your life. Give yourself up to four hours to run the 7.8 km (4.8 mile) section from the Takakkaw Falls Campground to the take-out, which is 3.8 km (2.3 miles) above the bridge on the Takakkaw Falls Road.

Parks
(National and Provincial Parks)

National Parks

The Canadian Rocky Mountain National Parks contain some of the most dramatic scenery in the world, let alone the country. While Alberta's Banff and Jasper remain the flagships of the National Park system, the BC parks are nothing to sneeze at, with towering mountains, thundering waterfalls, dramatic glaciers and lots of wildlife. This section looks at the parks with an eye toward camping. For information on other pursuits in the parks (hiking, fishing, etc.), please turn to the appropriate section.

Glacier National Park (Maps 31, 32, 37, 38)

This national park offers tremendous recreation pursuits in the shadows of the Rockies. Unknown to many travelers, Glacier Park is actually found in the Columbia Mountains, not the Rocky Mountains. The park is famous for its glaciers (422 in all) and heavy snowfall, which can reach over 15 metres (50 feet) at Rogers Pass in the winter. The world-renowned Nakimu Caves, which stretch 5.9 km (3.5 miles) underground, are also found in the park. Access to these caves is restricted.

Before starting out on your adventure, make sure you obtain the necessary permit and check in at the park headquarters for the rules and regulations of the park. Permits and information can be obtained at the Rogers Pass Visitor Centre or at the park headquarters in Revelstoke. Call (250) 837-7500 for more information.

Several picnic areas are found along the Trans-Canada Highway. These sites offer travellers a perfect place to rest and enjoy the mountain views. The two principal road access campgrounds are the Illecillewaet and Loop Brook Campgrounds. They are found a few kilometres west of Rogers Pass and are set in large cedar/hemlock forests. There are no electric hookups at either campground, which are only open in the summer.

> **Illecillewaet Campground** (Map 31/F1) has 57 sites, flush toilets, kitchen shelters, firewood and drinking water. The campground marks the trailhead for 8 trails leading to be the Asulkan and Illecillewaet Valleys. Depending on snow conditions, it is open from early June until late September.

> **Loop Brook Campground** (Map 31/E1) offers 20 campsites, kitchen shelters, firewood, drinking water and flush toilets. It is open from June to September.

Backcountry explorers have a few options to choose from, including alpine huts and backcountry campsites. The alpine huts include the **Asulkan Hut** (31/D1), **Balu Hut** (37/C4), **Glacier Circle Hut** (31/D1) and **Sapphire Col Hut** (31/C1), which can all be used for a fee. These huts are used year-round and require mountaineering knowledge to access. Call (250) 814-5232 or (403) 678-3200 for more information and reservations.

There are three designated backcountry campsites. All are primitive in nature and offer bear poles and tent pads. They are not snow free until mid-July and require reservations. These campsites can be found at **Copperstain Pass**, **Caribou Pass** and **20-mile**. Random camping is also permitted, but you have to be at least 5 km (3 miles) away from the paved roads.

Kootenay National Park (Maps 27, 33, 34, 39)

This impressive national park is home to the popular Radium Hot Springs and some spectacular peaks of the Rocky Mountain Range. There are several excellent campgrounds and over 200 km (120 miles) of trails that help you explore the low valley bottom and high alpine tundra. Mountain biking is only allowed on the fire roads and if you plan to horseback, you must check with park staff before heading out. Although this park is not a popular cross-country ski destination, most of the trails in the park can provide for a pleasant backcountry pursuit. None of the trails are track set so be prepared to break trail.

Before starting out on your adventure, make sure you obtain the necessary permit and check the rules and regulations of the park. Permits and information can be obtained at all national park visitor centres or at the main visitor

centre at the hot spring pools, east of Radium Hot Springs. Call (250) 347-9505 for more information.

The drive-in campgrounds on Highway 93, the main artery through the park, are available on a first-come first-serve basis unless otherwise stated. Summer camping is possible from mid-May until late September.

> **Crook's Meadow Group Campground** (Map 27/C1) is located 34 km (20.7 miles) from the West Gate entrance and is for group camping only. A maximum of 90 groups are allowed at the campground, which allows tenting only. You must reserve space with Parks Canada.

> **Redstreak Campground** (Map 27/C3) is 0.5 km (0.3 miles) from the Highway 93 and Highway 95 junction. There are 242 vehicle/tent sites, including 50 fully service sites (38 with electric hook ups). The campground contains a sani-station, showers, interpretive programs and trails that link to the popular hot springs.

> **Marble Canyon Campground** (Map 34/B2) has 61 unserviced vehicle/tent sites as well as a sani-station and interpretive program. The campground is located 17.2 km (10.5 miles) from the Banff-Kootenay boundary on Highway 93 and is open from mid-June to September.

> **MacLeod Meadows Campground** (Map 27/D1) is located 26.9 km (16.4 miles) from Radium on Highway 93. There are a total of 98 vehicle/tent sites.

> **Dolly Varden Campground** (Map 34/D7) is a designated winter camping area found 35.6 km (21.7 miles) from the West Gate entrance on Highway 93. The seven primitive vehicle/tent sites are for off-season use only (late September to May) and available free of charge.

There are also a total of nine designated backcountry campsites that must be reserved. These sites are very primitive in nature and offer tent pads for 6 to 18 tenters. Bear poles are provided at all sites while pit toilets and fireboxes may or may not be provided, depending on the site. Look for these sites at **Floe Lake** (Map 34/B4), **Helmut/Ottertail Pass Trail Junction** (Map 34/A1), **Helmut Falls** (Map 33/G2), **Kaufmann Lake** (Map 34/A1), **Numa Creek** (Map 34/A3), **Tokumm Valley** (Map 34/A1), **Tumbling Creek** (Map 34/A3), **Tumbling/ Ottertail Pass Trail Junction** (Map 34/A2), and **Verdant Creek** (Map 34/E4).

Mount Revelstoke National Park (Maps 30, 31)

Set in the rugged Columbia Mountains, the attraction to this park is the snow-covered peaks, avalanche chutes and alpine meadows filled with summer wildflowers. The impressive Clachnacudainn Icefield, which is 260 square kilometres, covers the center of the park. A variety of animals including caribou, black bear and mountain birds (including owls, grouse and eagles) can be seen. A drive up the scenic Summit Parkway is an enjoyable day trip with a few picnic areas and easy trails to walk. Away from the core area the steep mountains and narrow valleys with dense rainforests limit the opportunities for exploring.

Before starting out on your adventure, make sure you obtain the necessary permit and check in at the park headquarters for the rules and regulations of the park. Permits and information can be obtained at the Parkway Kiosk or at the park headquarters in Revelstoke. Call (250) 837-7500 for more information.

Unlike other Rocky Mountain National Parks, Mount Revelstoke does not have vehicle accessible camping. There is one cabin (Caribou Cabin on the Summit Parkway) and one backcountry shelter (Eva Lake) in the park, which can be used for $15/night. Heather Lake also offers a hut and there are designated backcountry campsites at Eva and Jade Lakes.

Random camping is available in the **Amiskwi**, **Otterhead** and **Ice River valleys**, while alpine camping is also possible. Be sure to check with the park wardens for certain restrictions.

Vehicle accessed campgrounds are available on a first-come, first-serve basis. These campgrounds can open as early as mid-May and are open throughout the summer travel season. Tenters, trailers and motor homes all share these campgrounds:

Chancellor Peak Campground (33/C1) is open from mid-May to mid-September and has 58 vehicle and 10 tenting sites. There are pit toilets, picnic tables, firewood and a kitchen shelter.

Hoodoo Creek Campground (33/D1) is open from June until September and has 106 vehicle/tent sites as well as picnic tables, kitchen shelter, firewood, flush toilets, an adventure playground and a sani-dump. A short but steep 3.2 m hike leads to the impressive Hoodoos.

Kicking Horse Campground (39/E5) is open from mid-May to October and has 86 vehicle/tent sites as well as picnic tables, showers, kitchen shelter, firewood, flush toilets, an adventure playground and a sani-dump.

Monarch Campground (39/E5) has 46 sites including eight walk-in, tenting only sites. There is a kitchen shelter, picnic tables and toilets at the campground. The campground is located on the Yoho Valley Road and open from late June until September.

Takakkaw Falls Campground (39/D4), which is set near one of Canada's highest waterfalls at 254 m (770 feet), offers picnic tables, kitchen shelter and toilets. There are 35 walk-in, tenting only sites. The campground is located at the Yoho Valley Road and open from late June until mid-September.

Yoho National Park (Maps 33, 39)

Set in the Rocky Mountains with glaciated peaks, waterfalls, alpine meadows and mountain streams, this national park is a spectacular place to visit and explore. Enjoy the view of 28 snow capped mountain peaks over 3,000 m (9,900 ft) high, marvel at the impressive 254 m (833 ft) Takakkaw Falls or look for the abundant wildlife, including elk, moose, deer, grizzly and black bears, mountain goats and sheep.

There are numerous rules and regulations to follow while in the park. Also, permits and reservations are needed for most everything. We suggest you contact the Parks Canada Visitor Centre, at Field, before heading out on your adventure. Call (250) 343-6783 for more information

In order to camp in the backcountry, you require a wilderness pass, which you can purchase for a fee. The pass is available at the Parks Canada Visitor Centre. There is a wide range of backcountry accommodations available and reservations are necessary:

The Alpine Club of Canada offers cabins at **Lake O'Hara** (39/G7), **Abbott Pass** (39/G6), **Little Yoho Valley** (39/C4) and on **Mount Daily** (39/F4). Call (403) 678-3200 for more information and to make reservations.

Twin Falls Chalet (39/D3) offers rooms and meals during July and August.

Lake O'Hara Campground (39/G7) has 30 primitive sites with a kitchen shelter, firewood and chemical toilets. It is open from June 19 to September 30 and can be used for a fee. Call (250) 343-6433 for more information.

Lake O'Hara Lodge (39/G7) offers rooms and meals. Call (250) 343-6418 for more information.

Designated backcountry campsites include **McArthur Creek** (33/F1), **Float Creek** (39/E7), **Yoho Lake** (39/E5), **Laughing Falls** (39/D4), **Twin Falls** (39/D3) and **Little Yoho Campsites** (39/C4). These sites are very primitive and offer few facilities other than bear poles, pit toilets and up to ten tent pads. No fires are allowed.

Symbols Used in Reference Section	
🏕	Campsite /Trailer Park
🔺	Road Access Recreation Site
🔺	Trail or Boat Access Recreation Site
⛱	Day-use, Picnic Site
🏖	Beach
🚤	Boat Launch
🚶	Hiking Trail
🚵	Mountain Biking Trail
🐎	Horseback Riding
⛷	Cross Country Skiing
🛷	Snowmobiling
⛷	Downhill Skiing
❄	Snowshoeing
🧗	Mountaineering /Rock Climbing
🛶	Paddling (Canoe /Kayak)
🏍	Motorbiking /ATV
🏊	Swimming
♠	Cabin /Hut /Resort
📖	Interpretive Brochure
🐟	Fishing
📷	Viewpoint
🎯	Hunt
♿	Wheel Chair Accessible
☽	Reservations
$ - $ $ $	Enhanced Wilderness Campsite

Provincial Parks

The provincial parks of the Kootenays offer an excellent way to explore the true beauty of the southeastern portion of British Columbia. The parks range from vast wilderness retreats to roadside campgrounds and picnic areas.

Between 1993 and 1996, many new parks were created in the government's intense push to preserve 12% of the provincial land base. Most of the newer parks have little in the way of developed facilities and are best left to the backcountry enthusiast.

The older, more established parks offer a full range of facilities. The roadside campgrounds are ideal locations to get acquainted with the outdoors while the large destination parks offer a more rugged, wilderness adventure. Regardless of your interest, you are certain to find a park that suits your needs.

Provincial parks with campgrounds generally operate from May through to October. Camping fees have recently been increased and range in price depending on facilities and popularity. Generally speaking, you can pay anywhere from $4.00/night for a designated wilderness campsite to over $18.00/night for a campground with full facilities, including showers.

Since many provincial park campgrounds are full during the summer, you can phone Discover Camping at 1-800-689-9025 (604-689-9025 in Greater Vancouver) to reserve a space. Not all parks in the Kootenays can be reserved through this system.

Akamina-Kishinena Provincial Recreation Area (Map 8/F7)

This internationally recognized park provides wilderness hiking, mountain biking, cross-country skiing, mountaineering, camping and fishing opportunities. The park is accessed by trail beginning in the Flathead River Valley or in Waterton Lakes National Park via Akamina Pass. The best lakes to fish are Forum and Wall Lakes, with both providing good trout fishing. Tenting pads and a pit toilet are provided at Akamina Creek.

Arrow Lakes Provincial Park (Maps 2, 6, 9,17)

Upper Arrow and Lower Arrow Lakes are a widening of the Columbia River and lie between the Selkirk Mountains on the east and the Monashee Mountains on the west. Both lakes are popular with recreational boaters and have endless bays and sandy beaches to explore. The park is divided into four units that are mostly popular day-use areas.

> **Burton** (Map 17/A6) is located on the eastern shores of the Upper Arrow Lake off Highway 6 near Burton. This unit provides a picnic site as well as a boat launch and beach.

> **Eagle Creek** (Map 9/D3) is located south of Edgewood on the western shores of the Lower Arrow Lake. The park has a picnic area, a sandy beach and a boat launch.

> **Fauquier** (Map 9/F1) is situated off Highway 6 on the eastern shores of the Lower Arrow Lake, and has a boat launch, picnic area and beach.

> **Shelter Bay** (Map 23/G3) is located at the Galena Bay Ferry terminal off Highway 23. This park has 23 tightly spaced and exposed campsites together with picnic tables, pit toilets, pump water and a boat launch. It is open from April 1 to October 31 and is often used as a rest area for travellers waiting for the ferry to Galena.

Blanket Creek Provincial Park (Map 30/F7)

Found on the old Domke Homestead at the northwestern end of the Upper Arrow Lake, this park has 64 private campsites, a large picnic area and sandy beach as well as a place to launch small boats or canoes (by portage only). It is open from April to October. Lake fishing the 12 m (40 foot) high Sutherland Falls and the lagoon are the big attractions to the park. Look for spawning kokanee in the fall.

Bugaboo Glacier Provincial Park (Maps 25/G1, 26/A1, 32/G7, 33/A7)

The 13,646 hectare park was created in 1995 because of its rugged mountain wilderness area, which attracts mountaineers worldwide. Massive glaciers, vast alpine meadows and rugged granite spires highlight the park. Mountain goats and grizzly bear are commonly sited in the park, while a series of alpine lakes and mountain cabins are popular destinations. Access

into the park is by trail from Bugaboo FSR and many visitors enjoy the services of Canadian Mountain Holidays (CMH), which operates a lodge near the entrance to the park and provide heli-hiking and heli-skiing. A steep 5 km (3 mile) one-way trail heads to the Conrad Cain Hut, climbing 700 m (2,295 feet) along the way. The hut has space for up to 40. A second hut, the Malloy Igloo, is located deeper in the park, and can hold six. Access to this hut is via a technical route, and should only be attempted by experienced climbers.

Burges and James Gadsen Provincial Park (Map 38/D5)

This wildlife sanctuary and nature study area is located in the Moberly Marsh on the north side of the Columbia River off Highway 1, near Golden. No facilities are offered but there is plenty of waterfowl to view. The park is open from April to October.

Canal Flats Provincial Park (Map 20/F3)

This park is a small lakeside picnic area located at the south end of Columbia Lake. The park is a popular destination for windsurfers. There is a good boat launch, pit toilets, a water tap, picnic tables and a developed beach at the park. Visitors can also explore the old canal connecting the Columbia and Kootenay Rivers or try their luck fishing on Columbia Lake.

Champion Lakes Provincial Park (Map 2/C5)

This 1,408 hectare provincial park is home to three lakes and is very popular among locals. The park is accessed by a windy, paved road from Highway 3B north of Fruitvale and is open from June to September. The hub of the park is the Third Lake. There is an 89 unit treed campground and separate beach and picnic area next to the lake. The attractions include the warm water, easy to catch minnows, sandy beach and nature trail around the lake. The First and Second lakes offer the better spring and fall rainbow fishing.

Christina Lake Provincial Park (Map 1/B7)

This is a popular sandy beach and picnic site on the south end of Canada's warmest recreation lake. There are unlimited water activities at the park, plenty of picnic tables, a large sandy beach and good bass fishing. While there is no boat launch at the park, there are marinas and a public launch nearby.

Cody Cave Provincial Park (Map 11/F3) $

Accessed off a forestry road 3 km (1.8 miles) north of Ainsworth, it is a 1.6 km (1 mile) 35 minute uphill walk to the caves. The caves are opened from June to September (10:00 am to 5:00 pm) and can only be viewed with a guide. Reservations are a must so call 250-353-7425. The current cost of the tour, which includes rental of a hard hat, light and coveralls, is $15/adult and $10/child but it is well worth it. Within the caves is a 1 km (0.6 mile) long underground stream, some small waterfalls, stalactites and stalagmites. Since the caves are cold and dirty, come dressed appropriately and with good foot wear.

Columbia Lake Provincial Park (Map 20/F1)

A popular lakeshore site offering a beach and water sports including excellent windsurfing. In winter, the area comes alive with animals and both sides of the lake are designated wildlife reserves.

Columbia View Provincial Park (Map 30/D4)

A picnic site with a fantastic view of Revelstoke Dam is found off Highway 23 north of Revelstoke.

Crowsnest Provincial Park (Map 15/F5)

At 1,350m (4,388 feet) in elevation, this small, cool day-use park is located on the pass through the Rocky Mountains. There is a group picnic shelter, day-use tables and hiking/biking opportunities around the park. The area is a winter range for elk and deer, which are often seen by cross-country skiers and snowmobilers.

Cummins Lakes Provincial Park (Map 41/G1)

This is a remote park on the east side of Kinbasket Lake at the head of the Cummins River. The park is set just below and west of the vast Clemenceau Icefields in Jasper National Park and features spectacular glacier fed waterfalls and lakes. The area has nationally significant scenic and recreation values for wilderness mountaineering and ski-touring and is home to grizzly bear, caribou and mountain goat. The park is rarely patrolled, so anyone venturing into the park should be self-sufficient.

Dry Gulch Provincial Park (Map 27/C4)

This park is located five minutes south of Radium Hot Springs on Highway 3 in the heart of the Columbia Valley. The park contains 26 vehicle/tenting campsites in a quiet, shaded pine forest. The campground is offered on a first come first serve basis from May 1- September 15 for a fee.

Elk Lakes Provincial Park (Maps 28, 29A/A6)

The attraction of this expanded, 17,325 hectare park is the rugged peaks, delicate sub-alpine, mountain lakes and glaciers. The two largest lakes of the park are Upper Elk Lake at 1,800 m (5,905 feet) and Lower Elk Lake at 1,700 m (5,525 feet), both of which are ice-free from mid-June to November. Both lakes are glacier-fed lakes offering fishing for small whitefish, cut-throat or bull trout. Fishing is also provided in the Elk River and Cadorna Creek. A wide variety of wildlife is abundant in the park including grizzly, black bear, cougar, wolf, moose, elk and deer. There are many mountaineering and rock climbing routes but limited winter activities due to the avalanche potential, and the fact that the road to the park is not plowed. No mountain biking is allowed in the park.

There are four camping areas in the park, which are available for a fee:

Lower Elk Lake Campground (Map 29/A5) has several tent pads, a food cache, fire pits, and a toilet.

Park Headquarters Campground (Map 29/A5) is located in the parking lot at the park entrance and has no facilities.

Petain Basin Campground (Map 28/G5) is a mountaineering bivouac site located near Petain Glacier and above Petain Falls.

Petain Creek Campground (Map 29/A5) located 1 km (0.6 miles) past the south end of Upper Elk Lake has a toilet, a food cache, tent pads and group fire rings.

Elk Valley Provincial Park (Map 22/C7)

This park is a small picnic site found near the Elk River, north of Sparwood.

Fort Steele Historical Park (Map 14/A5)

Outside of Cranbrook on Highway 93, this historic turn-of-the-century town has been re-created as a live museum. 60 restored buildings, musical shows and wagon rides are yours to discover.

Gilnockie Provincial Park (Maps 5/G6, 6/A7)

This is a 2,842 hectare park, which encompasses an undeveloped wilderness area protecting large larch and fir stands and wildlife habitat (including deer, elk, grizzly bear, moose and the endangered northern leopard frog). No off-road vehicles are allowed in the park and there are no marked trails. Hunting, wildlife viewing and creek fishing are the principal recreational activities.

Gladstone Provincial Park (Map 1/A1-B6)

Although this 40,000 hectare park covers vast stretches of wilderness, most of the recreational activity occurs around the northern half of Christina Lake.

The main access is from the Texas Creek Campground where it is possible to camp, launch a boat or access the Deer Point Trail. There are also a series of seven boat access only campgrounds and other trails climbing from the low-elevation forests into the rugged alpine terrain. The shores around Christina Lake are prime deer and elk wintering areas and several streams flowing into the lake have spawning kokanee in the fall. Also, look for historical pictographs and Doukhobor Settlements in the park. The 48 shaded vehicle/tent campsites at Texas Creek are often full and reservations are highly recommended.

Goat Range Provincial Park (Maps 17/G3-18/C5, 24/G7-25/B6)

Stretching from Trout Lake, high into the Goat Mountain Range, this large, 78,947 hectare wilderness park contains old-growth forests, alpine meadows and lakes. The park was established to protect the only natural spawning area of the Gerrard Trout as well as an important caribou, grizzly and mountain goat wintering area. Fishing, hunting, hiking, camping, mountaineering, snowmobiling, backcountry skiing and biking are some of the activities offered in the park. The principal access routes into the park include the Wilson Creek Falls Trail at the south end of the park, the Popular Creek Road and Highway 31. The most accessible campground is at the south end of Trout Lake were you will find five camping units and a picnic area. From there, you can enjoy watching the world famous Gerrard Trout (up to 14 kg/30 lbs) spawn in April and May.

Granby Provincial Park (Map 9/A1-A5)

Since only the eastern portion of this large, 40,845 hectare, park is shown in this mapbook, we recommend reviewing the Kamloops/Okanagan edition before venturing further west. In this book, the best access is along the 4wd Mount Scala Road. There are no developed facilities within park.

Grohman Narrows Provincial Park (Map 11/A7)

Located off Highway 3 west of Nelson, this small park offers a 30 minute, nature walk around a small pond and through the surrounding forest. In the winter, the nature trail is open for cross-country skiing, while skating is popular on the pond. Highway travellers will also enjoy the 15 picnic sites and the opportunities to explore some wetland habitat and the shores of Kootenay River.

Height-of-the-Rockies Provincial Park (Maps 21/G1-22/C1, 28/D2-29/B7)

This 54,208 hectare wilderness park covers the high alpine area from Connor Lake to Banff National Park. The prominent feature here is the Rocky Mountains, including 26 mountains over 3,000 m (9,800 feet) high, and an abundance of wildlife, especially mountain goats (over 1,200 known). In the remote park, there are wilderness campsites at both ends of the bigger Connor Lake, a cabin at Connor Lake (first come first serve) and an 8 person cabin at Queen Mary Lake (you must make a reservation through the Invermere Forest District). Hike/backpackers, horseback riders, hunters, mountaineers and backcountry skiers use the extensive trail systems found throughout the park. Connor Lakes are also popular lake fishing destinations.

James Chabot Provincial Park (Map 27/C5)

On the northern shores of Windermere Lake in Invermere, this popular day-use park offers a picnic site, sandy beach and grassy play fields. Sunbathing, swimming, windsurfing and waters sports are the attraction to the park. The facilities are open from May 1 to September 30 at no charge.

Jimsmith Lake Provincial Park (Map 13/F7)

This park, which is open to camping from May 1 to October 31, is a popular retreat to the west of Cranbrook. The park contains 29 large, well spaced vehicles/tent campsites, a picnic area, beach, canoe launch and pit toilets. Cross-country skiing, tobogganing and ice-skating are the winter recreational activities whereas paddling, sunbathing and swimming are the summer recreation activities. **Jimsmith Lake** offers good fishing for bass as well as rainbow and brook trout.

Kianuko Provincial Park (Maps 4/E2-12/D7)

Found at the headwaters of Kianuko Creek, this 11,638 hectare wilderness park contains several small lakes, meadows and old-growth forests. Caribou, grizzly bears and moose are common to the area, which doesn't see many visitors outside of hunters and mountaineers. There are several rustic campgrounds and a few trails to explore.

Kikomun Creek Provincial Park (Map 6/F4)

Located on the eastern shores of Lake Koocanusa, this park has 135 full service campsites in addition to picnic tables, pit and flush toilets, showers, tap water, a boat launch, two developed beaches, a playground and pay phones. Activities in the park include canoeing, windsurfing, swimming and cross-country skiing. Lake Koocanusa is known for its great kokanee fishing, while Surveyor's Lake holds plenty of bass and some good sized brook trout and rainbows. If you are interested in hiking, try the trail around Hidden Lake, the trail to the top of the drumlins behind the campground or the Engineer's Lake Loop. A big attraction to Kokomum Creek is the spawning kokanee in the fall. The park is open for camping from May 1 to October 31 and the overnight facilities can be used for a fee. Reservations for camping are highly recommended.

King George VI Provincial Park (Map 1/G7)

Just north of the Patterson border crossing on Highway 22, this park offers a shady picnic site next to the old Red Mountain Railway bed.

Kokanee Creek Provincial Park (Map 11/C5)

Offering sandy beaches and impressive displays of spawning salmon, this popular, full facility park offers 132 vehicles/tent campsites at two sites (Redfish and Sandspit). Other facilities include a boat launch, cross-country skiing trails (2 km/1.2 miles of groomed trails), toilets, water and an adventure playground. From the visitors centre within the park, there are eight different walking trails taking a total of 1.5 hours to hike. The primary attraction is the spawning channels, which have spawning kokanee in August. Reservations for camping are highly recommended, as the park can be busy on weekends.

Kokanee Glacier Provincial Park (Map 11/A1-E4)

With over 85+km (52.7 miles) of trails, 30 glacial fed lakes and magnificent peaks all over the 1,800m (5,905 foot) elevation level, Kokanee Glacier Park is a gem of the Kootenays. Kokanee Glacier Peak, at 2,775m (9,105 ft), is the dominant feature of the 32,035 hectare park, which also features several glaciers. Backcountry explorers will find three cabins (Slocan Chief, Woodberry and Silver Spray Cabins), one picnic shelter and several designated wilderness campsites. The hiking season runs from July to October while backcountry skiing is popular in the winter. Anglers will find the small, sub-alpine lakes are home to abundant but small cutthroat trout.

Kootenay Lake Marine Parks (Maps 3, 4, 18)

On the shores of Kootenay Lake are several small parks for people exploring the large lake by boat. In addition to sheltered mooring sites for boaters, there are endless water sports. Eagles, osprey and waterfowl are commonly sighted around the parks.

Campbell Bay (Map 18/G7) is found on the eastern shores of Kootenay Lake across from Kaslo. A rustic campsite, pit toilets and three mooring buoys are available at the park. Hikes in the area access the remote Clute Lake and the good trout fishing at Leviathan Lake.

Coffee Creek (Map 11/F4) is found at the estuary to Coffee Creek north of Balfour and has five tent sites, pit toilets and a sandy beach. The park is reached by boat or by walking down from Highway 31. Shore fishing at the creek mouth can produce large rainbow.

Davis Creek (Map 18/F4) contains 10 rustic, semi-private campsites south of Lardeau on Highway 31. The park is open to camping from May 15 to September 15. Visitors often enjoy fishing at the creek mouth or swimming in the lake.

Drewry Point (Map 3/G1) is a boat access only park on the western shores of Kootenay Lake. The area has several sandy coves, picnic tables, a pit toilet, a mooring buoy and three tenting pads.

Lost Ledge (Map 18/F5) offers 14 shaded, secluded campsites, a picnic area, pit toilets, water pump and a boat launch. The park is found on the western shores of Kootenay Lake south of Davis Creek next to Highway 31. The park is open to camping from May 15 to September 15.

Midge Creek (Map 3/G2) is a boat access only site that boasts a large sandy beach, picnic tables, toilets and tenting pads. There is an opportunity to see spawning bull trout, kokanee and rainbow trout in season. These sites are unserviced, and are user maintained.

Pilot Bay (Map 11/G5) is a scenic park on the eastern shores of Kootenay Lake with two sheltered anchorages and nine mooring buoys. There are also tent sites, picnic tables, fire pits and pit toilets at the park. Visit the historic smelter explore the extensive network of hiking trails throughout Pilot Peninsula or fish for bull and rainbow trout.

Lockhart Beach Provincial Park (Map 12/A7)

Found on the shores of Kootenay Lake, this small park offers a broad sandy beach and a separate camping area. There are 12 treed campsites that fill up quickly in the summer, picnic tables and pit toilets. Access is provided by Highway 3A, north of Boswell. Kokanee can be seen spawning in the nearby creek in fall.

Lockhart Creek Provincial Park (Map 12/A7)

This 3,751 hectare park contains a pristine watershed rising steeply from the slopes of Kootenay Lake to some beautiful alpine meadows. The park preserves old-growth cedar-hemlock forests and offers creek fishing for bull trout and rainbow. The only access into the park is by way of the Lockhart Creek Trail, which leads from the shores of Kootenay Lake to Baker Lake.

Martha Creek Provincial Park (Map 30/D2)

Located on an old river terrace on the western slopes of Lake Revelstoke, this park offers 25 vehicles/tent campsites, a picnic area, cooking shelters, an unpaved boat launch, tap water and pit and flush toilets. The beach and adventure playground are a hit with the children, while trails lead up the hillside. The park is open to camping from May 15 to September 15 and is easily accessed off Highway 23, north of Revelstoke.

McDonald Creek Provincial Park (Map 17/B4)

Found next to the Upper Arrow Lake, there are 38 vehicles/tent camping sites in this park, which are located 10 km south of Nakusp on Highway 6. The park is popular with water enthusiasts as there is an 800 m (2,600 foot) beach and a boat launch off Upper Brouse Road. Two loop trails offer good hiking, biking and horseback riding. The park is open for camping from April 1 to October 31.

Monashee Provincial Park (Map 23/C6)

Known as the jewel of the Monashees, this remote park offers 7,513 hectares of pristine wilderness ideal for a backcountry trek or high elevation fishing. The only access to the park is via the Rainbow Falls Trail from north of Sugar Lake. In addition to the 30 km (18.3 mile) network of maintained trails, there are several wilderness camping areas. Most visitors use Spectrum Lake, which is 6 km (3.7 miles) one-way from the trailhead, as a staging ground for day trips to the surrounding mountains and other lakes. There are a total of 16 wilderness campsites with bear caches at Spectrum. A second camping option is found at Peters Lake, 12 km (7.3 miles) from the trailhead. There are ten wooden tent platforms at the south end of the bigger lake. There are also undeveloped campsites at Mikes Lake and Fawn Lake among other places. Hiking beyond Peters Lake should be left to the experienced backpacker prepared to climb some steep terrain.

Morrissey Provincial Park (Map 7/A1)

On the north bank of the Elk River south of Fernie, the park offers a pleasant picnic site. Explore some old coke ovens or try your luck fishing.

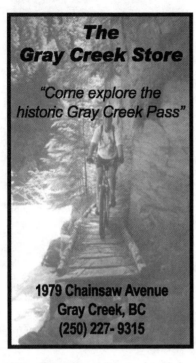
Mount Assiniboine Provincial Park (Maps 29B/A2, 34/G6)

This beautiful wilderness park is dotted with high elevation lakes and meadows surrounded by snow capped peaks. The 3,561m (11,443 foot) high Mount Assiniboine overshadows the whole park. Most visitors hike into the park from Spray Lakes in Alberta and use Lake Magog as a staging ground. At Lake Magog, there is a campground, four cabins and the Mount Assiniboine Lodge (call 1-403-678-2882 for reservations). Trails lead past several lakes worth fishing and into the surrounding mountains. Mountain biking is allowed on the Assiniboine Pass Trail, while horseback riding is only possible after receiving a letter of authority with route directions from the Parks branch. The park has long been a popular backcountry skiing destination as the meadows below Mount Assiniboine offer some good terrain with great scenery and lots of powder. The season runs from early December to mid April with accommodation at Naiset Cabins, Bryant Creek shelter or Mount Assiniboine Lodge. Reserve your accommodation before you go. Most skiers prefer a helicopter ride to Lake Magog and then ski out at the end of the trip. The more adventurous can follow one of the long routes into the area.

Mount Fernie Provincial Park (Map 15/A7)

The 38 treed vehicle/tent campsites, diverse vegetation and picturesque waterfall are part of the attractions of this beautiful park. Visitors can explore the Lizard Creek Nature Trail along the old Elk Lumber Co Railgrade, mountain bike the nearby trails or fish Lizard Creek for cutthroat and bull trout. There is also a good chance to see wildlife as there is an abundance of (over friendly) black bear, deer and elk. The park is open to camping from June 1 to October 15, with tap water, pay phones and pit and flush toilets being available. Reservations for camping are highly recommended.

Moyie Lake Provincial Park (Map 5/E2)

Set on the shores of beautiful Moyie Lake, this popular park has a 111 unit vehicle/tent campground, a nice beach, picnic area, flush toilets, showers, water taps, an amphitheater and a boat launch. There is also a 2 km/1.2 mile (45 minute) interpretive trail through the forest on the west side of the campground called the Meadow Interpretive Trail. Water sports and fishing are the main attractions to the park, which is open to camping from April 1 to October 31. Reservations for camping are highly recommended.

Nancy Green Provincial Park (Map 1/F4)

At the junction of Highway 3A and Highway 3, this high elevation park surrounds Nancy Green Lake. You can fish for rainbow, swim in the lake or walk/cross-country ski around the lake depending on the season. The park has 10 lakeshore campsites, a cartop boat launch, picnic tables and shelter, pump water, pit toilets, fire pits, firewood and an enclosed kitchen. It is open for camping from May 1 to September 30. Ice skating and ice fishing are also popular winter activities at the park.

Nancy Greene Recreation Area (Map 1/G6)

Found in the Rossland Range of the Monashee Mountains, this recreation area is best known for its downhill skiing at Red Mountain. The area also offers excellent backcountry ski touring and a breathtaking hike up Old Glory (the highest peak in the area). Access to the recreation area is by way of the old Cascade Highway or Highway 3B.

Norbury Lake Provincial Park (Map 14/C7)

This park, located on the Wardner-Fort Steele Road, offers 46 vehicle/tent campsites, a picnic area, pit toilets, water pump and a boat launch. The main activities at the park are the swimming and fishing at Norbury Lake and Peckhams Lake. The beautiful park is set below the Steeples and is open for camping from May 15 to the September long weekend.

Pilot Bay (Map 11/D3)

See Kootenay Lake Marine Parks.

Premier Lake Provincial Park (Maps 14/A1-21/A7)

A popular retreat for angling enthusiasts, this park offers 57 vehicle/tent camping sites, a boat launch, an adventure playground, showers, water and toilet facilities. In addition to good fishing for rainbows and brook trout in 5 lakes, hiking, and swimming at the beach are popular pastimes. Starting from the campground, a one hour one-way hike leads to Yankee Lake and Canuck Lake whereas an easy, 15 minute one-way walk reaches Cat's Eye Lake. The road easily accesses Quartz Lake. The park is a good wildlife viewing area with bighorn sheep, elk and deer. Be sure to follow the Staple Creek Trail for 10 minutes to the spawning area where rainbow are trapped so that they can provide the egg source for stocking 350 lakes and streams throughout the province. The park is open for camping from May 1 to September 15. Reservations for camping are highly recommended.

Purcell Wilderness Conservancy (East) (Maps 19-20, 26-27)

This is a spectacular, 34,947 hectare Wilderness Park with alpine lakes and grasslands surrounded by mountain peaks. The park is virtually untouched and boasts a large elk population. Access to the park is via horse trails up the major valleys (Dutch Creek Trail, Finlay Creek Trail, Mineral Creek Trail and Brewer Creek Trail) or via the historic Earl Grey Pass Trail. Heli-hiking and heli-ski touring are a popular alternative to the long hike into the park. Hiking, horseback riding, fishing, hunting and wildlife viewing are all popular recreational activities.

Purcell Wilderness Conservancy (West) (Maps 18-19)

Rising above the north end of Kootenay Lake, this 32,662 hectare park encompasses a virtually untouched wilderness. Access into the park is by way of a series of trails (Earl Grey Pass Trail, Fry Creek Trail and Kootenay Joe Ridge Road Trail). The southern portion of the park includes rugged canyons, alpine meadows and lakes as well as glacier covered mountains. Caribou, grizzly bear and wolverines abound. Activities include caving, fishing, hiking, mountaineering, hunting, ski touring and snowmobiling.

Rosebery Provincial Park (Map 17/G6)

Just off Highway 6 on the eastern slopes of Slocan Lake, this small park has 36 quiet, treed campsites next to Wilson Creek. There is also a picnic site, pit toilets and water pump for visitors wishing to enjoy the lake. The park is open from May 1 to September 15.

St. Mary's Alpine Provincial Park (Maps 12/F1-19/F7)

Another remote, undeveloped park tucked in the Monashee Mountains, St. Mary's Alpine Park offers endless alpine hiking on undeveloped bushwhacking trails or ridge routes. The 9,164 hectare wilderness park is also home to 29 alpine lakes with **Huggard Lake**, at 2,134m (7,000 feet), and **Spade Lake**, at 1,646m (5,400 feet) being the most popular fishing destinations. The 4wd mining road found at 7.5 km (4.6 miles) on the Dewar Creek Road provides the best access with the least amount of bushwhacking. The other main trails into the park include the **Westley Creek Trail**, the **Skookumchuck Creek Trail**, and the **White Creek/Spade Creek Trail**, which starts at the washed out Spade Creek Bridge. Once you have accessed the park, you can explore the park along any of a number of informal routes. To do so requires crossing rough terrain and talus slopes. A compass and topographic map is a must since these routes are not marked, and may be difficult to follow.

Stagleap Provincial Park (Map 3/C7)

A beautiful lakeside picnic spot lies at Kootenay Pass on the scenic Salmo-Creston Highway. More adventurous people like to explore the short, 3.5 km trail systems by foot, bike or skis into the alpine ridges. In winter migrating caribou are often seen in the area, while the warm up cabin helps take the chill off. Anglers will find **Bridal Lake** has many small rainbows to 25 cm (10 inches) that are best caught during summer evenings.

Summit Lake Provincial Park (Map 17/C4)

Summit Lake Provincial Park is located on Highway 6, 13 km (8 miles) south-west of Nakusp at the height of land between Slocan Lake and Upper Arrow Lake. The Nakusp Range of the Selkirk Mountains rises above the lake, providing a magnificent backdrop to the many recreational opportunities in the park. Fish for rainbow trout or swim in the lake's clear, refreshing mountain water. Mountain Goats can often be viewed on rocky outcroppings and each fall a natural spectacle occurs as thousands of toads emerge from the lake and migrate to the nearby forest to hibernate for the winter.

Syringa Provincial Park (Map 1/G1)

Home to a large sandy beach and a 60 unit, full service campground, this park is a popular retreat for Kootenay area visitors. There are actually three separate areas, the campground, the picnic area and the boat launching area. Other amenities include pit and flush toilets, water taps, sani-station and the ever-popular adventure playground. In addition to water sports, Lower Arrow Lake offers good rainbow and kokanee fishing. Both the Yellow Pine and Syringa Creek Nature Trails offer several viewpoints from the dry hillside dotted with Ponderosa pine trees. Rocky Mountain Bighorn Sheep, elk and mule deer are common to the area. The park is open to camping from May 1 to September 30.

Top of the World Provincial Park (Map 14/D1)

This park is truly at the top of the world, as much of its terrain is in the alpine and above the 2,200m (7,200 foot) level. Because of its elevation, the numerous hiking opportunities do not become accessible until early June or after November. Fish Lake is the hub of the park and has a cabin as well as numerous designated campsites around the sub-alpine lake. The cabin, which sleeps 20–25 hikers, can be used for a fee and has firewood and a stove. The main trailhead is accessed off the South Lussier River Road. Fishing is another popular activity as the lakes are stocked.

Upper Cummins Provincial Park (Map 41/F1)

Remote is the operative word here. This 6,109 hectare wilderness park is set below the Clemenceau Icefields at the headwaters of Cummins River. Mountaineers and ski tourers can explore the series of three spectacular waterfalls and two glacial lakes. Also, there is an opportunity to see wildlife such as caribou, grizzly bears and mountain goats. The easiest way to access the park is to take a helicopter to the Alpine Club of Canada hut, which is located just outside of the park.

Valhalla Provincial Park (Maps 10/C2-17/G6)

Located on the western shores of Slocan Lake, this magnificent 49,600 hect-are wilderness park is defined by the rugged sub-alpine and alpine terrain of the Valhalla Range. The park has limited development except for several primitive campsites, some trails and nine lakeshore camping/beach areas with outhouses and bear caches. Visitors should be prepared for a remote wilderness experience when they explore this vast park. To access the park, there are several boat access trails beginning along the shores of Slocan Lake as well as a popular trail leading from Slocan City. Trails also lead from the Hoder-Drinnon Creek, Shannon Creek or Wragge Creek Forest Service Roads. Your best bet is probably one of the logging roads if you wish to avoid the hike up the forested slope from Slocan Lake. There are several sub-alpine and alpine lakes in the park, which offer good fishing throughout the summer and early fall.

Victor Lake Provincial Park (Map 30/A5)

Although found beside the Trans-Canada Highway west of Revelstoke, there is no marked access to this small 14.7 hectare park. It is possible to walk in along a rustic trail and try your luck fishing in this pretty mountain lake.

Wardner Lake Provincial Park (Map 6/C1)

This is a small waterfront park on the west side of Lake Koocanusa. The park offers a beach, picnic sites and fishing opportunities.

Wasa Lake Provincial Park (Map 13/G3)

This is a popular park on Highway 93/95 north of Cranbrook, which has 104 vehicle/tent campsites, a separate beach and picnic area, as well as a boat launch. Facilities include pit and flush toilets, water taps, sani-station and the ever-popular adventure playground. Wasa Lake is a warm lake that offers good largemouth bass fishing and scuba diving around the rare freshwater reef. There are 8 km (4.9 miles) of walking/biking trails around the lake as well as the opportunity for mountain bikers to take a 33 km (20.1 mile) loop via Lazy Lake. During the winter months, cross-country skiing and skating are popular activities. Reservations for camping are highly recommended, as the park can be busy on weekends.

West Arm Provincial Park (Maps 3/C1-11/C5)

Protecting the undeveloped portion of the West Arm of Kootenay Lake, this 25,319 hectare wilderness park is home to caribou and grizzly bears. The northern reaches of the park next to Kootenay Lake can be reached by road or boat but the principal access into the remote sub-alpine portion of the park is by way of trail (Mount Station Trails and Lasca Creek Trail).

Whiteswan Lake Provincial Park (Map 21/C4)

Found in the Kootenay Range of the Rockies, this beautiful park offers five campgrounds (Alces Lake, Packrat Point, Home Basin, Inlet Creek and White River) with a total of 114 vehicle/tent sites. In addition, there are natural hot springs (Lussier Hot Springs), four boat launches (the Home Basin launch is paved) and four picnic sites. For lake fishermen, good fishing for stocked rainbow is offered at both Alces and Whiteswan Lakes. You can also hike the 8 km (4.9 mile) one-way trail from Home Basin Campground along the northern shores of Whiteswan Lake to Alces Lake. The park is also a good wildlife viewing area with moose and spawning rainbow trout (in May-June). The park is open to camping from May 1 to September 30.

Yahk Provincial Park (Map 5/A7)

On the banks of the Moyie River, this park offers a stopover for highway travellers. There are 26 forested vehicle/tent sites, tap water, pit toilets and a picnic site. Fishing is the main pastime here. The park is open from May 1 to September 15. Please note that the campground is located next to Highway 3 and the railroad so it can be quite noisy at times.

Trails

(Hiking, biking, ATV, horseback and more)

The Kootenays offer the explorer some of the best trails in the world. The spectacular mountain vistas, cascading waterfalls, retreating glaciers and natural hot springs are just some of the possible destinations. The Kootenays have all the spectacular scenery of Banff and Jasper, but with a fraction of the people. While some trails are very popular, it is not unusual to hike to some spectacular destination without seeing another soul on the trip.

Below we have included information on over 500 (yes that says 500!) trails. Our multi-use trails have been described from a hiking standpoint. All distances and times are for return hikes, unless otherwise noted in the description. We have also included a symbol to indicate the other trail users including mountain bikers, horseback riders, cross-country skiers, snowmobilers and ATVs/motorbikers. However, there is a separate section devoted to winter recreation (cross-country skiing and snowmobiling).

Finding the trailhead is sometimes half the fun (and half the work). For this reason, you should refer to the appropriate map in this book to determine where the trail begins. But remember our maps are designed only as a general access guide. They are not intended to navigate you through a hidden mountain pass or across an expansive ridge network. If you are attempting to travel an unmarked trail or route, we recommend that you have mountaineering knowledge and are equipped with a topographic map and a compass.

The hiking/biking season is often limited, especially when heading for high elevations. Snow can stay on the higher peaks (over 1,500 m or 5,000 feet), until late July. Another concern for trail users exploring the Kootenays is bears and other large animals. Bear bells and common sense should help you avoid any unnecessary encounters.

In this section, where we refer to the difficulty of the trail we mean the following:

Easy is a gentle grade excellent for family excursions.

Moderate is a fairly strenuous trail with climbing involved. These trails will challenge most trail users and should not be underestimated.

Difficult is for experienced users as the trails are often rough and or unmarked.

The trails are grouped into three main sections: East Kootenay Trails, West Kootenay Trails and National Park Trails.

East Kootenays

The southeastern corner of BC ranges from the farmlands around Creston to the lush green Elk Valley surrounded by the snow capped peaks of the Rocky Mountains. Stretching north the area extends through the hot, dry Rocky Mountain Trench around Cranbrook to the dramatic peaks of the Purcell and Columbia Mountains west of Invermere and Golden. Add in the lowlands around the Columbia River and several high alpine parks and you have all the variety a trail user could ask for. The trails range from easy valley strolls to steep glacier ascents. Waterfalls, fantastic mountain vistas and beautiful mountain lakes are just some of the highlights in this quiet corner of BC.

Akamina-Kishinena Provincial Park (Map 8/F7) 🚶 🚵 🐟 ⛺

Tucked in the extreme southeast corner of the province, this spectacular area is far removed from most any form of civilization, which makes this a great destination for recreationists. Cyclists usually stick to the old road system while hikers like to venture up the ridges and into the small lakes.

Akamina Ridge

This is arguably one of the most spectacular viewpoints in the province, bringing hikers almost to the three point border of BC, Alberta and Montana. The first part of the trail from Forum Lake (in itself 2 km/1.2 miles from the nearest road access) is signed and well marked. You will gain 890 m (2892 ft) over 7 km (4.3 miles) one-way to the top.

Bennett Pass to Akamina Ridge

From the Akamina Creek Campsite, it is a 6.5 km (4 miles) hike to Bennett Pass, along a signed trail, then another 4 km (2.4 miles) along the spine of the ridge to Forum Peak. The views over two countries are amazing.

Akamina Pass

This old road built in the 1920s transects the park from Akamina Pass through the Kishinena Creeks to eventually reach the Flathead River valley. Cyclists use this route for day excursions from Waterton Lakes.

Forum Lake

From the Ranger Station, it is a 2 km (1.2 mile) hike to Forum Lake, gaining 200 m (650 ft) along the way. A short side trail at the start of the hike brings hikers to Forum Falls.

Wall Lake

So named because it sits at the base of a 600 m (2,000 foot) wall of rock, this lake is a 2 km (1.2 mile) hike from the Ranger Station, gaining 50 m (163 ft) along the way. This is an easy hike along well-marked trails that is often used by anglers. The campsite that once was here has been removed, due to concerns over human/grizzly conflicts.

Akunam Creek Trail (Map 28/E7) 🚶 ⛺

If you follow the North White River Road to near its end, you will find the trailhead on the north side of the creek. The trail, which was cut by a trapper, begins off a skid road and is fairly obvious for the first 1.8 km (1.1 miles) before it descends into some old-growth timber near the creek. At that stage, cross over to the south side of the creek and continue upstream. The trail fades out as you near the headwaters of Akunam Creek.

Alexander Creek Drainage (Map 15/C2) 🚶 🐎 🚵 🏍 🛶 ⛺

This drainage offers great riding along a 2wd/4wd forestry road. From the main road, you can access nine different alpine bowls along very challenging road and trails. The Deadman Pass Trail is the most exciting side route to try. The area is popular with snowmobilers in the winter.

Alki Creek Trail (Map 13/A5) 🚶 ⛺

Off the St Mary River Road at the west end of St Mary Lake, this trail follows Alki Creek and passes several old mine workings before reaching Murray Pass. From there, you can explore the high benches and rock gardens. Expect a long day trip as you gain over 1,200 m (3,900 ft) to the pass at 2,317 m (7,600 ft). Also expect to get your feet wet, as it is necessary to ford the creek on several occasions.

Amiskwi Pass Trail (Map 39/B2) ⛰ 🚶 🐎 ⛺

From the Blaeberry River Road, a 22 km (13.4 mile) difficult route follows a horse trail to Amiskwi Pass and the border of Yoho National Park. It is possible to continue past the lodge and along the Amiskwi River to the fire road leading down towards Field.

Andy Good Creek Trail (Map 15/G7) 🚶 🚵 ⛺

From just before the railroad tracks on the Byron Creek Mine Road, an old road leads to the left. It offers a good hike or bike travelling about 7 km (4.3 miles) one-way. The experienced bushwhacker can continue on to a series of caves, which are difficult to find.

Baker Lake Trail (Map 12/B7) 🚶 🐟 ⛺

It is a 6 km (3.7 mile) 3 hour moderate one-way hike to Baker Lake. At the lovely Baker Creek Meadows, the trail connects with the Lockhart Creek Trail, which leads steeply down to Kootenay Lake. The trailhead is found at the end of the Redding Creek Road.

Balancing Rock Trail (Map 4/A6) 🚶 📖 ⛺

From the Creston Valley Wildlife Centre, this interpretive trail gains 730 m (2,373 ft) as it switchbacks up the slopes of Creston Mountain ending at 1,360 m (4,420 ft) in elevation. The trail passes by the Balancing Rock and Ralph's Bridge before leading to a viewpoint over the Creston Valley. A short side trip brings you to a small waterfall. An interpretive guide is available at the sign box (or at the Creston Travel Information Centre).

Baldy Lake Trail (Map 7/B7) 🚶 🐎 🏍

Found 11.2 km (6.8 miles) up the Phillips-Rabbit Road, this moderate hike leads to an alpine lake. Hikers and horseback riders share the trail.

Bare Hill Viewpoint Trail (Map 22/B6) 🚶 🚵 🎿

From the power sub-station on Galbraith Road, it is a short one kilometre (0.6 mile) 30 minute hike gaining 90 m (295 ft) in elevation. The hill offers a scenic view over Elkford.

Bear Lake Trail (Map 14/C3) ⛺ 🚶 🏍

It's a stiff climb from the parking area at the end of Bear Lake Road to the lake, gaining 300 m (975 feet) over 2.5 km (1.5 miles). People with low clearance vehicles may have to walk an extra 2.3 km (1.4 miles) along the road to get to the trailhead. From the lake it is possible to hike up another couple hundred metres to a pass between Bear and Rault Lakes.

Ben Abel Lake Trail

(see Mineral Creek Trail)

Big Ranch Trail (Map 15/D1) 🚶 🚵 🎿 🏍

Located on the Lower Elk Valley Road, these grasslands offer a leisurely stroll, bike or ski in a well-known Elk wintering range. The Sparwood District Fish and Wildlife Association manage the area.

Black Diamond Basin Trail (Map 26/E7) 🚶 🚵 🏍

From the Jumbo Creek Road, an old logging road leads up an unnamed creek draw through a series of large clearcuts to the base of Black Diamond Mountain. Since the road is virtually undrivable, you will have to hike/bike most of the way. From the end of the logging road, the trail continues through a sub-alpine forest to the open meadows below the mountain. Depending on how far you can drive up the road, the hike is approximately 5 km (3 miles) and 2–3 hours one-way gaining 1,000 m (3,280 ft).

Blue Lake Trails (Map 20/C4) 🚶 🚵 🎿

The Blue Lake Forest Education Society has created a 12 km (7.3 mile) network of multi-use trails. All levels of hikers/bikers and cross-country skiers can enjoy the trails (depending on the season), which follow old roads in a forested setting.

Boivin Creek Peace Park Trail (Map 22/B6) 🚶 🚵 🎿

Starting on Fording Drive in Elkford, a 1.2 km (0.7 mile), 30 minute interpretive loop helps visitors enjoy the wildlife and unique flora in the area. Benches and picnic tables are found en route. If you want a longer hike or bike, continue west along the creek and gradually climb 300 m (385 ft) to the end point. This part of the trail, which is 7.5 km (4.6 miles) 2 hours one-way, is also used in the winter for cross-country skiing.

Boivin Creek South Fork Trail (Map 22/B6) 🚶 🚵 🏍

Also known as Wildcat Creek, this route is mostly a road walk, which is why many people bike it. The road starts from the end of Natal Road in Elkford, and forks twice. Stay left, then right until you get to an old cut line that leads directly to the base of Phillips Peak. (If you've biked in, you'll probably want to leave it here.) From here you can head up to a small lake, and, if you are feeling very energetic, you can bushwhack into the Weigert Creek drainage, and hike out along the road. Another option is to hike up to a meadow near the steep face of Phillips Peak.

Brewer Creek Trail (Maps 19/G1, 20/A1, 26/G7, 27/A7) 🚶 🏍

The Brewer Creek Trail climbs steadily, although not too steeply, as it gains 670 m (2,200 ft) from the end of the Brewer Creek Road (Map 27/A7) to Brewer Pass, 6 km (4.6 miles) southwest of the parking area. (There may be an extra 1.7 km/1 mile distance and 180 m/585 ft if the last bridge is out). The hiking is fairly easy, but the trail is hard to follow at times. Experienced scramblers can get to the top of Mount Brewer, a 3 km (1.8 mile) ridge walk from the pass. You can also take the Hopeful Creek Trail to the Panorama Ski Resort, which will add the better part of a day to your hike.

Bruce Creek Route (Maps 26/G6–27/B5) 🏍 🚵 🏍

By riding the old mining road uphill from the Toby Creek Road, mountain bikers/ATVers can make a loop down to Wilmer via the Bruce Creek drainage. It is 16 km (9.8 miles) up and 35 km (21.3 miles) down. Uphill is painful, downhill is fast and fun. Leave a vehicle in Wilmer, unless you want to climb back up the Toby Creek Road.

Brule Creek Trail (Maps 14/G1-15/B1) ⛺ 🚶 🐎 🏍

At about 75.5 km (46 miles) along the Bull River Road, a 28 km (17 mile) day + hike follows a poorly marked historic trail next to Norboe Creek and Brule Creek. The trail leads to Hornaday Pass where the views from the alpine meadows are impressive. You can take a side trip to tiny Josephine and Big Lakes if you wish.

Bugaboo Provincial Park (Maps 25, 26, 32, 33) ⛺ 🚶 🚵 🛶 📷 ⛷ 🏍

An international climbing destination, the rugged granite spires of the Bugaboos are a sight to behold. Most of the activity occurs around the Conrad Cain Hut, although there is also a second hut located near Mount Malloy that experienced climbers can access. Outside of the park are several other trails to explore.

Cobalt Lake Trail (Map 26/A1)

This is an 8 km (5.5 mile) 4–5 hour difficult hike from the CMH Lodge, switchbacking up a steep slope until it reaches the open ridge above Cobalt Lake. The trail then descends 55 m (180 ft) to this beautiful lake surrounded by a large glacier with the granite spires of the Bugaboo Mountains looming in the background. Overall, there is an 885 m (2,905 foot) elevation gain to the lake at 2,330 m (7,645 feet). It is possible to continue on to the Conrad Kain Hut but this trek is best left to experienced mountaineers prepared to cross a glacier.

Conrad Kain Hut Hike (Map 26/A1)

Very popular with rock climbers, the hut provides overnight accommodation and a propane stove for up to 40 people for a fee. To access the hut requires walking a 5 km (3 mile) 2.5 hour one-way steep, difficult trail gaining 700 m (2,295 ft) in elevation. The first part of the hike follows the valley bottom on a well-used trail, which has several boardwalks to cross. Eventually, the trail leads up a lateral moraine of the Bugaboo Glacier to the hut. For tenters, the Applebee Dome Campsite is on a rocky ridge overlooking the hut, about 1.5 hours one-way. There is also the Boulder Camp, 75 m (244 feet) below the hut.

Bugaboo Pass Trail (Map 26/A2) 🚶 🚵 🏍

From the end of the Bugaboo Road, this trail rises steadily to the pass at 2,250 m (7,380 ft). The beginning of the trail is overgrown in places requiring some bushwhacking. You soon break out into some beautiful alpine meadows for a steady climb to the pass. The trail is 5 km (3 miles) 2–3 hours one-way gaining 650 m (2,130 ft). Highlights of the trail include fantastic displays of wildflowers in July-August and views of Quintet Peaks and the surrounding glaciers.

Canyon Creek Loop (Maps 38/E7-32/E1) 🚵

From the blue wooden bridge outside of Golden, this fantastic cycling loop begins. The trail initially climbs along logging roads that head up and over to Canyon Creek. From there, a single-track trail descends towards Nicholson. Pick your way back to Golden along any of the various roads. We recommend the low road, as it is the flattest. The main route takes about 2.5 hours to ride, but there are numerous side routes to explore.

Canyon Creek/Moonraker Trails (Map 32/E1) 🚶 🐎 🚵 🎿

Including the much talked about Moonraker Trails, there is a series of about 40 km (24 miles) of former ski trails, which extend from Cedar Lake south to Canyon Creek. This trail system is ideal for a scenic day hike, bike or horseback ride and is very popular with locals from Golden. To reach the trail system, follow the Dogtooth-Canyon Road to the end and you will find the unmarked trail heading steeply uphill near the creek, just past the cattleguard. Alternatively, you can reach the north end of the trail system by following the signs up the ski hill road to Cedar Lake.

Canyon Lake Trail (Map 32/F1) 🚶

From the Twelve Mile Road west of Nicholson, a 4 km (2.4 mile) 1 hour hike begins on a skid trail in a recent clear-cut. The route leads to a wilderness lake.

Caribou Creek Trail (Map 32/B3) ⛺ 🚶 🚵 🏍

From the end of the Caribou Creek Road, a rough, water barred logging road, you will find the signed trailhead for the Caribou Creek Trail. The well-defined trail leads in an eastward direction, climbing up to a rustic campsite set next to a small mountain lake. The trail is about 2 km (1.2 miles) 1–1.5

alpine forest to the summit. The latter part of the hike involves scrambling up a steep, rocky ridge. You will gain 1,300 m (4,265 ft) to reach the summit at 2,700 m (8,860 ft).

Cliff Lake Trail (Map 14/D5) 🚶 🐟 ⛺

At 41.2 km (25.1 miles) on the Bull-Van Road, this 8.5 km (5.2 mile) 4 hour trail leads to Cliff Lake. The first kilometre is an easy walk to Lemon Lake, but after that it is a steep climb past some waterfalls to Cliff Lake. Cliff Lake offers good fishing for trout as well as an opportunity to connect with the Mause/Tanglefoot Trails along the Tanglefoot/Cliff Lake Trail. This 3.6 km (2.2 mile) 3 hour one-way route is for the experienced hiker as the trail is unmarked and difficult to follow.

Coal Creek Area Trails (Map 15/A7) 🚶 🚲

In the Coal Creek area outside of Fernie there are a number of challenging mountain bike routes and easy walking trails. There are many, many trails in the area, including the Educational Forest Trail and The Fernie Ridge Trail (both described elsewhere in this section). It is recommended to pick up a copy of the biking map from the Fernie Travel Information Centre to properly explore the bike routes. Hikers will enjoy the Coal Creek Historical Trail, which follows an old rail grade, then an old road to the old town-site. Interpretive markings are not yet up, and no buildings remain but it is a nice easy three hour walk.

Cooper Lake Trail (Map 5/A2) 🚶 🐟

Just prior to 17 km (10.4 miles) on the Moyie-South Road, it is a 6 km (4.6 mile) 2 hour easy hike to this sub-alpine fishing lake.

Coppercrown Creek Trail (Map 19/F1) 🚶 ⛺

Hikers are blessed with an abundance of old mine sites to explore around the Kootenays and the old Coppercrown Mine will not disappoint. It is set in a sub-alpine bowl that requires a 12 km (6.1 mile) 5 hour steep hike along an unmaintained trail.

Corn Creek Trail (Map 4/B6) 🚶 🚲 ⛺

From the West Creston Road 3 km (1.8 miles) south of Highway 3, this 6 km (3.7 mile) 2 hour hike takes you through a coniferous forest to the Old Kootenay River. The trail leads back to the road via a dyke and open marshland.

Cranbrook Community Forest Trail (Map 13/D7) 🚶 🚲 🎿

The Cranbrook Community Forest is located to the east of Cranbrook and is dissected by the Community Forest Road off of Mount Baker View Road. Within the Forest are three lakes (Sylvan, Four and Kettle Lake) that are accessed by a series of extensive hiking and biking trails. In total, there are 15 trails within the Forest ranging in length from 200 m to 9.5 km (650 ft to 5.8 miles). The trails are generally easy walking given the lack of elevation gain in the area. To obtain full details on the trails in the area, please obtain a brochure from the Cranbrook Ministry of Forests at (250) 426-1700.

Creston Valley Wildlife Centre Trails (Map 4/B6-B5)
🚶 🚲 🎿 ⛺

This is a popular area to take an easy walk to observe some of the 265 species of birds that inhabit the marshlands. With a 30 km (18.3 mile) network of dykes, there are many different trails to take (the Boardwalk, the Levee Trail, Bird Watcher's Trail and Campground Trail) ranging from a few hundred meters to 5.8 km (3.5 miles). Hikers, bikers and cross-country skiers can enjoy the trails in season. Detailed maps are available at the Creston Valley Wildlife Centre.

Crossing Creek (Koko Claims) Trail (Map 22/B5)
🚶 🚲 🏍 🛶

From Round Prairie, follow the old road along the north side of Crossing Creek. The route leads over the pass and then down to the Bull River Valley. The first 7 km (6.1 miles) is a moderate climb while the last 2.5 km (1.5 miles) is a steep ascent and descent through the alpine. This is a popular area for hunters and ATVers in the fall that makes a great mountain biking trip.

Crystaline Creek Trail (Map 32/E6) 🚶 ⛺

Found off the Vowell Creek Road, this 8.5 km (5.2 mile) one-way trail is rarely used. The route may be difficult to follow but does offer an excellent backcountry trek into the Purcell Mountains.

---

hours one-way with an elevation gain of 200 m (650 metres) from the road to a sub-alpine campsite at 2,100 m (6,890 ft). From the campsite, set in a sparse spruce/fir forest, it is possible to continue on to the pass through an alpine meadow filled with picturesque tarns on an unmarked route.

Castlerock Trail (Map 27/B6) 🚶 ⛺

To reach the trailhead, follow the Johnson Road past Patti Ryan Lakes to the signed trailhead near the powerline. From there, it is a 4 km (2.4 mile) 2 hour one-way hike to the top of the Castlerock and a fantastic view overlooking the Columbia Valley and Invermere. The trail is steep with numerous switchbacks and an elevation gain of 700 m (2,295 ft). You can continue on to Mount Taynton, which involves a 3 km (1.8 mile) 2 hour one-way hike along the south side of the ridge. Continue through some open slides to the summit at 2,380 m (7,810 ft). This extension is hard to find initially but becomes well defined as you proceed along the ridge. The elevation gain is 320 m (1,040 ft).

Catamount Glacier Trail (Map 26/D3) 🚶 🎿 📷 ⛺

The signed trailhead is found at the parking lot past the 42 km mark on the Forster Creek Road (high clearance vehicle required). It is the same trailhead as for the Thunderwater-Whirlpool Lake Trail. The trail initially starts on an overgrown road for about 2 km (1.2 miles) to the General Store Cabin, a private heli-skiing hut. After the cabin, the trail takes off to the left across the Catamount Glacier to Olive Hut, a six person stone shelter overlooking the glacier. If you want to stay in the hut, reserve a spot with the Ministry of Forests in Invermere (250-342-4200) before heading out. The trail is 7.5 km (4.6 miles) 3-4 hours one-way gaining 950 m (3,088 ft) to the hut at 2,670 m (8,760 ft).

Certainty Mine Trail (12 Mile Creek Trail) (Map 32/F2) 🚶

Off the Twelve Mile Road and depending on how far you can drive, it is about a 9.5 km (5.8 mile) 3-4 hour moderate hike to the turn-of-the-century mine site. The trailhead is not easy to find and is located on the northwest corner of a cut-block to the east of Twelve Mile Creek. Look for red rectangular markers.

Chalice Creek Trail (Map 26/B2) 🚶 ⛺

This trail begins by following an old road from the parking area and descending gently through a forested and swampy area on the south side of Chalice Creek. The trail soon crosses the creek and heads sharply upward and switchbacks through the sub-alpine forest and eventually breaking out into the alpine meadows. From there, you get a spectacular view of the surrounding mountains. The trail eventually culminates at a small lake after 6 km (3.8 miles) 1.5-2 hours one-way. Overall, the elevation gain is 610 m (1,983 ft). It is possible to follow the ridge to Septet Pass Trail and down to the Frances Creek Drainage.

Chauncey Creek Route (Map 22/E4) 🚶 🚲

This isn't an official trail, but some people come here for that very reason. You can make your way up the creek, which widens into open sub-alpine meadows, and lots of room to roam.

Chisel Peak Trail (Map 27/F7) 🚶 ⛺

This difficult 5 km (3 mile) 4 hour one-way hike begins from the washout at the end of the Madias Creek Road. Initially, the trail follows the old road for 3 km (1.8 miles) before leading uphill through open meadows and a sub-

Cummings Creek Road (Map 15/C3)

The Cummings Creek area is well known for its good mountain biking and ATV opportunities. The right fork takes you 17 km (8.5 miles) 5 hours one-way along Cummings Creek to Mount Frayn. The left fork heads to Mount Washburn along Telford Creek.

Dainard Lake Trail (Map 33/G3)

It is a 5 km (3 mile) 1.5 hour easy hike to a good fishing lake. The tricky road access and the remoteness of the area limit visitors to the area.

David Thompson Trail (Map 39/A1)

From the north end of the Blaeberry River Road, it is a 28 km (17.1 mile) 8 hour hike to Howse Pass. The historic route continues to Saskatchewan River Crossing in Banff National Park (see the Southwestern Alberta Backroad Mapbook). This route was once proposed as a highway shortcut through the Rockies.

Dawn Mountain Trails (Map 38/D7)

The Dawn Mountain Trail is the most popular summer hike within the Nordic trail system. The trail, which climbs to 1,300 m (4265 ft) in elevation, has a shelter and a good view. Recently, the entire trail network underwent a radical improvement to cater to mountain bike riders.

Delphine Glacier Trail (Map 26/F7)

Mountaineers will find this glacier hike very challenging. It starts from the washout on Delphine Creek Road about 2 km (1.2 miles) from the Toby Creek Road. Hike along the washed out logging road until a trail takes off to the right of an unnamed creek draw. The trail leads steadily uphill until it peters out and you will have to make your way on an unmarked route. After 12 km (7.3 miles) 5–6 hours you will come to the foot of the glacier, which overhangs an impressive headwall. You should expect an elevation gain in the order at 1,500 m to 2,800 m (4,875 ft-9,185 ft), depending on how close to the glacier you hike.

Dewar Creek Trail (Maps 12/E1-19/C4)

Off the end of the Dewar Creek Road, an outfitter's trail follows the creek and continues past the Dewar Creek Hot Springs. The undeveloped hot springs are the obvious attraction to this picturesque area and can be visited year round. Be careful as the water can be very hot. The hot springs are reached after a 9 km (5.5 mile) 3 hour one-way day hike. The trail crosses the creek on several occasions and may be tough to follow given the overlapping game trails in the area.

Dewdney Trail (Map 4/A5)

From the Summit Creek Campground, this section of the historic Dewdney Trail begins at a suspension bridge over Summit Creek. The trail then ascends the hills above Leach Lake where good views of the valley are afforded. Although fragments of the trail continue to the Kootenay River, the main part of the trail ends at Williams Creek Falls, which is 5 km (3 miles), 2 hours return. It is also possible follow one of the many dyke roads in the area. Kokanee spawning in late August to September in Summit Creek is a popular attraction in the area.

Diana Lake Trail (Map 34/A7)

From 24 km (14.6 miles) on the Pinnacle Road, the trail follows an old roadway to an aluminum bridge crossing over Pinnacle Creek. After about one kilometre, the trail leaves the roadway and climbs quickly along the forested slopes. The trail then passes through several small avalanche chutes before again descending to Pinnacle Creek. At this point, you have reached the halfway point. Thankfully, the trail becomes less steep as you approach the lake. In all, the trail is 6 km (3.6 miles), 2–2.5 hours one-way gaining 600 m (1,970 ft). From the lake, there are possibilities to hike to the high alpine ridges for a great view of the surrounding country.

Duck Lake Trails (Map 4/B5)

Duck Lake is part of the Creston Valley Wildlife Management Area, which offers seemingly endless dyke trails through some of the best wildlife habitat in British Columbia. To reach the south end of the trail system, take the lower Wynndel Road from Creston and follow the dyke along a narrow strip of land between Duck Lake and a meandering man-made water coarse. Alternatively, to reach the north end of the dyke system simply drive 2 km (1.2 miles) north of Sirdar on Highway 3A and park just as the highway begins to climb steeply uphill (where you can see a railway bridge to the left). Mountain bikers and cross-country skiers also use these trails.

Dutch Creek Trail (Maps 20/B2-19/E4)

Off the Whitetail Lake Road, this long pack trail provides access through the undeveloped East Purcell Wilderness Conservancy. The popular horse trail is 80 km (48.8 miles) 2–3 days long and accesses some remote yet beautiful backcountry.

Earl Grey Pass Trail (Maps 19/E1-18/F2)

This historic trail begins near the abandoned Mineral King Mine off Toby Creek Road and climbs to Earl Grey Pass. The popular trail is 18 km (11 miles), 1–2 days one-way and gains 905 m (2,970 ft) along the way. The trail begins in the forested valley bottom on the north side of Toby Creek and crosses several tricky avalanche chutes. Approximately 20 minutes along the hike you will pass by the remains of the Earl Grey Cabin, which was built in 1912. Beyond the pass, the trail becomes rough and unmarked as it descends towards Kootenay Lake north of Argenta.

Echoes Lakes (Map 13/F1)

It is only about 4 km (2.4 miles) from the parking area on the road south of Echoes Lake to the lakes themselves, following the old road. (The usual parking spot is about 200 m (650 ft) past the underground pipeline, which crosses the road.) Riders will find many old roads in the area that are perfect for spending the day exploring.

Educational Forest Trail (Map 15/A7)

This mountain bike route begins 0.7 km (0.4 miles) on the Coal Creek Road outside of Fernie. Riders will find a series of narrow single-track loops as well as a number of trails that join with the Ridgemont Trail (see below). The EFT (as locals call it) offers easy riding, but connects to a number of more challenging technical rides, including The Roots Trail.

Elk Lakes Provincial Park (Map 29A)

Rugged peaks, mountain lakes, glaciers and an abundance of wildlife are a few of the attractions of this provincial park. Most of the trail activity takes place around the Elk Lakes and the West Elk Pass but there are also many mountaineering and rock climbing routes to explore. Winter activities are limited due to the avalanche potential, and the fact that the road to the park is not plowed. No mountain biking is allowed in the park, but the Trans Canada Trail allows bikers to follow the powerline road along the park border up to Elk Pass and over the Great Divide to Alberta.

Cadorna Lake Trail (Map 29A/B6)

The main route to Cadorna Lake starts from the Elk Valley Bighorn Outfitter's Lodge off the Elk Valley FSR. It is a 13 km (7.9 miles) 6–8 hour one-way hike through the valley bottom to the good fishing lake. The trail is best hiked in the summer to avoid the fall hunting season and the wet, soggy conditions in the spring. Many windfalls and wet areas impede your travel in the valley and it is necessary to scramble up a slide to the pass where superb views can be had. From there, it is an easy descent to the beautiful lake set in a cirque basin. This route also accesses the climbing opportunities at Mount Aosta. You can also take a side trip to Abruzzi Lake by following the fork up Abruzzi Creek (5 hours one-way).

Coral Pass Route (Map 29A/A5)

From Upper Elk Lake Campsite, there are a number of routes for expert mountaineers only. Like many, the route to Coral Pass requires traversing over treacherous snow in the Nivelle Creek drainage (ropes use of ropes).

Fox Lake Trail (Map 29A/A5)

From the east side of Upper Elk Lake, this 3.9 km (2.4 mile) 1.5–2 hour one-way trail gains 250 m (820 ft) crossing several open avalanche chutes and offering great views of the Elk Valley and Neville Basin. The trail continues past Fox Lake to the West Elk Pass.

Kananskis Lakes to Lower Elk Lake (Map 29A/A4)

The Elk Lakes are often accessed from hikers in Peter Lougheed Provincial Park, Alberta. The trail is found at the south end of Kananskis Lake and initially climbs for 1.5 km (0.9 miles) gaining 50 m (163 ft) to West Elk Pass. It then descends to a trail junction at the park boundary. The left fork takes you to the Elk Lakes Park Headquarters and the right fork takes you to the Lower Elk Lake. Along the trail, you cross Elkin Creek several times and a swampy meadow on a long boardwalk. Views of Mount Aosta are offered on route. Overall, the hike is 4 km (2.4 miles) 1.5 hour one-way, descending 240 m (785 ft).

Lower Elk Lake (Map 29A/A5)

Lower Elk Lake is accessed on a short, easy 1 km (0.6 mile) 20 minute one-way walk from the park headquarters. At the lake a popular destination is the viewpoint, which requires an additional 1.2 km (0.7 miles) 45 minute one-way hike gaining 122 m (400 ft) in elevation. The steep incline after you leave the lakeshore is fairly strenuous.

Petain Creek Waterfall (Map 29A/A5)

This easy trail is 3 km (1.8 mile) 1–1.5 hours one-way from Upper Elk Lake and takes you to a view of the waterfall and the Castineau Hanging Glacier west of the lake. The trail straddles the banks of the Upper Elk Lake before following a bench above Petain Creek to the falls. If you want to continue onward, try the scramble up the steep slopes to Petain Basin, which is another 4 km (2.4 mile) 4 hour return gaining 520 m (1705 ft) in elevation along a sporadically marked trail.

Upper Elk Lake (Map 29A/A5)

From the park headquarters, it is an easy 2 km (1.2 km) 40 minute one-way walk past Lower Elk Lake to Upper Elk Lake. The hike leads through old growth spruce forests, meadows, and rock slopes gaining 30 m (100 ft) along the way.

West Elk Pass to Frozen Lake/Taiga Viewpoint (Map 29A/A4)

From the West Elk Pass, it is 2 km (1.2 mile) 1 hour to Frozen Lake gaining 300 m (985 ft) in elevation. This trail is best hiked in August or September when the lake is no longer frozen. The trail is not maintained, and is steep in places. From Frozen Lake, it is possible to scramble to the top of Taiga Viewpoint, at 2,360 m (7,740 ft), where you get a fantastic view of Frozen Lake and its surrounding talus slopes. The latter hike is 2 km (1.2 miles) 1 hour one-way gaining 225 m (738 ft).

West Elk Pass via Elkan Creek (Map 29A/A4)

From the park headquarters, it is a 4 km (2.4 mile) 1.5 hour one-way moderate hike through a spruce forest and meadows gaining 240 m (785 ft). The trail takes you to the boundary between Elk Lakes Park and Peter Lougheed Park in Alberta. When you reach the park boundary, you can access the old powerline road into Peter Lougheed Park or make a circuit back to the park headquarters via Upper Elk Lake on the Fox Lake Trail.

Fairy Creek Trail (Map 15/A6)

The trail is accessed from the Fairy Creek Road just after a small dam site and a wooden bridge. The trail leads through the woods paralleling the creek to its headwaters. Overall, the trail is 4 km (2.4 miles) 1.5 hours one-way gaining 260 m (855 ft) to the base of the Three Sisters. A shorter option is to hike the 4.6 km (2.8 miles) return trip to Fairy Creek Falls, a pretty, 5m (16 ft) high waterfall.

Farnham Creek Trail (Map 26/D6)

The hike up Farnham Creek begins at 46 km (28 miles) on the Horsethief Creek Road. The trail initially crosses the creek via a footbridge that is often washed away. Fording the creek is a rather precarious alternative. The trail continues on a former logging road to an old cabin gaining 275 m (894 ft) over 8.4 km (5.1 miles), 3–4 hours one-way. Along the way, you get a great view of the Commander Glacier. From the old cabin, it is possible to continue on the old road toward Black Diamond Mountain or take the right hand branch on an overgrown trail to the foot of Commander Glacier.

Fernie Alpine Resort (Map 15/A7)

Fernie Alpine Resort was the first resort in North America to open their lifts to mountain bikers. They have developed one of the province's biggest lift-assisted trail systems, with 32 runs, ranging from easy to double black diamond (extremely difficult). There are also a number of lift-assisted hiking trails, like Boom Trail, Lost Boy Lookout and the 5 km (3 mile) Timber Ridge Trail.

Fernie High Trail (Map 15/A7)

The Fernie High Trail begins from the parking lot at Fernie Alpine Resort. Either climb Cedar Trail to the top of Snake Ridge or take the chairlift to Bear's Den and hike to the ridge via Cedar Bowl. When on the ridge there is the opportunity to travel to Thunder Meadows Cabin or to the Timber Bowls via Polar Peak. The route is marked with red rocks and has many tricky spots including cliffs. From Timber Bowl you descend back to the ski hill for a 7+ hour strenuous loop. Wildflowers, views and huckleberries are among the attractions.

Fernie Ridge Trail (Map 15/C7) 🚶 🐎 🚴 🏍 ℹ️
From the gate off an old road near Coal Creek Road, follow the road steadily up hill to what is called the Bear Chutes (about a two hour hike), at the end of the road. From there, it is a scramble up to Fernie Ridge, which can be traversed to the small community of Hosmer. The alternate route is to drive south of Hosmer on the powerline road to a gate then climb up the ridge from there.

Findlay Creek Trail (Maps 20/A3-19/F5) ⛺ 🚶 🐎 ℹ️
Frequented in the fall by hunters, this 80 km (48.8 mile) 2–3 day hike follows a popular horse trail. It provides the main access into the southern tip of the East Purcell Wilderness Conservancy. West of the park, you will find yourself in a very remote mountainous area. It is possible to continue south to the Dewar Creek Trail.

Fording Pass (Map 22/D1) ⛺ 🚶 ℹ️
The Fording River Pass connects the Fording River Valley to the Aldridge Creek drainage and hooks up with the Baril Creek Trail in Kananaskis Country, Alberta. It is 12.3 km (7.6 miles) from the trailhead to the Fording River Pass (at 2,299 m/7,472 ft), gaining 765 m (2,510 ft) along the way. This is a difficult but rewarding trip that possible to do in a day. Most people take two and enjoy the scenery, and explore the amazing alpine landscape.

Giant Cedars Interpretive Trails (Map 37/F1) 🚶 📖
Off the Bush River Road, there is a short, wheelchair accessible, interpretive walk through a stand of old growth cedar.

Gibraltar Lookout Trail (Map 21/A1) 🚶 ℹ️
Drive about 7.5 km (4.6 miles) on the Kootenay-Gibraltar Road. From there, the old road continues for 200 m (650 ft) before the actual trail starts. The well-defined trail gains 775 m (2,519 ft) to an active, concrete lookout station at 2,400 m (7,875 m). The trail is 4.5 km (2.7 miles) 2–2.5 hours one-way passing by several avalanche chutes on the way to the top. You can either admire the view of White River Valley or try some ridge running.

Glenogle Ridge Trail (Maps 39/A7-38/G7) 🚶 🐎 ℹ️
This is an 8 km (4.8 mile) moderate horse trail accessing Glenogle Ridge, east of Golden. The trailhead is found off Glenogle Creek Road.

Goldrun Lake Trail (Map 5/A1) 🚶 🐟
It is an easy 1.1 km (0.7 mile) hike from the end of Perry Creek Road to this quiet mountain lake, gaining 122 m (397 ft). The name comes from the gold rush in the area, though the name is the only thing remaining of that bygone era; even the gold is gone.

Gorman Lake Trail (Map 38/C7) ⛺ 🚶 🐟 ℹ️
From the west end of the Gorman Lake Road, this popular hike leads 6 km (3.6 mile) 2 hours through a sub-alpine forest on a well developed trail. About half way along the trail, it breaks out into an alpine meadow full of glacier lilies in the spring. In the alpine of the Dogtooth Range, rocks sporadically mark the trail. The lake itself is set beneath several alpine slides and offers good fishing. There are tent pads and picnic tables at the lake to help enjoy the peace and tranquility of the area.

Graves Lookout Trail (Map 21/G3) 🚶 🚴 ℹ️
Drive the deactivated White-Grave Lookout Road as far as you can. Soon, a huge washbar marks the end of the drive. Hike/bike uphill and about 1.5 km (0.9 miles) later you reach an old landing and the start of a well-defined trail, which switchbacks through the forest up to the abandoned lookout. From the lookout, at 2,280 m (7,480 ft), you get a great view of the White River Valley and the signs of logging activity below. The hike is 5 km (3 miles) 2–3 hour one-way gaining 800 m (2,625 ft).

Hall Lake Trail (Map 12/E5) 🚶 🐟
About 100 m (325 ft) before the Hall Creek Bridge, a 12 km (7.3 mile) 5 hour return moderate hike leads to a mountain lake. Expect a poorly maintained, wet trail with two creek crossings. The reward for your effort is pan-sized trout in a lake surrounded by forests.

Harrogate Pass Trail (Map 33/F5) 🚶 🐎 ℹ️
Harrogate is a small East Kootenay community on Highway 95 southeast of Golden. From the roads above the community, a steep horse trail climbs 12 km (7.3 mile) over 6 hours to the pass. There are great views of the Columbia Valley. The trail can also be accessed from the Marion Lake Road to the north.

Haystack Alpine Trail (Maps 4/C1-12/D7) ⛺ 🚶 🐎 ℹ️
A 13 km (7.9 mile) one-way hike follows a horse trail over the pass between Meachen and Sanca Creeks. The moderate 5 hour trail provides good access to sub-alpine lakes and the surrounding peaks and ridges of Kianuko Provincial Park. The trailheads are found on both the Meachen Creek and the Sanca Creek Roads and require a high clearance vehicle to access. Wilderness camping is possible. You can also make side trips to Meachen Lake, Haystack Lake and Kianuko Creek. A shuttle vehicle system is recommended.

Height-of-the-Rockies Provincial Park (Maps 21, 22, 28, 29) ⛺ 🚶 🐎 🚶 🛶 🐟 ℹ️
This high alpine area is distinguished by its 26 mountains that rise over 3,000m (9,800 feet) high. Trail enthusiasts will find several trails, in various states of repair, leading up many of the river and creek drainages to the alpine. There are cabins found at Connor Lakes and Queen Mary Lake as well as wilderness campsites. Wildlife enthusiasts will find the area is home to a large number of mountain goats and other large animals.

Connor Lakes (Maiyuk Creek) Trail (Maps 21/G1-22/A1)
This trail initially follows a seismic line before reaching a pass and descending to the north end of Connor Lake. The trail is 7 km (4.3 miles) 4 hours one-way.

Forsyth Creek Trail (Maps 22/B2-29A/A7)
The trail along Forsyth Creek begins on a seismic road before climbing through a second growth forest to the north end of Connor Lakes and eventually to the cabin. You can continue past the lake but the route becomes hard to follow as you traverse open terrain, eventually leading to the headwaters of Forsyth Creek and the foot of Abruzzi Glacier. Conner Lake is a beautiful sub-alpine lake with a hanging glacier. It is 7 km (4.3 mile), 2.5–3.5 hours from the Forsyth Creek Forest Service Site to Connor Lakes.

Goat Lake Trail (Maps 21/G1-29A/A7)
From the Maiyuk Creek Forest Service Site, this 9 km (5.5 mile), 4–5 hour one-way hike gains 400 m (1,310 ft) to Maiyuk Pass before dropping 125 m (406 ft) to tiny Goat Lake. The remote mountain lake does offer good fishing for small but feisty trout.

Joffre Creek Trail (Map 28/F5)
The easiest way into the Sylvan Pass area and the beautiful Limestone Lakes is from the north along Joffre Creek. It is 11 km (6.7 miles) one-way to the pass. The trail continues beyond on a rugged horse trail that follows the White River (see below) to the Maiyuk Creek Recreation Site.

LeRoy & Beatty Creek Trails (Map 28/E2)
From the Palliser River Trail a pair of trails lead in an eastward direction to Peter Lougheed Park in Alberta. The LeRoy Creek Trail is 5 km (3 miles) 4 hour one-way from the river to the North Kananaskis Pass. The Beatty Creek Trail branches south past Beatty Lake and on to the South Kananaskis Pass.

Palliser River Trail (Map 28/E5-E2)
Linking the Palliser River with the Spray River in Banff National Park, this trail begins at the end of the Palliser River FSR. The southern portion of the hike involves bushwhacking through thick alder or walking along the creek bank and crossing the river channel on numerous occasions. As you climb past the outfitter cabin to Palliser Pass, the trail improves. The trail to the pass is a 20 km (12.2 mile) one-way day jaunt. Many continue north to Spray Lakes Reservoir in Alberta or visit Tipperary Lake and North Kananaskis Pass via side trails.

Quarrie Creek Trail (Map 22/B1)
An old guide outfitter horse trail leads up Quarrie Creek for about 14 km (8.5 miles) one-way. The trail is not maintained and the trailhead is difficult to locate.

Queen Mary Trail (Map 28/D4)
The Queen Mary Trail begins on the Palliser River FSR and soon crosses the Palliser River. The well defined but muddy horse trail leads northward eventually climbing to Queen Mary Lake. The difficult day hike is

12 km (7.3 miles) one-way and involves 17 tough creek crossings but the fishing is excellent.

Ralph Lake Trail (Map 28/C3)

Ralph Lake is a beautiful emerald colored lake set in a scenic alpine basin. The unmaintained 5 km (3 mile) 3 hour one-way trail is steep, gaining 850 m (2,790 ft) to the good fishing lake. Mountaineers can continue on to Queen Mary Lake.

Tipperary Lake Trail (Map 28/E3)

Branching from the Palliser River Trail is a short but steep and rough side trail climbing to Tipperary Lake. The trail is 2 km (1.2 miles) long one-way and should take 2 hours to hike.

Hoodoos Trail (Map 20/E1) 🚶 🚲 🛶

At the north end of Columbia Lake, the 120 m (395 ft) high hoodoos often catch the attention of highway travellers. Conservationists have recently purchased the area and the roads have been closed in order to protect this unique and diverse area. To reach the top of the Hoodoos, take the Westside Road and look for the first dirt road to the left. From there, you can hike or bike 1.5 km (0.9 miles) to the end of the road. A trail takes off to the left and soon you are looking over the top of the Hoodoos and down at the Columbia Lake area. In all, the trail is about 4.5 km (2.7 miles) one-way with an elevation gain of 100 m (325 ft).

Hopeful Creek Trail (Map 27/A7) 🚶 🛶

The Hopeful Creek Trail is one of several trails south of Panorama Resort and has several access points. The hike leads to the pass between Goldie and Brewer Creeks. You can continue on the Brewer Creek Trail via a 10 km (6.1 mile) 4 hour route. This difficult trail accesses several alpine lakes at the headwaters of Brewer Creek and continues onto the Mineral Creek Pass.

Horse Barn Valley Interpretive Forest (Map 13/B3)
🚶 🚲 🛶 🚶

The Kimberley Nature Park Society maintains a patch of land just outside of Kimberley. They also manage this new interpretive forest that was recently established, adjacent to the Nature Park. The forest covers 204 ha, and is open to non-motorized recreation (hiking, biking, skiing, snowshoeing).

Hourglass Trail (Map 12/D7) 🚶 🛶

The two Hourglass Lakes are a magnificent destination set high in the Purcell Mountains. The upper lake is 330 m (1,073 ft) higher than the lower lake, and the short creek between the two is half waterfall, half rapid as it pours down the steep slope. The first lake is 270 m (878 ft) higher than your starting point, near the km 29 signboard. The trail is about 3 km (1.8 miles) to the lower lake; from there, you can beat your way up to the upper lake or to a smaller lake north of the first lake.

International Basin Route (Map 32/C4) ⛰ 🚶 📷 👤 🛶

From the end of the rough McMurdo Creek Road, this two-day mountaineering trek leads to a tiny lake at the headwaters of Bobby Burns Creek. The route involves crossing the Spillimacheen Glacier and following an alpine ridge, which offers fantastic views of the surrounding area. This route is best left for well equipped and experienced backcountry hikers.

Isadore Canyon Trail (Maps 13/G6-14/A6) 🚶 🐎 🚲 🛶 🛶

Part of the Trans Canada Trail, the Isadore Canyon Trail follows a turn of the century railway. The popular trail is well marked and offers picnic areas, breathtaking views of the Rocky Mountains and old rock ovens. The TCT branches north at the 8 km marker but the old railway continues south toward Wardner.

Island Lake Loop (Map 14/G7) 🚶 🚲 🛶

From the Island Lake Lodge an easy walk (or bike) skirts the lake through an old growth cedar forest.

Jurak Lake Trail (Map 12/G2) 🚶 🐟

This is a difficult 5 km (3 mile) 3 hour one-way hike into a remote lake. A route continues over to White Creek and it is possible to access to St Mary's Alpine Park along another difficult route in the area.

Jumbo Pass Trail (Maps 19/E1-26/B7) 🚶 🛶 🏊 📷 👤 🛶

From the Jumbo Creek Road, it is a 10.4 km (6.3 mile) 4–5 hour hike gaining 670 m (2,200 ft) to the cabin in the pass. For an alternate, less popular

access route, try accessing the pass from the Glacier Road to the northwest. This trail is 8.4 km (5.1 miles) return. The quaint mountain cabin sleeps six and is often used as a base camp to explore the surrounding peaks. (Reservations for the cabin are needed and can be made through the Invermere Forest District (250) 342-4200). From Jumbo Pass it is possible to scramble to the summit of Bastille Mountain gaining an additional 350 m (1,150 ft) over 2 km (1.2 miles) 1.5 hours one-way. There is also a trail leading north to the unnamed peak (locally referred to as Mount Anubis) that offers a breathtaking panoramic view. Mountaineers can continue north to the next summit (known as Mount Thoth) to take in the best view in the area.

Kicking Horse Mountain Resort (Map 38/E7) 🚶 🚲 🛶

The new Kicking Horse Resort is doing all it can to become BC's best year-round resort. Part of that includes developing North America's longest unguided lift-assisted descents, and a series of 18 rides that range from easy to expert. There are also a few easy hikes available from the top of the gondola to explore.

Kimberley Alpine Resort Trails (Map 13/C4) 🚶 🚲 🛶

There are four lift-accessed biking trails at Kimberley Resort that range from easy to expert. Hikers will find the North Star Express accesses some easy alpine hiking.

Kimberley Nature Park Trails (Map 13/C4)
🚶 🐎 🚲 🛶 🐟 🛶

On the southeastern slopes of North Star Mountain, this nature park offers over 100 km (60 miles) of multi-use trails. They are open to hikers, mountain bikers, horseback riders and, in winter, cross-country skiers. Due to the complex nature of the trail system, it is recommended to pick up a copy of the detailed trail map, which is available at most Kimberley retailers. Below is a description of some of the more popular trails in the park:

Eimer Lake Trail

Accessed from the end of Higgins Street, there is a one hour easy walk along an access road to the small pond called Eimer Lake. At the pond, there are trout fishing and wildlife viewing opportunities. A trail circles the lake.

Duck Pond Loop

From the south end of Swan Avenue, this is a two hour moderate hike following a variety of trails to the pond found at the foot of Myrtle Mountain. Spring flowers, sub-alpine fir forests and wildlife viewing (deer and moose) are the attractions.

Dipper Lake

From the Nordic Ski Area parking lot, which is found at the end of the road to the ski hill, it takes about two and a half hours to hike to this small lake. Take the Centennial and Trapline Trails to Five Corners. From there, follow the Rockslide Trail across the talus slope to the lake. For the return trip, hike down the Creek Trail to Army Road, which brings you through a forest of large cedar trees and lush ferns. The lake is quite marshy in the summer.

Lady Slipper Trail (Map 4/D6) 🚶 📖 🛶

Off the Goat Mountain Road north of Creston, a 3 km (1.8 mile) 1 hour one-way hike brings you to the summit of Arrow Mountain. The moderate trail gains 380 m (1,235 ft) to the top at 1,700 m (5,577 ft). This interpretive trail was established by East Kootenay Environmental Society. A brochure with 30 stops of interest is available at the Ministry of Forest office in Creston.

Lake Enid Trail (Map 27/B5) 🚶 🚲

This trail is accessed off the Bruce Creek Road, west of Wilmer. The 2.4 km (1.5 mile) 1 hour hike begins at the Lake Enid Recreation Site and circles the lake. There is little elevation along the way so makes for an enjoyable family walk.

Lake of the Hanging Glacier Trail (Map 26/C6) ⛰ 🚶 📷 🛶

From the 49.5 km (30.2 mile) mark on the Horsethief Creek Road, this is an 8 km (4.8 mile) 2–3 hour one-way moderate hike. The trail takes you along the east bank of Horsethief Creek to a gorgeous lake surrounded by rugged glacier covered peaks. Although the trail is well maintained, you should expect to ford the creek and gain 720 m (2,360 ft) along the way. From the lake, there are several mountaineering opportunities available.

Lakit Lookout Trail (Map 14/A3) 🚶 🚴

This scenic trail is found off the Lakit Lookout Road. It is a 2 km (1.2 mile) 1 hour one-way hike into the alpine gaining 460 m (1,495 feet) to the lookout at 2,355 m (7,726 ft). From the top, there is a panoramic view of Rocky Mountain Trench and Wildhorse River Valley.

Lakit Lookout to Teepee Mountain Route (Map 14/A3-A1) 🚶 🚴

While not a formal trail, this ridge walk offers great views of the surrounding mountains. It is not, however, for the unprepared. It will take the better part of three days to hike the nearly 30 km (18.3 miles) between the two mountains, along some very narrow ridges. It is best to have a second vehicle waiting at the end of the hike.

Lang Lake Trail (Map 38/C6) 🚶 🐟

A 4wd vehicle is needed to access the trailhead off the Dogtooth Road. Otherwise you can expect a longer walk than the 7 km (4.3 mile) 4 hour long trail. The destination is a beautiful wilderness lake.

Lazy Lake Loop (Maps 13/D2–14/A2) 🚴 🏍 🐟

From the campground at Wasa Provincial Park, this is a 33 km (20.1 mile) 8 hour moderate bike ride gaining 300 m (985 ft). It follows Wolf Creek Road to Lazy Lake before returning via the Wolf Lewis FSR to the south.

Lemon Lake Trail (Map 28/D2) 🚶 🐟 🚴

Bringing you into Banff National Park in Alberta, this trail is accessed at the end of the Albert River Road. It is a 5 km (3 mile) 2–3 hour moderate hike to an alpine lake that offers fishing lake. From the lake, a series of trails lead into the Spray River valley.

Lisbon Lake Trail (Map 13/C6) 🚶 🐟

This is a 4 km (2.4 mile) 1.5 hour easy hike to a small fishing lake. Access is provided off the Perry Creek Road.

Lizard Lake-Lizard Ridge Walk (Map 15/A7) 🚶 🚴 ⛺ 🚴

The trailhead to this moderate trail is difficult to locate. It is found at the 3 km (1.8 mile) mark on the Cedar Valley Road south of Fernie. From the road, a 10 km (6.1 mile) 5 hour trail leads to the tiny Lizard Lake. From the lake, you can scramble to the top of Lizard Ridge, where a route to the southwest connects with the Fernie Alpine Resort. The route to the northwest takes you to Thunder Meadow Cabin and the Cabin Bowl Trail.

Lone Pine Hill Trail (Map 4/B6) 🚶 🚴

From the West Creston Road, 800 m (2,600 ft) south of the Wildlife centre, it is a 3.2 km (2 mile) 1.5 hour fairly steep ascent to the hill overlooking the Creston Valley. It is best to park at the Wildlife Centre and walk to the trailhead.

Lost-Lily Lakes Trails (Map 22/D6) 🚶 🚴 🏊 🐟 🚴

To reach the trailhead, turn east off of Highway 43 at the 4 way stop and travel past the Greenhills Viewpoint to the gravel parking lot. An alternative access point is to take the Fording Road and travel to the first bridge. Immediately after the bridge, park in the open area and walk to the trailhead, which is 350 m (1,138 ft) north of the bridge.

> From there, **Josephine Falls Trail** is a 2.3 km (1.4 mile) 40 minute one-way hike to the base of the waterfalls. You can continue past the fenced area another 150 m (488 ft) for a better view of the 25 m (80 ft) high falls or you can continue to Lost and Lily Lakes.

> **Lily Lake Walk** is a 2.7 km (1.6 mile) 55 minute one-way hike that requires many ups and downs. The trail leads past several marshy areas and crosses a 10 m (33 ft) bridge. The tiny lake offers good opportunities to see wetland birds and ducks. Mountain biking and cross-country skiing are popular in season.

> **Lost Lake Trail** is a 4.6 km (2.8 mile) 2 hour one-way hike gaining 260 m (855 ft) over a steady uphill climb. The trail leads through a second growth Lodgepole pine stand past the waterfalls at 2.3 km (1.4 miles) and then along the rim of a canyon to the lake. At the lake, you will find a picnic area, two docks and good fishing for stocked rainbow.

Lost-Sunken Trail (Map 14/C6) 🚶 🚴

About 2.5 km (1.5 miles) past the Horseshoe Lake Recreation Site on the Horseshoe Lake Road, this 11.7 km (7.6 mile) 4 hour one-way moderate hike takes you to the Sunken-Dibble Pass of the Steeples. The trail passes the historic Dibble Mine while gaining 1,500 m (4,920 ft) on a steady incline. Once at the summit, you can continue on to Tanglefoot/Cliff Lakes via a 3.6 km (2.2 mile) 3 hour one-way route.

Lower Bugaboo Falls Trail (Map 33/F7) 🚶 🚴

The signed trailhead is found on the Westside Road north of Brisco. The trail passes through a livestock gate and through a second growth coniferous stand for 1.5 km (0.9 miles) 30 minutes to the 25 m (80 ft) high waterfalls. You can access the viewpoint above the two tier falls or stand at the water's edge at the top of the falls. Please be careful.

Lower Canyon Creek Trails (Map 32/F1) 🚶 🚴 🏊 🚴

Accessed off the 12 Mile Road south of Golden, this 6 km (3.7 mile) 3 hour hike follows a well developed trail along the edge of the scenic canyon. Cross-country skiers use the trail in the winter.

Lumberton Ski Trails (Map 5/C1) 🚶 🚴 🏊 🐕

There are over 30 km (18 miles) of trails, many of which utilize the logging road network in this wilderness area. The trails are found off the Moyie River Road, west of Lumberton and are managed by the Kootenay Nordic Outdoor Club.

Mallandaine Pass Trail (Map 12/G6) 🚶 🚴

There are actually two ways up to Mallandaine Pass; the first is an old mining trail accessed off the Mount Evans Trail. The second is from the end of Fiddler Creek Road. The latter is shorter, at 2 km (1.2 miles), while the former is 5 km (3 miles).

Marvel Pass Trail (Maps 28/B1-29B/A2) 🚶 🚵 🚴

A 20 km (12.2 mile) hike on a moderate well-marked trail leads to the alpine meadows of Marvel Pass in Banff National Park. From the scenic pass, you can continue onto Marvel Lake or Mount Assiniboine Provincial Park. The trailhead is located off the Cross River Road.

Mary Anne Falls (Map 13/A5) 🚶 🚴

The trailhead for this hike is found along a steep skid road from Musser's Cabin, off the St Mary Lake Road. It is a 3 km (1.8 mile) 2 hour long hike gaining 458 m (1,489 ft) to the falls at 1,433 m (4,701 ft). Along the trail, there is a good view of the St Mary Valley or you can take a side trip to Parachute Springs. The springs are another 4 km (2.4 miles) 1.5 hours down the trail.

Mause/Tanglefoot Trail (Map 14/C5) 🚶 🐟 🚴

Eight kilometres up Mause Creek Road a 7.8 km (4.8 mile) 3 hour one-way hike climbs to Tanglefoot Lake gaining 900 m (2,950 ft). The first 4 km (2.4 miles) to the historic Victor Mine are an easy walk. Here you can explore the remnants of old mine buildings as well as an abandoned railway bed complete with a trestle and tunnel. Beyond the mine site, the climb stiffens as you hike upward through the gorgeous alpine meadows before crossing the summit and descending to the lake where wilderness camping/fishing is offered. You can also access Cliff Lake, which is another 3.6 km (2.2 miles) 3 hours one-way hike along the Tanglefoot/Cliff Lake Trail.

Mayo-Ailsa Trail (Map 12/F6) 🚶 🐟

Located off the Meachen Creek Road, this is a 3 km (1.8 mile) 1 hour easy hike to two small wilderness lakes.

McLean Lake Trail (Map 26/D3) 🚶 🚴

Park your vehicle (4wd, preferably) about 17.5 km (10.7 miles) up the Frances Creek Road just past the bridge and walk the remaining 1.5 km (0.9 miles) to the actual trailhead along the brushed-in road. Taking the right fork leads to Septet Pass. The first 2.7 km (1.6 miles) of the trail follows an old mining road which switchbacks up the hillside on a fairly steep grade, crossing several avalanche paths. The mining road ends where the creek meets a small canyon some 300 m (975 ft) from McLean Lake. As a result, the last section of the trail is steep and narrow as you ascend uphill to a rocky knoll overlooking McLean Lake. In total, the trail is 4 km (2.4 miles) 1.5–2 hours one-way gaining 550 m (1,805 ft).

Meachen Creek Falls (Map 12/G5) 🚶 🚴

At the 8 km sign on the Meachen Creek Road, look for an unsigned trail heading northwest. It's only 300 m (975 ft) to the 35 m (114 ft) high falls.

Mineral Creek Trail (Maps 26/G7-19/G1)

One of several trails in the area, this 14 km (8.5 mile) 5 hour one-way hike begins off Toby Creek Road on a skid trail leading into a cut-block. From the cut-block, a well maintained horse trail follows the Mineral Creek Valley crossing the creek on three occasions (without the luxury of a bridge). At 6 km (3.6 miles), the trail leads past an outfitter cabin and shortly after, the trail begins to peter out. It is possible to continue uphill to the Mineral/Ben Abel Pass and then walk down the treeless alpine to Ben Abel Lake. The elevation gain to the pass at 2,400 m (7,800 ft) is 1,140 m (3,705 ft).

Mitchell Lake Trail (Map 14/D5)

An easy hike for the family is found at the 47.5 km (29 mile) mark on the Bull-Van Road. The trail is 1.3 km (.8 miles) half an hour one-way, gaining 100 m (325 feet) to the lake at 1,600 m (5,250 ft). The first part of the trail follows a skid road through a logged-off area before entering the forest. Mitchell Lake is surrounded by trees and offers some fishing opportunities.

Mitchell River Trail (Maps 28/A1-34/G6)

Backpackers and horse packers will find a seldom used 24 km (14.6 mile) day + horse trail that starts from Bay Mag Mine and leads to Fero Pass in Mount Assiniboine Provincial Park. Along the way, there are several side routes, camping locations and scenic vistas. Expect to ford the river on several occasions and to do some bushwhacking while gaining 1,100 m (3,610 ft). It is another 6 km to Lake Magog on a much more developed trail.

Moose Creek Trail (Map 33/F2)

It is an 8 km (4.8 mile) 2–3 hour moderate hike along a horse trail to the base of Helmet Mountain. Backcountry skiers use the remote area in the winter.

Morrissey Ridge Route (Maps 15/C7-7/B1)

Preferred by bikers, this road route follows an old logging road up to a microwave tower across from Morrissey Ridge. The 9.8 km (6 mile) route gains 830 m (2,720 ft) to the tower, which offers good views of the Elk Valley. The hike starts from a gate on the Matheson Creek Road.

Mount 7 Trails (Maps 32/D1–38/D4)

Ground Zero for some of the best and most challenging mountain biking in the province. The Mount 7 area outside of Golden has nearly 1,540 m (5,000 ft) of vertical descents across six main trails, plus a number of side runs. This is big bike country, and most of the rides are rated expert. A 14 km (8.5 mile) long logging road takes cyclists to the top (most people arrange for a shuttle to the top).

Mount Assiniboine Provincial Park (Maps 29/B, 34)

The combination of high elevation lakes and meadows surrounded by snow capped peaks makes this park a hikers paradise. Lake Magog, with a campground, cabins and the Mount Assiniboine Lodge, forms the hub of the park and most people make day trips from here. Of course, visitors need to hike into the core area. Mountain biking is allowed on the Assiniboine Pass Trail, while horseback riding is only possible after approval from the Parks branch. The park is also a popular backcountry skiing destination with the Naiset Cabins, Bryant Creek shelter or Mount Assiniboine Lodge adding comfort to the fantastic scenery.

Allenby Pass Trail to Lake Magog (Map 29B/B1-A2)

Beginning in Banff National Park (see Southwestern Alberta Mapbook), this route takes you up Brewster Creek to Allenby Pass gaining 1,070 m (3,510 ft) along the way. The trail then dips 500 m (1,625 ft) from Allenby Pass to Bryant Creek before climbing back over Assiniboine Pass for another 216 m (702 ft) elevation gain. Overall, the scenic but challenging hike is 44 km (27 miles) one-way. The maximum elevation is 2,440 m (7,875 ft) at Allenby Pass.

Assiniboine Lakes Loop Trail (Map 29B/A2)

This short, three-hour hike provides access to three beautiful lakes. Access to the trailhead is found at the Lake Magog Campsite. Mid-June through September is the best time to hike the trail.

Assiniboine Pass Trail (Map 29B/A2)

Accessed from the Lake Magog Campground, this hike is a 3.7 km (2.3 mile) 2 hour round trip. It runs through meadows and forested land to the ridge, before descending into the Bryant Creek Valley.

Bryant Creek Trail to Lake Magog (Map 29B/C3-A2)

This is the most popular route into Lake Magog. It takes you from Canyon Dam off the Spray Lakes West Road along Bryant Creek and over Assiniboine Pass to Lake Magog. The first 14.5 km (8.8 miles) follows several dirt roads before 7 km of rough trail leads to the pass. The total distance of the hike is 25 km (15.2 miles) 7–8 hours one-way gaining 520 m (1,700 ft) to the Assiniboine Pass at 2,195 m (7,200 ft). An alternate route is to travel past Marvel Lake to Wonder Pass. That route is 26 km (15.8 miles) 7–8 hours one-way with an elevation gain of 700 m (2,275 ft) to a maximum of 2,378 m (7,800 ft).

Ferro Pass Trail (Maps 29B/A2-34/G6)

Accessed from the Lake Magog Campground, this hike is 9 km (5.5 miles) 6 hours one-way, gaining 275 m (900 ft) along the way. The trail runs past several lakes and provides an excellent view from the pass, at 2,270 m (7,450 ft) in elevation. Many hikers prefer the higher route towards tiny Elizabeth Lake and Ferro Pass as opposed to the lower route to Ferro Pass.

Mitchell River Trail to Lake Magog (Maps 28/A1-29B/A2)

From the Bay Mag Mine at Mitchell River, it is a 30 km (18.3 mile) 8 hour one-way hike gaining 1,100 m (3,610 ft) to Lake Magog. The trail is seldom used and requires river crossings and bushwhacking.

Moose Bath (Map 29B/A2)

From Lake Magog, this hike is 8 km (4.8 miles) 4 hours return and involves an initial climb of 140 m (460 ft) to the pass near Elizabeth Lake. The Moose Bath is 150 m (488 ft) below. On the return to Assiniboine Lodge, the trail climbs about 100 m (325 ft) to a view overlooking Cerulean Lake. The maximum elevation reached is 2,290 m (7,515 ft).

Og Lake Trail (Map 29B/A1)

To reach Og Lake from the Lake Magog Campground, it is an easy 11 km (6.7 mile) 4 hour return valley walk gaining 185 m (605 ft) in elevation. The trail leads through a sparse sub-alpine forest and large alpine meadows, including the vast Og Meadows, before reaching the Valley of the Rocks and Og Lake. Bring your fishing rod.

Og Pass Trail (Maps 29B/A2-34/G4)

Og Pass is reached by an 11.5 km (7 mile) 5–6 hour strenuous hike from the Lake Magog Campground, gaining 470 m (1,540 ft) in elevation. The trail is well worn, as it is the main horse trail leading into the park from Sunshine Village, in Banff National Park. Once you reach the pass, you will be rewarded by one of the best panoramic views in the park. Also, the wildflowers below Windy Ridge are spectacular. Mid-June through September is the recommended time to visit this trail.

Sunburst Valley Trail (Map 29B/A2)

From the Lake Magog Campground, the trail leads in a northwest direction passing by Sunburst Lake after about 1 km (0.6 miles) and Cerulean Lake half a kilometre later. Soon, the trail reaches the height of land at 2,300 m (7,545 ft) and descends north to Elizabeth Lake. From there, you can retrace your footsteps back to Lake Magog, try climbing to Ferro Pass or visiting Wedgwood Lake. Overall, the trail is 8 km (4.8 miles) 3 hours return gaining 150 m (488 ft). It is one of the most popular routes in Mount Assiniboine Park.

Sunshine Ski Village to Lake Magog (Map 34/G4-29B/A2)

From the Sunshine Village in Banff, this hike stretches 27 km (16.5 miles) 8 hours one-way past Og Lake to Lake Magog. The advantage of this route is that although it is longer than other routes, the elevation gain is only 488 m (1,600 ft) to a maximum of 2,408 m (7,900 ft).

Surprise Creek Trail to Lake Magog (Maps 34/E5-29B/A2)

From Highway 93 in Kootenay National Park, take the Simpson Valley Trail for 9.5 km (5.8 miles) and then hang a right on the Surprise Creek Trail at the hiker's cabin (free to use by all travelers). From there, the trail climbs 825 m (2,705 ft) up the Surprise Creek Valley to Ferro Pass at 2,270 m (7,450 ft) before dropping down to Lake Magog. This seldom used route into Mount Assiniboine Park is 29 km (17.7 miles) one-way leading primarily through a forested setting.

The Nub (Map 29B/A2)

This trail is reached off the trail from Lake Magog to Elizabeth Lake about 0.5 km (0.3 miles) south of the tiny lake. The hike leads steadily uphill to Nub Peak gaining 400 m (1,310 ft) to the summit. The latter part of the hike is a scramble to the top on a poorly defined trail. From the top, you get a view of four mountain lakes and the sub-alpine meadows below. Overall, the trail is 3.8 km (2.3 miles) 2 hours one-way.

Wedgewood Lake Trail (Maps 29B/A2-34/G6)

Starting at Sunburst Lake west of Lake Magog, this moderate trail extends 5.1 km (3.1 miles) one-way. Gorgeous lakes and scenery highlight this trail, which is best done in early summer to early fall.

Wonder Pass Viewpoint Trail (Map 29B/A1)

From Lake Magog, this 10.5 km (6.4 mile) 3–4 hour easy hike passes through beautiful sub-alpine meadows with wildflowers and past Og Lake. The elevation gain is 230 m (748 ft) to the pass at 2,400 m (7,875 ft). At the viewpoint, you overlook a couple of turquoise lakes and the spectacular mountain terrain.

Mount Evans Trail (Map 12/F6) 🚶 🏕

From the 1.2 km mark on the Fiddler Creek Road, it is a 12 km (7.3 mile) 5 hour return hike to an old mine in the sub-alpine below Mount Evans. A route continues south to Malandaine Pass.

Mount Fernie Trail (Map 15/A7) 🚶 🏕

To reach the trailhead, take the first right after the south Fernie highway bridge and proceed 0.5 km (0.3 miles) on Beach Street before taking an old road to the left. The trail follows Mutz Creek on an old road leading up the south face of Mount Fernie. Expect a steep, strenuous, 2–3 hour hike up to the top offering a great view of Fernie and the Lizard Range.

Mount Fisher Trail (Map 14/C5) 🚶 📷 🏕

Mount Fisher is the highest peak in the area and despite the grueling 1,600 m (5,250 ft) climb it is a popular destination. The trail begins from the 8 km mark on the rough Mause Creek Road and leads 5 km (3 mile) 3–4 hour one-way to the base of the mountain. From there, you can scramble up the steep slope to the top at 2,846 m (9,337 ft). It is a tough climb but the view from the top is worth it. Mountaineering opportunities exist.

Mount Hosmer Trail (Map 15/B5) 🚶 🏕

From the 7 km (6.1 mile) mark on the Hartley Lake Road, it is a moderate 3 km (1.8 mile) 2–3 hour one-way hike to the Ghostrider Peak on Mount Hosmer. The elevation gain is 700 m (2,275 ft) to the peak at 2,340 m (7,675 ft). The trail is well maintained and offers excellent views of the Fernie area. Many visitors continue along the ridge and/or climb to the peak of Hosmer.

Mount Nelson Trail (Map 26/G7) 🚶 🏕

From the washout on Delphine Creek Road, 2 km (1.2 miles) from the Toby Creek Road, this difficult hike begins. The trail leads straight uphill for 12 km (7.3 miles) 5–7 hours gaining 2,000 m (6,560 ft) to the summit where you will find a large aluminum cross. The trail peters out before the actual summit but it is possible to scramble up the southwest face to get to the top. You will be rewarded with a great view from one of the highest mountains in the Purcell Mountains at 3,307 m (10,850 ft).

Mount Proctor/Proctor Creek Trail (Map 15/A6) 🚶 🏕

The Mount Proctor Trail is a long day hike that covers 22 km (13.4 miles) from the trailhead just north of Ferry Creek on Highway 3. It is also a steep climb to the summit at 2,391 m (7,771 ft) gaining 1,330 m (4,365 ft). An alternative route to reach the summit is to hike to the end of the Fairy Creek Trail (4 km/2.4 miles) and then head north on the Proctor Creek Trail. After climbing for 200 m (650 ft), you will break out into the alpine at 1,500 m (4,920 ft) in elevation. From there, it is a steep hike through the alpine to the summit.

Mount Stevens Trail (Map 14/B1) 🚶 🏕

Off the Estella Mine Road, it is a 13 km (7.9 mile) 5 hour one-way hike past Mount Stevens to the Nicol Creek drainage. A second car left at the end of the Lussier River Road is recommended. It is also possible to summit both Mount Stevens and the neighbouring Teepee Mountain.

Mount Swansea Lookout Trail (Map 27/D6) 🚶 🏕

Depending on how far you drive, this popular viewpoint overlooking the Columbia Valley can be as short as a 0.5 km (0.3 mile) walk. The steep and rough Mount Swansea Road can shave off 5 km (3 miles) of the walk from the signed trailhead, which is actually 200 m (650 ft) up the road. The well-defined trail parallels the logging road to the top of Mount Swansea for an elevation gain of 745 m (2,421 ft). The viewpoint is used by hang-gliders and is at 1,733 m (5,685 ft). The trail then loops back down to the trailhead for a 10 km (6.1 mile) 3 hour return hike.

Mount Tegart Trail (Map 27/F6) 🚶 🏕

This trail begins from the Madias Creek Road and initially follows an old road for 1.5 km (0.9 miles). The trail then climbs steadily uphill through a large avalanche path before reaching a grassy ridge, which will take you to the summit at 2,385 m (7,825 ft). The hike covers 3.5 km (2.1 miles) gaining 800 m (2,625 ft) over 2–3 hours. You are rewarded with a great view from the summit.

Mountain Shadows Trail (Map 15/D3) 🚶 🚴

So named because this trail starts at the Mountain Shadows Campground in Sparwood, this easy trail circles the Sparwood Golf Course. You will gain only about 40 m (135 ft) along the 4.7 km (2.9 mile) trail.

Mountain Walk Trail (Map 22/C5) 🚶 🚴 🎿 🏕

It is an 8 km (4.8 mile) 2 hour one-way moderate hike from the northwest corner of the parking lot of the Wapiti Ski Hill, found west of Elkford. The trail climbs through the sub-alpine forest to the ridge before descending towards Round Prairie and the River Walk Trail (see above). Mountain biking and cross-country skiing are popular alternatives.

Mummery Glacier Trail (Map 39/A1) 🚶 🏔 🏕

This 6 km (3.6 mile) 3 hour hike begins off a signed secondary road about 60 km (36.6 miles) along the Blaeberry Road. The trail begins by dissecting an old growth cedar and hemlock stand where you get a number of promising views of the glacier. From there, the trail leads up the old creek bed and across a wooden bridge bringing you onto an immense moraine. The trail then leads up the moraine to the top where you will get a spectacular view of the glacier and waterfall. The trail is very popular, particularly during the summer months.

Natural Bridge Cross-Country Cross-ski Trails (Map 27/F3) 🚶 🚴 🎿 🏕

The parking lot to the ski area is 16 km (9.8 miles) from Highway 93 on the Cross River Road. In the summer, you can hike/bike the old road system through a mixed coniferous forest. The longest route is a moderate 5 km (3 mile) bike to the spectacular upper canyon and the Natural Bridge over the Cross River.

North Galbraith Aldertree Trail (Map 14/F1-3) ⛺ 🚶 🏇 🏕

This is a popular 48 km (29.3 mile) trail up the North Galbraith Creek drainage. The trail is used mainly by hunters and horseback riders and can be accessed from both the north (via the Bull-Quinn Road) and south (Galbraith Road) ends.

North Shore Trail (Map 21/B4) 🚶 🚴 🐟

Located in Whiteswan Provincial Park, this is a 16 km (9.8 mile) 5 hour return hike from Home Basin to Alces Lake. As the name implies, it skirts along the northern shores of Whiteswan Lake passing the remnants of an old trapper's cabin along the way.

Number Nine Mine Trail (Map 15/B7) 🚶 🚲 🏕

East of Fernie on Coal Creek Road, this historic mine site is found at the end of an old mining road. The road climbs 325 m (1,065 ft) over 3.8 km (2.4 miles) from a large coal pile just past the bridge on Coal Creek. The mine was abandoned due to a high incident rate of tunnel collapse. Although the tunnels are closed, there are still a lot of hazards around the site to be wary of.

Palmer Creek Trail (Map 37/B1) ⛰ 🚶 🏔

This is a 35 km (21.4 mile) difficult day hike along an overgrown trail that requires bushwhacking. The trail begins at Gold Arm on Kinbasket Lake and leads to the base of Azimuth Mountain where mountaineering opportunities exist.

Panorama Trail System (Map 27/A6) 🚶 🐎 🚲 ⛷

At the Panorama Ski Resort, there are 20 km (12.2 miles) of well-developed cross-country ski trails. The trails are also used for horseback riding, mountain biking and hiking in the spring through fall. For the more adventurous, it is possible to follow the elaborate trail system into the surrounding backcountry. In recent years, Panorama has also opened up its lifts to mountain bikers, catering to hardcore bikers, with a biker-cross course, a bike park, and the double-black diamond run Crazy Trail. There are stunts that rival those made famous by the fanatics on the North Shore of Vancouver.

Paradise Basin Trail (Map 26/G6) 🚶 🏕

By driving the old mining road uphill from the Toby Creek Road, you will reach the treeless alpine ridge at 2,450 m (8,040 ft). From the end of the road, it is possible to hike along the ridge in either direction for a fantastic view of the Panorama Ski Hill and the surrounding mountains. This hike is nice since it gets you into the alpine without the usual climb. The long access road with 4wd sections discourages would be explorers.

Pedley Pass Trail (Map 27/G7) 🚶 🏕

Follow the Westroc Mine Road then an old road to its end and you will find the trailhead at the west side of a clearing. From there, the 2 km (1.2 mile) 1.5 hour one-way trail takes you steadily uphill through a large meadow with grassy humps called Bumpy Meadows. You continue to the alpine pass at 2,250 m (7,380 ft) gaining 300 m from the trailhead. The trail is popular in July and August because it is relatively easy to access the alpine. From the pass, it is possible to scramble to the summit of Mount Aeneas located to the south. This route is 2.5 km (1.5 miles) 2–3 hours one-way gaining 425 m (1,395 ft). A route also continues south to Pedley Creek and beyond.

Perry Creek Falls Trail (Map 13/C6) 🚶 🏕

This short (1.2 km) easy trail is accessed off the Perry Creek Road. At the 8 km sign, watch for a parking spot, just before the road begins to climb. From here, the falls, and remains of old gold mining operations, are an easy walk southwest.

Perry Pass Trail (Maps 5/A1-4/G1) 🚶 🏕

In 1895, the Perry Pass Trail was built to access gold claims in the Goldrun Lake area. While the claims were not as fruitful as first predicted and a mine was never built, the trail was. These days, the trail is known only to a few, even though part of it is still is in very good condition. From Perry Pass, it is possible to hike to Hellroaring Creek, Mount Flett, Kamma Pass and Nogalski Peak.

Phillips Pass Trail (Map 15/F5) 🚶 🐎 🚲 ⛷ 🛶 🏍 🏕

Beginning off Highway 3 near the Crowsnest Provincial Park, a pipeline road climbs to Phillips Pass gaining 245 m (805 ft). A steep gravel road on the east side of the pass leads to Crowsnest Lake and on to Highway 3 in Alberta.

Pinto Mountain Trail (Map 27/E5) 🚶 🏕

Fantastic views of the Columbia Valley and Windermere Lake are offered from the summit, which is accessed on a 2 km (1.2 miles) 2–3 hour hike. The trail starts from the southeast edge of a cut-block north of the Westroc Mine Road and follows flagging tape through a second growth forest. It is a steady uphill climb before reaching a grassy avalanche chute and the challenging route to the summit. Overall, the hike gains 850 m (2,763 ft) to the summit at 2,550 m (8,365 ft).

Ptarmigan Lake Trail (Map 21/B3) ⛰ 🚶 🚲 🐟

This 6 km (3.7 mile) 2–3 hour one-way trail initially follows an old road. Eventually, a trail leads steeply through a sub-alpine forest to the lake at 1,900 m (6,235 ft). The lake is beautifully set beneath the rugged White Knight Peak and has a small campground at the north end. The lake also offers good fishing.

Quartz Lake Trail (Map 38/A5) ⛰ 🚶 🐟

Leading to a pristine wilderness lake, this trail is located about 7.5 km (4.6 miles) along the Quartz Creek Road. The difficult 3 hour trail climbs uphill covering 5 km (3 miles) one-way. The trail is grown-in in places adding to the difficulty of the hike.

Queen Mary Lake Trail (Map 28/B3) 🚶 🐎 🏔 🐟 🏕

See Height of the Rockies Park above.

Richmond Lake Trail (Map 5/A1) 🚶 🐟

From just past the 32 km sign on the Perry Creek Road, is a 2.8 km (1.7 mile) 1.5 hour steep hike leading to a sub-alpine fishing lake.

Ridgemont (Fernie Ridge) Trail (Map 15/B7) 🚲 🏕

This bike trail can be reached either from the graveyard, or by taking a left fork off the Coal Creek Road on Ridgemont Road. Follow this road uphill past another fork to the top of the ridge. The real fun begins as you descend the north side of the mountain. Eventually, you'll hit a powerline. Turning left will bring you back to town. There are a number of other trails accessed off Ridgemont Road, including Eric's Trail, Sidewinder Trail and Deadfall Trail. All three feature strenuous uphill climbs. Part of this trail follows the Fernie Ridge route (see above).

Rim Trail (Map 4/E7) 🚶 🏕

If you drive to the Mount Thompson Lookout, which is found at 2,187 m (7,175 ft) in elevation, a trail continues along the ridge top. The easy 8 km (4.8 mile) 2 hour one-way hike offers great views of the Creston Valley.

River Walk (Map 22/C5) 🚶 🚲 ⛷ 🏕

This easy 4.2 km (2.6 mile) trail allows hikers to walk along the edge of the Elk River north of Elkford. The trail is relatively flat as it cuts through forests and meadows next to the river. This route hooks up with the Mountain Walk (see below) at Round Prairie.

Rockypoint Creek Trail (Map 33/B7) 🚶 🏔 🏕

Near the 29 km marker of Bugaboo Road, an old road takes off to the right and marks the beginning of the trail up Rockypoint Creek. This trail leads 8.5 km (5.2 miles) 2–3 hours to an open alpine meadow and treeless ridge top with great views of the Bugaboo Spires. The trail, which is difficult to follow in places, initially passes through a second growth forest crossing several avalanche chutes before breaking out into the alpine full of wildflowers in July-August. At 6.5 km (4 miles), you pass by an old cabin. The elevation gain to the ridge at 2,450 m (8,040 ft) is a grueling 1,050 m (3,445 ft).

Rault Lake Trail (Map 14/C3) 🚶 🚲 🐟 🏕

The trailhead for the 9 km (5.6 mile) trail to Rault Lake is found past the Summer Lake Recreation Site. There is a rough road leading up the north side of Rault Creek that climbs up to the lake. 4wd vehicles can make it part way up the road before having to hike. The trail is often overgrown, and can be difficult to follow in places as it climbs 590 m (1,935 ft) to the lake. From the lake, you can scramble up the ridge to your west, then down to Bear Lake, which holds a good population of small cutthroat trout.

Russell Lake Trail (Map 28/G7) 🚶 🐟 🏕

This trail begins where a bridge has been removed on the White-North Fork Road. From the old bridge crossing, hike up the old road 3.5 km (2.1 miles) to a cut-block where you will find the marked trail. The 4–5 hour trail continues up the North White River drainage to Russell Lake gaining 500 m (1,640 ft) over 8 km (4.9 miles) one-way. Alternative routes are to scramble to the summit of Russell Peak on a poorly defined trail or continue on to the Sinna Pass at the boundary to the Height of the Rockies Provincial Park.

Saddleback Trail (Maps 14/A1, 21/A7) 🚶 🏕

Found in Premier Lake Provincial Park, this trail can be accessed from Cats Eye Lake. It is a moderate 16 km (9.8 mile) 5 hour hike to the ridge overlooking Premier Lake and the Kootenay River Valley.

Septet Pass Trail (Map 26/C2) 🚶 🏕

Septet Pass Trail begins about 17.5 km along the Frances Creek Road. You will have to park at the washed out bridge and then walk approximately 1.5 km (0.9 miles) to the actual trailhead because the road is brushed in. From there, the trail follows Frances Creek for 2.8 km (1.7 miles), passing several large avalanche slides on an old road. Soon, the trail leaves the valley bottom and rises sharply through a mature spruce and balsam forest. Towards the top, a series of switchbacks brings the hiker into the high elevation meadows of Septet Pass. In all, the trail is 4.7 km (2.9 miles) 2–3 hours one-way gaining 500 m (1,640 ft). At the meadows it is possible to follow game trails and link to Chalice Creek Trail.

Sheep Creek/Premier Lake/Wolf Creek Route (Map 13/G1-21/A7) 🚴 🏍 🏕

This is a popular 40 km (24 mile) ride that starts from the campground at Wasa Provincial Park. There are some steep climbs, great views and nice picnic areas. From Wasa Lake, follow the Sheep Creek Road past Premier Lake Park. Continue south to the Wolf Creek Road for a downhill ride back to Wasa Lake.

Sheep Mountain Route (Map 7/A3) 🚶 🐴 🚴 🏍 🏕

An easy walk up an old road leads to the site of a former fire lookout tower that has been removed. The 5 km (3 mile) route gains 340 m (1,000 ft) to the top.

Sherman Lakes Trail (Map 4/B1) ⛺ 🚶 🎣 🏕

Found off the Sanca Creek Road is a 5.5 km (3.3 mile) 3 hour moderate hike to a small lake set in an alpine basin below Mount Sherman. Many prefer to base camp at the lake and explore the surrounding ridges.

Silent Pass Trail (Map 32/C4) ⛺ 🚶 🚵 🚵 ⚓ 🏕

From the end of the McMurdo Creek Road, a deteriorating logging road, the Silent Pass Trail leads 2 km (1.2 miles) 1 hour to Silent Lake, a tiny lake set in some sub-alpine meadows. The lake is at 2,040 m (6,695 ft) in elevation and the elevation gain is 360 m (1170 ft). From Silent Lake, you can continue over Silent Pass to McMurdo Cabin but there is no defined trail. Route finding skills are essential. Alternatively, the cabin can be reached from the end of the road via a short 0.5 km (0.3 mile) walk on an old road with little elevation gain. The cabin is available for public use and can be reserved with the Ministry of Forests in Invermere (250-342-4200). It is very popular, so book ahead. Beyond the cabin, continue up the old road and you'll soon come across an old mine to explore.

Silver Basin Trail (Map 26/A2) 🚶 🏕

Bringing you into a beautiful alpine basin full of wildflowers in July-August and offering a great view of the Bugaboos, the hike is 2.2 km (1.3 miles) 1–1.5 hours one-way. The elevation gain from the Bugaboo South Road is 230 m (748 ft). The trail initially follows a deactivated road for over one km to an old cut-block. The trail then follows the creek to the basin at 2,050 m (6,725 ft). From the basin, it is possible to access the ridgeline at 2,325 m (7,630 ft).

Silver Spring Lakes Trail (Map 7/A3) 🚶 🐴 🚴 🏍 🎣

A stiff climb, gaining 100 m (325 ft) in about 0.5 km (1,625 ft) along an old logging road brings you to the first Silver Spring Lake. You will only gain a few more metres in elevation as you make your way to the second and third lakes beyond (2.9 km/1.8 miles one-way to the third lake). The first is the prettiest and most popular of the lakes west of Elko.

Slide Lake Trail (Map 26/e1) 🚶 🎣

An easy 4 km (2.4 mile) trail starts from the Leadqueen Frances Road and leads to this small lake.

Snowshoe Lake Trail (Map 7/C5) 🚶 ⚓

From the Wigwam Road, it is a 2.5 km (1.5 mile) one-way walk to the trailhead along an old road. From there, you must cross the Wigwam River (which is only possible in low water) and climb another one kilometre to the lake.

Sparwood Ridge Trail (Map 15/D3) 🚶 🐴 🚴 🏕

Found near the powerlines off Sycamore Road, a well maintained horse trail leads to the top of Sparwood Ridge. It is an 8 km (4.8 mile) 3 hours difficult hike gaining 600 m (1,950 ft). The view of Sparwood and area is impressive.

Spillimacheen River Trail (Map 32/A1) ⛺ 🚶 🚵 🏊 🏕

At the end of the Spillimacheen Road (which requires a high clearance vehicle), you will find the signed trailhead for this moderate trail. The hike begins on an old road along the river. Follow the road to its end (about 1.5 km/0.9 miles) before a well maintained trail begins. You will pass an outfitter cabin at 2.5 km (1.5 miles) and reach the Yurt Hollow Campground at 10.5 km (6.4 miles) near the headwaters of the river. Along the way, you will be required to make a major creek crossing. From the campground, you can either take the steady climb up to the Purcell Lodge at the base of Bald Mountain or hike to Copperstain Mountain. The total distance to the Purcell Lodge at 2,150 m (7,055 ft) is 12.5 km (7.6 miles) 3–4 hours one-way gaining 500 m (1,625 ft). To reach the summit of Copperstain Mountain involves a total hike of 14.5 km (8.8 miles) 4–5 hours one-way gaining 930 m (3,050 ft).

Spirit Trail (Map 20/F2) 🚶 🏕

A 16 km (9.8 mile) day hike leads along the eastern shores of Columbia Lake providing good opportunities to see wintering animals such as deer, elk and mountain goats. The trail connects the popular day-use Columbia Lake and Canal Flats Provincial Parks.

South Star Recreation Trails (Map 5/F1) 🚶 🐴 🚴 🎿

At the end of 38th Ave in Cranbrook there are 30+km (18 miles) of trails designed for a variety of recreational pursuits including hiking, biking, horseback riding and cross-country skiing. The trails are well developed and can be enjoyed by all levels of users.

St Mary's Alpine Park (maps 12, 19) 🚶 🏕

While there are no established trails within St. Mary's Alpine Park, you can explore the beautiful park along any of a number of informal routes. To do so requires crossing rough terrain and talus slopes. A compass and topographic map is essential since these routes are not marked, and may be difficult to follow. The following trails can be used to access routes leading into the park.

Wesley Creek Trail (Maps 12/E1-19/E7)

Beginning 200 m (650 ft) before the end of Dewar Creek Road, this 5 km (3 mile) one-way trail follows the north side of Wesley Creek to Mount St Mary. The trail degenerates into a route before you hit the top, climbing 1,523 m (5,000 ft) to the 2,896 m (9,500 ft) summit. Side routes hook up with the Dewar Creek Trail and lead into St Marys Alpine Park. It is the most popular access point into the park.

Skookumchuck Creek Trail (Maps 20/A7-19/G7)

From the trailhead at Greenland Creek, this trail takes you up the north side of the creek to the divide where the trail continues down into the headwaters of Alton Creek at the north end of the park. From there, the trail continues 2 km (1.2 miles) one-way south through open meadows to a point overlooking White Creek.

White Creek/Spade Creek Trail (Map 12/G2)

From the washed out Spade Creek Bridge, this trail follows the old road for another 0.5 km (0.3 miles) one-way before a poorly marked trail leads along the north side of Spade Creek to a small mountain lake. From the lake, you can continue along a difficult to follow route past Stair Lakes to access the height of land. This route is not popular, nor is it recommended.

St Mary River Trail (Maps 12/C1-19/C7) ⛺ 🥾 🐎 🎣

From the end of St Mary River Road (around the 69 km/42 mile mark), an outfitter's trail follows the St Mary River through open stands of spruce. The trail takes 1–2 days return to hike and has an elevation gain of only 240 m (785 ft). You can take a side trip near the headwaters to reach an attractive alpine lake to the east.

Starbird Glacier Trail (Map 26/C6) 🥾 🎣

The highlight of the trail is exploring the caves of Starbird Glacier. To get to the caves requires a 12 km (7.3 mile) 6 hour steep, difficult trail leading to the nose of the glacier.

Stockdale Creek Trail (Map 26/D5) ⛺ 🥾 🎣

There is a 32 km (19.5 mile) overgrown trail found on the west side of Stockdale Creek. The difficult trail accesses some remote mountainous terrain of the Purcell Mountains.

Swan Creek Trail (Map 42/A7) 🥾 🚵 🎣

From the Columbia West Road, this steep 18 km (11 mile) 4–5 hour hike provides access to a glorious alpine meadow. The trail dissects a stand of giant cedar and hemlock trees as it gains a thigh burning 1,400 m (4,595 ft) in elevation. From the meadows, you can continue on to Adamant Range, a world-class mountain climbing area.

Taynton Creek Trail (Map 27/A7) 🥾 🎣

From the Panorama Ski Hill, this trail begins on an overgrown road leading towards the Platter Ski Lift. It gains a grueling 1,050 m (3,445 ft) over 7 km (4.3 miles) one-way to a treed column at 2,200 m (7,220 ft) south of Mount Taynton. Allow 2–3 hours to get to the column and another half an hour to climb the summit of Mount Taynton at 2,380 m (7,810 ft). Mount Goldie to the south can also be accessed after scrambling up an open ridge to the summit. You climb 480 m (1,575 ft) over a distance of 4 km (2.4 miles) to reach the higher peak.

Tegart Pass Trail (Map 27/G6) 🥾 🎣

A seldom used, difficult 13 km (7.9 mile) trail climbs from the Kootenay River to Tegart Pass. It should take about 6 hours to hike over the pass and down into the Windermere Creek drainage and the Westroc Mine.

Templeton Lake Trail (Map 26/C1) ⛺ 🥾 🚵 🎣

From the Templeton River Bridge on the Templeton River Road, it is a 12 km (7.3 mile) 4.5 hour return hike along the river. Initially you follow an old logging road to a footbridge about (2 km/1.2 miles) later. From the south side of the river, the moderate trail is sporadically marked as it crosses several talus slopes eventually reaching the turquoise colored lake. At the lake, you can admire the hanging glacier, camp or try a mountaineering route to the Shangri-La, an alpine basin formally called the Dunbar Lakes. The total elevation gain to Templeton Lake is 305 m (1,000 ft).

Thompson Falls Trail (Map 38/F4) 🥾 🎣

More of a walk than a hike, the destination is a waterfall on the Blaeberry River. Allow half an hour to walk 2 km (1.2 miles) return.

Three Sisters Trail (Map 15/A6) 🥾 🎣

From the end of an old 4wd road off the Hartley Lake Road, a strenuous but popular hike follows a well maintained trail (marked by red triangles on trees or rock cairns) to the unique alpine setting. The trail is about 8 km (4.8 miles) 4–5 hours long. There are several scenic vistas to enjoy and a lot of alpine to explore.

Thunderbird Mine Trail (Map 26/F7) 🥾 🚵 ⛷ 🎣

From the washout on Delphine Creek Road, about 2 km (1.2 miles) from the Toby Creek Road, follow the old washed out logging road to a skid road, just east of Sultana Creek. The skid road leads uphill to a trail, which switchbacks uphill along an old pack trail leading to the former Thunderbird Mine Townsite. Backcountry skiers maintain one of the four buildings at the townsite. The trail is 8 km (4.9 miles) 3–4 hours one-way gaining 900 m (2,955 ft) to the townsite at 2,225 m (7,231 ft). From the townsite, it is possible to scramble uphill on an unmaintained route to Sultana Peak at 3,220 m (10,565 ft).

Thunderwater–Whirlpool Lake Trail (Map 26/D3) 🥾 🐟 🎣

The signed trailhead to these two sub-alpine fishing lakes is found at the parking lot past the 42 km mark on the Forster Creek Road (high clearance vehicle required). The trail initially starts on an overgrown road that passes the General Store Cabin, a private heli-skiing hut, about 2 km later. From there, a poorly defined trail that requires strong route-finding skills continues. As you approach Thunderwater Lake, you will break out into the treeless alpine meadows with a fantastic view of the glaciated peak surrounding the lake. Whirlpool Lake is a short hike from Thunderwater Lake. This trail is best hiked after mid-July because the lakes are iced over until that time. Overall it is a difficult 6 km (3.6 mile) 2.5–3 hour one-way hike gaining 435 m (1,425 ft). It is possible to hike beyond the two lakes to Forster Pass, which is another 2 km (1.2 miles) 1.5 hours one-way from Thunderwater Lake. The pass provides a great view of the rugged, untouched mountains to the south.

Tiger Pass/Dunbar Lakes Trail (Map 26/D1) 🥾 🚵 🎣

This trail system begins at the end of a steep, deteriorating and heavily wash barred mining road off the Frances Creek Road. The main trail rises steeply through a larch stand and meadows with wildflowers in July-August. Soon, you break out onto a talus slope and the final scramble to Tiger Pass at 2,570 m (8,430 ft) in elevation. At the pass, you descend 355 m (1,154 ft) across a glacier and into a remote valley filled with over ten small lakes and pools collectively called Dunbar Lakes. Locally the area is called Shangri-La. The distance to Tiger Pass is 2 km (1.2 miles) 1–2 hours one-way gaining 390 m (1,280 ft). To Dunbar Lakes, it is 4 km (2.4 miles) 3–4 hours one-way. From the Dunbar Lakes, it is possible to hike over to Templeton Lake and eventually down to the Templeton River Road. A two-car system is recommended for this extension. You can also hike to the summit of **Mount Ethelbert**, which is 3 km (1.8 miles) 2–3 hours from Upper Dunbar Lake. To reach the summit, head straight up the avalanche chute on the face of the mountain and then circle around the backside of the peak on the left hand side. The whole route requires walking over talus slopes.

Top of the World Provincial Park (Map 14/D1) ⛺ 🥾 🐎 🚵 🚶 🐟 🎣

The high alpine setting makes this park a spectacular hiking destination. Since most of its terrain is above the 2,200m (7,200 foot) level, the numerous hiking opportunities do not become accessible until early June or after November (for backcountry skiers). Fish Lake is the hub of the park and has a cabin as well as numerous designated campsites. The main trailhead is accessed off the South Lussier River Road.

Access to Fish Lake (Map 14/C1)

This is a 6.7 km (4.1 mile) 1.5–2 hour one-way easy walk along a fairly good trail gaining 212 m (695 ft). The forested trail climbs alongside the Lussier River with snow-covered peaks in the background. While at beautiful Fish Lake try your luck fishing for the plentiful but small bull trout and cutthroat.

Fish Lake to Alpine Viewpoint (Map 14/C1)

Beginning 100 m (325 ft) north of Fish Lake, the 3.2 km (2 mile) 2–3 hour trail gains 600 m (1,970 ft) on a steady uphill grade eventually ending at a large slide. From the top, you get a panoramic view of Fish Lake and the surrounding park.

Fish Lake to Coyote Creek Campsite (Map 14/D1)

This 7 km (4.3 mile) 1.5–2 hour one-way hike gains 370 m (1,203 ft). The trail starts 100 m (325 ft) to the north of Fish Lake and involves a strenuous hike. At 5.6 km (3.4 miles), take the left branch if you what to reach The Sugarloaf.

Fish Lake to Sparkle Lake (Map 14/C1)

Start on the Wildhorse Ridge Trail (below) and at the top of first steep pitch, take the branch that crosses the creek. From there, the trail leads steadily uphill and ends at a slide. Cross the slide and you will reach Sparkle Lake. Overall, the trail is 2.8 km (1.7 miles) 1–2 hours one-way with an elevation gain of 350 m (1,150 ft).

Fish Lake to Summer Pass (Map 14/C1)

A 4 km (2.4 mile) 2–3 hour one-way trail climbs 430 m (1,410 ft) to the pass. The steep trail takes you through alpine meadows with wild flowers in season.

Fish Lake to Wildhorse Ridge (Map 14/C1)

This 3.2 km (2 mile) 2–3 hour one-way hike gains 640 m (2,100 ft). The trail starts at the bottom of the slide west of Fish Lake and involves a steady uphill climb to the ridge.

Lakeshore Trail (Map 14/C1)

A 2 km (1.2 mile) half hour stroll leads around the forested banks of Fish Lake. It is often used to access fishing holes.

Valenciennes Canyon Trail (Map 43/A7) 🚶 👣

This is a 4 km (2.4 mile) 2.5 hour moderate trail with a fabulous canyon view. The trail is fairly steep and found after a long trip up the Bush River Road.

VOR Tower/Very Outrageous Ride (Map 13/B7) 🚶 🚵 👣

The name given to the ridge route between Angus Creek and Perry Creek gives you a sense of what you're in for. (VOR actually stands for VHF Omni Range, and is an aircraft navigation tower.) The hike/bike follows an old road off the Angus Creek Road and up the summit of Puddingburn Mountain. This is a steep uphill grunt, gaining 1,400 m (4,595 feet) as it switchbacks its way up to the ridge known for meadows filled with wildflowers and sub-alpine larch. From here, bikers can either return the way you came, or connect with a logging road network in the Pitt Creek or Perry Creek Valleys. Either way, take a few moments to enjoy the scenery at the top.

Wapiti Mountain Trail (Map 22/B6) 🚶 👣

From the Ski Hill parking lot a tough climb will take you to the top along the main ski run. It leads to a nice view over Elkford and area.

Warren Creek Trail (Map 33/A6) 🚶 👣

Another remote route is accessed off the Bobbie Burns Road south of Parson. This trail is 16 km (9.8 mile) 8 hours return as it follows an old mining road and unmarked trail to the alpine.

Weary Creek Gap Trail (Map 29A/C7) 🚶 👣

An old, overgrown logging road heads up into the alpine at the headwaters of Weary Creek. You will cover about 6.2 km (3.8 miles) to the gap between Mount Muir and Mount McPhail on the BC/Alberta boundary. Expect to climb 625 m (2,050 feet) to the gap, at 2,240 m (7,350 feet). Wandering into Alberta will lead to a gorgeous headwall above McPhail Creek.

Welsh Lakes Trail (Map 26/E3) 🚶 👣

From 36 km on the Forster Creek Road, it is a 4 km (2.4 mile) 2–2.5 hour one-way hike gaining 675 m (2,215 ft) to Lower Welsh Lake. The moderate trail begins by following an old road for the first 3.5 km (2.1 miles) before crossing some steep rocky sections on the traverse to the lake. The last 1.5 km (0.9 miles) climbs over a steep, rocky landscape on a faint, hard to follow trail. From the lake, you can make your own route to the three other wilderness lakes in the area. All four lakes are a remarkable turquoise colour.

Wesley Creek Trail (Map 12/E1–19/E7) 🚶 👣

See St Marys Alpine Park above.

West Bench Area (Maps 32, 38) 🚵 🏍 🛷

The West Bench Area around Golden offers a great variety of terrain and difficulty for all types of mountain bikers and ATV riders. Endless logging roads with a fine mix of single-track gives riders a fabulous playground to explore. The Canyon Creek Loop, Kicking Horse Ski Hill and Wiseman Lake routes are described elsewhere, but there are a number of other popular biking routes in this area.

Whiteman Pass Trail (Map 28/C1) 🚶 👣

This scenic, well developed trail leads along the Upper Cross River into Banff National Park. The pass is 5.5 km (3.4 miles) from the trailhead on the north side of the river.

White River Trail (Maps 21/G1-28/G6) ⛺ 🚶 🐎 👣

A long rough horse trail follows the middle fork of the White River from the Maiyuk River Recreation Site up to Sylvan Pass. This is a difficult trail, with lots of mud and plenty of rough sections. Add in a number of river crossings and you have a trail better left to horseback riders, although backpackers still head this way. It's 21.5 km (13.1 miles) to the pass, gaining 645 m (2,096 feet). Along the route, you can take side trips to any one of five sub-alpine lakes (Deep Lake, Limestone Lakes or Driftwood Lake). For those people who don't like retracing their footsteps, an interesting two or three-day trek can be planned by continuing down the Joffre Creek Trail in Height of the Rockies Park.

Wigwam Flats Trail (Map 7/B3) 🐎 🚵 🛷

The Wigwam Flats are part of the Mount Broadwood Heritage Area (and Trans Canada Trail). The area is best explored by bike, as the long, dusty roads don't make for the most exciting hiking. The trail begins on River Road, and heads south along the Elk River to a viewpoint over the Wigwam Canyon, climbing 105 m (345 ft) to reach the flats. The canyon is found 8.5 km (5.3 miles) along the road. About halfway along, the road splits; left takes you to the flats, right takes you to a viewpoint over the Elk/Wigwam confluence.

Wigwam Lookout Trail (Map 7/B4) 🚶 👣

Old forestry lookouts are popular hiking destinations because of the panoramic view they offer. This moderate hike is 12 km (7.3 miles) 5 hours long and follows an old road to the abandoned lookout. The route involves fording Wigwam River from the Lodgepole-Cabin Road.

Wiseman Lake to Golden (Map 38/C5-E7) 🐎 🚵 🏍 🛷

This 40 km (24.4 mile) ride starts on the Donald FSR, off the Trans-Canada Highway. The route takes you along the west bench above the Columbia River via a series of active and old logging roads to Golden. The long wilderness route has very little elevation gain, and can be enjoyed by any level of riders. Horseback riders, ATVers and motorcyclists also use the route.

Wooden Shoe Trail (Map 4/B2) ⛺ 🚶 🎣

The once beautiful sub-alpine lake was ravaged by fire in 2003. It is still possible to hike in to camp and enjoy the sandy beaches but anglers will need to be patient and hope that the stocking program will resurrect the cutthroat fishery.

Wolverine Pass Trail (Map 33/G3) ⛺ 🚶 🐎 ⛷ 👣

The Wolverine Pass Trail is popular backcountry skiing route in the winter that sees a fair bit of activity in the summer. The 30 km (18.3 mile) moderate horse trail follows Dalhard Creek to the pass at 2,250 m (7,380 ft). From there, you can approach the Rockwall Pass or Tumbling Creek Trails in Kootenay National Park.

Yankee, Canuck and Turtle Lakes Loop (Map 21/A7) 🚶 🎣

It is an easy 7.4 km (4.5 mile) hike past this trio of small, scenic lakes in the eastern section of Premier Lake Provincial Park. Because of the relatively low elevation of the lakes (the high point is about 1,050 m/3,460ft), this is a good early season hike. The trail is well signed and should take about half a day to hike unless you bring your fishing rod.

Dewdney Trail

The Dewdney Trail is a historic pack trail that once stretched from Hope to Fort Steele. Originally constructed in 1865 the trail was soon replaced by more trains and modern transportation routes. With the recent development of the Trans Canada Trail pieces of the trail are being restored. The most popular section is found east of Christina Lake (Map 1/B7) and climbs up and over the summit toward Rossland. The actual route continued east to the old Fort Sheppard site south of Trail, along the Pend D'Oreille River to the Salmo River and up Lost Creek to the Kootenay Summit. The route continued towards Creston along Summit Creek (a restored section of trail is found around the Summit Creek Campsite on Map 4/A5) and over the Kootenay River. From Creston to Cranbrook there is not much to find but the trail once followed the Kid Creek drainage over to the Upper Moyie River valley. The last section of trail is actually found northeast of Fort Steele at the old Fisherville Townsite (Map 14/A5). Look for the sign off the Wildhorse River Road. Back in 1865, this was a booming mining town of 8,000 people.

West Kootenays

The West Kootenays are notorious for big lakes and big mountains. With the mountains comes trails and there are plenty to choose from in this quaint area of the province. In the south around the cities of Trail, Castlegar and Nelson, the Selkirk Mountains make a scenic backdrop. East of Kootenay Lake visitors will find the wild Purcell Mountains and further north around Revelstoke the Columbia Mountains take over. West of the Arrow Lakes the impressive Monashee Mountains are yours to explore. The West Kootenays are also the inspiration for the Backroad Mapbook series, as it is the birthplace of Russell and Wesley Mussio.

Alps Alturas Trail (Map 18/A4) 🚶 📷 👣

This high elevation trail is an alpine paradise. The moderate 5 km (3.1 mile) one-way trail cuts through a sub-alpine forest and alpine meadows. It follows an old mining trail to the pass between Mount Dolly Varden and Martin Mountain climbing 580 m (1,900 feet). A 4wd is required to access the trail.

Arrow Lakes Riding Area (Maps 23, 16, 9)
🏕 🚵 🏍 🐎 🎣 👣

Roads leading along the western side of Upper Arrow Lake are ideal for ATV riders to explore. It is possible to ride all the way from Shelter Bay (Map 23/G3) to Needles (Map 9/E1). Popular destinations include the Pingston Valley and Paint Lake (both described below) as well as Catherine and Cameron Lakes, the Fosthall Canyon, Mosquito Lake and Whatshan Lake. There are endless logging and deactivated roads to explore, lakes to camp and fish and plenty of wildlife to see (including bear, moose and deer). When travelling on logging roads, please obey the rules of the road and keep alert for other traffic.

Badshot Mountain Route (Map 25/A2) 🚶 🚵 🏍 👣

Beyond Bunker Hill Creek, the Gainer Creek Road becomes undriveable. Hikers and off-road riders can continue to the foot of Badshot Mountain where the road becomes overgrown and difficult to follow. The road improves higher up. Also in the area is an overgrown road that leads up to the old Mohican Mountain Mine. Once you break through the alder, the road becomes easier to follow.

Barnes Creek Trail (Map 16/B4) 🚶 🐎 👣

This 8 km (4.8 mile) trail heads into the South Pinnacles of the Monashee Mountains and links up with the Vista Pass Trail at the pass. The trailhead is found off the Keefer Lake Road on a 4wd road. This is a very scenic route.

Beaven Mountain Trail (Map 16/A2) 🚶 👣

Accessed off South Fork Road east of Lumby, this steep 7 km (4.3 mile) trail climbs 700m (2,275 ft) to the top of Beaven Mountain. Although well developed, there are rough sections along the trail. Be careful, this is Grizzly bear country.

Trans Canada Trail (TCT)

Due to the mountainous terrain, the West Kootenay and Rocky Mountain portions of the Trans Canada Trail are considered the most challenging sections in British Columbia if not Canada. With the mountains comes some of the most breathtaking scenery you will find anywhere. As a general rule, the TCT follows the course of the historic Dewdney Trail from Christina Lake to Fort Steele. This old pack trail climbed the mountain ranges between Christina Lake and Rossland and between Salmo and Creston. Today, the TCT follows a similar route that links existing trail systems with logging roads, old railgrades and even paved roads. The final section of the route in BC ends at the Elk Pass in Alberta. For a complete step-by-step description of the route, check out *Trans Canada Trail: The British Columbia Route*, produced in cooperation with Trails BC.

Begbie Creek Trail (Map 30/D6) 🚶 🐎 🚵 📷

The trailhead can be reached by travelling about 9 km (5.5 miles) south along Highway 23 from the junction at Highway 1. From there, it is a 1 km (0.6 mile) 45 minute one-way hike culminating at the Begbie Falls Recreation Site. A side spur provides access to a popular rock-climbing wall.

Begbie Falls Trail (Map 30/D6) 🚶 🐎 🚵 📷 👣

It is a 30 minute easy walk through the forest to the falls. A series of steps leads to a viewpoint at the base of the falls. The trail starts at the second quarry (off Mount Begbie Road) and is signed.

Bluebird Lake Trail (Map 3/E5) 🚶

A 6 km (3.6 mile) 2–3 hour moderate hike to a small shallow sub-alpine lake, this trail is located off Blazed Road in the Nelson Range of the Selkirk Mountains.

Bonanza Recreation Area (Map 1/D5) 🚵 🎿 🏍 🏂 👣

Found at the summit of Highway 3 east of Christina Lake, this high alpine area offers endless biking, cross-country skiing and snowmobile routes. The trails start off of the highway on the gravel pit on Bonanza Creek Road and follow a series of old logging roads. It is possible to join up with the old roads to Mount St Thomas and make your way down to Christina Lake.

Boundary Pathway Trail (Maps 2/A2-1/A7)
🚶 🐎 🚵 🎿 🏍 🏂 👣 ⛷

Beginning just south of Hugh Keenleyside Dam, the Boundary Pathway forms an integral link along the Trans Canada Trail. The trail follows the old CPR Columbia and Western Railway initially along the southern slopes of the Lower Arrow Lake before proceeding southward through the Dog Creek and McRae Creek drainages. Along the way, there are ten spectacular bridge crossings together with seven tunnels, including one over one kilometre long that requires a light. Although bumpy, the railgrade, bridges and tunnels remain in generally good condition. There is a 2.2% maximum grade along the route so it makes for a steady uphill climb to the summit (near the old Farron Station) before the cruise down to Christina Lake. Many people start from the Blueberry-Paulson bridge on Highway 3 (Map 1/C5) and ride the 80 km (2 day) route to the Celgar Pulp Mill (west of Castlegar). Allow 3 days to cover the 123.6 km (75.4 mile) route to Christina Lake or 4 days for the 152.5 km (93 mile) route to Grand Forks. Due to the distance involved, most people ride a bike, although it is becoming a popular ATV route.

Box Lake Loop (Map 17/B3) 🚵 🎿 🏂

From Hwy 6, head east on the old railgrade up to Box Lake. A trail leads from the railgrade to Box Lake Road at around the 12 km (7.3 miles) mark. Continue past the recreation site and around the lake along the old road that eventually meets up with Brouse Road. Follow this road north back to Hwy 6. It is a 28 km (17 mile) route along an easy mix of road, old railgrade and trail.

Brilliant Overlook Trail (Map 2/C2) 🚶 👣

Developed and maintained by the Friends of Trails Society, this rugged trail climbs up to the Brilliant Overlook, above the Brilliant Dam. There are actually three trailheads, at Skattebo Reach Junction (found 2 km/1.2 miles along the Skattebo Reach Trail), and two on the Little McPhee Creek FSR (one on the old road, one on the new). The Overlook offers great views over the Columbia and Kootenay Valleys. Some sections are fairly steep; others skirt the edges of drop-offs. From the Skattebo Reach Junction to the overlook is 2.5 km (1.5 miles), and should take about four hours for a round trip. From the Little McPhee trailheads it is 3.5 km (2.1 miles) to the overlook. The old forest service road can be followed down the hill to the Golf Course Road and the trailhead for the Skattebo Reach Trailhead, making an 11 km (6.7 mile) loop.

Buchanan Lookout Trail (Map 18/F7) 🚶 📄 👣

From the end of the Buchanan Lookout Road, there is a 2 km (1.2 mile) walking trail, which leads around the 1965 Fire Lookout building. Interpretative signs along the trail and the great view from the 1,912 m (6,275 ft) summit are two of the main attractions to the area. Day-use facilities (picnic table, fire ring and outhouse) as well as two hang gliding launches are located near the lookout.

Carnes Creek Trail (Map 36/D7)

From the Carnes Creek Recreation Site, this moderate 29 km (17.7 mile) 8 hour return hike follows the north side of the creek. After climbing 400 m (1,310 ft) you will meet up with a spur road from the Carnes Creek Road. It is also possible to access the Kelly-Burke Trail, which climbs along the creek to the foot of Roseberry Mountain.

Castlegar Millennium Walkway (Map 2/B2) blade

This paved walkway is found in Twin Rivers Park, and is built on part of the old Twin Rivers Trail. The trail is 1.6 km (1 mile) long, although it is possible to follow the old trail all the way to Zuckerberg Island (see Riverside Trails, below).

Cedar Grove Loop Trail (Map 17/D1)

At the 4 km mark on the Kuskanax Logging Road, take the left branch one kilometre to the trailhead. From there, the trail is an easy 1 km (0.6 mile) 30 minute walk, which takes you along an old spur road through an impressive stand of western red cedar trees.

Centennial Trail (Map 1/G6)

Several years back, the Trails for Rossland Society officially opened its first trail, a 2.5 km (1.5 mile) one-way trail running from the base of the Red Mountain Ski Hill to Rossland. The popular multi-use trail skirts the Rossland reservoir before passing under Highway 3B to the parking area off Kirkup Avenue.

Clearwater Creek Trail (Map 3/B2)

See Huckleberry Pass Route.

Clute Lake Trail (Map 18/G7)

Accessed by boat on the Kootenay Lake at Verandah Point, this 6 hour moderate hike covers 15 km (9 mile) return. The trail follows an old road to a mountain lake where it is possible to camp.

Columbia River Trail (Map 2/A3)

This popular 7 km (3.6 miles) trail follows the eastern shore of the Columbia River from a trailhead north of Trail to Jordan Creek west of Champion Lakes Provincial Park. It is possible to access the trail from the north end, although there is a gate on the Columbia Road that may be locked. The open trail stays close to the river, and is easy to follow.

Curtis Lake Trail (Map 3/D6)

One of several small, picturesque mountain lakes in the area, Curtis Lake offers a fine camping and fishing destination. Washouts often affect the road access and you may need to walk the road from Sheep Creek. This will add considerable length and elevation gain to the modest 2 km (1.2 mile) one hour trail found at the end of the road.

Cusson Lake Trail (Map 16/C2)

Found west of Upper Arrow Lake, this remote lake offers good fishing in a sub-alpine setting. The moderate 10 km (6.1 mile) 5 hour return hike follows the creek to the lake.

Davis Creek Trail (Map 18/E4)

A moderate 10 km (6 mile) 4–5 hour return hike accesses a small plateau above the small town of Lardeau. The trailhead is off Highway 31.

Dennis Creek Trail (Map 18/A5)

It is a 5 km (3 mile) 2 hour moderate hike through a clear-cut and then over the ridge to the Dennis Creek drainage. The attraction includes the summer wildflowers and the sub-alpine terrain above Slocan Lake. Watch for Grizzly bears.

Deer Creek Trail (Map 1/E1)

An easy 2 km (1.2 mile) 45 minute walk leads to Deer Creek Falls. The trail is found off the Deer Park Road on the east side of the creek.

Deer Point Trail (Map 1/A5)

See Gladstone Park below.

Dewdney Trail (Map 1/B7-G7)

Between Christina Lake and Rossland the Trans Canada Trail has helped restore portions of this historic pack trail. The 43 km (26.2 miles) trail takes you over two summits and through some challenging terrain. For this reason, mountain bikers are well advised to climb the Old Cascade Highway.

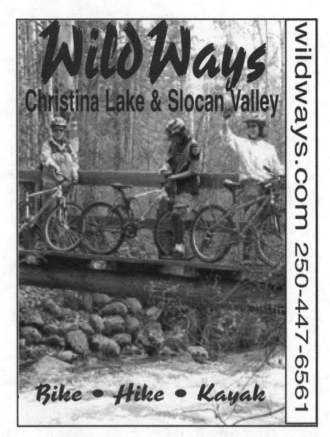

The **West Dewdney Trail** begins off of Santa Rosa Road near Christina Lake and follows a mix of trails and logging roads as it climbs past the Trout Creek Recreation Site and the Santa Rosa Summit to the Santa Rosa Recreation Site. This section of the trail is about 26 km (15.9 miles) long.

The **East Dewdney Trail** is 17 km (10.4 miles) long and offers it share of great views as it drops down to Highway 22 south of Rossland. In fact, the steep section between the Old Cascade Highway and Highway 22 loses 905 m (2,970 ft) in elevation. The combination of forested trail and logging roads requires paying close attention to the TCT signs. From the Cascade Summit at 1,070 m (3,510 ft) to the Santa Rosa Summit, the recent improvements to the gasline has played havoc with the original trail and it may be easier to take advantage of their right of way.

Dirk Diggler/Twinkle Toes (Map 2/B3)

These two trails are showcases for Castlegar area downhill mountain bikers. Both trails feature long, steep descents, with a bunch of stunts and drops just to keep things interesting. Both these rides should be left to the experts. There is a 675 m (2200 ft) vertical drop from start to finish. The trails are accessed from the Merry Creek FSR.

Doukhobor Draw (Map 1/G7)

Accessed off the end of Southbelt Road in Rossland, this 4.5 km (2.7 mile) trail descends to the old railgrade above Hwy 22. Mountain bikers should expect a fun 300 m (985 ft) descent with some tricky sections. The route is difficult and best left to advanced riders.

Doukhobor Waterline Trail (Map 2/C2)

This new trail follows an old heritage trail along McPhee Creek. The route leads to a water intake, which used to bring water to the Doukhobor Community at Ootischenia. The trail follows 4 km (2.4 mile) of wooden piping and is accessed off the Skattebo Reach Trail. The last section up to the intake is very steep. It's 3.5 km (2.1 miles) to the top from the junction with Skattebo Reach Trail, which in turn is 3 km from the trailhead. It is also possible to follow the short but steep McPhee Canyon Trail, which climbs 150 m (488 ft) over 0.75 km, to create a loop. This trail passes by the McPhee Creek Canyon, offering occasional glimpses of the frothing water below.

Dove Hill Trail (Map 2/C3)

From the road to the Castlegar Golf Club, a narrow dirt road signed "Dove Trail" leads to the parking area. From the parking area, the trail switchbacks gently up the hill soon breaking out onto the dry hillside where you will find three lookouts: Dove Hill, Surrey Hill and the Golf Course Panorama. The trail has been extended down the backside of Dove Hill to a new parking lot and trailhead near the Brilliant Substation, a distance of 2.8 km (1.7 miles) one-way gaining 180 m (590 ft) along the way. There is also a new spur trail, the Elk Cutoff Trail, a very good option to return to the original trailhead via a different route.

Dunn Creek Trail (Map 25/F5)

This is a remote 12 km (7.3 mile) 5 hour unmaintained trail to Four Squatters Icefield. Along the way, there is a deteriorating cabin available to use as a base camp but experienced mountaineers should only explore the icefield. The trail is accessed off the good 2wd Duncan Road.

Eagle Creek Trail (Map 9/D2-A2)

A 40 km (24.4 mile) day + horse trail leads up the Eagle Creek Valley. You eventually access the height of land in the remote Granby Provincial Park where experienced route finders can follow the ridges north and south to access any of the several mountains in the area.

Earl Grey Pass Trail (Maps 18/F2-19/E1)

This historic trail begins north of Argenta at the head of Kootenay Lake. The trail begins easy enough as you climb through the West Purcell Wilderness Conservancy Park towards the pass. Eventually, the route becomes rough and hard to follow as you climb towards the pass. Those that make it through can reach the remains of the Earl Grey Cabin and the abandoned Mineral King Mine off Toby Creek Road west of Invermere. Most settle for a day or overnight hike in the Hamill Creek drainage.

Fairview Loop (Map 2/B3)

This 18 km (11 mile) bike loop is located in Fairview, which is a few kilometres south of Castlegar on Highway 22. Take the road to Fairview and then Jesse Road to the right. Where you see the sign "Hair It Is", start hiking/biking the old road to reach the technical single-track trails.

Ferguson Creek Trail (Maps 24/G2-25/A1)

An old horse trail once took travellers on a 30 km (18.3 mile) day + route from the headwaters of Ferguson Creek over the divide into the Westfall River Valley. Unfortunately, the trail has fallen into disuse and is difficult to locate and follow. On the Trout Lake side, the crossing of Mountain Goat Creek is a serious obstacle except in the fall. The trail around Marsh Adams Creek on the Westfall River end is overgrown.

Fishermaiden Lake/Billy Valentine Trail (Map 11/B1)

An easy 4 km (2.4 mile) 1.5 hour hike access Fishermaiden Lake. It is recommended to bring a fishing rod to test the lake. Hikers with good route finding skills can continue onto Natenek Lake. Also in the area is the Billy Valentine Trail, which extends southeast from the north end of Fishermaiden Lake. The moderate trail accesses the sub-alpine terrain and peaks along Wilfred Ridge in Kokanee Glacier Park.

Fletcher Lake Trail (Map 11/E2)

The difficult to locate trailhead and the prime grizzly bear habitat may discourage some visitors from visiting this picturesque mountain lake. The trail is found at the end of a spur road to the right about 7.3 km (4.5 miles) on the Fletcher Lake Road. From there, it is a 3 km (1.8 mile) steep hike to the lower lake. The first part of the 2 hour trail is tricky because of the numerous roots and ledges. The last part requires you to walk along the steep walled creek draw where the trail is continuously washed away by mudslides. Once at the lower lake, try some fishing or bushwhack to the upper lake.

Fry Creek Trail (Maps 18/G5-19/C5)

An old mining trail follows Fry Creek to the remote mountainous area above Kootenay Lake. The distance of the hike depends on how long you want to hike but can be up to 24 km (14.6 miles) 8 hours one-way gaining 240 m (785 ft). Although well used, the forested trail is narrow in places and offers good views.

Galena Trail (Maps 17/G6-18/A6)

This popular hiking, biking and cross-country skiing trail follows the abandoned 1894 CPR railgrade around New Denver. The well signed route offers an easy 1.5 hour one-way walk from New Denver north to Rosebery Park or a 6 km (3.7 mile) 2 hour one-way walk east to Three Forks. The route to Three Forks is easily found off Denver Siding Road off Highway 31A and passes by the old townsite of Alamo and an old mining concentrator.

Giveout Creek Trails (Maps 2, 3, 10, 11)

The road systems found south of Nelson offer fine off-road biking and snowmobiling. Most visitors start from the Giveout Creek Road.

The Cottonwood Route starts along the Giveout Creek FSR (Map 10/A7) and climbs up the Giveout Creek Valley to the foot of Todd Mountain (Map 2/G1). Make your way over the pass to the east, which will bring you into the Cottonwood Creek drainage. From here, there are a number of options to choose from that will take you back to the Giveout Creek FSR or Hwy 6.

The Kenville Mine Route is another intermediate ride that follows main roads and offers spectacular views of the Valhalla Mountains, Nelson, and the Kokanee Glacier. The route ascends the Giveout Creek FSR, and then follows the Kenville Mine Road (Map 10/G7), returning to Nelson via Blewett Road. The total distance is 42 km (25.6 miles), gaining 850 m (2,790 ft).

The King of the Mountain Trail is a bike route that intersects both Giveout Creek FSR and Gold Creek FSR (Map 3/A1) making a figure 8. The trail covers about 8 km (4.8 miles) with an elevation gain of 300 m (985 ft).

The Silver-Stanley Loop is perhaps the easiest route in the Giveout Creek Road area. Locate Vancouver Street, in Nelson (Map 11/A7), which turns into Silverking Road. Bike to the end of the road, and follow the gravel road. An immediate left and you are climbing up the generally smooth (though there are some rocky sections and creek crossings) single-track trail. The trail ends on the Giveout Creek Road. If that is enough for you, head left to Hwy 6. If you still want to do some more riding, turn right and climb up to the gravel pit, which is on the left of the road. A trail taking off to the left from the logging road brings you downhill to an old railgrade. Head right, and, after the second trestle a trail descends to the left. Follow this back to Stanley Street. Total distance for this route is about 14 km (8.5 miles).

Gladstone Provincial Park (Map 1)

This park encompasses most of Christina Lake and the pristine forests to the north of the lake. There are a number of well-developed trails in the park that will allow you to explore the park. Access from the west is better shown in the Backroad Mapbook for the Kamloops/Okanagan region.

Deer Point Trail (Map 1/A5)

From the Texas Creek Campground, this 16 km (9.8 mile) 5 hour return hike takes you along the eastern shores of Christina Lake. The trail is initially steep and then involves traversing over rolling terrain along an old roadbed, which was partly completed in the early 1900s. Many great vistas of Christina Lake are found along this moderate trail. Popular destinations include the campsites at Deer Point (6 km one-way) and Troy Creek. It is possible to connect with the Sadner Creek Trail at the north end of the lake but you will have to obtain permission in order to cross private property. Bikers should expect an up-n-down single-track ride with lots of roots, narrow corners and obstacles.

Mount Faith Trail (Map 1/A2)

This trail begins at the end of Lynch Creek FSR (4wd required), which is west of our maps. The very well maintained horse trail leads 36 km (22 miles) return to the top of Mount Faith within Gladstone Provincial Park. Guide outfitters looking to access the rich Mule Deer hunting grounds below the mountain use the trail extensively. Hikers will need two days, since the trail is moderately steep and is fairly difficult to hike. Horseback riders can do the trail in a day and will find it fairly easy to ride.

Sandner Creek Trail (Map 1/A4)

Give yourself the better part of a day (or two) to explore the old homestead and unique geological formations that are accessed by this trail that follows Sander Creek. It begins at the north end of Christina Lake and extends some 18 km (11 miles) return. Please respect private property at the north end of the lake.

Xenia–Christina Lake Trail (Map 1/A4)

This trail begins at the end of the Miller Creek FSR (2wd access), which is west of our maps. It extends 6 km (3.7 miles) one-way over the summit from the Granby River Valley to Christina Lake. The trail is steep and difficult so it is not a good choice for a family outing. The hike should take less than three hours.

Great Northern Mountain Trail (Map 25/E3) 🚶 ⛷ 🧗

It is possible to hike to the top of this peak found north of Trout Lake. Although a road takes you close to the summit, it is better to park further down and hike up. There are also a series of old roads found in the alpine between Great Northern Mountain and Mount Thompson to explore. This is a popular backcountry skiing area with most of the activity happening during the winter.

Hall Creek Trail (Map 25/C3) ▲ 🚶 🧗

A few years ago, the North Kootenay Lake Trail Society tried brushing out the lower section of this 20 km (12.2 mile) mining trail. They never finished, although they still have plans to complete the trail. For now, the remote trail that once connected Healy Creek Road with the Duncan Road by climbing over an alpine pass is impassible.

Hamilton Creek Trail (Map 30/F4) 🚶 🧗

This is a 4 km (2.4 mile) 2 hour hike leading into Revelstoke National Park. If you plan to explore the park from here, it requires some bushwhacking on an unmaintained trail.

Heather Lake Trail (Map 3/D7) 🚶 🐟 🧗

This 1.5 hour easy hike climbs 2 km (1.2 miles) to a small sub-alpine lake in an alpine basin. Fishing opportunities exist at the lake.

Hiren Creek Trail (Map 30/A3) ▲ 🚶 🐎 🏍 🚵 🛷 🐟 🧗

It is a 20 km (12.2 mile) 6–7 hour hike along an abandoned mining road that accesses sub-alpine terrain and several mountain lakes. Once you reach the old mine site, you can scout the old workings or try your luck fishing at

Hiren Lakes, which can be accessed by climbing to the pass at the 2,300 m (7,545 ft) elevation level. The trail is shared with mountain bikers and horseback riders and requires an elevation gain of 525 m (1,720 ft).

Huckleberry Pass Route (Map 3/B2) 🚶 🚵 🛷 🧗

An old mining road-cum trail follows Clearwater Creek through Huckleberry Pass then down Huckleberry Creek and onto Wildhorse Road. This route is popular with mountain bikers and backcountry skiers (there are avalanche hazards). The system is best accessed from the Clearwater Road side since the Huckleberry side is littered with fallen debris and logging activity. This makes finding the way down from the pass rather difficult. Also in the Clearwater Creek Road area is a cross-country ski network that offers a nice area for all levels of hikers and mountain bikers to explore in the summer.

Hufty Mountain Lookout Trail (Map 17/B1) 🚶 🚵 🛷 🧗

From the 4wd Hufty Mountain Lookout Road, it is a 3 km (1.8 mile) one-way hike along an old road to the lookout. Although considered moderate, the hike is a steady 1.5 hour uphill grind with few breaks along the way. A great view of Nakusp and area makes the climb worthwhile.

Idaho Peak Trail (Map 18/A7) 🚶 🧗

The brilliant wildflower display throughout July and August and great view of the Slocan Valley makes this trail a popular area attraction. Accessing the trailhead is half the fun as it is a 12 km (7.3 mile) drive on the steep and narrow Idaho Peak Road from Sandon to the parking lot. The actual trail is only 2.8 km (1.7 miles) long and should take about an hour to wind through the open alpine slopes covered with wildflowers. The scenic trail culminates at a lookout at 2,280 m (7,480 ft) and is best hiked from early July to October when there is little or no snow.

Jackson Basin Trail (Map 18/C6) 🚶 🧗

This 6 km (3.7 mile) 3 hour easy route begins along an old logging road before scrambling up the ridge. The trailhead is located off Highway 31A between Bear and Fish Lakes. The elevation gain is 500 m (1,625 ft) and a good view of Kokanee Glacier is offered along the way.

Joss Mountain Trails (Map 23/A1, 30/A7) 🚶 🧗 🛷

There is an old lookout on top Joss Mountain that few people visit, as the climb to the top of the 2,385 m (7,750 ft) mountain is difficult, no matter how

you decide to travel. Area trail riders have recently discovered this route, but it's doubtful that ATVs could make it up the narrow trail. The views from the top are spectacular, and the stone lookout, despite having been built in 1921 (and closed in 1930), is still in remarkably good shape.

K & S Railway Trail (Map 18/A6) 🚶 🐎 🚴 ⛷ 🏕

The K & S (Kaslo & Sandon) Railway is a historic trail through a once bustling silver valley. Today, the railgrade is in various stages of disrepair. The best way to explore the old mining sites is to start in Sandon and proceed in a northwest direction along the abandoned railgrade. The walk/bike brings you past Altoona Mine to Cody Junction where the K & S Railway meets with the abandoned railgrade to Cody. From there, the K & S Railgrade continues towards Three Forks past the Payne Concentrator, the Payne Siding and finally the Payne Bluffs. After the Bluffs, the railgrade becomes rather difficult to follow before reaching Three Forks. Overall, the 3 hour historical route is 9.2 km (5.6 miles) one-way and gains 275 m (900 ft). It is possible to join up with the Galena Trail, which takes you down to New Denver.

Kaslo River Trailway (Map 18/E7) 🚶 🐎 🚴 ⛷ 🏍

This multi-use trail system is found parallel to Highway 31A just north of the river. The 18 km (11 mile) one-way trail is an ideal family biking or horseback riding trail. Active roads interrupt sections so pay attention to the signs.

Kaslo Walking Trails (Map 11/F1) 🚶 🐎 🚴 ⛷ 🏕

Kaslo is a quaint heritage community next to Kootenay Lake. There are two short walking trails in town that visitors can explore. The **Wardner Trail** begins from the signed trailhead off of Wardner Street. The trail switchbacks up a small hill overlooking Kaslo and the Kootenay Lake. Overall, the 20 minute trail is about 0.75 km long (0.45 miles). The **River Walk Trail** is found off of 5th Street next to the Kaslo River. The trail leads upstream for one kilometre and takes about half an hour to walk to its end and back.

Kate Lake Trail (Map 23/A6) ⛺ 🚶 🐎 🚴 ⛷ 🏍 🐟

Kate Lake is a pretty destination found tucked in the Monashee Mountains. The access to the trailhead is along a 4wd road and many people walk (or bike) the extra 5.5 km to the trailhead. From the trailhead, it is a steep 2.5 km (1.5 mile) one-way hike through boggy sections to the picturesque lake.

Kelly-Burke Creek Trail (Map 36/D7) ⛺ 🚶 🏕

This is a 16 km (9.8 mile) difficult hike along a trail that is overgrown and difficult to follow. The trail begins about 4.5 km (2.7 miles) along the Carnes Creek Trail and accesses Rosebury Mountain. This 2,456 m (8,057 ft) remote peak offers a fine vantage point.

Keystone-Standard Basin Trail (Map 36/C6) 🚶 🚴 ⛷ ⛏ 🏕

From the 15 km mark on the logging road, a large sign marks the start of the trail. Luckily, most of the elevation gain is done on the drive up to the trailhead. Most visitors take two days to cover the 36 km (22 mile) return trip to Standard Peak. The trail leads through Grizzly bear country and a spectacular mix of alpine forests, ridges and small mountain lakes. A good

start to the hike is to travel 11 km (6.7 miles) one-way to the Standard Cabin and stay the night.

Kimbol Lake Trail (Map 17/D2) ⛺ 🚶 🐟

From the Nakusp Hot Springs, this 5 km (3 mile) 2 hour one-way hike requires a 600 m (1,970 ft) climb to a beautiful mountain lake. At the south end of the lake, you will find an old cabin as well as some rustic camping spots. The actual trailhead starts at the Old Pool, which is one kilometre from the hot springs resort. The trail leads through a cedar/hemlock forest and has many creek crossings and wet areas that are not suitable for mountain biking.

Kinnaird Bluffs Trail System (Map 2/B3) 🚶 🚴 🏕

On the south facing bluffs above Castlegar is a series of trails, which are ideal for spring and fall but are generally too hot and dry for hiking during hot summer days. The trail system is reached off of 37th Avenue, which, in turn, leads from Columbia Avenue. There are a total of eight different trails on the bluffs ranging in length from a few hundred metres to several kilometres in length. There are several nice viewpoints on the bluffs overlooking the Columbia River. Also in the area is a popular bike trail that follows a dirt road behind Kinnard Middle School to the United Buy and Sell south of Castlegar. The **Kinnaird Pipeline Trail** is a flat, easy 6 km (3.7 mile) ride that should take most riders about an hour.

Kokanee Glacier Provincial Park (Map 11/A1-E4)
⛺ 🚶 ⛷ ⛏ 🐟 🏕

Found in the heart of the West Kootenays, Kokanee Glacier Park is a world renowned hiking and backcountry skiing destination. There are over 85 km (52.7 miles) of trails, excellent fishing lakes, old mining works, mountain peaks and several glaciers to explore. Of the three cabins, Slocan Chief is by far the most popular. It sleeps 12 campers on a first come first serve basis in hiking season but must be reserved (by lottery in mid-October) for winter use. Contact the park service for more information. Designated wilderness campsites (tent pads and bear proof food cache provided) are found at the cabins and many of the lakes. The hiking season runs from July to October while backcountry skiing is popular in the winter.

Blue Grouse Basin Trail (Map 11/A2)

From the park boundary on the Enterprise Creek Road, it is a 6.4 km (3.9 mile) 4 hour one-way hike along Paupo Creek to the basin. The elevation gain is 790 m (2,590 ft) as you pass through some avalanche chutes as well as some alpine meadows with spectacular wildflowers in season.

Enterprise Creek Trail (Map 11/B2)

This 9 km (5.5 mile) 4.5 hour one-way trail leads past both Tanal and Kaslo Lakes before reaching the Slocan Chief Cabin, which was built in 1886. The elevation gain of the moderate hike is 652 m (2,140 ft) from the trailhead at 1,340 m. Both Tanal and Kaslo Lakes offer good cutthroat fishing and designated camping areas.

Gibson Lake Loop (Map 11/C3)

From the end of Kokanee Glacier Road, a trail circles Gibson Lake for an easy 5 km (3 mile) 2 hour hike. In addition to nice views of the surrounding peaks and wildflowers in season, there are some old mine workings to explore. Anglers will find good fishing at Gibson Lake. At the trailhead, which is located at 1,536 m (5,040 ft) in elevation, there are picnic tables, an outhouse and a day-use shelter.

Gibson Lake to Slocan Chief Cabin (Map 11/B3)

From Gibson Lake, it is a 7.5 km (4.6 mile) 4.5 hour one-way trip gaining 490 m (1,610 ft) to the Slocan Chief Cabin. The trail traverses Kokanee Pass before passing by Kokanee and Kaslo Lakes.

Joker Millsite to Joker Lakes (Map 11/C3)

The trail leading to Joker Lakes starts at Joker Millsite and covers 5 km (3 miles) one-way and should take about 2.5 hours to hike. You will gain 450 m (1,475 ft) on the way to the unique lakes. One of the lakes is a clouded turquoise colour, while the other lake is crystal clear.

Joker Millsite to Slocan Chief Cabin (Map 11/B3)

It is a 5 km (3 mile) 3 hour one-way moderate hike to the cabin from the mill gaining 540 m (1,770 ft). The area is closed from mid-August to September because of the possibility of a bear encounter. You may wish to stop at Helen Deane Lake to try the good fishing.

Lemon Creek Trail (Map 11/A3)

From the park boundary at Lemon Creek, it is a difficult hike to Sapphire Lakes along a 9.8 km (6 mile) 5 hour one-way trail gaining 950 m (3,115 ft). The hike follows an old mining trail through old-growth forest, past several waterfalls and past an old mining cabin. The trail is poorly maintained and difficult to follow in places. From Sapphire Lakes, the trail continues over Lemon Pass and past Kaslo Lake before reaching the cabin after an additional 4.5 km (2.75 miles) 2.5 hours. The latter part of the trail involves a 320 m (1,040 ft) elevation drop.

Nilsik Creek Trail (Map 11/A3)

This is a 14 km (8.5 mile) 8 hour difficult hike that begins along the Lemon Creek Trail before traversing up Nilsik Creek to Outlook Mountain. The elevation gain is 1,100 m (3,575 ft) to the 2,585 m (8,480 ft) peak.

Silver Spray Cabin Trail (Map 11/D2)

From the end of the Woodbury Creek Road, this 8 km (4.9 mile) one-way difficult hike takes about 5 hours to access the cabin, which is found in Clover Basin. The scenic hike crosses Woodbury Creek, takes you past remnants of gold mining from the turn of the century and offers wildflowers in season. Expect to climb a grueling 1,015 m (3,330 ft) to the cabin, which sleeps eight on a first come, first serve basis. A tenting area is available at the cabin as well.

Sunset Lakes Trail (Map 11/D2)

This is one of the few easy trails in Kootenay Glacier Park. The 1.5 hour hike is 3 km (1.8 miles) one-way, initially following the deteriorating Stranton Mine Road. Towards the lake, you depart from the road and follow a worn trail to the lake. Overall, there is an elevation gain of 195 m (640 ft). Sunset Lake provides good fishing.

Wheeler Lake Trail (Map 11/E3)

An 8 km (4.9 mile) 3–4 hour hike climbs along Lendrum Creek to a good fishing lake. The trail is hard to find but is located off the Cedar Creek FSR.

Woodbury Cabin Trail (Map 11/D2)

This moderately difficult trail follows Woodbury Creek to the Woodbury Basin before descending to the cabin. It is a 9 km (5.5 mile) 4.5 hour one-way hike gaining 1,005 m (3,295 ft) to the pass, but only 762 m (2,477 ft) to the cabin itself. The cabin sleeps six on a first come, first serve basis. A tenting area is also available at the cabin.

Kootenay Joe Ridge Road (Maps 18/G5-19/A5)

Found south of Argenta, this road will keep you on the edge of your seat. For this reason many people prefer to hike, bike or ride an ATV up the scenic ridge and into the West Purcell Wilderness Conservancy Park. It is possible to link up with the Fry Creek Trail.

Kuskanax Hot Springs Trail (Map 17/B2)

Accessed from Alexander Road east of Nakusp, this is a 19 km (11.6 mile) 6 hour return hike, which leads through an old clear-cut and forested slope to the hot springs. It is possible to continue on to Kimbol Lake. The trail is well maintained and crosses the creek on many occasions.

Laforme Creek Trail (Map 30/E1)

Off Highway 23, this is a 22 km (13.4 mile) 6 hour moderate hike with an elevation gain of 400 m (1,300 ft). Remains of an old ghost town make for an interesting destination.

Lasca Creek Trail (Map 11/C6)

This trail is accessed by the Harrop Ferry or boat launched at Sandspit Provincial Park. From the shores of Kootenay Lake, it is a 35 km (21.4 mile) difficult hike to the headwaters of Lasca Creek. Allow two or three days to explore the extensive alpine area of the West Arm Park.

Leviathan Lake Trail (Map 18/G7)

Accessed by boat on Kootenay Lake, this 6 km (3.7 mile) 2–3 hour easy walk takes you along the Campbell Creek Road to the lake. The road continues up the creek draw for a few more kilometres.

Lockhart Creek Trail (Map 12/A7)

Beginning on the north side of the creek at the Lockhart Beach Provincial Park, the trail leads 15 km (9.2 miles) one-way into a pristine wilderness valley. The first 7 km (4.3 miles) of the trail are generally well maintained as it meanders alongside the creek through old growth timber. After the second bridge, the going gets tough, eventually climbing into the Purcell Mountains. You will reach a summit at 2,134 m (7,001 ft) where you get a great view of the Kootenay Lake Region. From the summit, you can access Baker Lake on the Baker Lake Trail. As one of the fleet-footed authors can attest, be careful of Grizzly bears in the area.

London Ridge Trail (Map 18/B6)

The London Ridge Trail is a 16 km (9.8 mile) 7 hour moderate hike gaining up to 1,180 m (3,870 ft) along a steep old mining road. The route is very popular with backcountry skiers as it offers a great view of the surrounding mountains. The trailhead is easily located off Highway 31 at Fish Lake.

Lyle Creek Trail (Map 18/D6)

A 9.6 km (5.9 mile) 6 hour moderate hike follows a narrow steep trail that climbs 944 m (3,095 ft) to a tiny mountain lake. You can continue on to old mining claims as well as Mount Brennan. The area is popular with backcountry skiers. The trailhead is located off the Lyle Road, which passes through private property.

MacBeth Icefield Trail (Maps 18/G1-26A7)

Access into this remote icefield involves climbing 640 m (2,100 ft) from the end of the spur road off the Glacier Road. Allow 6 hours to cover the moderate 12 km (7.3 mile) return trail that takes you through the valley bottom before a steep climb to the foot of the icefield. The bridge over Dunsinane Creek is often out.

Mark Berger Traverse (Map 16/C2)

A difficult 20 km (12.2 mile) route, the Mark Berger Traverse is mostly unmarked and leads along a series of alpine peaks and narrow ridges. The trail connects the Twin Lakes and Monashee Mountain Trails and features panoramic views. Be careful, this is Grizzly bear country.

Marten Creek/Dolly-Varden Trail (Map 18/A5)

From the Kane Creek Road, this moderate 14 km (8.5 mile) 6 hour hike follows a well developed trail along Kane and Martens Creek to the foot of Mount Dolly Varden. From there, mountaineering opportunities exist.

Martha Creek Trail (Map 30/E2)

Just north of the Martha Provincial Park on Highway 23, a 14 km (8.5 mile) 5 hour trail begins. The well marked but difficult trail climbs over 1,100 m (3,575 ft) in elevation on the slopes above Lake Revelstoke.

McRae Lake Trail (Maps 23/G1, 30/G7) 🚶 🥾

This is a 5 km (3 mile) 2.5 hour hike into a sub-alpine lake surrounded by alpine meadows. This remote trail is found south of Revelstoke off the Akolkolex-Dumont Road.

Meadow Mountain Trail (Map 18/D2) 🚶 🐎 🥾

Allow 4 hours to cover the 10 km (6.1 mile) trail along an old, forested road that cuts through open meadows. The attraction is the great view of the Purcell Mountain Range. The gentle trail climbs 200 m (650 ft) and provides access into the Goat Range Provincial Park.

Mel DeAnna Trail (Map 2/C4) 🚶 🚲 📱 🥾

Off Highway 3 at the viewpoint southeast of Castlegar, this is a 5 km (3 mile) 1 hour easy loop on a well maintained nature trail. The trail circles Champion Ponds, a good waterfowl and wildlife viewing area, and accesses a popular mountain biking system. There are single-track trails with good technical sections to explore. Make sure you grab a copy of the interpretive guide at the Ministry of Forests in Castlegar before heading out.

Merry Creek Trails (Map 2/B3) 🚶 🚲 🛶 📱 🥾

Accessed via the Merry Creek FSR, these trails are set in the 100 hectare recreation reserve of the Merry Creek watershed. The trail network includes three interconnecting loops totaling 5.5 km (3.3 miles) in length and provides an easy stroll through the timber. Except the moderate climb up to the Columbia Viewpoint overlooking Castlegar and area, there is not much elevation gain. An interpretive guide is available at the Ministry of Forests in Castlegar.

Mill Lake (Harrop Creek) Trail (Map 11/D6) ▲ 🚶 🎣 🥾

Recent work has re-routed the old Harrop Creek Trail to provide access up to Mill Lake. The difficult 20 km+ (12.2 mile) day hike climbs into the wilderness area south of Mount Lasca.

Monashee Lake Trail (Map 16/C3) ▲ 🚶 📷 🎣 🥾

The trail to the beautiful glacier-fed Monashee Lake is one of the main access routes into the Pinnacles area. The Pinnacles are a spectacular destination with towering spires that provide lots of options for rock climbers. To the lake, the trail climbs 700 m (2,275 ft) over 4.5 km (2.7 miles) but it is possible to continue north on the Mark Berger Traverse.

Monashee Provincial Park Trails (Map 23/A6-D6)
▲ 🚶 🐎 🚲 🎣 🥾

This remote park offers 24 km (14.6 miles) of multi-use trails through a pristine wilderness area. From the parking lot north of Sugar Lake, the easy 4-5 hour **Rainbow Falls Trail** leads 12 km (7.2 miles) one-way to Spectrum Lake and the site of the first wilderness campsite. Many visitors use this campsite as a staging ground for day trips to the surrounding mountains and other lakes. There are a total of ten wilderness campsites as well as six overnight shelters in the park. Peters Lake, Mikes Lake and Fawn Lakes are other popular resting areas.

From Spectrum Lake, the trail system gets more difficult as you climb 4 km (3+ hours) to **Little Peters Lake** or 6 km to the south end of **Peters Lake**. There is an elevation gain of about 800 m (2,625 ft) to the bigger lake. From here there are several difficult alpine routes to explore. These trails traverse steep terrain, and should be left to the experienced backpacker only:

Fawn Lake is found west of Peters Lake and requires a moderate 300 m (985 ft) climb from the trail to Margie Lake. Allow 3-4 hours to cover the 5 km return route.

Margie Lake is found in the southeast portion of the park, about 8 km (4.9 miles) 2-3 hours return from Peters Lake. The gentle trail is one of the easier to follow in the area.

Mount Fosthall is the prominent peak to the south. To access the mountain requires a 1,000 m (3,281 ft) climb over 7-9 return km. Allow at least 6 hours since climbing gear is advantageous on this difficult route.

South Caribou Pass must be climbed on the first leg of the difficult route to Mount Fosthall. Due to the distance involved, most day hikers enjoy the views from the pass before returning to Peters Lake. The open ridges can easily be extended into a 9-11 km (8-10 hour) return route.

Valley of the Moon is another enticing area of Monashee. The trail into the valley climbs 600-700 m (2,000 ft) over 7-9 km return. Allow 6-7 hours to complete this moderate route.

Monica Meadows Trail (Map 26/B7) ▲ 🚶 🥾

The moderate trail to Monica Meadows is a 7 km (4.3 mile) 3 hour return trail accessing a beautiful alpine plateau. You climb over 550 m (1,805 ft) and are rewarded with great views. If you camp, please help protect the sensitive alpine meadows and camp below the plateau. The signed trailhead is accessed off the Glacier North Road.

Monte Christo Trail (Map 2/A6) 🚶 🚲 🥾

This local hiking/biking trail is found in upper Rossland at the junction of Plewman Way and Kirkup Ave, just east of Highway 3B. The 3 km (1.8 mile) 2 hour hike climbs the water station road to a marked trail. It is a popular teenage tobogganing route in the winter.

Mount Begbie Trail (Map 30/C6) 🚶 🐎 🚲 📷 🥾

Popular with both hikers and mountaineers, a 7 km (4.3 mile) steep hike leads up the southeast side of Mount Begbie to the sub-alpine. Beyond the main trail a route continues across a glacier to reach the summit at 2,732 m (8,965 ft). Once in the alpine, you can explore the tiny alpine lakes near the Monashee Divide. Mountain bikers and horseback riders can use the lower part of the trail.

Mount Cartier Trail (Map 30/E6) 🚶 🏔 🥾

Allow a couple days to the alpine area of Mount Cartier along the steep 32 km (19.5 mile) trail. There is a cabin below the summit, which can be used as a base camp to explore the surrounding alpine. The trailhead is located at 9.5 km (5.8 miles) on Airport Way.

Mount Loki Trail (Map 12/A1) 🚶 📷 🥾

A 6 km (3.7 mile) 3 hour moderate route leads to the foot of Mount Loki. This route is popular with mountaineers accessing the climbing routes on Mount Loki.

Mount MacPherson Demonstration Forest (Map 30/C5)
🚶 🐎 🚲 🛶 📱

This demonstration forest has several multi-use interpretive trail systems ideal for the explorer who wishes for an easy walk while learning about the ecology/forestry of the area. We have provided a sample of the 26 km (15.9 miles) of trails in the area. Brochures are available at the Ministry of Forests office in Revelstoke.

The Silviculture Trail is a 2.5 km (1.5 mile) 1 hour loop, which passes through several old and recent clearcuts.

The Beaver Lake Trail is an easy 3 km (1.8 mile) 1 hour walk around Beaver Lake.

The Biodiversity Trail is a 2.6 km (1.6 mile) 1 hour self-guided tour demonstrating both naturally regenerated and planted forests.

Mount Shields Trail (Map 1/E2)

Off Summs Road, an 8 km (4.8 mile) 4 hour moderate hike leads to the summit of Mount Shields at 1,789 m (5,869 ft). The view of the Lower Arrow Lakes is fabulous.

Mount Sophia Trail (Map 1/G7)

Beginning from the Rossland Summit on the Old Cascade Highway, a poorly marked trail leads 6.5 km (4 miles) to the summit. The route starts along an old logging road before entering a clearing where the actual trail begins. After climbing 250 m (820 ft), you will be rewarded with a panoramic view of the Sheep Creek Valleys.

Mountain Station Trails (Map 11/A7)

Starting at the old Great Northern/Burlington Northern Station in Nelson (Mountain Station), there is a series of six single-track mountain bike routes known for their steep vertical and technical challenge. Best left for expert riders, the trails range in length from 2.5 km to 6 km (1.5–3.7 miles), with vertical descents of up to 500 m (1,625 ft). The trail system connects the gravel pit above Nelson with Mount Station Road and is shared with hikers. Also in the area is the trail known as **Silverking**. This mountain bike route connects the old Burlington Northern Railway Line with Silverking Road. You will climb about 400 m (1,310 ft) over 14 km (8.5 miles).

Natural Arch Trail (Map 1/D1)

This impressive 20 m (65 ft) high, 44 m (144 ft) long natural archway requires a boat to access the trailhead. From the lake it is a 4.5 km (2.7 mile) 1.5 hour steep hike to the arch found 250 m (813 ft) above the Lower Arrow Lake.

Noble Five Mine Trail (Map 18/C7)

A historic route starting in the old town of Cody, this maintained trail switchbacks up behind the remains of the Noble Five Mine. This is a difficult route that leads past remnants of the old aerial tramline, cookhouses, and more. As with most trails around old mines, it can be dangerous in places. Please be careful. Also in the area is an unnamed route that extends from the end of the Cody Creek Road to the height of land and the alpine between Mount Cody and Mount Carlyle.

Nun Lake Trail (Map 3/E7)

Located off the Monk Creek Road, this 6 km (3.7 mile) 3 hour return hike leads to two small picturesque lakes. It is a steep trail leading into a beautiful alpine area.

Old Glory Trail (Map 1/G5)

From the parking spot on Highway 3B just south of Hanna Creek, this popular hike offers panoramic views from the highest peak in the Rossland Range. The summit is a breathtaking 2,376 m (7,795 ft) above sea level and requires climbing 974 m (3195 ft) over 19 km (11.6 miles) to the old fire lookout. There are actually two trails. The shorter Plewman Trail cuts through Plewman Basin, while the main trail follows Unnecessary Ridge. Allow a full day for this hike. Due to the snow, the best time to hike is late June to October.

Old Growth/ Cedar Loop Trail (Map 11/C4)

About 11.5 km along the Kokanee Glacier Road, a sign marks the beginning of this self-guided interpretive trail system. The **Old Growth Trail** leads on the east side of Kokanee Creek whereas the **Cedar Grove Loop** is found on the west side of the creek. Both trails offer easy walking through a 600-year-old cedar forest. The walks range from 1.3 km to 3 km (0.8–1.8 miles) in length. A brochure is available to explain the 17 illustrated signs mounted along the trail.

Paint Lake Trail (Map 23/E6)

An old mining road cuts around the south shoulder of Mount Symonds and leads to Paint Lake. Allow about an hour to climb 520 m (1,705 ft) to the lake at 2,440 m (7,930 ft). The lake gets its name from the minerals that have leeched into the lake from an iron ore deposit higher up the mountain. It is also possible to scramble up the mountain, where you are treated to a view of two glacier fed lakes far below. This area has had extensive mining exploration but still retains the beauty of high alpine, including wildflowers in season.

Panther Lake Trail (Map 3/C5)

This beautiful mountain lake offers good fishing, wilderness camping as well as access to the Three Sisters Peaks in the summer and early fall. The easy 4 km (2.4 mile) 1.5 hour hike follows an old mining trail where a 4wd vehicle is needed to access the trailhead.

Pass Creek Trails (Map 2/B2)

This mountain bike trail system starts at the top of Clarke Drive in Robson. Climb about 10 km (6 miles) on the gravel road to access the first of a series of trails and old roads offering great single-track riding and even better views. Including the Robson Loop, there are almost 30 km (18 miles) of trails to discover here.

Paulson Cross-Country Ski Trails (Map 1/E4)

This 45 km (27.5 mile) ski trail system also provides an excellent alpine mountain biking and motor biking area. Three access points are found on Highway 3B, including Nancy Green Lake Park. Hikers can enjoy the easy, forested loop trail around the lake.

Pebble Beach Trail (Map 11/G2)

This trail is located about 7 km (4.3 miles) north of Riondel on the Kootenay Lake Road (watch for the sign on your left). The trail leads sharply downhill to a pebble beach on Kootenay Lake after about a 45 minute walk. The trip back to the vehicle is a lot longer given the steep grade. The attraction to the beach is the nice picnic/camping spot together with swimming and fishing.

Pilot Bay Trails (Map 11/G5)

In and around Pilot Bay are a series of trails to explore. They are found south of Crawford Bay and offer an alternate access to Pilot Bay Marine Park and Kootenay Lake.

The **Boomers Landing and Upper Levels Trails** are 2.5 km (1.5 miles) one-way and descend 280 m (920 ft) to Kootenay Lake. The trails are found close to Crawford Bay and join up with trails to Pilot Bay. The **Height of Land Trail** also starts near Crawford Bay. It is a 5 km (3 mile) one-way ridge walk that offers excellent views of Kootenay Lake and Pilot Peninsula.

Pilot Bay Lighthouse Trail is a short 10–15 minute stroll along a well maintained trail starting from the sign at 4.5 km (2.7 miles) on the Pilot Bay Road. The walk takes you along the forested shores of Kootenay Lake to an old lighthouse that was built in 1907. From the lighthouse, you can continue along the shoreline or explore the other trails in the area.

Sawmill Bay Trail starts at the sign marking Pilot Bay Marine Park, about 3 km (1.8 miles) from the ferry on Pilot Bay Road. The trail climbs uphill for a few hundred metres before passing a viewpoint overlooking Pilot Bay. The easy trail then follows the forested shoreline, heading towards the tip of the peninsula and Cape Horn.

Pingston Lake Trail (Map 23/E3) 🥾 🐟 ⛺

Pingston Lake is a pretty mountain lake that is accessed by a 5 km (3 mile) 2 hour return hike. The easy trail is located off the Coursier Lake Road, which is part of a popular ATV and snowmobile area.

Pingston Valley/Mt Hall Area (Map 23/E2-G7) 🏍 🏍 🚴 ⛺

The Pingston Valley offers some of the most beautiful scenery for off-road riders in the Revelstoke area. There are miles and miles of active and deactivated logging roads within this area. One route not to miss is the road over the shoulder of Mt Hall that overlook a small valley stretched out before you. Rugged mountains, glaciers and waterfalls are other highlights in this area.

Pinnacles Lake Trail (Map 16/B3) ⛺ 🥾 📷 🐟 ⛺

The Pinnacles are a popular destination with those in the know; towering spires with lots of options for scrambling. The trail to beautiful Pinnacles Lake is one of the main access routes into the area, and is about 4.5 km (2.7 miles) one-way from the trailhead, gaining 450 m (1,463 ft) to the lake.

Placer Lake Trail (Map 3/E6) 🥾 🐟

The Placer Lake Trail is a 6 km (3.7 mile) 2–3 hour moderate hike to two small sub-alpine lakes in the Nelson Range of the Selkirk Mountains. The trailhead is located at the north end of the Placer Creek Road.

Plaid Lake Trail (Map 12/A3) 🥾 🐟 ⛺

The trailhead to the sub-alpine hike is reached by following the signs up the rough Spring Creek Road. It is 4.5 km (2.7 miles) 2 hours one-way to Plaid Lake, which is set approximately 400 m (1,300 ft) below the summit. If you are not there to enjoy the good fishing, then try scrambling up Razorback Ridge to the height of land where you will be rewarded with great views of Crawford Bay. Given its high elevation, the moderate hike is best left until late July to early October.

Rainbow Falls Trail (Map 23/B5) ⛺ 🥾 🐎 🚴 🐟 ⛺

See Monashee Provincial Park Trails.

Record Ridge Trail (Map 1/G7) 🥾 📷 ⛺

From the Cascade Summit on the Old Cascade Highway, it is a 6.5 km (4 mile) one-way hike gaining 175 m (471 ft) to the ridge. From there, you can climb the 2,039 m (6,690 ft) Record Mountain or continue to Squaw Basin of the Red Mountain Ski Hill or even Old Glory. Allow 6–8 hours for the hike to Squaw Basin. The scenic ridge makes for a great backcountry ski route starting from the top of the Granite Mountain Chairlift.

Retallack Cedars Trail (Map 18/C6) 🥾 📖

Found just south of Highway 31A, near the historic Retallack Railway Station, this short easy trail provides a nice chance to stretch your legs. The 1.5 km (0.9 mile) interpretive trail cuts through a lovely cedar grove. The hollow trees are used by bears as dens for the winter.

Ripple Ridge Trail (Map 3/C7) 🥾 📷 🏕 ⛺

Found just south of Stagleap Park, this 4 km (2.4 mile) trail climbs the scenic Ripple Ridge. It is a popular backcountry ski route complete with a cabin.

Riverside Trails/Zuckerburg Island Trails (Map 2/B3) 🥾 🚴 ⛺

A self-guided trail circles the tiny Zuckerburg Island in Castlegar. For a longer hike, continue in a westward direction along the riverbank to the ballpark on the Riverside Trail. This walk will take about an hour to complete. To reach the parking lot off of 7th Avenue, follow Highway 22 to the Pioneer Area (9th Street).

Rockslide Lake Trail (Map 10/E6) 🥾 🐟 ⛺

Off the rough Pedro Creek Road, this 2 km (1.2 mile) 1.5 hour easy trail leads to a small mountain lake. Fishing is popular at the scenic lake.

Ross Lake Trail (Map 11/D5) ⛺ 🥾 🐟

A 4 km (2.4 mile) 1.5 hour easy hike leads to Ross Lake, set below Mount Yuill. Fishing and rustic camping are popular pastimes at the lake. The trailhead is located at the 11.5 km mark on the Redfish Creek Road.

Rossland-Trail Railgrade Trail (Map 2/A7) 🥾 🐎 🚴 📷

Part of the Trans Canada Trail, this historic railgrade was used to haul gold from the mines in Rossland to Trail. Today, the popular multi-use trail is found in a semi-wilderness area linking the City of Rossland with the Village of Warfield. The 9.6 km (5.9 mile) 1.5 hour one-way route gently climbs 300 m (985 ft) along Trail Creek. The trailheads are found behind the community hall in Warfield and off Union Avenue in Rossland. The Railgrade Trail provides access to many other mountain bike trails in the area, including the Rubberhead Loop. These Rubberheads were created to allow the trains to switchback down the hillside.

Rossland-Trail Old Wagon Road Trail (Map 2/A7) 🥾 🐎 🚴

From Esling Drive in Rossland, the old wagon road to Trail is found. It now makes an excellent multi-use trail leading past the Rossland Gold Course, through the open fields above Trail Creek to join up with the Railgrade Trail (see above) outside of Warfield. It is an easy downhill walk best done outside the heat of the afternoon.

Rottacker Lake (Maps 23/B7-16/B1) ⛺ 🥾 🐟

It is only 3 km to Rottacker Lake from the trailhead, but the trail can be overgrown. There is a forest service site at the lake.

Saddle Mountain Lookout Trail (Map 17/A4) 🥾 ⛺

From the 8 km mark on the Saddle Mountain Road, it is a 4.5 km (2.7 mile) 2–3 hour one-way trail up the forested slopes below Saddle Mountain. You will eventually break out into the alpine meadows near the summit. The elevation gain of this moderate hike is 650 m (2,113 ft) to the lookout, which offers a fantastic view of the Upper Arrow Lake.

Sandon to Stenson Creek Route (Map 18/C7) 🏍 🚴 ⛺

Beyond Sandon are a series of roads that make fine ATV and biking routes. In particular, it is possible to climb the pass east of Rec Mountain and link up with the Stenson Creek Road. Another favourite to explore is the Cody Creek Road south to the shoulder of Mount Cody.

Selkirk Circuit Trails (Map 2/B3) 🥾 🚴 ⛺

On the bench above the Columbia River across from Castlegar, the hot, dry landscape of Selkirk College offers a series of trails. The best place to start is at the beginning of the road to the museum, which turns off College Road near the airport junction. A sign on the right hand side of the road marks the start of the trail system. From there, a trail leads northward along the riverbank and around the college, while providing views of the Columbia River as well as the Kootenay River. Eventually, the trail loops around the student plantation and back to College Road, about 2 km (1.2 mile) later.

Shannon Creek Trail (Map 17/E5) 🥾 🐟 ⛺

It used to be a real strenuous hike to this mountain lake with the reward of great cutthroat fishing. However, with the Shannon Creek FSR close by, it is now only 1.5 km (.9 mile) moderately steep hike along Shannon Creek to the lake. The scenic lake still makes a fine fishing destination.

Sitkum Lake Trail (Map 23/B7) ⛺ 🥾 🐟 ⛺

The road to the Sitkum Lake/Goat Mountain Trailhead is found 12 km (7.3 miles) along the Kate Creek Road. It is a difficult 8 km (4.9 mile) hike to Twin Peaks Lake passing by Sitkum Lake and Goat Mountain along the way. The trail is steep and rocky in places and traverses through Grizzly bear country.

Skattebo Reach Trail (Map 2/C2) 🥾 ⛺

The Skattebo Reach is part of the Kootenay River found above the Brilliant Dam. A semi-wilderness trail skirts the east side of the river from the Highway

3A bridge below the Brilliant Dam to Glade. The moderate trail does require crossing some rockslides. It is best to use a two vehicle shuttle system, leaving one at Glade (by crossing the ferry) and the other at the road to the Castlegar Golf Course. The golf course access to Brilliant Dam is an easier route. It is possible to create a loop with some of the other trails in the area. There is also a short (five minute) side trail to the Little McPhee Waterfall.

Silver Cup Trails (Maps 24/G3-25/A5)
Northeast of Trout Lake is a multi-use trail that stretches 20 km (12.2 miles) one-way through the alpine meadows of Silver Cup Ridge. The old mining trail provides fantastic views and is popular for mountain biking, horseback riding and wilderness camping. A 4wd vehicle is required to access the trail.

Smuggler's Loop/007 (Map 2/A7)
This 22 km (13.4 mile) difficult mountain bike loop is so named because it follows an old route used to smuggle whiskey from Canada into the US during prohibition. These days the ride, which circles Baldy Mountain, is a tough, hot climb along a steep, old road that switchbacks to the top. There are some tricky sections to cross before you connect with another old road that descends to Rossland. The loop is accessed off the end of Southbelt Road.

Sproat Mountain Lookout Trail (Map 24/A2)
It is a 16 km (9.8 mile) 5 hour steep climb on a forested trail which switchbacks up the face of the mountain to an old forestry lookout. The reward of the 590 m (1,918 ft) climb is the great view of Upper Arrow Lake from the lookout at 2,445 m (8,020 ft). The old road system in the area makes finding the trailhead quite tricky.

Sproule Creek Trail (Map 10/G6)
From the end of Sproule Creek Road (3.5 km/2.1 miles along the road), an easy 10 km (6.1 mile) 4 hour trail follows an old railgrade to a historic mill and beautiful meadow area. Expect a climb of 200 m (655 ft). It is possible to climb the surrounding ridges for extended touring.

St Leon Waterfall Trail (Map 24/A6)
Found on the north side of the Halfway River on Highway 23, an easy trail follows the north side of the creek to a cascading waterfall. The heavily forested trail makes for an ideal place for highway travellers to stretch their legs.

Sugar Mountain Trail (Map 23/A7)
An old 4wd road heads up to an abandoned fire lookout on Sugar Mountain. Depending on how far you drive up the Kate Creek Road, this can be a steep 14 km (8.5 mile) return route. The spectacular views from the top help compensate for the tough 900 m (2,925 ft) elevation gain. Beware of bears.

Syringa Creek Park Trails (Map 1/G2)
Within Syringa Provincial Park are three different trailheads, one at the boat launch, one at the campsite and one at the picnic area, accessing two nature trails. The **Yellow Pine Trail** is 2.6 km (1.6 miles) long while the **Syringa Trail** is 3.3 km (2 miles) long. You should allow a few hours to explore these interconnected trails that climb through the Ponderosa pine trees to a hot, dry bench above Lower Arrow Lake. Several viewpoints offer great views of the lake and there is a chance to view wildlife, including deer and grouse. Watch for poison ivy along the trails. Also in the park is a leisurely one kilometre self-guided interpretive trail along **Tulip Creek**. It should take about 25 minutes to walk from the bench above Lower Arrow Lake to a waterfall.

Tsuius Mountain Trail (Maps 23/A3-30/A7)
This is a difficult route, with three different trailheads—Tsuius Creek, Tourmaline Creek, and just east of Mirror Lake. The latter is the shortest and most popular, and it will take strong hikers about six hours to hike 12 km (7.4 miles) to the mountain and back. The trail gains 900 m (2,925 ft). Of course it is possible to extend the route north or south to enjoy the spectacular scenery and views of distant snowfields.

Twin Lakes Trail (Map 16/C2)
Twin Lakes are located at the north end of the Pinnacles and best accessed from the end of Severide Road, a deteriorating 4wd road. It should take about 1.5 hours for hikers to cover the 6 km (3.6 miles) to the lakes climb-

ing 500 m (1,625 feet). It is possible to continue south on the Mark Berger Traverse to the beautiful Monashee Lake.

Valhalla Provincial Park (Maps 10, 17)
Stretching from the western shore of Slocan Lake into the rugged alpine terrain of the Valhalla Range, this wilderness park has limited access. Most visitors hike or fly into one of the lakes to enjoy the fishing and rustic camping opportunities. The designated backcountry campsites offer bear proof food caches and outhouses.

Beatrice Lake Trail (Map 10/E1)
The trail along Beatrice Creek passes two lakes that offer good fishing and nice campsites. Tiny Emerald Lake is found after a 4 km (2.4 mile) 2.5 hour one-way hike. The trail gains 500 m (1,640 ft) mostly in the first 1.5 km (0.9 miles). Cahill Lake is another 2 km (1.2 miles) 1.5 hours further along. The trail climbs an additional 215 m (705 ft) as it follows the old White Road where you will see several old dams that were once used for logging flumes. The final part of the trail leads to Beatrice Lake gaining 215 m (705 ft), with the steepest portion of the trail being near Beatrice Lake. The hike is 2.5 km (1.5 miles) 1.5 hour one-way. Beyond Beatrice Lake, numerous mountaineering opportunities exist but remember this is prime Grizzly bear habitat.

Cove Creek Trail (Map 10/G1)
From the Cove Creek Cabin and beach on Slocan Lake, this 3.5 km (2.1 mile) 2 hour one-way hike gains 280 m (920 ft). It leads through a Ponderosa pine stand and a patch of rare coastal salal on an old logging skid trail.

Drinnon Pass/Gwillim Lakes Trail (Map 10/C2)
This trail rises sharply to Drinnon Lake climbing 435 m (1,425 ft) over 2 km (1.2 miles). Allow 1.5 hours to access the lake, which offers good fishing as well as a three site campground. From Drinnon Lake, the trail continues climbing an additional 125 m (410 ft) over 1.5 km (0.9 miles). At the pass, you can tent in the beautiful alpine meadows or continue onto Gwillim Lakes. The last section of trail gains an additional 120 m (395 ft) before losing 250 m (813 ft) on the way down to the lake. Another campsite and cooking centre is found at Gwillim Lakes.

Evans Creek Trail (Map 10/F3)
The trailhead for this popular hike is located in Slocan City just over the Slocan River Bridge. Walk across the bridge, turn right, and follow a narrow residential road for 200 m (650 ft) to the trailhead. The first 8 km (2.4 miles) of the trail is called the Evans Creek Trail. Allow 2.5 hours one-way to hike the relatively flat shoreline trail to the campsite at South Evans Beach. Once at the Evans Creek estuary, the trail follows Beatrice Creek in a northwest direction.

Nemo Creek Trail (Map 17/F7)
There are plenty of highlights on this trail including a 4 km (2.4 mile) one-way hike along the north side of Nemo Creek. After 200 m (650

ft), you pass by Nemo Falls. At 3.5 km (2.1 miles), you come across the Rock Castles and then at 4 km, you reach an old cabin. Another highlight of the 4 hour moderate trail is the old-growth cedar/hemlock forest. Be wary, this is Grizzly bear country.

Sharp Creek Trail (Map 17/G7)

The attraction to this steep trail is the New Denver Glacier. The 8 hour trail climbs 1,720 m (5,645 ft) over 8.8 km (5.4 miles) to the foot of the glacier. As you trek up the Sharp Creek Valley, you pass several waterfalls and cascades.

Wee Sandy Creek Trail (Map 17/F6)

From the mouth of Wee Sandy Creek on the shores of Slocan Lake, this 14.4 km (8.8 mile) one-way hike gains 1,370 m (4,495 ft) to Wee Sandy Lake. The initial part of the 10 hour difficult trail follows a historic logging trail and passes by two old trappers' cabins. Overnight accommodation is offered at 11.2 km (6.8 miles) where there is a good log shelter with stove. Wee Sandy Lake offers excellent fishing but no facilities. Mountaineering opportunities exist beyond the lake.

Vista Pass Trail (Map 16/C4)

The steep, difficult trail to Vista Pass climbs 700 m (2,275 ft) over 6 km (3.6 miles) one-way to the South Pinnacles Ridge. The trailhead is found near the end of the logging road that runs up Railroad Creek. The trail hooks up with the Barnes Creek Trail, creating a 14 km (8.5 mile) one-way hike through the beautiful pass. It is best to have a second vehicle waiting at the Barnes Creek Trailhead.

Wakefield Trail (Map 18/A7)

A 10 km (6.1 mile) 4–5 hour moderate hike leads from the Wakefield Mine to the parking lot at Idaho Peak. In addition to the old mine workings and good views, the trail is known to be snow free early in the year. The trail starts 4.6 km (2.8 miles) up the Silverton-Aylwin Road before climbing 805 m (2,640 ft) to the peak. Extreme cyclists often cruise down from the top so hikers should be wary.

Waldie Island Trail (Map 2/C2)

Developed in 1996, this trail follows the north shore of the Columbia River from the CPR bridge below the Brilliant Dam to the small community of Brilliant. The 1.5 km (1 mile) one-way walk is designed as a self-guided interpretive trail providing insight into the local economy and the Columbia River ecosystem. Along the route, there are 16 interpretative stops, a number of long boardwalk sections and chances to see a variety of birds. It is well advised to obtain a brochure from the Castlegar Travel Information Centre before heading out.

Waterfront Trail (Map 11/G3)

Taking you from the North Bay Beach Campground to the abandoned mine concentrator along the Riondel waterfront is a 1.5 km (0.9 mile) trail. Riondel was once a booming mining community that has turned into a quiet West Kootenay town.

Wensley Creek Cross-Country Ski Trails (Map 17/B2)

Located on Upper Brouse Road east of Nakusp, this 9.6 km (5.9 mile) ski trail system also offers easy hiking or biking from spring through fall. The forested trails are generally flat and follow old logging roads.

West Kokanee Creek Trail (Map 11/C5)

Located off the Kokanee Glacier Road is a short 2 km (1.2 mile) trail with interpretive signs. Allow about 45 minutes to walk the easy creek side trail.

Whitewater Creek Trail (Map 18/C5)

This is a 12.8 km (7.8 mile) 6 hour moderate hike to an old mine site and some small alpine lakes set below Whitewater Mountain. Mountaineers can base camp at the lakes and explore the Whitewater Glacier. To reach the lakes requires a strenuous climb of 914 m (3,000 ft) through prime Grizzly bear habitat. Be careful! The trailhead is located off the Lyle Road, which passes through private property.

Wilson Creek Falls and Trails (Maps 17/G4-18/A3)

This popular waterfalls trail is found off the East Wilson Creek Road at the 11.5 km (7 mile) mark. From the trailhead, it is a steep 3 km (1.8 mile) trail that actual descends 90 m (300 ft) to the cascading falls. The **Wilson Creek Trail** is found another kilometre up the East Wilson Creek Road off a narrow, rough 4wd road. From the signed trailhead, the easy, well developed trail climbs 120 m (400 ft) over 6 km (3.7 miles) one-way. The forested trail follows the creek as it dissects the Goat Range Provincial Park. This area is home to many large animals including caribou, elk, mountain goats and Grizzly bears.

Wragge Creek Trail (Map 17/E5)

Off the Wragge Creek Road, where the bridge has been removed, an old overgrown road leads to a mountain lake. Motorbikes and ATVs share the trail with fishermen hiking into the picturesque lake that holds plenty of small trout.

Wulf (Waldie) Lake Trail (Map 3/C6)

Locally known as Wulf Lake, the trailhead to this beautiful mountain lake requires a high clearance 4wd to access. At the end of the road, a marked but deteriorating trail climbs 4 km (2.4 miles) 1.5 hours return. Good fishing and rustic camping are offered at the scenic lake.

National Park Trails

The Kootenays are blessed with four national parks for visitors to explore. The easy access and spectacular scenery makes these parks a favourite place to hike, ski or bike. Be sure to pick up a park permit and let the park staff know where you are travelling before heading into the backcountry.

Glacier National Park Trails (Maps 31, 32, 37, 38)

Found in the Columbia Mountains east of Revelstoke, most of the recreational activity is centred around Rogers Pass. In this area, there are a variety of trails leading up to the many glaciers that frame the highway. Further into the park, steep mountains and dense rainforest impede travel. The hiking and backpacking season is also restricted by snow. For the lower elevation trails (600 to 1,300 m), you can hike between May and early November whereas the high elevation treks (over 1,900 m) are limited to late July to mid-September. Be aware that you are travelling in Grizzly bear country and some of the trails may be closed.

Abbott Ridge Trail (Map 31/F1)

Allow 7 to 8 hours to hike 10 km (6.1 miles) into the alpine from the Illecillewaet Campground gaining 1,040 m (3,380 ft) to 2,290 m (7,443 ft). There are opportunities to continue on the ridge after the trail ends. Those looking for a shorter, easier hike or ski may choose to stop at Marion Lake. It is a 4.4 km (2.7 mile) 2.5 hour hike to the barren (holds no fish) mountain lake. This section of trail gains 425 m (1,381 ft).

Asulkan Valley Trail (Map 31/F1)

From the Illecillewaet Campground, it is a 13 km (7.9 mile) 7 to 8 hour hike along the slowly rising trail through the Asulkan Valley bottom. The attraction is the mountain scenery, waterfalls, and glacier views. The elevation gain along the trail is 925 m (3,006 ft) to 2,175 m (7,069 ft). Backcountry skiers use the trail in the winter.

Avalanche Crest Trail (Maps 31/F1-37/G7)

From the Illecillewaet Campground, this hike covers 8.4 km (5.1 miles) over 5.5 hours offering excellent views of the surrounding mountains and valleys. The trail ends on Avalanche Crest, at 2,045 m (6,646 ft), after gaining 795 m (2,584 ft) in elevation.

Balu Pass Trail (Map 37/F7)

From the Rogers Pass parking lot, it is a 10 km (6.1 mile) 4 hour hike through several avalanche chutes into the alpine meadows of Balu Pass. The trail follows the valley bottom and then ascends sharply to the pass where glacier views and wildflowers in August reward the hikers. This is a popular backcountry ski area that provides access to Bruins Pass (there is no established trail). Beware of bears in the area!

Beaver Falls Trail (Map 37/G6)

It is a 2 km (1.8 mile) easy walk descending to the falls on Connaught Creek. Allow 40 minutes.

Beaver Valley Trail (Maps 37/G6-32/A4)

This 42 km (25.6 mile) one-way trail takes you to the southern park boundary. The 2 to 3 day hike travels through a valley bottom noted for its old growth forests before ascending to higher ground. The total elevation gain is 445 m (1,446 ft) so it s a gentle incline. From this trail, you can connect with Glacier Circle Trail or the Copperstrain Trail. Backcountry skiers use the trail in the winter.

Bostock Creek Trail (Maps 31/D1-37/B4)

Off the Trans Canada Highway, it is a 36 km (22 mile) day + moderate hike to Bostock Pass and down into the Casualty Creek drainage. The elevation gain is 732 m (2,379 ft) to the beautiful sub-alpine pass at 1,753 m (5,697 ft). With two cabins, this are makes a fine backcountry skiing destination.

Copperstain Trail (Maps 37/G6-38/A7)

This is a 32 km (19.5 mile) day+ difficult hike, which provides you with access to the endless alpine of Bald Mountain. Expect a steep uphill climb gaining 1,092 m (3,549 ft) to 2,050 m (6,663 ft). Access starts on the Beaver Valley Trail off the Trans Canada Highway.

Glacier Circle Trail (Maps 32/A2-31/G2)

From the Forkes Cabin along the Beaver Valley Trail, it is a 16 km (9.8 mile) 10 hour difficult hike gaining 600 m (1950 ft) to the Glacier Circle Cabin. The cabin is popular with both backcountry skiers and mountaineers who often explore further.

Great Glacier Trail (Map 31/F1)

This 9.6 km (5.9 mile) 5 to 6 hour hike starts on the Asulkan Valley Trail and offers great glacial views over the Illecillewaet Glacier as you follow a switchbacking trail. You will climb over 1,000 m (3,250 ft) to the 2,255 m (7,329 ft) summit of the crest where you are rewarded with a panoramic view of several glaciers.

Hemlock Grove Boardwalk (Map 31/D1)

From the picnic site next to the highway, this 400 m (1,300 ft) long boardwalk offers an easy walk through an old Western Hemlock forest. Some of the trees are over 350 years old.

Loop Brook Interpretive Trail (Map 31/E1)

This is a 1.6 km (1 mile) circuit through the forest and along an abandoned railroad. The 1 hour trail starts at the first highway viewpoint east of the Loop Brook Campground.

Sir Donald Trail/Perley Rock Trail (Map 31/G1)

From the Illecillewaet Campground, the **Sir Donald Trail** is a steep, rigorous 4.5 hour hike to the basin below Vaux Glacier. The gain in elevation is a thigh burning 895 m (2,909 ft) to 2,165 m (7,036 ft). From the base of the glacier, mountaineers can access the popular northwest ridge of Mount Sir Donald. Another alternative is to take the right branch of the Sir Donald Trail along the **Perley Rock Trail** to the summit of Perley Rock. Allow 6 hours to hike the 11.2 km (6.8 miles) from the campground to the rock, gaining 1,160 m (3,770 ft) in total.

Kootenay National Park Trails (Maps 27, 33, 34, 39)

Bisected by Highway 93, there are over 200 km (120 miles) of trails to explore in this park. This park offers a good variety of valley trails as well as some dynamic mountain trails leading into the alpine. Mountain biking is only allowed on the fire roads and if you plan to horseback, you must check with park staff before heading out. Backcountry skiing and snowshoeing is a fine alternative during the winter.

Cobb Lake Trail (Map 27/E3)

From the parking lot on Highway 93, the trail initially switchbacks downhill losing 150 m (488 ft) in elevation before crossing Swede Creek at about 1.5 km (0.9 miles). The 1.5 hour trail continues through a dense second growth forest and reaches the lake at 3 km (1.8 miles), gaining 50 m (163 ft) in elevation from the creek. The lake provides fairly good fishing and can be accessed from May-November.

Dog Lake Trail (Map 27/E1)

Beginning at the McLeod Meadows Campground, this easy 6.5 km (4 mile) 2 hour trail initially crosses the Kootenay River on a wooden suspension bridge. The trail is well maintained and has an elevation gain of 60 m (195 ft) before you reach the boggy shoreline of Dog Lake. If you do not want to return the way you came, take the lesser-used and wetter trail to the northwest of Dog Lake. This alternative leads to the East Kootenay Fire Road and back to the suspension bridge. The trail is open year round with the hiking season extending from April-October. The lake does hold fish.

Dolly Varden Trail (Maps 34/C7-27/C1)

From the warden station at Kootenay Crossing, it is an 8.8 km (5.4 mile) 3 hour one-way hike leading to the Crook's Meadows Group camping site. The trail follows an old fire road and gains 185 m (601 ft) in total but it is up and down terrain the entire distance. The lower elevation trail can be hiked or biked from April to October or skied in the winter. If you employ a two car shuttle system, you can avoid the long trek back to the wardens' stations.

East Kootenay Fire Road (Maps 27/C1, 34/C4)

This fire road was constructed in 1926 to service the east side of the Kootenay River Valley. To reach the northern access point, travel 5.3 km

(3.2 miles) south of the warden's station at Kootenay Crossing. From there, it is 29.5 km (18 miles) one-way trek to the south end of the road. There is little elevation gain along the way making the 4 to 5 hour hike a long but easy venture. The road is generally away from the river and passes through a second growth coniferous forest. You can shorten the route by crossing the footbridge near McLeod Meadows Campsite. This is a popular bike trail that can be skied or snowshoed in the winter.

Floe Lake Trail (Map 34/B4)

A footbridge leads across the Vermilion River and Floe Creek before the steady climb to the sub-alpine. Soon, the trail begins to switchback up Numa Mountain before traversing across several avalanche chutes along Floe Creek. The final 3 km (1.8 miles) involves a steep hike to the lake. It is all worth it as Floe Lake is set beneath a rugged rock wall covered by a cascading glacier. There is a warden cabin as well as three separate campsites at the lake. The 8 hour, 20 km (12.2 mile) return hike requires a 700 m (2,275 ft) climb to the lake at 2,500 m (8,125 ft). It is best taken in late June to September. Beyond the lake, it is possible to hike to Numa Pass and on to the Tumbling Creek Trail, which is another 9 km (5.5 miles) 6 hours to the Numa Creek Trail junction gaining 340 m (1,105 ft), through a vast alpine meadow. This hike involves walking through Numa Pass at 2,392 m (7,774 ft) about 1.5 km (0.9 miles) from Floe Lake and then dropping down into the Numa Creek Drainage.

Haffner Creek Trail (Map 34/B2)

From the Marble Canyon Campsite, this unmaintained but marked trail leads up the north side of Haffner Creek, approximately 1.5 km (0.9 miles) one-way. It is possible to extend beyond this point but you should expect to bushwhack and straddle windfalls as the trek is little more than a series of game trails.

Hawk Creek Trail (Map 34/C3)

This trail extends 9.5 km (5.8 miles) 3 to 4 hours one-way to Ball Pass gaining 900 m (2,925 ft) along the way. The trail begins on the north side of Hawk Creek, about 350 m (1,138 ft) north of the Floe Lake parking lot on Highway 93. A steep climb through the forest and over avalanche chutes and rockslides leads to the pass. The surrounding snow-capped mountain peaks and the beautiful alpine meadows with wildflowers makes the tough climb worthwhile.

Helmet Creek Trail (Maps 34/A1-33/G1)

From the Paint Pots parking area, this trail follows the Ochre Creek Trail for about 6.5 km (4 miles) before branching left. The trail up Helmet Creek crosses Ochre Creek on a suspension bridge and then switchbacks uphill before reaching the Helmet Creek Valley and a view of a spectacular 365 m (1,186 ft) high waterfall. Overall, it is a 15 km (9.1 mile) 6 hour one-way trip to Helmet Falls, gaining 750 m (2,438 ft) along the way. Due to the elevation, the hike is best done in late June to early October. Hikers wishing to continue past Helmet Falls can hike to Goodsir Pass, an additional 3.5 km (2.1 miles) 2 hours one-way gaining 450 m (1,463 ft) or Rockwall Pass, an additional 4 km (2.4 miles) 2 hours one-way.

Honeymoon Pass/Verdant Creek Trail (Map 34/D4)

Beginning at Vermilion Crossing on Highway 93, a difficult, unmaintained trail system leads up to Honeymoon Pass and Banff National Park. The pass, at 2,000 m (6,500 ft) in elevation, requires following a 2.5 hour 5.5 km (3.4 mile) trail. It begins on a boardwalk over a marshy lowland area before the steep 700 m (2,275 ft) uphill climb through the forest to the pass. Continuing on takes you down into the Verdant Creek Valley where the trail leads to the southeast and eventually up the East Verdant Creek. Soon, you will reach Redearth Pass. A popular destination is Egypt Lake in Banff National Park, which is a 21.6 km (13.2 mile) 1–2 day one-way trip gaining 1,150 m (3,738 ft) along the way. You also descend 320 m (1,040 ft). The route continuing through the Verdant Creek Drainage beyond East Verdant Creek is non-existent in places.

Kimpton Creek Trail (Map 27/D3)

Beginning about 7 km (4.3 miles) from the western park gate on Highway 93, this trail initially crosses Sinclair Creek and then travels up the east side of Kimpton Creek for a 5.5 km (3.4 miles) 2 hour trek. As the

trail begins to deteriorate into little more than a game trail, there is a sign marking the end of the maintained route. Overall, there is a 150 m (488 ft) elevation gain as the trail passes through a dense second growth forest next to the creek. The best time to take this hike is in April to October.

Kindersley Pass Trail (Map 27/D3)

Beginning just north of the Kootenay Viewpoint on Highway 93, this 10 km (6.1 mile) 3–4 hour hike leads to the scenic pass. At first, the trail dissects a thick second growth forest before breaking out into the sub-alpine. At 8.5 km (5.2 miles), you pass through Kindersley Pass at 2,210 m (7,183 ft). From there, the trail climbs steadily to 2,395 m (7,784 ft) and the open alpine, which provides spectacular views of the surrounding valleys. It is possible to hike into the Sinclair Creek Valley and return to Highway 93 without retracing your steps. Overall, the elevation gain is 1,050 m (3,413 ft) and the hike is best left to mid-July to early September.

Luxor Pass Trail (Map 34/B7)

The trail to Luxor Pass begins on the Dolly Varden Trail at Kootenay Crossing. The trail branches from the fire road at 4.1 km and is a steady 4.3 km (2 hour) climb up a steep, densely forested mountainside to the pass at 1,900 m (6,235 ft) in elevation. It is not a highly recommended route since the trail is not maintained and offers few viewpoints.

Nixon Lake Trail (Map 27/C1) hike

The signed trailhead begins about 2.8 km (1.7 miles) south of McLeod Meadows Campsite. The easy trail leads through a second growth forest full of wildflowers in the spring to the shores of marshy, Nixon Lake. Allow an hour to hike the flat 2 km (1.2 mile) return trail.

Numa Creek Trail (Map 34/A3)

Beginning at the Numa Picnic Area on Highway 93, the 2.5 hour trail crosses the Vermilion River and then Numa Creek before ascending up a narrow forested valley for 6.4 km (3.9 miles) to a fork in the trail. The trail gains about 120 m (390 ft) in elevation and can be hiked any time from early June to late October. In addition to a swinging suspension bridge, the scenic trail accesses a vast alpine area surrounded by glacier covered mountains. At the fork, a left leads to Numa Pass, which is a 13 km (7.9 mile) 4 hour hike gaining 915 m (2,974 ft) from Highway 93. A right takes you to Tumbling Pass, at 2,269 m (7,374 ft). This hike is 11.4 km (7 miles) 5.5 hours one-way from Highway 93.

Ochre Creek/Ottertail Pass Trail (Maps 34/A2-33/G1)

From the Paint Pots parking area, this trail follows Ochre Creek for about 6.5 km (4 miles) to a campsite at Helmut Creek. Continuing northwest results in hiking the difficult to follow Ottertail Pass Trail, which stretches into Yoho National Park. That trail has not been maintained for years and is overgrown.

Paint Pots/Marble Canyon Loop (Map 34/A2)

Natives and commercial ventures once used the Paint Pots for painting purposes. A popular trail leads past the pots, to the Ochre Creek Trail and the Marble Canyon Loop. The canyon loop brings you through a narrow gorge with a number of natural rock bridges. Allow 3 hours for this 9 km (5.5 mile) return hike gaining 100 m (325 ft) in elevation.

Redstreak Trail (Map 27/C4)

This trail begins 4.4 km (2.7 miles) from the western park gate on Highway 93. You immediately cross Sinclair Creek on a small wooden bridge and then begin the ascent up the Redstreak Creek Valley through a lush second growth forest of Douglas-fir and Lodgepole pine. The trail ends below Redstreak Mountain about 2.4 km (1.5 miles) from the start. The elevation gain is 150 m (488 ft).

Simpson River/Mount Shanks Lookout Trail (Map 34/E5)

North of the Simpson River an easy trail system begins at the wooden bridge crossing over the Vermilion River. The old lookout road past the gates branching left leads to a scenic lookout tower and an old cabin on the south side of Mount Shanks. This hike is 9.5 km (5.8 miles) 4 hours return, gaining 365 m (1,186 ft) to the tower at 1,645 m (5,346 ft). The right branch leads 16 km (9.8 miles) up the Simpson Valley to the boundary of Kootenay National Park, gaining 120 m (390 ft) along the way. From here, difficult routes access the Surprise Creek Shelter in Mount Assiniboine Provincial Park (2 km/1.2 miles), or follow the river up through the Simpson Pass and down into Sunshine Village in Banff. This is a popular backcountry skiing destination.

Sinclair Canyon/Juniper Trail Circuit (Map 27/C3)

This popular 6.5 km (4 mile) 2–3 hour return hike combines several shorter trails in the most commercial part of Kootenay National Park. The best place to start is at the Redstreak Campground. The trail begins in an open Douglas-fir forest, continues east on the south side of Highway 97 with views of the canyon before reaching the Aquacourt. From the Aquacourt, take the pedestrian tunnel crossing under Highway 93 and head up the road to the Juniper Trail. This trail switchbacks up the forested slopes before heading west to the canyon and then Sinclair Falls. Eventually, you will have to cross Highway 93 and return to the campground entrance kiosk. The well-maintained route provides excellent views of Sinclair Canyon and has an elevation gain of 190 m (618 ft).

Sinclair Creek Trail (Map 27/D3)

Across from the radio tower on Highway 93 just below Sinclair Pass, this hike climbs steadily up Sinclair Creek Valley into the alpine meadows below Brisco Range. Once in the meadows, the trail becomes hard to follow but it does continue past Sinclair Meadows to Kindersley Pass at 2,200 m (7,150 ft), where you can descend back to Highway 93. To reach Sinclair Meadows involves a hike of 5 km (3 miles) 2–3 hours one-way gaining 550 m (1,788 ft) in elevation. The total circuit is 16 km (9.8 miles) 3–4 hours.

Stanley Glacier Trail (Map 34/C2)

This popular 8.5 km (5.2 mile) trail leads to the foot of the steep rock wall upon which Stanley Glacier lies. The best views of the glacier come when you reach the open talus slopes near the foot of the glacier. The trail gains 300 m (975 ft) over 6 hours return and is used in the winter by backcountry skiers.

Tumbling Creek Trail (Map 34/A2)

This is a 22 km (13.4 mile) 1–2 day hike, which begins off Highway 93 on the Ochre Creek Trail. The Tumbling Creek Trail makes five river crossings, with two of them on suspension bridges and another on a log bridge over a narrow canyon. The trail also passes by a 100 m (325 ft) high waterfall and ultimately culminates at a sub-alpine camping area below the Tumbling Glacier. The elevation gain along the way is 450 m (1,463 ft) to a high point of 1,900 m (6,175 ft). From the camping area it is possible to access Wolverine Pass at 2,250 m (7,313 ft) in elevation.

Valley View Trail (Map 27/C3)

This 1.2 km (.7 mile) easy trail begins at the Redstreak Campground entrance kiosk. The trail leads to a viewpoint overlooking the Columbia Valley, where picnic tables are offered. There are also self-guided interpretive signs to help you enjoy the natural beauty of the area.

West Kootenay Fire Road (Map 34/C7-A5)

From Kootenay Crossing, the West Kootenay Fire Road leads to the Beaverfoot Road outside of Kootenay National Park. This is the beginning of a popular mountain biking route that leads all the way to the Trans-Canada Highway at the boundary of Yoho National Park. This mountain biking trek is 66 km long (40.3 miles) 5–8 hours one-way and is best completed by using a two car shuttle system. The actual fire road involves an initial climb before leveling out near the park boundary. Continuing on, the road deteriorates and is extremely rutted and grown-in in places. Allow about 4 hours to walk the 8 km (4.8 mile) one-way trail, which is also shared with horseback riders and cross-country skiers.

Mount Revelstoke National Park (Maps 30, 31)

Like many other national parks, the hiking season in Mount Revelstoke is restricted by snow. For the lower elevation trails (600 to 1,300 m/1,950–4,225 ft), you can hike between May and early November whereas the high elevation treks (over 1,900 m/6,175 ft) are limited to late July to mid-September.

No horseback riding is allowed in the park and the only mountain biking trails are found at the base of Mount Revelstoke. Be aware that you are traveling in bear country.

Balsam Lake Trail (Map 30/E4)

This is a 2 km (1.2 mile) easy walk from the parking lot at the top of the Summit Parkway gaining a modest 90 m (293 ft). The trail leads through sub-alpine meadows and Douglas-fir forest.

Eva and Jade Lakes Trail (Map 30/E3)

From the top of the Summit Parkway, this 12 km (7.3 mile) 4 hour hike crosses the beautiful alpine terrain to Eva Lake, located at the 1,930 m level (6,330 ft). The attractions of the area are the wildflowers in late July and August, the wilderness camping (including a cabin), and the fishing for small cutthroat trout. You can take a short branch trail to the right to reach Miller Lake, or continue on to Jade Lake. The hike into Jade Lake is an additional 6 km (3.7 miles) 2–3 hours return climbing 240 m (785 ft) to the summit at 2,160 m (7,085 ft) before descending to the lake at 1,825 m (5,931 ft). The area offers an endless view (at the summit) and wilderness camping and fishing at the lake.

Giant Cedars Interpretive Trail (Map 31/A3)

This 600 m (1,950 ft) boardwalk trail takes you into a stand of old growth cedar trees, some over 800 years of age. Interpretive signs describe the importance of the ecosystem and there are benches available so you can sit and relax in the cool forest on a hot summer day. The trailhead is at the Giants Cedar Picnic Area.

Inspiration Woods Trail (Map 30/D5)

This is an easy 3 km (1.8 mile) forested walk from the first switchback on the Summit Parkway. There is little elevation gain and it offers early and late season hiking opportunities due to its low elevation (61 m/198 ft).

Lindmark Trail (Map 30/D4)

From the Monashee Lookout on the Summit Parkway, it is an 8 km (4.8 mile) 3.5 hour one-way hike gaining 960 m (3,120 ft) to the Balsam Lake picnic shelter, at 1,830 m (5,948 ft).

Meadows-in-the-Sky Interpretive Trail (Map 30/C4)

This short, one kilometre interpretive loop has little elevation gain and is paved to allow wheelchair access. The trail starts at the Heather Lake parking lot at the summit of Mount Revelstoke (1,920 m/6,240 ft). It passes through the sub-alpine meadows full of wildflowers blooming in late July and early August. A point of interest is the Icebox, a shaded rock cleft with snow year-round.

Skunk Cabbage Interpretive Trail (Map 31/A3)

This short 1.2 km (0.7 mile) circuit starts at the Skunk Cabbage Picnic Area off the Trans Canada Hwy. The trail follows a boardwalk through swampland along the Illecillewaet River. The name of the plant comes from its pungent smell it gives off when it blooms in spring.

Summit Trail (Map 30/A3)

This is a rigorous 10 km (6.1 mile) one-way hike or ski that begins at the base of Summit Parkway and leads to Balsam Lake at the top of Summit Parkway. From the valley floor to the alpine meadows (which contain beautiful summer wildflowers) you gain 600 m (1,950 ft) to 1,830 m (5,948 ft) in elevation. Allow 4 to 5 hours to hike up, but since the trail crosses the road on seven occasions, you can shorten the hike if desired.

Yoho National Park (Maps 33, 39)

There are over 400 km (240 miles) of hiking trails in the park ranging from easy valley walks to rugged treks into the alpine. The hiking season on the lower elevation hikes begins in May and ends in early October. Hikes into the sub-alpine are not accessible until mid-June at the earliest and can be used until mid-September. Mountaineering opportunities are endless but mountain biking is limited to designated fire roads and certain portions of a few trails (Kicking Horse Trail, Amiskwi Trail, Otterhead Trail, Ice River Trail, Tally-ho Trail and Ottertail Trail). As with all national parks, Grizzly bears are a concern.

The Lake O'Hara area is the most popular destination within Yoho National Park and the lodge and the campground are usually fully booked throughout the summer months. It is well advised to reserve your spot months ahead.

Alpine Circuit (Map 39/D4)

This difficult, 11.8 km (7.2 mile) 4.5 hour trail is one of the more popular routes, but also one of the most difficult in the Lake O'Hara area. The trail is reached by passing the Lake O'Hara Warden Cabin and walking 150 m (488 ft) along the lakeshore to the outlet bridge. From here, it quickly ascends up Wiwaxy Gap to run along some exposed and narrow ledges overlooking Lake O'Hara and the surrounding mountains. The trail then descends to join up with the Opabin Plateau Trail and then the All Soul's Alpine Route.

Amiskwi River Fire Road (Map 39/D6-B2)

This gravel road proceeds 24 km (14.6 mile) one-way to the Amiskwi III Campsite gaining 520 m (3,172 ft) to 1,675 m (5,495 ft) in elevation. Given the distance, it is more common to bike up the road, which usually takes between 4 and 5 hours as you pass by remnants of logging and an old mill site. From the campsite, the Amiskwi Pass Trail climbs 305 m (991 ft) past the Amiskwi Falls to the remote pass at 1,980 m (6,435 ft) in elevation. It is possible to descend from Amiskwi Pass into the Blaeberry River Valley on a flagged trail, which begins on the east slope of the valley. This trail leads past the Greens Lodge (for use of the lodge call 250-343-6397) before reaching Branch 27 off the Blaeberry FSR. Mountain biking is not allowed north of the Amiskwi III Campground. In the winter, backcountry skiers use the trail.

Burgess Highland Trail (Map 39/E5)

Beginning at the Emerald Lake parking area, the route initially starts along the Emerald Lake Nature Trail before beginning a steady climb to Yoho Pass at 1,840 m (5,980 ft). To reach the pass involves a 7 km (4.3 mile) 3 hour hike gaining 530 m (1,723 ft) in elevation. From the Yoho Pass, a trail heads south some 6.5 km (4 miles) 2-3 hours to Burgess Pass at 2,200 m (7,150 ft). Then, the trail heads downhill to Emerald Lake and the start. In total, the hike is 21 km (12.8 miles) and is an excellent choice if you want a day hike around the alpine with great views of the Emerald Lake Valley.

Cataract Brook Trail (Map 39/G6)

This 13 km (7.9 mile) 3-4 hour hike provides foot access into the Lake O'Hara area. The trail climbs 410 m (1,333 ft) from the O'Hara parking lot off the Trans Canada Hwy to the Hector Gorge. Along the way it crosses several creeks and swampy meadows before reaching the Lake O'Hara Campground.

Centennial Trail (Map 39/E6)

From the Kicking Horse Campground, this short 2.5 km (1.5 mile) hike begins at the bridge on Yoho Valley Road. There is little elevation gain

and the trail offers views of old mine portals on the cliffs above. Mountain goat also graces the cliffs.

Emerald Basin (Map 39/D5)

From the Emerald Lake parking lot, the trail brings you along the western shores of the lake. At about 1.6 km (1 mile), you will reach a junction at the north end of the lake. Take the left branch of the trail, which brings you to a short, steep hike to a natural amphitheatre of hanging glaciers and avalanche chutes. Overall, the hike is 8.6 km (5.2 miles) 3-4 hours return gaining 275 m (894 ft) in elevation.

Emerald Lake Circuit Trail (Map 39/D5)

This easy, relatively flat walking trail follows the shoreline of Emerald Lake for 4.8 km (3 miles) 1.5-2 hours). It is a very scenic route with lots of vegetation and a great view of Mount Burgess and the lodge area. In the winter, cross-country skiers use the trail.

Emerald River Trail (Map 39/D6)

The best way to hike this trail is to use a two car shuttle system, one parked at Emerald Lake and one at the Amiskwi Picnic Area. The 7.5 km (4.6 mile) 2-3 hours hike starts at the lake and cuts through the dense forest next to the Emerald River as it drops 140 m (455 ft) to the access road 200 m (650 ft) east of the picnic area.

Hamilton Lake & Falls Trail (Map 39/C5)

This easy 1.5 km (0.9 mile) return walk starts from the Emerald Lake parking area and leads to a spectacular falls eroding into a bedrock fault. The hike requires a 50 m (163 ft) elevation gain. For the more adventurous, try the 11 km (6.7 mile) 4 hour hike past the falls to Hamilton Lake. This hike involves a climb of 850 m (2,763 ft) along a steep, forested trail. It is best tried after mid-July due to snow accumulations on the trail and ice on the lake at 2,149 m (6,984 ft) in elevation.

Hoodoos Trail (Map 33/D1)

From the Hoodoo Creek Campground, a 3 km (1.8 mile) 1.5 hour hike climbs a steep trail along Hoodoo Creek to several viewpoints of the Hoodoos. These Hoodoos are the most spectacular in all the national parks.

Ice River Fire Road (Map 33/C1-E2)

From the gate at the Hoodoo Trail parking lot, an old fire road leads along the eastern side of the Beaverfoot River to the Lower Ice River Warden Cabin. It is a gentle 19 km (11.6 mile) 4-5 hour one-way trek through a forested valley that is shared with mountain bikers as well as cross-country skiers and snowshoers in winter. Beyond the warden cabin, the trail crosses the Ice River, leading up the east side of thevalley to the Upper Ice River Warden Cabin about 6.5 km (4 miles) 2-3 hours further along. This section is best left to hikers and experienced backcountry skiers since most of the 375 m (1,219 ft) elevation gain occurs after crossing the river.

Iceline Trail (Map 39/D4)

From the Whiskey Jack Hostel on Yoho Valley Road, follow the Yoho Pass Trail as it switchbacks through a large avalanche path to a sub-alpine forest. After passing the Hidden Lakes Trail heading off to the left, you will come to the Iceline Trail, which leads to the right. Hikers can either descend into the Little Yoho Valley for a 22 km (13.4 mile) return circuit or connect to the Lake Celeste Trail for an 18 km (11 mile) circuit. Either way, you can expect to gain about 695 m (2,280 ft) along a very scenic route.

Lake McArthur Trail (Map 39/G7)

Accessed from the warden cabin on the Lake O'Hara Road, Lake McArthur is a favourite destination for artists and photographers. It is a beautiful lake surrounded by alpine meadows and a hanging glacier. It is a 7 km (4.3 mile) return climb that takes four hours to complete while climbing 310 m (1,008 ft) in elevation. Since the lake often remains frozen until mid-July, this trip is best taken during the late summer.

Lake Oesa Trail (Map 39/G6)

A popular 3.6 km (2.2 mile) 1.5 hour one-way hike, starts at the north end of Lake O'Hara. Follow the lake shoreline about 0.8 km (0.5 miles) to a noticeable fork. Take the left branch and you will begin a steady climb gaining 250 m (813 ft) to the beautiful turquoise-coloured lake at 2,275 m (7,465 ft). From the northern shores of Lake Oesa, you can scramble uphill to Abbott Pass and the Great Divide. The tough, steep climb leads to the windswept pass that is home to a cabin used by mountaineers (for reservations, phone the Alpine Club of Canada at 403-678-3200).

Linda Lake/Cathedral Lake Trail (Map 39/F6)

This trail begins 2.9 km (1.8 miles) south of the Lake O'Hara Campground off of the fire road. The trail crosses the Morning Glory Creek bridge before reaching Linda Lake for a total distance of 1.8 km (1.1 miles) one-way gaining 85 m (280 ft). The tree-lined lake is set below some spectacular peaks of the Great Divide. The trail continues along the north shore of the lake before ascending through a sub-alpine forest and open meadows to Cathedral Lake. This 1 km (0.6 mile) one-way extension gains 225 m (731 ft) and is little more than a scramble up a rocky slope. Allow 3-4 hours to access Cathedral Lake from Lake O'Hara.

Little Yoho Valley Trail (Map 39/D4)

The trailhead to the Little Yoho Valley is found at Laughing Falls on the Yoho Valley Trail, about 4.3 km (2.6 miles) from the Takakkaw Falls parking lot. The trail climbs steadily up the north side of the Little Yoho River to an inviting alpine meadow, which contains the Stanley Mitchell Cabin and the Little Yoho Campground. The total distance is 10 km (6.1 miles) 4 hours one-way from Takakkaw Falls, with an elevation gain of 520 m (1,690 ft). Backcountry skiers use the trail in winter. Once at the camp, it is possible to take the 2.5 km (1.5 mile) 1.5 hour one-way hike to Kiwetinok Pass, at 2,450 m (7,963 ft) in elevation. This very steep, hard to follow trail brings you to a rocky windswept pass with a small lake.

McArthur Creek Trail (Map 39/F7)

From the Lake O'Hara Warden Cabin, this trail ascends McArthur Pass at 2,200 m (7,150 ft) gaining 165 m (536 ft). Enjoy the view before you begin a steady, 750 m (2,438 ft) descent along McArthur Creek to Ottertail River. This hike is 12.5 km (7.6 miles) 4–5 hours one-way.

Mount Hunter Lookout Trail (Map 33/C1)

From the Trans-Canada Highway at the Wapta Falls turnoff, this trail climbs steadily upwards to the old fire lookout at 1,530 m (4,973 ft). The elevation gain is 400 m (1,300 ft) over the 7 km (4.3 mile) 3.5 hour return trip. You can continue on to the Upper Lookout at 1,965 m (6,386 ft), which is another 6 km (3.7 miles) return. Both lookouts provide excellent views of the Kicking Horse and Beaverfoot Valleys and are used by backcountry skiers in the winter.

Odaray Prospect Trail (Map 39/F7)

Beginning at the Lake O'Hara Warden Cabin, this trail first brings you to Alpine Meadows before heading off to the right at the Alpine Club Cabin. From there, climb to one of the best vistas in the Lake O'Hara area where you get a great view of Upper Morning Glory Lake and the Great Divide. The trail is 2.5 km (1.5 miles) 1.5 hours one-way gaining 250 m (813 ft) to the Prospect, at 2,285 m (7,426 ft). From the Prospect, it is possible to access McArthur Pass, Odaray Plateau and Odaray Grandview Prospect.

Opabin Plateau Trail (Map 39/G7)

From the Lake O'Hara Lodge, follow the southwest lakeshore for a few hundred metres. From here, a trail climbs the west side of the plateau to Opabin Lake, gaining 250 m (813 ft) along the way. The trail then loops downhill along the east side of the plateau making it a 6.5 km (4 mile) 4 hour return trip. This is one of the most scenic hikes in the Lake O'Hara area with snowcapped mountain ridges surrounding the alpine valley.

Ottertail Fire Road (Maps 39/D7-33/F1)

From the Trans-Canada Hwy, this old fire road gradually ascends the Ottertail River Valley ending at the McArthur Creek Warden Cabin. The route is about 15 km (9.2 miles) one-way with an elevation gain of 300 m (975 ft) and can be hiked or biked in the summer or skied in the winter. From the end of the road, the trail runs south, crossing the Ottertail River and reaching a fork in the trail about one kilometre later.

The left fork leads to Ottertail Falls and peters out (strong route finders can continue on to Ottertail Pass). The right branch leads to Goodsir Pass and other destinations within Kootenay National Park.

Ross Lake Trail (Map 39/G5)

From the Lake O'Hara parking area, this 2.6 km (1.6 mile) multi-use trail gains 90 m (293 ft) before reaching a small wilderness lake highlighted by a towering cliff face. It is possible to continue into Banff National Park.

Tally-Ho Trail (Map 39/D6)

This trail is a designated mountain biking route that is used by skiers in the winter. It extends 3 km (1.8 miles) one-way connecting the Trans Canada Hwy with Emerald Lake Road. The trail makes for an easy ride with an elevation gain of 35 m (114 ft).

Wapta Falls Trails (Map 33/C2)

From the end of the Falls Access Road, a 2 km (1.2 mile) gravel road, it is a 5 km (3 mile) return forested walk along the flat, easy trail to the spectacular 30 m (90 foot) high falls on the Kicking Horse River. The best view is from below the falls.

Whaleback Trail (Map 39/D4)

Linking the Yoho Valley Trail and the Iceline Trail is a moderate 20 km (12.2 mile) trail known as the Whaleback Trail. As the name implies, it climbs up and down a scenic ridge above the Yoho River. Most travellers start the circuit from the Takakkaw Falls Campsite and return on the Iceline Trail, which drops down to the Whiskey Jack Hostel. It is a short jaunt up the road to get back to the start.

Yoho Lake & Pass Trail (Map 39/D5)

This trail is found on the west side of the Whiskey Jack Hostel parking lot at the end of the Yoho Valley Road. The trail leads steadily uphill through an avalanche chute before reaching a sub-alpine forest. At about 1 km (0.6 miles), a side branch leads to the Hidden Lakes. After passing the Iceline Trail junction, the trail levels off as you reach Yoho Lake. Continue along the southern lakeshore and through an alpine meadow to Yoho Pass where you will find a trail junction, the left branch being the Burgess Highline Trail and the right branch being the Yoho Pass Trail. The hike to Yoho Lake is 3.5 km (2.1 miles) 1.5 hours one-way whereas the hike to Yoho Pass is 4.5 km (2.7 miles) 2.5 hours one-way. The elevation gain is 310 m (1,008 ft) to the pass. Beyond Yoho Pass, you have the opportunity to descend to Emerald Lake via the Yoho Pass Trail or to the town of Field via the Burgess Highline Trail.

Yoho Valley Trail (Map 39/D4)

Beginning at the Takakkaw Falls Campsite off Yoho Valley Road, this trail leads along Yoho River to Twin Falls. The 3 hour hike is 8 km (4.9 miles) one-way gaining 300 m (975 ft) in elevation. The trail passes a number of smaller waterfalls before eventually reaching the spectacular Twin Falls, where you will find a chalet at 1,800 m (5,850 ft) in elevation. The trail is the most popular one in the Yoho Valley area as it is fairly flat and easy throughout most of its length. For the more adventurous, you can make a circuit back to Takakkaw Falls along the Whaleback Trail, which is a total of 20 km (12.2 miles) in distance.

Wilderness Camping

(Forest Recreation Sites & Backcountry Huts)

The BC Forest Service has undergone a lot of changes in the last few years. Thankfully things have settled and the Forest Recreation Site system is being saved. Some of the recreation sites and backcountry huts are being managed in cooperation with organizations, First Nations and forest companies and others have reverted back to the user maintained system. This is particularly important in a region like the Kootenays where recreation sites are so important to the way of life.

Recreation Sites are now broken down into three categories:

Managed Recreation Sites with fees are being implied to the busier sites. Many of these sites have improved their services to become more like a provincial park campground. The fee is usually $10/night and the sites are usually open from mid May until mid September.

Managed Recreation Sites without fees are usually run by local communities or organizations that wanted to ensure the recreation sites in their area were not closed. There may or may not be an on-site supervisor and the sites are usually open year round. Also included in this category are a number of small cabins and huts that make backcountry hiking in the Kootenays so popular.

The **User Maintained Recreation Sites** are more primitive camping sites found in remote areas. Facilities are usually very limited and may include picnic tables, fire rings and pit toilets. Pump water is rarely provided at the site. Please help to keep these areas clean and pack out your garbage as well as any other garbage inconsiderate visitors may have left. In the Kootenays it is very important to be aware of bears in these remote areas.

Recreation sites are often found in remote locations and do not see the summer crowds common to the Provincial and National Park campgrounds. They are also usually found down often rough, sometimes active, logging roads. Because of this, families as well as travellers with trailers and RVs rarely venture to many of the sites. Although boat launches are often provided on the lakes, these launches range from portage (hand launch) sites to ramps suitable for small boats only.

Below we have grouped the sites according to the Forest District they are found in. We have also listed the Backcountry Huts that are available to the public at the end of this section. People may notice that the changes to the BC Forest Service have resulted in new Forest Districts. We have also added symbols next to the name to indicate the popular activities enjoyed in and around the area.

Arrow Forest District

The Arrow Forest District has been expanded to include the Boundary area around Grand Forks. In this book, most of the recreation is based around the Arrow Lakes. The Monashee Mountains in the west and the Selkirk Mountains in the east provide a scenic border. Unique to this region is a well-established backcountry hut system that is enjoyed by hikers, backcountry skiers and snowmobilers.

Bannock Point Recreation Site (Map 17/G7)

On the eastern shores of the Slocan Lake, this small, treed tent site is accessed by boat or an 800 m (2,600 feet) trail, which drops 70 m (229 foot) in elevation. At the site there is a pebble beach and most of the activity is water based.

Beaver Lake Recreation Site (Map 17/F3)

This popular but small (seven unit) site is located next to Beaver Lake. Fishing, swimming, paddling and a boat launch are offered at this treed site. An electric motor only restriction applies on the lake.

Big Sheep Creek Recreation Site (Map 1/F6)

There is space for one tenting party at this treed site on Big Sheep Creek. Fishing and hunting are the primary attractions.

Bluejoint Creek Recreation Site (Map 9/A7)

Located on the West Burrell Creek Road, this small site is set in a clearing at an old sawmill site next to Bluejoint Creek. Hunting is the primary attraction to the seldom-used site. Recent logging activities have taken away from the secluded nature of the site.

Bowman Point Recreation Site (Map 9/E7)

In a sheltered anchorage on the Lower Arrow Lake, this small, treed site is accessed by boat only. Fishing, swimming and boating are the primary attractions. Sailboats frequent the area.

Box Lake Recreation Site (Map 17/C2)

Off Highway 6, this popular site is set in a lush hemlock-spruce forest next to Box Lake. There is space enough for eight groups, a fishing dock and a primitive boat launch. Despite the close proximity to the highway, the narrow access road limits campers to smaller vehicles. There is an electric motor only restriction on the lake.

Cameron Lake Recreation Site (Map 16/G1)

In the hills above Lower Arrow Lake, this is a small (four unit), treed site with a cartop boat launch. Fishing and boating are the main attractions at the lake.

Caribou Lake Recreation Site (Map 16/F3)

On the Whatshan River Road, this is a small (three unit), semi-open lakeshore site set between two lakes. There is a rough boat launch for fishermen but know that there is an electric motor only restriction on the lake.

Catherine Lake Recreation Site (Map 23/G7)

Off the often-rough Shelter Bay Road, the forest service site at Catherine Lake is a small, semi-open lakeshore site with a cartop boat launch and space for four groups. The site receives heavy use during the summer, primarily by fishermen and paddlers.

Cooley Recreation Site (Map 10/D7)

Off the Goose Creek Road, this is a small, treed site near Cooley Lake. The site is actually located next to the 4wd road and requires a 200 m (650 feet) hike to the lake where there is space for ten or so tenting groups.

Crystal Lake Recreation Site (Map 11/A6)

This small site is accessed via a 2 km (1.2 mile) hike in to Crystal Lake. There is good fishing at the lake and, as you might expect, the site sees most of its use from anglers.

Erie Creek Recreation Site (Map 2/F3)

This is a semi-open site with a few picnic tables and nicely spaced spots to accommodate four groups. Despite the good creek fishing and a prolific crop of huckleberries, the site is rarely used in the summer. The good gravel road allows trailers to access the site.

Grizzly Creek Recreation Site (Map 10/A3)

At the junction of Koch and Grizzly Creeks, this is a semi-open two-unit site. Rock climbing is a popular activity in the area.

Horseshoe Lake Recreation Site (Map 17/C2)

Located on a 4wd road north of Wilson Lake, this small, open lakeshore site has space for one group. The main attraction to the site is fishing. No powerboats are allowed on the lake.

Larson Lake Recreation Site (Map 16/F2)

On the Mosquito Creek Road, this small, semi-open site is located next to the beautiful Larson Lake. The lake is known for its rich aquamarine coloured waters.

Little Slocan Lakes Recreation Site (Map 10/D4)

On the Little Slocan River Road, the site is found at the north end of the Upper Little Slocan Lake. It is a popular, semi-open site, which offers swimming, fishing and paddling. There is space for six groups at the lake. There is also a cabin in the area.

Little Wilson Lake Recreation Site (Map 17/F2)

This small, open lakeshore site is reached off the Wilson Lake Road. The three-unit site has a boat launch and tables and offers fishing and paddling. The access to the site limits RVs and trailers.

Mosquito Lake Recreation Site (Map 16/F1)

Next to Mosquito Lake, this is a small (three unit), treed site with fishing, swimming and boating. As the name indicates, the lake can be a real haven for mosquitoes.

Octopus Creek Recreation Site (Map 9/E3)

On the eastern shores of Lower Arrow Lake, this two-unit site has one table located next to the creek and another a short distance away. There is a boat launch and plenty of waterfront to suntan on. The site is located south of Applegrove and offers little shade.

Paulson/Mud Lake Recreation Site (Map 1/E4)

This small, high elevation site is found next to Mud Lake and Highway 3. The site has space for one group, and marks the trailhead and parking area for summer users of the Paulson Trail System.

Richy Recreation Site (Map 16/E5)

This small boat access only site has space for five tenting groups. Swimmers will find the lake much warmer than nearby Lower Arrow Lake.

Santa Rosa Creek Recreation Site (Map 1/E7)

On the Old Cascade Highway, there is space for one overnight group at this small, treed site. Travellers on the historic Dewdney Trail, which is now part of the Trans Canada Trail, frequent the area.

Sasquatch Lake Recreation Site (Map 11/A4)

On the Lemon Creek Road, this popular site is used by picnickers, swimmers and berry pickers (in season). Camping is possible as there is space for two groups.

Sheep Creek Recreation Site (Map 3/B6)

On the Sheep Creek Road, this small day-use site offers good stream fishing and hunting.

Snowshoe Lake Recreation Site (Maps 9/D1, 16/D7)

On a 4wd road off Highway 6, there is a small, treed site next to Snowshoe Lake. An electric motor only restriction applies at the lake. There is space for six groups at the lake.

St Anne Meadows Recreation Site (Map 9/A7)

This remote site is found along a deteriorating 2wd road in a large, grassy field overlooking Burrell Creek. The area is used primarily by hunters in the fall.

Stevens Creek Recreation Site (Map 16/E5)

At the north end of Whatshan Lake, this is a medium sized (11 units) site set in the forest. There is a boat launch and fishing and swimming in the warm lake are popular summertime activities.

Sunshine Bay Recreation Site (Map 9/E6)

On the eastern shores of the Lower Arrow Lake, this small, popular rec site is accessed by boat or 4wd vehicle. During low water, a nice beach is exposed and there is plenty of shade for campers. Mooring buoys are available for boaters.

Taite Creek Recreation Site (Map 9/E2)

Near Applegrove, this site has space for five vehicle-units, a boat launch and plenty of shade. At low water, there is a nice beach with lots of sun for water enthusiasts. The access road is not recommended for RVs.

Wilson Lake (West & East) Recreation Sites (Map 17/D2)

Wilson Lake is set in a steep, narrow valley and offers two sites, one at each end of the lake. Wilson Lake West is a small, forested lakeshore site that offers shade most of the day. Wilson Lake East is a semi open, medium sized site with a boat launch. The popular sites offer good fishing and paddling but are not recommended for a RV or trailer. There is space for ten groups between the two sites.

Wragge Beach Recreation Site (Map 17/F5) $$

On the western shores of Slocan Lake, this popular site is reached off the narrow Wragge Beach Road. The beautiful rec site is comprised of 5 tables right next to the lakeshore as well as 3 tables set in the heavily forested shoreline. There are also 5 walk-in tent sites with tables in the woods away from the beach. Boaters and backroad travellers both use the site, which offers a nice, pebble beach and fishing at the Wragge Creek estuary. There is a fee to camp here and the site is open from the end of May until mid September.

Columbia Forest District

This large area encompasses the majority of the upper Columbia River drainage as it flows north from Golden through Kinbasket Lake and loops south past Revelstoke to the Upper Arrow Lake. These large, man-made lakes are subject to severe water level fluctuations. Similar to most areas of the Kootenays, the Columbia Forest District is surrounded by spectacular mountain peaks of the Columbia and Rocky Mountains.

Begbie Falls Recreation Sites (Map 30/D6)

There are three day-use sites in this popular recreational area south of Revelstoke. The most popular location is the Begbie Falls site, which is found off Mount Begbie Road. It is set in a mature hemlock-cedar forest and offers hiking trails to the falls, back to Highway 23 (called the Begbie Creek Trail) and to the Upper Arrow Lake. Across the highway is the Begbie Bluffs, which is mainly used by rock climbers. There is also the Mount Begbie Trail system to explore.

Blackwater Lake Recreation Site (Map 37/G2)

At 24 km (14.4 miles) on the Bush River Road, this small, open lakeshore site has a cartop boat launch, four tables, a wheelchair–accessible fishing ramp and pit toilet. It is hard to ignore the constant stream of logging trucks that pass by the site on weekdays.

Bluewater Bridge Recreation Site (Map 38/B4)

This small, one-unit site is found on Bluewater Creek, beside the Bush River Road. It is mainly used as a put-in for paddlers but still makes a nice camping area.

Bluewater Creek Recreation Site (Map 38/B4)

Take a left at the 4.5 km mark on the busy Bush River Road and follow the rough road to the creek side site near the old bridge crossing. There is one site with a table and several others without. Hunters and paddlers are the principle users of the site.

Bush Arm Recreation Site (Map 37/F1, 42/F7)

At the 73.5 km mark on the Bush River Road, this small (four unit) site is set in a large opening on the southern shores of Kinbasket Lake. An improved boat launch allows fishermen to launch large boats at lower water levels. RVs and trailers can reach the site but be prepared for a long trip along a busy logging road.

Caribou Creek Recreation Site (Map 42/A6)

This is a two-unit, open lakeshore site on the Columbia Reach of the Kinbasket Lake. There is a cartop boat launch at the site along with picnic tables and fire pits. Fishing and boating are offered on the lake, which is subject to water fluctuations through the year. The site is found about 104 km (63.4 miles) along the Bush River-Sullivan Road.

Carnes Creek Recreation Site (Map 36/C7)

Located off Highway 23, this is a large, popular campsite on the western shores of Lake Revelstoke. RVs and trailers can reach the site with space for 17 vehicle units and another 10 or so tenting groups. The site has a boat launch and now charges a fee for camping from mid May to mid September.

Cedar Lake Recreation Site (Map 32/F1)

Off the Dogtooth-Canyon Road south of Golden, this is a popular site with four campsites, one table, a beach and a wharf. The lake is frequented by locals who enjoy water sports, sunbathing and fishing. In addition to the short 1 km walk to a small, secluded lake near Cedar Lake, there are several hiking and mountain biking trails in the area.

Echo Lake Recreation Site (Map 30/F7)

This four-unit site is located on the north side of Echo Lake a short distance from the Upper Arrow Lake. A hiking trail leads around the lake and there is good fishing at the lake, which has an electric motor only restriction. The site receives heavy weekend use.

Esplanade Bay Recreation Site (Map 37/E1)

Take a left at the 63.5 km mark on the Bush River Road, and drive down the secondary road to this nice site overlooking Kinbasket Lake. Because it is away from the road (and therefore away from the logging trucks), this site gets a lot of use in the summer. There are 14 campsites with a few units overlooking the lake and several located in the young second growth forest back from the lake. A boat launch is available for fishermen.

Five Mile Boat Launch Rec Site (Map 30/D3)

As you would expect with a name like that, this day-use site is mostly just a boat launch. Easily found off Highway 23, you will also find a beach and picnic site. The area is popular with locals due to its close proximity to Revelstoke and the water sports and fishing on Lake Revelstoke.

Giant Cedars Trail & Recreation Site (Map 37/F1)

There is space for one group near the short trail that leads to this stand of ancient red cedars.

Gorman Lake Recreation Site (Map 38/C7)

This site is located next to a popular, hike-in lake set in an open sub-alpine bowl. Fishing and the beautiful mountain scenery are the attractions to the site. There are picnic tables along with a few tenting pads next to the lake. No campfires are allowed.

Help Lake Recreation Sites (Map 37/G1)

Off the Bush River Road, a small, semi-open site is located between Help Lake and Aid Lake. Also in the area is an overflow site formally called the Help Lake Pull Out as well as cartop boat launches at Help and Aid Lakes. The three lakes in the area offer fairly good fishing.

Jeb Lake Recreation Site (Map 37/G3)

This grassy two-unit site is found on a small, fishing lake home to a decrepit dock and cartop boat launch. The road past Susan Lake is best left to 4wd drive vehicles. Bug spray is recommended.

Kootenay Crossing Recreation Site (Map 33/D4)

On the Beaverfoot Road, this is a small, semi-open site offering fishing and paddling. The site is located near the headwaters of the Kootenay River in a scenic mountainous area.

Marian Lake Recreation Site (Map 33/F4)

This is a small, open site with a boat launch onto a good fishing lake. Trailers can access the site, which is found at the headwaters of Kootenay River.

Mount Begbie Recreation Site (Map 30/D6)

Found just south of Revelstoke, this new site is popular with the hiking and mountaineering crowd.

Mummery Glacier Recreation Site (Map 39/A2)

On the Blaeberry River Road, this small, semi-open site is set in the valley below the popular Mummery Glacier. The site is used as a staging ground for hikers accessing the glacier.

Pitt Creek Recreation Site (Map 40/G4)
Found off of Highway 23, the good access allows trailers and RVs into the area. The six-unit site is found in a treed area next to Lake Revelstoke, where a boat launch is available.

Potlatch Creek Recreation Site (Map 40/G2)
This is a large, popular site on the eastern shores of Kinbasket Lake, located north of the Mica Dam at the end of Highway 23. There are 14 RV and trailer accessible campsites and a boat launch. Fishing is the main pastime in the area.

Split Creek Rec Site (Map 38/D4)
On the Blaeberry River Road, this is a small, grassy site next to the Blaeberry River.

Sprague Bay Recreation Site (Map 41/A2)
This mostly undeveloped site offers the traveller a good boat launch and camping area on Kinbasket Lake. Depending on the water level, the boat launch can be accessed throughout the year. The area has good logging road access.

Sullivan Bay Recreation Site (Map 42/A4)
This small, open site on a remote arm of Kinbasket Lake offers a boat launch, picnic tables, fire rings and a pit toilet. Trailers and RV's can access the site but remember the long haul up the busy logging road.

Susan Lake Recreation Site (Map 37/G3)
Found on the good 2wd access Susan Lake Road, there is a small, open site complete with a dock and a cartop boat launch on the east end of the lake. The terraced sites are mostly used as parking spots by locals (from Golden) trying to take advantage of the good brook trout fishing. Moose frequent the area, which is also home to an abundance of mosquitoes.

Thompson Falls Recreation Site (Map 38/F4)
There is one vehicle unit at this small site, located near Thompson Falls on the Blaeberry River. There is a short trail to the falls.

Valenciennes River Recreation Site (Map 43/A7)
This is a small (two-unit), treed site at the junction of the Bush and Valenciennes Rivers. From the remote site, a 2 km trail takes you to a canyon and natural springs. RVs and trailers can reach the site but remember the long haul up the busy logging road.

Waitabit Creek Recreation Site (Map 38/C4)
Take a left at the 2 km mark on the Big Bend Road, and you will find 13 well-spaced sites in an opening next to the creek. The site is easily accessed by RVs and trailers. There is an information kiosk and picnic area as well.

Wapta Falls Recreation Site (Map 33/C2)
On the Beaverfoot River Road, this small, partially treed picnic site overlooks Wapta Falls and Chancellor Peak. There are no camping facilities at the site.

Kootenay Lake Forest District

In the heart of the Kootenays, this area is renowned for its big lakes and big rivers. The Selkirk Mountains in the west and the Purcell Mountains in the east frame the area. The cool winters and warm summers allow recreationists to pursue activities throughout the year. While in the area, do not miss the chance to fish for the world famous Gerrard Trout.

America Creek Recreation Site (Map 5/C7)
On the Yahk-Meadow Creek Road, this is a popular, partially treed site next to America Creek. The site is used by fishermen and hunters and has six tables. RVs and trailers can use the site, which is busy on weekends and during hunting season.

Arkansas Lake Recreation Site (Map 3/D5)
Found in the mountainous region north of Highway 3, this is a fine destination for anglers and snowmobilers in winter. The small site is user maintained site, and is probably going to be closed soon. The outhouse has collapsed, and the picnic tables are in poor repair. There are no facilities, but a nice fishing lake.

Boundary Lake Recreation Site (Map 3/F7)
This medium sized, popular lakeshore site is located next to Boundary Lake. It has a cartop boat launch, a beach and a wharf. Fishing is fairly good at this sub-alpine, forested lake. The site receives heavy use during the summer.

Canuck Creek Recreation Site (Map 5/C7)
At 3.5 km on the Hawkins-Canuck Road, this site offers a nice campsite right next to the creek as well as several in a large, open area. Fishing, a scenic waterfall and a quiet, secluded camping site are the main attraction. RVs and trailers can use the site.

Cold Creek Recreation Site (Map 5/D7)
At the junction of the Yahk-Meadow Creek Road and the Cold Creek Road, this is a small, semi-open site offering fishing and camping space for three groups. RVs and trailers can use the site.

Coot Lake Recreation Site (Map 25/D3)
On the Duncan Road, this small, remote lake is used as a staging ground for the Hall Creek Trail. The site is no longer maintained but rustic camping is still possible.

Fletcher Falls Recreation Site (Map 11/F2)
This popular semi-open site is located next to a beach on Kootenay Lake. The site offers about five picnic tables and access to a gorgeous waterfall in a narrow canyon that is a short walk away. Designed as a boat access site, some visitor's park at the highway while others drive down the steep, narrow access road to the lake.

Garland Bay Recreation Site (Map 11/G1)
$$
Found next to Bernard Creek, the attraction to this popular site is the nice beach and good fishing in Kootenay Lake. The large site has a well-developed wharf in a sheltered bay and has room for up to 22 groups. Most of the RV and trailer accessible units are set in the trees away from the water. It is an excellent family destination. There is a fee for camping at the site, which is open from May through September.

Glacier Creek Recreation Sites (Map 18/F2)
On the Duncan River Road north of Argenta, there are two forest service sites that provide access to Duncan Lake. The main site offers a boat launch and a beach, while the northern site is little more than an overflow camping area. During the late summer, when the water level of Duncan Lake is low, the beach turns to a large, muddy area filled with stumps. Activities on the lake include windsurfing and fishing.

Goat River Canyon Recreation Site (Map 4/F4)
Found about 11km up the Goat River Road (take a left after the wooden bridge), this is a nice campsite on the forested banks of the Goat River. There is space for nine groups of campers. Visitors will find a streamside trail that leads to a scenic canyon. Swimming is also popular in the deep pools near the bridge.

Hart Creek Recreation Site (Map 5/F7)
This remote site is found at the junction of Hart Creek and the West Yahk River. It is a small (three unit), forested site.

Hawkins Creek Recreation Site (Map 5/B7)
A small, semi-open site is found next to Hawkins Creek. There is space for three groups here but the good access means they are often full, especially during summer weekends and hunting season.

Howser/Glay Recreation Site (Map 18/E1)

On Duncan Lake, this is a medium sized, very popular site with a nice beach and boat launch. Fishing, swimming, and windsurfing are popular pastimes on the lake. The campsite is handicapped accessible, and has space for up to ten groups.

Howser Canyon Rec Site (Map 18/E1)

This site has not been developed, and it might be the better for it. There are no facilities of any kind, and the site is often used as a day-use area, as it is located on a spit on Duncan Lake. It is possible to set up a tent here, too.

Milford Lake Recreation Site (Map 18/F6)

This small (three unit) site is located next to Milford Lake west of the North Arm of Kootenay Lake. The rough access limits vehicle access into the site. The main attractions here are fishing and hunting.

Monica Meadows Campsite (Map 26/B7)

One of the more popular hikes in the district, the trailhead to this site is found 23 km up the Glacier Creek Road. A nice hike leads to the meadows, where you will find wildflowers (in season) tarns, larch (lovely in the fall), and one alpine toilet set up for backcountry campers. The trail sees a lot of use despite the difficult hike that climbs 1500 m (4875 ft) in only 5 km. Be bear aware.

Next Creek Recreation Site (Map 3/G3)

On the western shores of Kootenay Lake, this boat access only site is popular due to the beach.

Oliver Lake Recreation Site (Map 12/A6)

Found along the renowned Gray Creek Pass Road, this nice picnic site is set on an alpine basin complete with a small lake. It is a short walk from the road to the beautiful lake where it is possible to circle the lake or continue onto the ridges in the area. Many of the visitors are travellers on the historic summertime backcountry road that takes you over the Purcell Mountains to Kimberley. The pass itself is found at the 1,869 m (6,100 ft) level making for a scenic drive.

Pebble Beach Recreation Site (Map 11/D2)

This site is either reached by boat on the North Arm of the Kootenay Lake or by hiking 2 km (1.2 miles) down from the Kootenay Lake East Road. There is a small, tenting site next to lake, which offers a beautiful pebbled beach.

Priest Falls Recreation Site (Map 3/D7)

A small day-use area overlooking the Priest River Falls, this picnic area can be accessed off the Monk Creek Road.

Six Mile Lakes Recreation Site (Map 11/A4)

A short hike brings you to this small, camping/picnic site on the shores of a beautiful sub-alpine lake. Anglers often test their luck while trail enthusiasts will find a 3 km (1.8 mile) trail around the lake, which is part of the domestic watershed.

Thompson Lookout (Map 4/F6)

An active lookout above the Creston Valley provides a nice area to picnic. The site also acts as a trailhead to the Rim Trail. The area can be quite hot and dry so bring water.

Tye Beach Recreation Site (Map 3/G2)

This forest service site is comprised of two small, lakeside campsites on the western shores of Kootenay Lake. The northern most site is accessed by boat or trail. The southern most site is accessed by boat or a private road owned by Darkwoods Forestry Ltd. in Nelson. The sites have a beach and offer fishing and swimming.

Rocky Mountain Forest District

A combination of the former Cranbrook & Invermere districts, the Rocky Mountain Forest District covers a large area of southeastern B.C. The area ranges from the Purcell Mountains north of Creston to the Rocky Mountains. The Rocky Mountain Trench, a broad U-shaped valley, separates the two mountain ranges and hosts the mighty Columbia and Kootenay rivers as well as several lakes. As with all regions of the Kootenays, locals pursue basically every type of outdoor activity imaginable. The deep valleys and glaciers within the Purcell Mountains and the endless ridges of the Rocky Mountains are popular backcountry retreats. Several excellent fishing lakes and extraordinary natural features are also found throughout the region.

Bittern Lake Recreation Site (Map 33/C5)

Follow the Mitten Lake Road and turn right before the marshy area. You will soon come to a forest service site on the shores of the tiny Bittern Lake. The site has a dock, one table and a couple places to camp. Fishing is the main attraction to the lake.

Blue Lake Recreation Site (Map 22/B3)

This four-unit, treed site is located on Blue Lake, which offers fair fishing. The site is accessed by the good 2wd Elk River Road.

Botts Lake Recreation Site (Map 26/F1)

The forest service site at Botts Lake is a small (one unit), partially treed site next to the lake. Fishing and hiking are the prime attractions. An electric motor only restriction applies at the lake.

Bugaboo Falls Recreation Site (Map 26/A1)

This is a day use rec site located at the popular Bugaboo Falls. There are picnic tables and three viewpoints at the well-developed site.

Bugaboo-Septet Recreation Site (Map 26/A2)

Accessed by a 4wd spur road off the Bugaboo Road, this small, treed site is located next to the creek and acts as a staging ground for travellers to the Bugaboo Provincial Park or up the Chalice Creek Trail. There are four campsites in a forested setting with fabulous views of the Bugaboos.

Buhl Creek Recreation Site (Map 20/C7)

Located on the Skookumchuck Road, this small (one unit) site is found in an open meadow. Visitors often enjoy the Buhl Creek Warm Springs east of the road or try their luck fishing in the creek.

Butts Recreation Site (Map 8/B6)

On the Flathead Road, this large, open site can be used by trailers and RVs. Beryl and Marl Lakes are a short hike away and offer fishing. There is also a cabin available for public use, which is very popular during hunting season.

Cartwright Lake Recreation Site (Map 26/E1)

On the Leadqueen Frances Road, there are two medium sized, treed sites on the lake complete with a boat launch and dock. Fishing is the main attraction to this popular area. There is space for up to 17 groups between the two sites.

Caven-Gold Creek Recreation Site (Map 6/D5)

This is a small (four unit), heavily treed site at the junction of Caven and Gold Creek. Paddlers, anglers and in fall hunters are the primary users of the site.

Cherry Lake Recreation Site (Map 6/B5)

This is a treed site on the east end of Cherry Lake with space for ten vehicle units. The lake is a good fishing and paddling destination, and there is a cartop boat launch at the site.

Cleland Lake Recreation Site (Map 33/F7)

Surrounded by the dramatic mountain peaks of the Purcell Range, this small fishing lake is a scenic destination. There is space for six groups set along the semi-open shoreline along with a boat launch and dock for anglers. There is a powerboat restriction on the lake.

Cranbrook Community Forest Rec Site (Map 13/G7)

This is a large site found in the popular Cranbrook Community Forest. There are all sorts of hiking, biking, and horseback riding trails in the forest, and space for thirty vehicle units.

Dog Leg Lake Recreation Site (Map 27/A3)

West of Radium Hot Springs, this is a small, forested campsite on a fishing lake.

Dorr Road Rec Site (Map 6/G6) $$$

This is a big site, or rather two sites, on the eastern shores of Lake Koocanusa. Between the two locations, Dorr Road North and Dorr Road South, there are a total of 53 sites, 25 in the north, 28 in the south. There is also a cartop boat launch as well as a few water-only access sites for canoers and boaters.

Dunbar Lake Recreation Site (Map 26/C1)

Frequented by anglers, this small shoreline site offers room for three campers. There is a cartop boat launch (note the engine restriction). The access road into the lake is difficult when wet.

Edwards Lake Recreation Site (Map 7/A6)

Located west of Grasmere, this small, semi-open site is set on the north side of Edwards Lake. Fishing is offered at the lake, which has an electric motor only restriction.

Englishman Creek Recreation Site (Map 6/F5) $$$

This site is one of the largest in the Kootenays, with space for 52 groups. It is found in a semi-open area next to a sheltered bay on Lake Koocanusa. Fishing and swimming are popular in the lake and there is a gravel boat launch. A camping fee is charged during the summer and over long weekends.

Engstrom Pond Recreation Site (Map 20/C4)

Off the Findlay Creek Road, this is a small, semi-open site next to a small, pothole lake. There are tables and a dock at the site, which is accessed by a rough road that can be impassable in wet weather.

Fenwick Lake Recreation Site (Map 28/A6)

Located on a 4wd road off the Kootenay River Road, this is a small, isolated, treed lakeshore site. There is space for three groups at the site.

Findlay Creek Recreation Site (Map 20/D4)

This is a small, partially treed site on the creek, just before it enters a canyon. Fishermen, hunters and paddlers are the primary users of the site. The short but rough access road off the Findlay Creek Road discourages trailers.

Findlay Falls Recreation Site (Map 20/E4)

This is a day-use site used by creek fishermen or visitors that want to take the short walk to the canyon viewpoint and the marvelous twin waterfalls.

Fish Lake Recreation Site (Map 6/B5)

This is a heavily treed site with space for five groups next to Fish Lake. Set in a larch stand this is a very pretty site when the trees turn colour in fall.

Forsyth Creek Recreation Site (Map 22/B2)

This six-unit rec site is used mainly as a staging area for hikers entering the Height of the Rockies Provincial Park. There is a corral for the horses and lots of parking space.

Forty Mile Recreation Site (Map 14/G3)

This is a six-unit, semi-open site at the junction of Quinn Creek and Bull River. The beautiful site is a popular fishing and paddling area. Hunters and hikers also frequent the scenic area.

Frozen Lake Recreation Site (Map 7/G7)

Near the U.S.A. border in the Flathead Valley, this is a five-unit, semi-open site on Frozen Lake. Fishing and paddling are offered at the lake along with a cartop boat launch.

Gilnockie Creek Recreation Site (Map 6/A7)

Used as a staging ground for Gilnockie Provincial Park, the site is found in an open meadow with space for trailers and RVs. There is also a cabin, which is a popular base camp for hunters in the fall.

Gold Creek Bay Recreation Site (Map 6/G7)

This is a six-unit, partially treed site located on a protected bay on Lake Koocanusa. It is accessed off the paved Kikomun-Newgate Road. Trailers and RVs can use the site.

Gold Creek #2 Recreation Site (Map 6/F6)

Located on the Kikomun-Newgate Road, this is a partially treed site with space for four groups. The access road into the site is fairly steep discouraging trailers. Fishing and hunting are the main attractions here.

Graves Creek Recreation Site (Map 21/F3)

On the North White River Road, this is a medium sized site set at the junction of White River and Graves Creek. Fishing and paddling are the attractions.

Halfway Lake Recreation Site (Map 26/F1)

Located on a rough 4wd road from the Westside Road, this is a small (two unit), partially treed site complete with a dock. The lake is visited mainly by anglers.

Halgrave Lake Recreation Site (Map 26/G2)

On a secondary road off the Westside Road, this is a small (two unit), partially treed site next to Halgrave Lake. Anglers and paddlers should note that boats must be hand launched over a muddy shoreline. An electric motor only restriction applies on the lake.

Hall Lake Recreation Site (Map 26/G1)

A small (two unit), forested site next to Hall Lake, this site is used mostly by anglers. There are handicap accessible picnic tables and a dock. An electric motor only restriction applies.

Hartley Lake Recreation Site (Map 15/A5)

The Hartley Lake Site is maintained by the Fernie Rod and Gun Club and is a small, open site next to the lake suitable for trailers and RVs. Fishing is the main draw to the site.

Horseshoe Lake Recreation Site (Map 14/C5)

This is a very popular site located in a pine-aspen stand next to the lake complete with pit toilets and tables. The site is large enough to hold 45 groups. There are many recreational pursuits offered in the area. You can either mountain bike around the grassy lakeshore, go fishing, or hike into the Steeples. Spring-fed Horseshoe Lake is beautifully set beneath the Steeples and is accessed off the Horseshoe Lake Road. There is a powerboat restriction on the lake.

Horseshoe Rapids Recreation Site (Map 27/G5)

This site is accessed 19 km down the Kootenay-Settlers Road on a rutted side road or by paddling the Kootenay River. There are two nice camping spots complete with tables next to a bend in the river known as the Horseshoe Rapids. Visitors often explore the portage trails developed to help scout the river.

Howell Creek Recreation Site (Map 8/A6)

On the Flathead Road, this is a partially treed site with space enough for five groups next to Howell Creek.

Jade Lake Recreation Site (Maps 26/F1, 33/F7)

There is space for one group and a dock at this site. The lake is a popular fly fishing only lake with an electric motor only restriction. The access road is steep and bumpy.

Johnson Lake Recreation Site (Map 20/G7)

Located on a signed road about 0.5 km from Highway 93/95, this site has seven vehicle units complete with tables around the lake. Fishing, a nice beach and turtle viewing are the main attractions to Johnson Lake. It is possible to bring a trailer to the site.

Kikomun Creek Recreation Site (Map 6/F3)

This site is found in a large grassy meadow next to the small, pretty creek. There are five well-spaced campsites with tables but shade is at a premium in the heat of the summer. The site is accessed off the Kikomun Road and trailers may have difficulty as the road into the site is rutted.

Kootenay-White Recreation Site (Map 21/A1)

This small (two unit) site is located at the confluence of the White and Kootenay Rivers. It is primarily used by anglers and paddlers. Road access does not allow trailers into the site.

Krivinsky Farm Recreation Site (Map 22/C5)

This is an open site located in an old homestead near the Elk River. The site is accessed by the Elk River Road and can be used by trailers and RVs. There is space for ten groups.

Lake Enid Recreation Site (Map 27/B5)

This small picnic site with a dock is located on Lake Enid, west of Wilmer. Enjoy the hiking/biking circuit around the lake, suntan on the beach or try fishing.

Lake Lillian Recreation Site (Map 27/B6)

On the paved Toby Creek Road west of Invermere, this is a small picnic site on the forested shores of Lillian Lake. It is used mainly by fishermen and has a beach and dock. There is an electric motor only restriction on the lake.

Lakit Lake Recreation Site (Map 14/A3)

This is an eight unit, semi-open site on a shallow, man-made lake. It is located on a secondary road north of Highway 93. Look for the old corduroy road under the water.

Larchwood Lake Recreation Site (Map 20/G7)

This is a scenic medium sized (eight unit), forested site on pretty Larchwood Lake. It is possible to bring a trailer to the site.

Lazy Lake Recreation Site (Map 14/A1)

Located on the Lazy Lake Road, this is a small, open site on the lake. There is space for 16 groups, and the site can be used as a staging ground for the Lakit Lookout Trail. Fishing is also offered at the lake.

Loon Lake Recreation Site (Map 7/A6) $$$

Found just west of Grasmere, this large, partially treed site is very busy during the summer. The close proximity to the highway attracts trailers and RVs to the 48-unit site. There is an electric motor only restriction on the lake, which is popular with anglers and warm enough to swim in summer. A camping fee is charged during the summer and over long weekends.

Loon Lake Recreation Site (Map 33/A4)

Accessed by a 2wd road, there are two medium sized sites, one on the north end and one on the south end of the lake. Both sites are forested and are quite busy during the summer as fishing can be good. There is a dock on the lake. There is space for four groups.

Lower Harvey Creek Recreation Site (Map 8/A4)

This small site has three camping spots, and is found alongside Harvey Creek. Anglers use this site year-round, as do hunters in the fall.

Maiyuk Creek Recreation Site (Map 21/G1)

This busy site is used as a staging ground for hikers/horseback riders into the Height of the Rockies Provincial Park. There are three campsites to choose from and the corral is popular with horse owners.

Mazur Meadows Recreation Site (Map 6/C5)

This is a large, open site next to Craven Creek. The site is suitable for trailers and RVs.

McLain Lake Recreation Site (Map 33/D5)

Accessed by a 4wd road, this small, treed site is next to McLain Lake. Locating the site can be difficult but the quiet lake and good fishing is well worth the effort. A 100 m (325 foot) portage is needed to launch a boat. There is space for two vehicles at the site.

Mineral Lake Recreation Site (Map 5/E2)
Just west of Moyie Lake, this is a small, open site located at a former sawmill and next to a good fishing lake. The close proximity to Cranbrook and good boat launch makes this a popular spot for local fishermen. There is no overnight parking allowed at the site, which has a couple of picnic tables.

Mitten Lake Recreation Site (Map 33/D5)
This is a large, 19-campsite site complete with a boat launch, tables dock and pit toilets. Since the water in the lake warms in the summer, the site has become a popular site for water skiing, swimming and boating. Fishing is fairly good in the spring. The site is accessed off the Mitten Lake Road and can be accessed with an RV.

Monroe Lake Recreation Site (Map 22/A4)
At the headwaters of the East White River, this small, semi-open site is next to Munroe Lake. The secluded, mountain lake is an ideal retreat for hunters, paddlers and fishermen. There is a cartop boat launch at the site, which has space for three groups.

Mount Forsyth Recreation Site (Map 21/G2)
On the White-Middle Fork Road (access is restricted during logging hours), this small, open site offers paddling and fishing. There is a corral popular with hunters on horseback riders as well as space for three vehicle units.

Nine Bay Lake Recreation Site (Map 33/D6)
This small, forested site is best accessed by trail from Mitten Lake to the north. The many bays on the lake make it a good lake to fish and paddle but a 100 m (325 foot) portage is needed to launch a boat. There is space for two vehicle units at the parking area, and another 11 tenting groups down by the lake.

Norboe Creek Recreation Site (Map 14/G1)
On the Bull River Road, this is a small, treed site next to the Bull River. The site is frequently used as base camp for people accessing Hornaday Pass.

North Star Lake Recreation Site (Map 6/F2) $$$
This is a lakeside site set in a dry, open ponderosa pine stand next to North Star Lake. There is a cartop boat launch for anglers and paddlers. In total, there are 12 units, well spaced to allow for some privacy and space for trailers and RVs. A camping fee is charged during the summer and over long weekends.

Palliser-Albert Recreation Site (Map 28/B5)
This is a medium sized (six unit), open site next to the bridge over the Palliser River. The site is accessed by the rough Palliser River Road and is found at the junction of the Albert and Palliser Rivers. Both rivers are very scenic and worth exploring.

Palmer Creek Recreation Site (Map 5/D1)
North of Lumberton, this small, (four unit) partially treed site is located on a small millpond where fishing is offered.

Pollock Creek Recreation Site (Map 8/A2)
This is a small, partially treed site next to the Flathead River. The site is found on the Flathead Road and is used as a base camp for hikers or bikers accessing the North Kootenay Pass. Fishing is offered at the creek.

Proctor Lake Recreation Site (Map 8/B7)
Accessed by 4wd vehicle, this is a small (three unit), treed site at the north end of Proctor Lake. Fishing is popular at the lake.

Ram-Wigwam Creek Recreation Site (Map 7/B5)
This is a small (two unit), semi-open site at the junction of the Bighorn Creek and the Wigwam River. The site is popular with anglers and hunters.

Riverside Recreation Site (Map 29A/B6)
Riverside is a small (3 unit), partially treed site next to the Elk River. The Elk Valley Road is part of the Trans Canada Trail and fishing is popular on the river.

Rock Creek Recreation Site (Map 6/G3)
This is a four unit site set in an open meadow along Kikomun Creek. The site is accessed off the Rock Lake Road.

Rocky Point Lake Recreation Site (Map 33/A5)
At the end of a 4wd road, this small (one unit), semi-open site is nestled in the forest next to Rocky Point Lake. There is a cartop boat launch and a dock at this rustic site.

Sage Creek Recreation Site (Map 8/B7)
At the junction of the Lower and Upper Sage Roads, this is a small (four unit), partially treed site on Sage Creek.

Sand Lake Recreation Site (Map 6/E1)
North of Jaffray on the good 2wd Bull River Road, this is a small, partially treed site at the east end of Sand Lake. The shallow lake is a prime mosquito breeding area.

Seven Mile Lake Recreation Site (Map 6/B6)
At the headwaters of Caven Creek, this small (six unit) site is found in a partially treed area next to a tiny lake.

Skookumchuck Creek Recreation Site (Map 20/C7)
On the Skookumchuck Road, it is a small, treed site near a waterfall. A short trail leads to the viewpoint overlooking the falls. The remote site is best suited for small units or tenting as there is only space for two groups.

St. Louis Campsite (Map 6/C3)
On the Gold Creek Road, this is a small (two unit), open site set along Gold Creek. The site used to be the location of a logging camp.

Steamboat Lake Recreation Site (Map 26/G1)
At the end of a deteriorating road, this small (three unit), semi-open site on Steamboat Lake. Fishing is the prime attraction.

Stockdale Creek Recreation Site (Map 26/E5)
At the 39 km mark on the Horsethief Road, you will find this small (two unit), treed site. The site is used as a staging ground for hikers on the Stockdale Creek Trail.

Sulphur Creek Recreation Site (Map 14/D4)
This is a small, open site located next to Sulphur Creek. Cold mineral springs are found to the east of the site. The Bull River Road is a good 2wd road that has restricted access during logging hours.

Summer Lake Recreation Site (Map 14/D3)

On Summer Lake, there are 20 treed sites that are often used as base camps for a trek into the Top of the World Provincial Park. There is fishing and paddling at the lake as well as a cartop boat launch.

Suzanne Lake Recreation Site (Map 6/F3)

There is a small, forested site on Suzanne Lake where you will find a cartop boat launch. There is space for ten groups.

Three Island Lake Recreation Site (Map 33/A5)

This is a small, treed site with a boat launch and space for one group. Fishing and paddling are possible on this quiet lake.

Tie Lake Rec Site (Map 6/E1) $$$

Found on Tie Lake Road north of Jaffray, this is a partially treed site on the southeast side of Tie Lake. The 16-unit site is popular during the summer months and offers picnicking, a beach, swimming and water sports. A camping fee is charged during the summer and over long weekends.

Tobermory Creek Recreation Site (Map 29A/B5)

This is a small, partially treed site next to the creek. Tenting spots are found in the parking lot or a short hike into the woods. There is also a cabin that can be used on a first-come first-serve basis. After September 10, the cabin is often full with hunters. The site is found on the Elk Valley Road, which is part of the Trans Canada Trail.

Twin Lakes Recreation Site (Map 26/G1)

There is a small, campsite complete with dock on Twin Lakes. The lakes are popular fishing retreats but have an electric motor only restriction. The site receives heavy use during the summer months.

Upper Elk River Recreation Site (Map 29A/A5)

Located near the end of the Elk Valley Road, this eight-unit site is set in a small, partially cleared area next to the river. The site offers fantastic views of the surrounding mountains and are used as a staging ground for hikers accessing Elk Lake Provincial Park.

Upper Harvey Creek Rec Site (Map 8/A4)

Located along Harvey Creek, this small site has six camping units on the banks of the creek. It is used mostly by anglers and found about 1 km upstream from the Lower Harvey site.

Wapiti Lake Recreation Site (Map 6/E1)

Located 2 km from Highway 3/93 on a good gravel road, there is space for ten groups in a large, grassy meadow at the north end of the lake. It is ideal for an overnight stop over and can be accessed by trailers and RVs. Fishing is offered year round.

Weary Creek Recreation Site (Map 29A/C7)

This is a small (two unit) site located next to the Elk River Road and can be accessed by trailers and RVs. Fishing and hunting are popular pastimes in the area.

White Boar Lake Recreation Site (Map 12/F7)

This spectacular mountain lake hosts a small lakeside camping area, which requires a 100 m (325 feet) walk from the end of the 4wd access road. Try fishing the lake or simply enjoy the great view of the cirque headwall.

Whitetail Lake Recreation Site (Map 20/C3) $$$

A very popular and productive fishing lake is found in the hills to the west of Columbia Lake. Due to the lake's popularity, there are now two large, forested sites with space for 22 groups located on the west side of the lake. There is a fee to camp from May until the end of September.

White River-East Fork Rec Site (Map 21/F3)

There is space for three camping groups at this site on the White River. There is good fishing on the river for bull trout, and anglers are the primary users. Wading or swimming in the river is also popular despite the frigid waters.

Wilbur Lake Recreation Site (Map 33/B5)

On the Crestbrook Mainline, this is a small, partially treed site next to Wilbur Lake. There is a small, boat launch, dock and fishing at the site.

Backcountry Huts

Included below is a listing of many of the backcountry huts and cabins that are open to the public. (More are described in the Parks section). Some of these are user maintained and available on a first-come, first-serve basis, while others must be reserved and charge a fee. The primary users of these huts are backcountry skiers and snowmobilers but there are several cabins that can be accessed by hikers and hunters. As always, we welcome our readers input on more cabins and their whereabouts.

A.O. Wheeler Hut (Map 37/F7)

Located at Rogers Pass in Glacier National Park, this area is considered the best road accessible backcountry skiing destination in North America. Contact the Alpine Club of Canada for more information on the hut.

Butts Recreation Site Cabin (Map 8/B6)

There is a cabin available for public use at this recreation site. Primarily hunters use it in the fall.

Char Creek Cabin (Map 3/E7)

This cabin is used primarily by snowmobilers and is maintained by the Kokanee Country Snowmobile Club. From the cabin there is a lot of alpine terrain to explore. Please take precautions, as this is avalanche terrain.

Copper Hut (Map 2/F1)

Part of the Bonnington Range of backcountry huts, this hut is found on the southwest slope of Copper Mountain in a dense forest. It is a popular hiking and backcountry ski destination.

Doctor Creek Hut (Map 20/A6)

Found at the headwaters of Doctor Creek, this old, renovated cabin is maintained by the local snowmobile club. The cabin, which can also be used by hikers, sleeps six. There is a fee for staying at the cabin. Call the forest district at (250) 426-1700 for more information.

Echo Basin Cabin

This is a snowmobile cabin, managed by Creston Valley Snowmobile Club. It is open to the public for use throughout the year and is user maintained. Please treat it with respect.

Elizabeth Park Hut (Map 39/F6)

Found west of Lake O'Hara in Yoho National Park, this is a beautiful location and a great ski touring destination. Contact the Alpine Club of Canada for more information.

Fay Hut (Map 39/F6)

This quiet ski destination is found above Tokumm Creek in Kootenay National Park. Contact the Alpine Club of Canada for more information.

Gilnockie Creek Recreation Site Cabin (Map 6/A7)

Used as a staging ground for Gilnockie Provincial Park, the recreation site is also home to a cabin. Hikers, snowmobilers and hunters enjoy the user maintained cabin.

Grassy Hut (Map 2/E3)

A difficult to find hut, especially in winter, the Grassy Hut is a popular hiking and backcountry ski destination. It is part of the Bonnington Range of backcountry huts. See Valleys & Vistas for more details on how to find the hut.

Great Cairn-Ben Ferris Hut (Map 37/A1)

Used by backcountry skiers, this hut is found northwest of Mount Sir Sandford in the northern Selkirk Mountains. Contact the Alpine Club of Canada for more information.

Huckleberry Hut (Map 2/G2)

This hut is the easiest to access hut in the Bonnington Range. It also offers the best backcountry skiing in the area.

International Basin Cabin (Map 32/C5)

A popular backcountry ski touring or mountaineer destination, this cabin is found in the remote alpine basin. Reservations are required and there is a fee for staying at the cabin. Call the forest district at (250) 426-1700 for more information.

Jumbo Pass Cabin (Map 19/C1, 26/C7)

Found along the Jumbo Pass Trail, this alpine cabin sleeps up to six hikers. It is a popular backcountry ski touring or backpacking destination. Reservations are required and there is a fee for staying at the cabin. Call the forest district at (250) 426-1700 for more information.

Keystone Standard Cabin (Map 36/C5)

The forest service helps maintain a small cabin high above Lake Revelstoke that is available on a first-come first-serve basis. The cabin is set in a beautiful alpine area that is popular with hikers as well as backcountry skiers and snowmobilers in the winter.

Ladybird Cabin (Map 10/A7)

This user maintained cabin is frequented by snowmobilers.

Lawrence Grassi (Clemenceau) Hut (Map 42/A1)

This hut is so remote that it is really only accessible by plane. It rests on the western edge of the Clemenceau Icefield. Backcountry skiers looking to getaway from it all should contact the Alpine Club of Canada for more information.

Little Slocan Lakes Recreation Site Cabin (Map 10/D4)

Found at the north end of the Upper Little Slocan Lake, the recreation site is found near a cabin. The cabin is user maintained so please help keep it clean

McMurdo Cabin (Map 32/B2)

On the Silent Pass Trail, this mountain cabin sleeps six. The old cabin is busy throughout the year as hikers, mountaineers, backcountry skiers and snowmobilers all explore the area. Reservations are required and there is a fee for staying at the cabin. Call the forest district at (250) 426-1700 for more information.

Mount Patrick Hut

A winter-only hut that is maintained in association with the Purcell Hut Association. It is used by ski tourers in the winter.

Olive Hut (Map 26/D3)

A mountaineering or ski touring hut overlooking the Catamount Glacier at the headwaters of Forester Creek. The stone structure sleeps up to six and is found at 2,650m (8,613 feet) in elevation. Also in the area are the Dave White and Forster Cabin. The latter is a snowmobile cabin. Reservations for all three are required and there is a fee for staying at the cabin. Call the forest district at (250) 426-1700 for more information.

Queen Mary Cabin (Map 28/D4)

Resting on the shores of a fine fishing lake, this cabin is a popular destination for anglers and horse packers.

Ram-Cabin Pass Cabin (Map 7/F6)

A winter-only hut used mostly by snowmobilers. It is designed as a day-use warming cabin, but does see some overnight use. Managed in conjunction with Fernie Snowmobile Association.

Ripple Cabin (Map 3/C7)

Found off the Monk Creek Road, this cabin is maintained by the Creston Valley Ski Club. It is used for backcountry ski touring. Snowmobiles are restricted.

Siwash Cabin (Map 2/E2)

This is a snowmobile cabin in the Bonnington Range northeast of Castlegar.

Stanley Mitchell Hut (Map 39/C4)

Known for it's great views and even better skiing, the Little Yoho Valley is a popular destination during summer and winter. The Alpine Club of Canada maintains a backcountry hut in the valley.

Steed Hut (Map 2/E2)

Located near Marble Lake it will take the better part of a day to access this hut. Hikers and backcountry skiers in the Bonnington Range use it.

Tobermory Creek Recreation Site Cabin (Map 29A/B5)

A cabin in the area can be used on a first-come first-serve basis. In the fall, the cabin is often full with hunters.

Wragge Hut (Map 17/E6)

Popular with anglers, this small shelter is found next to a trail access mountain lake.

Wildlife Viewing

The Kootenays are renowned for their dramatic mountain scenery and abundance of wildlife. People come from around the globe to get a chance to see the many large mammals that grace vast stretches of wilderness in the area. Add in the abundance of lowland areas that are home to waterfowl and other birds and the numerous streams that have spawning kokanee and trout and you can see why the Kootenays have long been a favourite wildlife viewing destination.

In order to improve your chances of spotting birds and animals, wear natural colours and unscented lotions. Bring along binoculars or scopes so you can observe from a distance and move slowly but steadily. Keep pets on a leash, or better yet, leave them at home, as they will only decrease your chances to spot wildlife. Early mornings and late evenings are usually the best time to see most birds and animals.

Never approach an animal directly and for heaven's sake, do not try and bring animals to you by offering them food. Animals can become conditioned to handouts, which may put both of you, into harm's way. Rather, figure out what natural foods they prefer, and situate yourself near where these animals will feed.

What follows isn't a complete list of where you can see animals and birds, but it is a fairly good start. Some of the sites below cater mostly to birders, while other sites feature large mammals like elk and mountain caribou. Still other sites focus on fish. All of them are worth checking out.

Airport Bay & Montana Slough (Map 30/D5)
Found just south of Revelstoke, are a couple areas that are home to a variety of waterfowl, shorebirds and songbirds. Airport Bay is found just north of the airport peninsula, while Montana Slough is a little further south and can be seen from Airport Way.

Akamina-Kishinena Provincial Recreation Area (Map 8/F7)
The habitat preserved in Akamina-Kishinena Provincial Recreation Area is home to a wide range of plants and animals including rare species like the Yellowstone moose and Pigmy poppy, which are found nowhere else in BC. However, the highlight for many people is the chance to see a grizzly bear. These mighty animals are best seen from spring through to fall. Other large mammals you may see include elk, mountain goat, bighorn sheep and deer. Access into this remote area can be difficult.

Arrow Lakes: Nakusp-Fauquir (Maps 9, 16, 17)
In the early spring, the shores of Arrow Lake are a prime place to see nesting osprey. The big nests can be easily spotted from either the highway or from a boat.

Arrow Lakes: Burton Provincial Park (Map 17/A7)
In September, this park is home to spawning kokanee. You can watch the spawning fish, or you can watch various birds (mostly seagulls) feeding on the dead kokanee.

Arrow Lakes: Kuskanax Bridge (Map 17/A2)
The Kuskanax River flows through Nakusp and into Arrow Lake. In September, kokanee spawn in the river and can be seen from a number of places. The best viewing area is from the Highway 23 Bridge.

Big Ranch (Map 15/D1)
Located just off Highway 43 north of Sparwood, this area is the largest uncultivated grassland habitat in the Elk Valley. The grasslands are a major source of winter forage for ungulates like moose and elk. In summer, you are more likely to see deer. It is also important habitat for small mammals, including badgers.

Bull River (Map 14/D7-G1)
The Bull River is home to one of the largest herds of Rocky Mountain Bighorn sheep in the Kootenays. Spotting them can sometimes be difficult, except in winter when they often come down from the hills to graze. Deer and elk can also be seen in the area.

Bummer's Flats (Map 14/A4)
The wetlands of Bummer's Flats are also known as Doran's Marsh. This extensive area is found just north of Fort Steele and is one of the prime stopovers in the Kootenays for waterfowl returning in the spring. In addition to birds, there is a good chance to see deer and elk in the wetlands. A series of dyke trails provide access to the area.

Canal Flats Provincial Park (Map 20/F3)
Found on the east site of Columbia Lake, Canal Flats is used as winter range for a number of large ungulates, like deer, elk and bighorn sheep. As you might expect, the best viewing time is winter. In the spring and summer, this area is home to waterfowl and shorebirds.

Columbia Wetlands: Brisco (Map 33/G7)
The Columbia Wetlands stretch alongside the meandering Columbia River for dozens of kilometres, offering shorebirds and waterfowl places to nest and feed. One of the best viewing areas is near Brisco, where you'll see all sorts of birds—raptors, shorebirds, songbirds and waterfowl— as well as various other critters, like deer and elk.

Columbia Wetlands: Wilmer (Map 27/C5)
While the access into this area isn't as easy as it is for the other Columbia Wetlands sites, it is well worth the effort. You'll see similar birds as with the other sites, as well as elk and deer. The area is also home to turtles, amphibians and beaver.

Columbia Wetlands: Parson (Map 33/C3)
Another in a series of viewing sites along the Columbia River, this area is a prime viewing area for all manner of birds, from raptors to songbirds to shorebirds and waterfowl. Both north and south of Parson, the highway passes by many marshes, many of them with nesting platforms.

Creston Valley Wildlife Management Area and Centre (Map 4/B6)
The wildlife watch checklist for the Creston Valley Wildlife Management area lists 266 species of birds, 56 species of mammals, 16 species of fish, and a handful of turtles, lizards, snakes, frogs and salamanders. This is indeed an excellent area to bring the family to enjoy the wonders of nature. There are dozens of dyke trails to walk as well as viewing platforms. Be sure to visit the Wildlife Centre to pick up the informative brochure.

Dewdney Trail (Map 4/A5)
At the Summit Creek Campground outside of Creston, kokanee can be seen spawning in Summit Creek in late August to September.

Downie Creek (Map 36/B4-D4)
Highway 23 skirts the eastern shore of Lake Revelstoke as it makes its way across the Kootenays. One of the many creeks it crosses is Downy Creek, which is a great place to see mountain caribou in November and December. While it is sometimes possible to see caribou along the highway, or along the Downie Creek FSR (unplowed in winter), you may also have to go for a bit of a hike/ski to see if you can find them.

Duncan-Lardeau Flats (Map 18/F3)
Found along the river connecting Duncan Lake with Kootenay Lake, these flats are home to numerous songbirds in the spring and summer.

Elizabeth Lake (Map 13/G7)
Located in Cranbrook, BC, the Elizabeth Lake wetlands provide nesting opportunities for many species of birds and are home to blue-listed Painted Turtles. In addition, Elizabeth Lake is one of only two known locations in Canada for the Dione Copper Butterfly.

Elko (Map 7/A3)

The area around Elko is used by ungulates such as moose, elk and bighorn sheep as a winter range. These large animals can often be spotted foraging in the fields from the highway.

Reflection Lake (Map 38/F7)

Reflection Lake is located just south of Golden. Access to this area is easy, and you'll see a variety of bird species, from waterfowl to shorebirds. There is also a heron rookery.

Glacier National Park (Maps 31, 32, 37, 38)

This large national park is a haven for wildlife, from moose to mountain goats, from bears to birds. Because man does not threaten the animals, they can often be seen alongside the Trans-Canada highway. For a more intimate experience, you can look for wildlife from one of the park's many trails.

Height of the Rockies Wilderness Area (Maps 21, 22, 28, 29A)

There is no road of access into this area, making access difficult. However, there are a couple main trails that will help you access the alpine. The park is home to numerous large ungulates, like moose, bighorn sheep and deer. In the winter, mountain goats are frequently seen on the slopes above Forsyth Creek.

Elk Lakes Provincial Park (Map 29A)

This provincial park is sandwiched between the Height of the Rockies and Peter Lougheed Provincial Parks. It shares many of the same wildlife viewing characteristics with large animals, like deer, elk, moose, bighorn sheep, mountain goats, and bears being the main attraction. You may also see various species of birds, including various raptors.

Highway 31A: Kaslo-New Denver (Map 18)

As you drive along Highway 31A, you will notice a number of beaver dams along Carpenter Creek and the Kaslo River. Not only are there good viewing opportunities for beavers, the ponds form great habitat for waterfowl and other birds.

Hill Creek (Map 24/A2)

Just outside Galena Bay on Upper Arrow Lake, this small creek provides a great opportunity to view spawning kokanee. These landlocked sockeye salmon create a brilliant display in September.

Hills (Map 17/F5)

The marshlands just outside of Hills are a migratory stopover in spring for a variety of waterfowl, shorebirds and songbirds.

James Chabot Provincial Park (Map 27/C6)

While there are a variety of birds to be found in this area, the big draw is the wide variety (over 40 species) of dragonflies.

Kikomun Creek Provincial Park (Map 6/F3)

Kikomun Creek plays host to thousands of returning kokanee every September and into October. This is a great place to watch the landlocked sockeye salmon as well as bears that feed on them.

Kimberley Nature Park (Map 13/B2)

The Kimberley Nature Park is a year-round wildlife viewing destination. You may see deer, moose, bear or birds as you wander the trails.

Kokanee Creek (Map 11/C5)

As you might gather from the name, this creek is a prime place to watch spawning kokanee in September.

Kootenay National Park (Maps 27, 33, 34)

Wildlife is a common sight along Highway 93 as it cuts through the heart of Kootenay National Park. Large ungulates, like moose, bighorn sheep, mountain goat, and elk are often seen grazing next to the highway. You may also see bears, and, on occasion the much more shy wolf.

Lardeau River (Map 25/A5)

Most of the rivers and streams in the Kootenays are known for their spawning kokanee. The Lardeau River, on the other hand, is a great place to watch

large rainbow (up to 14 kg/30 lbs) spawn in mid-May. The best viewing area is at the south end of Trout Lake where there is a viewing platform and interpretive signs.

Meadow Creek (Map 18/E2)

The Meadow Creek spawning channel is a good place to watch kokanee spawn in September. This is a huge channel—over 3 km (2 miles) long, with an annual return rate of about a quarter of a million salmon. It is a pretty amazing sight to see so many brilliant red fish in one area.

Moberly Marsh (Map 38/E6)

This wetland—part of the Columbia River matrix of wetland habitat—is a prime viewing area for waterfowl and shorebirds. The best viewing times are spring and fall. The area also provides habitat for deer and elk in the winter. A series of dikes provide access.

Mount Revelstoke National Park (Maps 30, 31)

This high elevation park is home to bears, caribou and a variety of birds. The park is also known for its prodigious wildflower bloom in summer.

Pend D'Oreille (Map 2/E7)

335 ha of land near the Seven Mile Dam have been set aside as white-tailed deer habitat. The deer frequent the area in the winter (certainly not during hunting season). The area also supports a population of marmots.

Premier Lake Provincial Park (Map 21/A7)

This popular provincial park plays host to spawning rainbow trout in June. Brood stock from these trout is used to stock thousands of lakes around the province.

Purcell Wilderness Conservancy (Maps 18, 19, 20)

This large protected area has no road access. However, backcountry explorers will have a good chance of seeing various large animals, like moose, bighorn sheep, mountain goat and bear.

Radium Hot Springs: Village (Map 27/C4)

The town sits at the Junction of the Columbia River Valley and the Sinclair Creek Valley, which are the traditional wintering grounds of bighorn sheep. It is possible to see these sheep on the nearby slopes, or even wandering through town.

Radium Wetlands (Map 27/B3)

Just north of the town of Radium Hot Springs are the Radium Wetlands. This area is home to a variety of water and shore birds. A viewpoint overlooking the Columbia River can be found along the Forestry Landing Road.

Stagleap Provincial Park (Map 3/C7)

This high elevation park is an excellent place to view mountain caribou during winter. Highway travellers can also see bears, bighorn sheep and mountain goats as they climb the shoulder of Lost Mountain.

Syringa Creek Provincial Park (Map 1/G2)

In the winter, bighorn sheep feed on the slopes above Syringa Creek. You will often find them down near the highway. You may also see deer and elk in the area.

Wasa Sloughs (Map 13/D2)

Highway 93/95 travels through a marshy area between Wasa and Fort Steele. This is a great place to see all manner of birds. In particular, the area is known for its large migratory birds such as Canada geese, great blue herons, ospreys, and eagles.

Whiteswan Lake Provincial Park (Map 21/B2)

Inlet Creek, in Whiteswan Provincial Park, is a good place to watch spawning rainbow trout in May and June.

Windermere Creek (Map 27/D6)

Windermere Creek plays host to spawning kokanee in September and October. It also plays host to various birds of prey, who feed on the spawned out fish.

Yoho National Park (Maps 33, 39)

This large mountain park is home to a variety of large ungulates and predators, like moose, bighorn sheep, mountain goat, cougars, wolves and bears. While bears are a fairly common sight, the other predators are much shyer and rarely seen. Many of these animals can be seen alongside the highway.

Backroads of the Kootenays

Generally speaking, Southeastern BC has an excellent backroad system that provides easy access into the backcountry. Cars or RV's can travel many of the secondary roads, most of which are paved or hard packed gravel. The paved roads are shown on the maps as thicker black lines with a white fill. Thicker black lines mark the better gravel or main roads. Branching from the main roads are side roads and trails of all shapes and sizes. These routes, marked by thinner black lines and dashed lines on our maps, should be left to the off-road enthusiasts and trail users.

Although we have done our best to classify the road systems on our maps, road and trail conditions can change very quickly. Weather, the status of road systems and the degree of maintenance can all affect the road systems. During logging hours (6am to 6pm) or at times of extreme fire hazard, logging and rural roads may be closed to the public. Other roads may be gated to protect equipment in the area. Further, with the change in the Forest Practices Code, more and more roads are becoming deactivated. This can result in bridges and culverts being removed, making the road virtually impassable. Be sure to pay attention to road signs and always watch for logging trucks. Please contact the nearest BC Forest District Office for information on specific road conditions.

Backroad travellers should also note that the BC Forest Service has undergone a lot of changes over the last few years. These changes include the amalgamation of several Forest Districts and the reduction in the number of Forest Service Recreation Sites. Luckily, industry, First Nations, clubs and various communities have stepped in to help maintain a portion of this spectacular resource. However, the Forest Service Roads (FSR) will not see the same level of maintenance as they have in the past. To be more specific, Wilderness Use Roads (the thin black lines on our maps) will not be maintained. This is going to restrict access to many of the recreation sites, and people without access to four-wheel drive or ATVs may find it more difficult to access the backcountry.

Our website, http://www.backroadmapbooks.com/bmupdates. htm, has updates on access issues, as well as any new or changed information. If you try to go somewhere and find that things have changed from what we've written, please send us an email and let us know. As always, we encourage comments, stories and pictures from our readers. Please drop us a line.

Winter Recreation
(Snowmobiling and Cross-country Skiing)

One of the most delightful times to explore the Kootenays is during the winter. The crisp, cool clean air and the lack of other human activity (not to mention lack of mosquitoes) will allow you to experience the peace and solitude local residents have known for years. The lack of development in the Kootenays also allows for a lot of informal routes to explore. Please help protect your sport and avoid private property.

Snow can hit the hills as early as late October. By late November, keen winter recreationists will be able to explore many of the higher elevation (above 1,500 m/4,875 feet) areas as well as a few of the lower elevation areas. The winter season usually lasts into March in the valleys and even as late as June in the mountains.

Snowmobiling

From the remote Flathead to the spectacular alpine around Revelstoke, the Kootenays offer world-class snowmobiling. Some of these areas are well known, and are being actively promoted. Other areas are known only to the locals, who would prefer to keep it that way. Many of these riding areas are maintained by local clubs and are usually brushed and marked with small triangular markers. In some cases cabins are available, and provide a great place to rendezvous and warm up.

Below we have provided write-ups on the more popular areas to ride in the Kootenays. If you are new to an area, we suggest you contact the local club to get more details on a route. Most clubs are more than willing to set you up with a guide. Call the BC Snowmobile Federation at (250) 566-4627 for more information.

As always, avalanches are a hazard when travelling through the mountains in the winter. Always carry an avalanche beacon, and never travel alone. When in doubt, stick to groomed routes.

East Kootenays

Abruzzi Creek/Cordona Creek (Map 29A/B6)
In Elk Lakes Provincial Park, these popular hiking trails are accessible by snowmobile in the winter. BC Parks is monitoring the impact of snowmobiles on wildlife in the area, and these trails may close. For now though, this remains a popular area with locals and visitors alike.

Aldridge Creek (Map 22/D1)
The Aldridge Creek trail heads up Aldridge Creek to Fording Pass, on the BC/Alberta boundary. There is good alpine riding up in the high country, and the trail hooks up with trails in Kananaskis Country around Etherington Creek and Cataract Creek.

Alexander Creek Valley (Map 15/F3)
Accessed off the Crowsnest Highway (Hwy 3) 1 km (0.6 mile) east of the weigh station, an unplowed 40 km (24.4 mile) logging road dissects the valley and offers easy riding. The real draw here, at least for hardcore snowmobilers, is the nine alpine basins with names like Nine Mile Basin, Fedorek Basin, Sheep Basin, Goat Basin and Mud Hole, along the way. The Elk Valley Mountaineers maintain two cabins in the valley.

Bingay Creek (Map 22/A2)
A logging road runs up Bingay Creek into the Mount Hornickel area. Snowmobilers can access this area off the Elk River FSR.

Blaeberry River Road (Maps 38/F4-39/A1)
Depending on whether the road is plowed, this logging road can offer a 160 km (97.6 mile) return trip. Overall, it's a fairly easy route that climbs slowly to the alpine.

Bobbie Burns (Map 33/A4-32/F4)
If the road is not plowed, riders will find an easy 80 km (48.8 mile) return route that follows a main-haul logging road. Before crossing Bobbie Burns Creek (Map 32/G5), branch north and follow the road and trail to the heli-skiing lodge. Access is found off the Crestbrook Mainline (which may be plowed) at the small town of Parson. The extensive logging road network extending on the bench northwest above the Columbia River towards Nicholson is also popular with snowmobilers.

Bull River Valley (Map 14/D3-F5)
This valley offers great riding opportunities along its extensive logging road network. The most popular route is to access Summer Lake from Galbraith or Tanglefoot Creek Road. You can also start on the Wildhorse Road or the Bull River Road.

Coal Creek Trails (Maps 15/A7-7/C2)
Starting at the Fas Gas in Fernie, riders can follow the groomed Coal Creek Road to the cabin at Minnesota Flats, as well as Flathead Ridge. The groomed trails offer fun riding for beginners, while expert riders can access the open alpine. Some old roads hook up with the Flathead area, which in turn hooks up with the Corban Creek area, which connects to trails in Alberta, which connect to...needless to say, there's a lot of riding to be had here.

Corbin Valley (Map 15/G7)
A maze of logging roads, a 30 m (100 ft) wide pipeline and huge alpine bowls, provide challenges for all levels of riding in the Corbin Valley. It is possible to sneak into Alberta (and another huge riding area) from here. Be sure to pick up the Southwestern Alberta Backroad Mapbook for more details.

Crossing Creek Trail (Map 22/B3)
Northwest of Elkford, this trail, also known as the Koko Claims Trail, takes riders up the valley, and then down into the Bull River/White River area. There are four large riding areas accessed off this trail, including Smith Basin and Mear Lake.

Cummings Creek (Map 15/C2)
North and west of Sparwood are logging roads leading up Cummings Creek and Telford Creek. In winter, these are reasonably popular, though ungroomed, snowmobile routes. Farther north, snowmobilers also ride along logging roads in the Brule Creek/Nordstrum Creek area.

Flathead Ridge (Map 7/D2)
The Flathead Ridge area is one of the most popular snowmobiling areas around Fernie. The defining feature of the area is a pipeline, from which you can access several large bowls for great alpine riding.

Forester Creek (Map 27/A4-26/D3)
North of Invermere, this valley is a very popular spot for snowmobilers. It offers a series of logging roads that access a large mountain meadow. More experienced riders can access Thunderbird Lake and Whirlpool Lake.

Forsyth Creek (Map 22/B1)
It is possible to follow the old road/trail up Forsyth Creek to the border of Height of the Rockies Provincial Park. Snowmobiles are not allowed in the park itself.

Glenogie Creek Road (Map 39/A7)
This logging road provides access to a 100 km (60 miles) return ride, which includes some fabulous alpine riding. Avalanche hazards exist making the ride suitable for the experienced rider only.

Gorman Creek/Lang Creek (Map 38/E7-B6)
Most riders begin at the golf course in Golden and ascend the slopes to these high elevation drainages. Bring lots of fuel as there is a lot of terrain and an elevation gain of about 2,150 m (6,988 feet) to cover. This area is best left to the experienced riders prepared to travel through avalanche shoots, narrow logging roads and several cut blocks. You eventually reach the sub-alpine.

Hartley Pass (Map 15/A5)
This is a popular area for the expert riders looking for deep snow and steep terrain. The route eventually breaks into the Bull River Valley on the west side of the Rockies. Depending on how far they plough, the ride could start off Dickens Road and follows the Hartley Lake Road over the pass.

Hope Creek (Maps 37-38, 42-43)

Another large riding area, this drainage offers a 100 km (60 mile) return ride accessing some alpine meadows. The route is recommended for experienced riders only. The best access is found on the F Road (Map 42/G7), off the plowed Bush River Road.

Hospital Creek (Map 38/F7)

The bench above Golden has many logging roads allowing you to make a 30 km (18 mile) return trip. Intermediate riders will enjoy the challenge of the steep incline.

Mount 7 Trail (Map 38/G7-32/G1)

Mount 7 is the prominent peak above Golden. Snowmobilers will find a fairly easy 25 km (15.3 mile) return route and a shelter along the way to the top.

Mount Bleasdell (Maps 22/C1-29A/C7)

The Elkford snowmobiling club maintains a cabin at the base of Mount Bleasdell, which can be accessed along a series of logging roads cum snowmobile routes. Also in the area is a looping, ungroomed route that takes riders into the Gardenev Creek drainage, then back to the cabin along a groomed trail.

Moyie Lake East (Map 5/G1-F6)

East of Moyie Lake, there are three different access sites to an extensive logging road network around Moyie Mountain. You can start at the Yahk River Road off Highway 3/95, take the Gold Creek Road, which leads south from Cranbrook, or ride the Sundown Creek Road to the Yahk River Road. The last route accesses Mount Olson.

Moyie Lake West (Maps 5/C3-13/C6)

The logging road network west of Moyie Lake also makes for some very good snowmobiling. You can either start on the Moyie River (Map 5/C1), Lamb Creek (Map 5/D2) or Perry Creek (Map 13/C6) roads. The most popular ride in the Perry Creek area is to access Grassy Mountain. The Cranbrook Snowmobile Club helps manage over 80 km (48.8 miles) of trails in the area.

Quartz Creek Road (Map 38/A5)

This logging road accesses a network of trails/roads and a shelter. If you are more interested in an easy ride, try the 40 km (24.4 mile) return trip along the logging road. For the more adventurous, you can ride the open terrain and choose your own path.

Sand Creek Area (Map 6/F1)

From Jaffray to Galloway, a backroad loop offers the snowmobiler open terrain with lots of untracked powder. The ride takes you past Tie Lake and Sand Lake. It joins the Tie Lake Road to the Bull River Road.

Spillimacheen River (Maps 33/A4-32/A1)

This main haul road leads to the spectacular alpine of Caribou Peak (Map 32/B3), Bald Mountain (Map 32/A1) and Silent Pass (Map 32/C4). The main road provides over 160 km (96 miles) return of easy riding, while experienced riders will find some serious climbing for added challenge. A couple cabins are also found in the area.

Susan Lake (Maps 38/A3-37/G3)

The Susan Lake Road, which is found off the Bush River Road, is generally unplowed and offers a steady incline to the lake. The ride can be over 100 km (60 miles) return and is best suited for the intermediate rider.

Toby Creek/Jumbo Creek (Maps 27/A6-19/F1)

From the Panorama Resort west of Invermere, the Toby Creek Road takes you to several historic mine sites where many of the structures are still standing. A side trip up the Jumbo Creek Road will take you to several large bowls. Please stay off the heli-skiing runs in the area!

Weary Creek (Map 29A/C7)

East of the Weary Creek Recreation Site, an old road up Weary Creek takes riders into the Weary Gap area, and some great alpine riding.

West Bench (Map 38/E7-C5)

The western slopes above the Columbia River from Golden to above Donald provide over 80 km (48.8 miles) return of easy riding. The route follows an old logging road system but riders should note that several bridges are out.

West Kootenays

Akolkolex River and Mount McCrae (Maps 30/E6-23/G1)

From the end of the plowed road off Airport Way south of Revelstoke, you can access a 75 km (45.8 mile) road network, which offers riding for all levels of experience. An ascent to Mount McCrae (Map 24/A1) is a scenic but more challenging alternative.

Bonnington Range (Maps 2, 10)

The Bonnington Range northeast of Champion Lakes Provincial Park offers hundreds of kilometres of logging roads to explore. Most of these wilderness areas provide fairly easy riding along heavily forested roads and the occasional viewpoint from a mountain vista. No matter what your level of riding, you will find something to make you happy.

South of Highway 3A, try the Rover Creek Road (Map 2/E1), Midslope Road (Map 2/E1), Copper Mountain Road (Map 2, 10/G7) or Giveout Creek Road (Map 2, 11/A7).

In the mountain range east of Castlegar and north of Salmo, try exploring the Beavervale Road (Map 2/E4), Bombi Summitt (Map 2/D4), Grassy Creek Road (Map 2/F3), Erie Creek Road (Map 2/G4) and Stewart Creek Road (Map 2, 3/A3).

In the area north of the Pend D'Oreille River and south of Highway 3B, try the Mount Kelly (Map 2/E5) and Blizzard Mountain (Map 2/D7) areas.

Boulder Mountain (Map 30/B5)

From the parking lot at Highway 1 or 4–6 km (2.4-3.6 miles) along the Jordan FSR (if it is plowed), this area is the most popular snowmobiling area near Revelstoke. The terrain is suitable for all levels of snowmobilers and the Revelstoke Snowmobile Club has developed the area by signing and grooming 40 km (24.4 miles) of trails. The chalet at the top of the mountain at 2,100 m (6,890 feet) is a popular rendezvous for snowmobilers who often access the 80 sq km (48.8 sq miles) of alpine riding opportunities. It is found at the end of Bezanson, Kirkup and Veideman Trails.

Cayuse Creek (Map 1/F1)

Located above Lower Arrow Lake, this series of logging roads hook up to roads in the Ladybird Creek area from the Deer Park Road.

Char Creek (Map 3/D6)

Near the summit of the Salmo/Creston Highway (Highway 3), the Char Creek Road leads to a cabin maintained by the local club. This is a very scenic alpine riding area.

Cooley Lake (Maps 2/B1-10/D7)

The Castlegar Snowmobile Association maintains a cabin in the Cooley Lake area. This area features deep powder and great views over the Slocan Valley. The unplowed Goose Creek FSR, off the Pass Creek Road, provides access from the south.

Creston Area Routes (Maps 3, 4)

Popular valleys around Creston that see plenty of riders in the winter are Sanca Creek (Map 4/A1), Blaze Creek (Map 3/F5), Goat River (Map 4/F5-E2), Little Moyie River (Map 4/G7) and Bayonne Creek (Map 3/E5). In these areas, most riders stick to the logging road networks. All routes are easily accessed off Highway 3 or Highway 3A.

Frisby Ridge Area (Map 30/C3)

From the parking near the Revelstoke Dam, you can access over 144 sq km (87.8 sq miles) of spectacular alpine via a 25 km (21.3 miles) one-way main trail. The snowmobile club grooms the main trails while the alpine is untracked. The chalet is shared with cross-country skiers and maintained by the Revelstoke Nordic Ski Club. Snowmobilers should stay clear of the areas that have been closed for wintering caribou (between Dec 15 and April 15) and should respect cross-country skiers. If caribou are spotted anywhere snowmobile activity takes place, shut your snowmobile off and let the animals leave the area.

Grizzly Creek (Maps 10/A5-9/G6)

The local club maintains a cabin 25 km (15.3 miles) along a groomed trail in the Grizzly Creek drainage. From the cabin, it is possible to access riding areas suitable for all levels of difficulty.

Hall Mountain Area (Map 23/F3)

From Highway 23, you can ride up the Vigue Road to access kilometres of logging roads and a few wilderness lakes, including Cousier Lake and Pingston Lake. Do not ride on Cousier Lake, as the ice can be unstable.

Keystone/Standard Basin (Map 36/B5)

Keystone is a very popular destination due to the amazing variety and scenery. However, it is also prime caribou habitat, and there are a number of restrictions on sledding in the area. The area south of the towers on Keystone is closed, as is the area south and west of the long ridge. Restricted areas are well marked along their closure boundary. If caribou are spotted anywhere snowmobile activity takes place, shut your snowmobile off and let the animals leave the area.

Kidd Creek (Map 4/D5-5/A3)

A main haul logging road in the Kidd Creek drainage is a popular snowmobiling area east of Creston. It is possible to continue north into the Moyie Lake area.

Koch Creek (Map 9/D2–10/A1&2)

The Koch Creek Road heads past the popular Grizzly Creek area, and into the Dago and McKean drainages. This area isn't as popular as, say, Grizzly Creek, as there is only one way in and out, and the riding is either easy (along the road) or expert.

Kokanee Range (Maps 10, 11)

In the Kokanee Range there are a number of valleys, which provide over 100 km (60 miles) of good riding opportunities via old logging roads. Some of the more popular routes are:

Cedar Creek Road (Map 11/F3) is found north of Ainsworth Hot Springs. The route leads to Cody Caves Park.

Duhamel Creek Road (Map 11/A5) leads from Highway 3A northeast of Nelson up to Six Mile Lake.

Kokanee Glacier Road (Map 11/C5) is an unplowed road that leads from Highway 3A to Gibson Lake, in Kokanee Glacier Provincial Park. Please avoid the temptation to explore the alpine areas in the park.

Lemon Creek Road (Maps 10/G4-11/A4) is a 22 km (13.4 mile) long route that starts from Highway 6, south of Slocan City.

North Star Mountain (Map 3/F6-G7)

Off the Salmo/Creston Highway (Highway 3), the Maryland Creek Road offers a good 17 km (10.4 miles) one-way ride below North Star Mountain. You can continue past Boundary Lake along Boundary Creek.

Pedro Creek (Map 10/E6)

An easy ride between Castlegar and Slocan City is found along Pedro Creek. Head for the towers via the Pedro Creek Road. An alternate, much more difficult route begins from Highway 6 near the Slocan Junction.

Rialto Creek (Map 2/A2)

Accessed off the Syringa Park Road, just past Keenleyside Dam, this is a smaller area, but with lots of logging roads to explore. The roads climb most of the way up Ladybird Mountain.

Sale Mountain Area (Map 30/E1)

For early season snowmobiling, take Highway 23 north from Revelstoke for about 18 km (11 miles) and park. From there, ride up the switchback road some 20 km (12.2 miles) to the microwave tower. If you head north from the tower, you will find open fields and plenty of slopes to climb. Please stay off the heli-skiing runs and keep out of the national park. Also, watch for backcountry skiers!

Cross-country Skiing

Cross-country and backcountry skiing is a popular pastime for recreationists wishing to experience the peace and tranquility of the Kootenays. Many of the cross-country ski trail systems are found in forested settings along old road systems, which allows for fairly easy skiing. The occasional viewpoint and warm-up hut helps you enjoy your visit. Backcountry skiers will have to be more adventurous when looking for a good route to explore. Several options are described in the multi-use trails as well as in the provincial and national park sections of this book. We also recommend picking up a copy of Valleys and Vistas. This book highlights a few of the premier routes found in the West Kootenays.

Apex Busk Ski Area (Map 3/A1)

Not to be confused with the popular ski hill near Penticton, this Apex Ski Area offers a relatively flat, 3 km (1.8 mile) loop ideal for beginners. There is also a 1.2 km (.7 mile) loop, which is lit for night skiing. Both these trails are suited for classic and skating. Further south on Highway 6, moderate skiers will find a 7 km (4.3 mile) loop leading to the old Euphrates Mine. This popular racing loop has two hills to challenge the skier. Trails also lead north to Cottonwood Lake and south to the Clearwater Creek Ski Trail. There is a rather hefty fee charged for day trippers.

Beaver Valley Cross-Country Ski Trails (Map 2/C5)

Found just east of Champion Lakes Park, this network of ski trails offers easy to advanced trails. The trails follow old roads through the pine forest and may be track set.

Blackjack Cross-Country Ski Trails (Map 1/G6)

Located off Highway 3B outside of Rossland, there are over 55 km (33.6 miles) of trails with 25 km (15.3 miles) being machine groomed awaiting skiers of all levels of experience. The trails are set in the forest and offer plenty of climbing, downhills as well as up and down terrain making the skiing highly technical. There is a log cabin at the beginning of the trail system, which offers wood heat and a waxing bench and another logging cabin 5 km (3 miles) along the main trail (Gibbard Trail). There is a fee for the use of the trails, which offer opportunities for both skating and classic skiing.

Boivin Creek Ski Area (Map 22/C6)

Next to the Elkford at the Wapiti Ski Hill, there is a network of 15 km (9.2 miles) of cross-country trails for you to enjoy. This is an alpine area that can have good snow as early as late November.

Bonnington Range Ski Touring Route (Map 2/D4-G1)

This classic alpine ski touring route follows the summits of the Bonnington Range east of Castlegar and south of Nelson. There are several cabins and huts strategically placed and available for public use (contact the Ministry of Forests in Castlegar at 250-365-8600 or pick up a copy of Valleys and Vistas for more information). Experienced backcountry skiers with good route finding skills can make a hut-to-hut traverse that can take from one to six days. Snowmobilers also frequent the area.

Brewer Creek (Map 27/A7)

A difficult route into the upper headwaters of Brewer Creek, this winter ski touring destination is not only a ski touring destination, but is also partially open to snowmobilers. Many people snowmobile from km 10 of the Hawke Road to km 26 of the Brewer Creek FSR, where they strap on skis. From here, the route generally follows the summer hiking trail into an area of meadows and ridges. It is 5 km (3 miles) from the trailhead south to the Brewer Mineral Pass, though your options are pretty limitless.

Catamount /North Star Glaciers (Map 26/D3)

This area is usually the domain of heli-skiers, but some backcountry skiers take a snowmobile to the Forster Creek Meadows, then ski in from there. (The glaciers are closed to snowmobiling.) Either way, this is a great ski touring area. Reservations are required at the Olive Hut, situated between the two glaciers.

Clearwater Creek Cross-Country Ski Trails (Map 3/B2)

This cross-country ski network is found off the Clearwater Creek Road and offers 6.5 km (4 miles) of beginner and intermediate cross-country ski trails. There is a fee to use maintained trails. A trail heading north connects this with Camp Busk and the Apex Busk Ski Area.

Cottonwood Lake Ski Area (Map 3/A1)

Cottonwood Lake offers 3 km (1.8 miles) of trails beginning just north of the Apex Ski Area and leading to the lake. Since there are two hills to climb near the lake, the trail is best left for moderate skiers. A fee is charged for use of the trail and there is a warm-up hut on site. A trail heading south connects this with the Apex Ski Area.

Creston Valley Wildlife Management Area (Map 4/B6-B4)

Like all the trails in the Creston area, this series of dikes and trails are not groomed, but are fairly easy to follow. The trails can be accessed from three places, Duck Lake, The Wildlife Centre and Summit Creek Park. There are many, many kilometres of trails and dikes that can be explored.

Cross River Canyon Trails (Map 27/F3)

Found near the southeast tip of the Kootenay National Park, this small site has long been a favourite of backroad travellers. For this reason, the Forest Service has created a user maintained recreation site here. The site is RV accessible.

Dawn Mountain Nordic Trails (Map 38/D7)

This series of 18.5 km (11.3 miles) of cross-country trails are found near the Kicking Horse Ski Area, west of Golden. There are trails for all levels of abilities with the loops ranging from 2.5 km (1.5 miles) to 7 km (4.3 miles) in length. Found at the 1,300 m (4,265 feet) level, the trails can provide good views. A shelter is also available.

Delphine Creek (Map 26/G7)

Found off the Toby Creek Road, just southwest of the Panorama Mountain Village, an old logging road system follows the Delphine Creek Valley bottom. The main route is a fairly easy ski, while the side routes climb up into much more difficult terrain.

Evening Ridge (Map 3/B1–11/B7)

Just before the Whitewater Ski Area, this 5 km (3 mile) difficult route heads north, along a road that crosses Hummingbird Creek. From here, head up the creek to Hummingbird Pass, and gain the ridge from the pass. There are a number of avalanche slopes to beware of.

Fernie Area (Map 14/G7, 15/A7)

Found in the scenic Elk Valley, Fernie offers two formal areas to explore south of town off of Highway 3. The Snow Valley Resort provides 10 km (6 miles) of groomed trails in a forested setting. Island Lake Lodge offers 15 km of backcountry skiing in the Cedar Valley Old Growth Reserve.

Frisby Ridge (Map 30/C4)

Better known as a snowmobile destination (see above for directions), this area is also popular with backcountry skiers. There is a cabin just below treeline that is shared with snowmobilers.

Glacier National Park/Balu Pass Trail (Map 37/F7)

Glacier National Park is famous for its snow and despite the avalanche risk, backcountry skiers love to explore the area. The most popular route is the Balu Pass Trail around Rogers Pass. In addition to this 10 km (6.1 mile) trail, backcountry skiers can head up Grizzly Shoulder, Grizzly and Ursus Minor Mountains or into Bruins Pass. More details and alternative routes can be found in the Valley & Vistas guidebook.

Huckleberry (Clearwater Creek) Pass (Map 3/B2)

To access this moderate backcountry ski trail, park at the Clearwater Creek Ski Trails Parking Lot, and ski east on the trails for 5 km (3 miles), until you join back up with the Clearwater Creek FSR. Ski up the road for the same distance via some very steep switchbacks. Watch for a road heading south; this logging road/old mining road follows Huckleberry Creek (stay left at intersections) down to the Wildhorse Road. Ski west until you hit km 4, which is how far the road is usually plowed. Oh yeah, you probably want to leave a second vehicle here, rather than retracing your route. Give yourself the better part of a day to ski this 20 km (12.2 mile) route, gaining 769 m (2,500 ft).

Jumbo Pass (Map 19/E1-C1)

This route is usually done is conjunction with an overnight stay at the Jumbo Pass Cabin (reservations required). This area is famous for its snow (a proposal is in the works to see the Jumbo Mountain area turned into a new ski resort), and features some great alpine or tree skiing. The ski route follows

the unplowed Jumbo Road to the hiking trail and may or may not include an extra jaunt down the Toby Creek Road (depending on if that road is plowed). Skiing the Jumbo Road adds an extra 16 km (9.8 miles) onto the 4.5 km (2.7 mile) hiking trail.

Kimberley Nordic Centre (Map 13/C4)

The Nordic Centre is found past the North Star Ski Hill in the Kimberley Nature Area. You will find 26 km of double track set and skating trails, 30 km (18.3 miles) of single-track trails and 3.5 km (2.1 miles) of lit tracks for night skiing. The trails are for all levels of ability and there is a warm-up hut on site. For the advanced skier, the Moe's Canyon Trail is a 7.5 km (4.6 mile) loop requiring a 110 m (360 feet) climb. The trail is not track set and is steep and narrow in places. At one point, it enters out on the ski hill.

Kitchener Trails (Map 4/F5)

There are a pair of trails that are used for cross-country skiing in the Kitchener area east of Creston. One of the trails is found on the Wyendel Brothers and Lumber Company property. It is a marked trail that is open to the public. The second trail is found by driving past the second bridge to Kitchener, and turning left at the café. A road leads about 1 km (0.6 miles) north to the powerlines. From here, it is possible to ski the old road for about 3 km (1.8 miles).

Kootenay National Park

Kootenay National Park lacks the development of other national parks. For backcountry skiers, this means that the area is wonderfully wild and often untracked. There are a number of relatively easy, but ungroomed routes for cross-country skiers, plus a few nice intermediate trips for folks looking for an introduction to backcountry skiing.

Chickadee Valley (Map 34/B1)

This moderate route follows the Chickadee Creek Valley for 5 km (3 miles), through an old burn area, to an open area at the head of the valley. The surrounding valley slopes are very open, and are good places to practice telemarking.

East Kootenay Fire Road (Maps 34/C7-27/F3)

The East Kootenay Fire Road runs parallel to the Kootenay River for the better part of 30 km (18 miles). There are numerous access points near the northern section of the road, while the southern end of the road hooks up with the Natural Bridge Cross-Country Ski area (see below).

Hector Gorge (Map 34/6)

This easy 11 km (6.7 mile) trail follows an old fire road as it loops away from, then back to, Highway 93. Overall, you gain 150m (488 ft) in elevation.

Simpson River (Map 34/E5)

It is an easy 16 km (9.8 miles) from where the Simpson River flows into the Vermillion to the boundary of Kootenay National Park, gaining 120 m (390 ft) along the way. From here, it is possible to ski to the Surprise Creek Shelter in Mount Assiniboine Provincial Park (2 km/1.2 miles), or follow the river up through the Simpson Pass and down into Sunshine Village in Banff. This difficult extension is also shown in the Southwestern Alberta Backroad Mapbook.

Stanley Glacier Trail (Map 34/C2)

Take the moderately difficult trail (most people need skins, or at least a good wax), as you climb 275 m/894 ft up the Stanley Creek Valley to the treeline. From here it is possible to head up onto the slopes to put in a few turns, or return to the parking lot, via the creek.

Tokumm Creek Trail (Map 34/A1)

While many skiers heading up Tokumm Creek are destined for Fay Hut (about 12 km/7 miles), this is not the only route in the Tokumm area. A popular option is to ski to Kaufmann Lake and back in a long day (30 km/18.3 miles), or to continue beyond to the Eagle Eyre, near Opabin Pass (in Yoho). Another option is to ski beyond Fay Hut to Colgan Hut. The Kaufmann Lake route is considered moderate, while all the other routes are difficult.

West Kootenay Trail (Map 34/B6)

From the Kootenay River Crossing Warden Station, this easy 19 km (11.6 mile) route follows an old fire road to the park boundary. There is a bridge that crosses the river and it is possible to return along the less developed trail on the other side of the river.

Lumberton Ski Trails (Map 5/C1)

Over 30 km (18 miles) of trails utilize the unplowed logging road network in this wilderness area. The trails are found off the Moyie River Road, west of Lumberton and are managed by the Kootenay Nordic Outdoor Club.

McMurdo/Spillimacheen Glacier (Map 32/C4)

While the silent pass area is a popular snowmobiling area, the McMurdo/Spillimacheen Glacier area is zoned for ski touring. You can use the McMurdo Cabin as a base to explore the area but reservations are required. The usual parking is at km 21 or km 27 on the Spillimacheen Forest Service Road (depending on how much snow there is). Since you would have to ski about 38 km of road to get to the start of the Silent Pass Trail, most people snowmobile into McMurdo Cabin and ski from there.

Mount MacPherson Cross-Country Ski Trails (Map 30/C6)

Located off Highway 23 about 7.6 km (4.6 miles) south of the Trans-Canada Highway/Highway 23 junction, there are 25 km of groomed trails and 5 km of untracked trails. The routes, for all levels of skiers, range from relatively flat trails to ones with steep hills and are ideal for both skating and classic skiing. A large trail map is found at the trailhead and there is a warm-up hut available on the trail system.

Mount Plewman/Old Glory (Map 1/G5)

This backcountry touring route starts out along the Old Glory Trail and climbs onto the summit of Mount Plewman. From here, there are numerous options for descents from the top, and a couple of alpine bowls to play in. It is also possible to continue on to Old Glory.

Mount Revelstoke National Park (Map 30/E4)

For cross-country skiers, most of the Summit Parkway is left unplowed in winter but you can still reach the trailer drop-off. From there, you can take one of two loops, which are track set by Parks Canada. The loops are 5 km (3 miles) and 2 km (1.2 miles) in length and take skiers to the ski chalet. For the more adventurous, the steep Summit Trail (20 km/12.2 miles return), which is not track set, takes you to the alpine.

Natural Bridge Cross-Country Ski Trails (Map 27/F3)

The parking lot to this remote ski area is 16 km (9.8 miles) from Highway 93 on the Cross River Road. There are four loops, two for beginners and one each for intermediate and advanced skiers. In total, there are 12 km (7.3 miles) of groomed trails with the longest and most difficult being the highlight

of the area. This 5 km (3 mile) advanced route crosses the natural bridge at the spectacular upper canyon of the Cross River. A warming hut on the Oochucks Loop overlooks the Kootenay River.

Nipika Cross-Country Centre (Map 27/G3)

At 14 km (8.5 miles) along the Cross River Road is this series of trails and a warm-up hut. These trails are maintained by donations from users, and are mostly easy or intermediate. The only exception is where this trail system links up with the Natural Bridge trails by crossing the natural bridge, along a fairly difficult trail.

Panorama Cross-Country Ski Trail (Map 27/A6)

At the Panorama Resort, there are 20 km (12.2 miles) of well-developed cross-country trails to explore. The trails are also used for horseback riding, mountain biking and hiking in the spring through fall.

Paulson Cross-Country Ski Trails (Map 1/E4)

With three access points on Highway 3B and a 45 km (27.4 mile) trail system to explore, there is plenty of variety for skiers of all abilities. The forested loop trail around Nancy Green Lake (at 1,300m/4,225 feet) is the easiest and most popular route. The advanced skiers can explore the various routes along the alpine ridges further west. The Castlegar Nordic Ski Club maintains a few day-use shelters and provides some track setting..

Sale Mountain Area (Map 30/E2)

A popular snowmobiling and backcountry skiing area is found about 18 km (11 miles) north of Revelstoke on Highway 23. This area is very challenging, as you must climb up a switchback road about 20 km (12.2 miles) to the microwave tower. North of the tower there are open fields to explore. Be careful of heli-skiers and snowmobilers in the area.

South Star Cross-Country Ski Trails (Map 5/G1)

From the end of 38th Avenue in Cranbrook, a network of 30+km (18.3 mile) of groomed forested trails is offered for skiers of all ability. The trails are located between the powerline and Hogg Creek Road and offer a warm-up hut as well as some nice vantage points.

Stagleap Provincial Park (Map 4/D7)

At the infamous Kootenay Summit on Highway 3, Stagleap Park offers everything from an easy 3 km (1.8 miles) route along an old road around the lake to some difficult but scenic ridge routes. The warm-up cabin is a popular spot for skiers and highway travellers alike and it is not uncommon to see caribou in and around the area in the winter.

Welsh Lakes (Map 26/E3)

Access into this area is the same as for the Catamount/North Star Glaciers (see above), which means that you'll either be skiing up Forster Creek Road, or taking a snowmobile to the end of the road. Either way, it is a challenging route that climbs up to the lakes and the beautiful alpine areas that surround.

Wensley Creek Cross-Country Ski Trails (Map 17/B2)

Located on Upper Brouse Road east of Nakusp, this 9.6 km (5.9 mile) trail network is formed in a figure 8 to allow skiers to explore as many different options as they want to. The trails, which are forested and groomed, are rated for beginner to intermediate skiers since they are generally flat and follow old logging roads. An A-frame shelter is also available. The system is used for biking and hiking in the non-snow seasons.

Yoho

Yoho is a great place for cross-country and backcountry skiers alike. The trails are ungroomed, but the easy and moderate trails are usually quickly tracked, making them easy to follow. Some trails cross avalanche paths and anyone skiing a moderate or difficult trail should have backcountry skiing experience. Yoho is also home to a number of classic winter ski traverses (like the Bow-Yoho Traverse and the Wapta Traverse), but these are best left to experienced mountaineers.

Amiskwi Trail to Amiskwi Pass (Map 39/D6-B2)

The long, difficult trail starts at the Natural Bridge and follows part of an old First Nations trade route, which traversed Amiskwi Pass. After crossing the bridge over the Amiskwi River, turn north along the Amiskwi Trail for a daunting 35.5 km (21.7 miles). A large burnt area at Fire Creek provides views in an otherwise heavily forested valley. However, the open slopes of Amiskwi Pass offer terrific views of the Mummery Icefield in the Blaeberry Valley. Backcountry camping is permitted in the Amiskwi Valley if you obtain a wilderness pass. The trip is 75.8 km (46.2 miles) return.

Chancellor Peak Road (Map 33/C1)

From the Trans-Canada Highway, the summer access road to Chancellor Peak Campground parallels the Kicking Horse River and offers easy skiing and great views of the Ottertail and Beaverfoot ranges. The trail is 4 km (2.4 miles) return and is an excellent place to see a variety of animal tracks.

Emerald Lake Circuit Trail (Map 39/D5)

The groomed trail begins at Emerald Sports, and crosses the lake to by-pass the run-out area of a large avalanche slope on Emerald Peak. On the east side of the avalanche path, the trail angles up from the lakeshore onto the summer horse trail. The easy 5.2 km (3.2 mile) trail follows gently undulating terrain to the end of the lake where it connects with the Emerald Basin Loop (a 5.3 km side route around the alluvial fan, through trees and glades back to the Emerald Lake Circuit). Continue around the east side of Emerald Lake to a junction where the groomed trail once again goes across the lake back to Emerald Sports. The other fork is an unmaintained trail. It climbs over a moraine, passes Peaceful Pond and ends at the parking lot and is recommended for experienced skiers only. Stay off the lake, except where there is a maintained trail (thermal springs in the lake can cause weak sections in the ice).

Emerald Lake Connector Trail (Map 39/F6)

Start at the Field Visitor Centre, and follow the trail along the Kicking Horse River then cross the Trans-Canada Highway and ski up the Tally Ho Trail to the junction for the Natural Bridge or Emerald Lake. The right hand fork continues on to the Emerald Lake Road, and then parallels the road through rolling terrain that provides skiers with opportunities to work on technique. After crossing the bottom of an avalanche slope, the trail drops down to follow the Emerald River, with many lovely views, and brings you directly to Emerald Lake. You can stop for rest or refreshments, or continue on a variety of trails at the lake (see above). This is a 22 km (13.4 mile) return, intermediate route.

Ice River Trail (Map 33/D2)

From Hoodoo Creek Campground follow the road south for 1 km (0.6 miles) to the gate at the beginning of the Ice River Trail. The trail is a former fire road, which ascends gradually over slightly rolling terrain, with some moderately steep hills, to the Lower Ice River Warden Cabin. It is 37 km (22.3 miles) return through a beautiful valley.

Kicking Horse Trail (Map 39/C6)

From the Natural Bridge it is possible to access the Otterhead River along the Kicking Horse River. Ski 2.4 km (1.5 miles) along the road down a gradual hill, past the Emerald River to the Amiskwi River Bridge. Cross the bridge and continue left along the fire road for 4.1 km (2.5 miles) to the Otterhead River. If you add in the Tally Ho Trail (below), it is a 13 km (7.9 miles) return trip from the Visitor Centre in Field.

Lake O'Hara Fire Road (Map 39/D3)

From the Lake O'Hara parking lot, just east of Wapta Lake, the trail climbs moderately to the shores of Lake O'Hara. The trail crosses several avalanche paths and is 23.4 km (14.3 miles) return to the lake. At the 10 km (6 mile) mark strong skiers can take the trail to Linda Lake. It is 2 km (1.2 miles) one-way to the lake or 5 km (3 miles) one-way to Duchesnay Basin. Detailed maps of the Lake O'Hara area are recommended and lunch is available at the lodge from February to April. The day-use only cabin, Le Relais, is open on weekends.

Lake O'Hara Parking Lot to the Great Divide (Map 39/G5)

From the Lake O'Hara parking lot, just east of Wapta Lake, ski along the road to the picnic shelter and interpretive display. This is an easy 11 km (6.7 mile) return trip. For other options, continue east along the road to Lake Louise in Banff National Park (7.5 km/4.6 miles one-way), or take a side trip to Ross Lake (see below).

Little Yoho Valley (Map 39/E4)

From the trailhead on the Yoho Valley Road, ski 13 km (7.9 miles) to Takakkaw Falls (see Yoho Valley Road) and continue up the Yoho Valley

to Laughing Falls. This last stretch is a gradual climb except for a steep section on Hollingsworth Hill. It is possible to continue on the summer trail from Laughing Falls into the Little Yoho Valley. After a series of switchbacks, the climb moderates to an easy grade until the ACC's Stanley Mitchell Hut. The trail is 44.4 km (27 miles) return.

Monarch Trail (Map 39/C5)

This easy 12 km (7.3 mile) trail begins from Yoho Brothers parking lot, across the road from the Field Visitor Centre and extends to Monarch Campground on the Yoho Valley Road. From the parking lot, it drops down to follow along the north bank of the Kicking Horse River for 1 km (0.6 miles). Cross the Trans-Canada Highway and follow the trail along the base of Mt Field, across two small avalanche paths and on to Monarch Campground. Here you can see the old portals from Kicking Horse Mine in Mt Field, and from Monarch Mine across the valley in Mt Stephen.

Ottertail Trail (Map 39/E7)

From the Trans-Canada Highway, 7.8 km (4.8 miles) west of Field, the fire road climbs moderately for the first few kilometres then becomes more gradual for the remainder of the trip. At McArthur Creek, the view of the Goodsir Towers dominates the scene. The moderate trip is 28 km (17 miles) return, but skiers can travel an additional 6 km (3.7 miles) to the base of Mount Goodsir.

Ross Lake Circuit (Map 39/G5)

From the Lake O'Hara parking lot, follow Highway 1A until you reach the Ross Lake trailhead sign on your right. The trail climbs gradually for 1.3 km (.8 miles) to this small lake bounded by a great rock wall. Turn west at the lake and continue for 3.2 km (2 miles) to the Lake O'Hara Fire Road. Turn north (right) at the fire road to return to the parking lot. There are some narrow and fast sections on this circuit, which is 9.5 km (5.8 miles) total.

Sherbrooke Lake (Map 39/F5)

From the parking lot behind West Louise Lodge on Wapta Lake, the intermediate trail climbs steadily for 2 km (1.2 miles), leveling off before reaching the lake at kilometre 3.1 (mile 1.9). The lake sits in a narrow valley surrounded by steep avalanche slopes. If you continue to the back of the lake, a further 1.4 km (0.9 miles), you will be in avalanche terrain. The return trip is an exciting run, best accomplished on fresh snow. This route is 6.2 km (3.8 miles) return.

Tally Ho Trail (Map 39/D6)

From the Visitor Centre, this easy trail follows the Kicking Horse River downstream for 0.5 km (0.3 miles) then crosses the Trans-Canada Highway to join the Tally Ho Trail. This trail, originally a carriage road, was built at the turn of the century so visitors could travel to the Natural Bridge and Emerald Lake. The trail climbs gradually for about 1.5 km (0.9 miles) through an avalanche area before descending to a junction. The left trail descends to the Natural Bridge, where it links to the Kicking Horse Trail. The trail on the right is the Emerald Lake Connector trail. The return trip is 7 km (4.3 miles).

Wapta Falls (Map 33/C1)

This easy trail is 8.2 km (5 miles) return, and starts from the Trans-Canada Highway in the park's west end. The first 1.6 km starts on the summer access road before joining the hiking trail. There are a few rolling hills but the effort is rewarded with a spectacular view of frozen Wapta Falls. The trail continues to a lower viewpoint down river from the falls. Mist makes this lower section too icy to ski.

Yoho Valley Road (Map 39/E5)

In winter, the Yoho Valley Road is not plowed beyond Monarch Campground, but it is track set to the base of the switchbacks (7 km/4.3 miles). On the way, you pass the Upper Spiral Tunnel Viewpoint and the Meeting of the Waters, where the Yoho River flows into the Kicking Horse River. Skiers continuing beyond the switchbacks to Mt Field, Takakkaw Falls and the Upper Yoho and Little Yoho Valleys (see Little Yoho Valley) should be equipped for backcountry travel. The trail crosses several avalanche paths on Mt Wapta (do not stop in the avalanche zones) and winter camping is available at Takakkaw Falls Campground if you have a wilderness pass. The moderate route to Takakkaw Falls is a 26 km (15.9 mile) return.

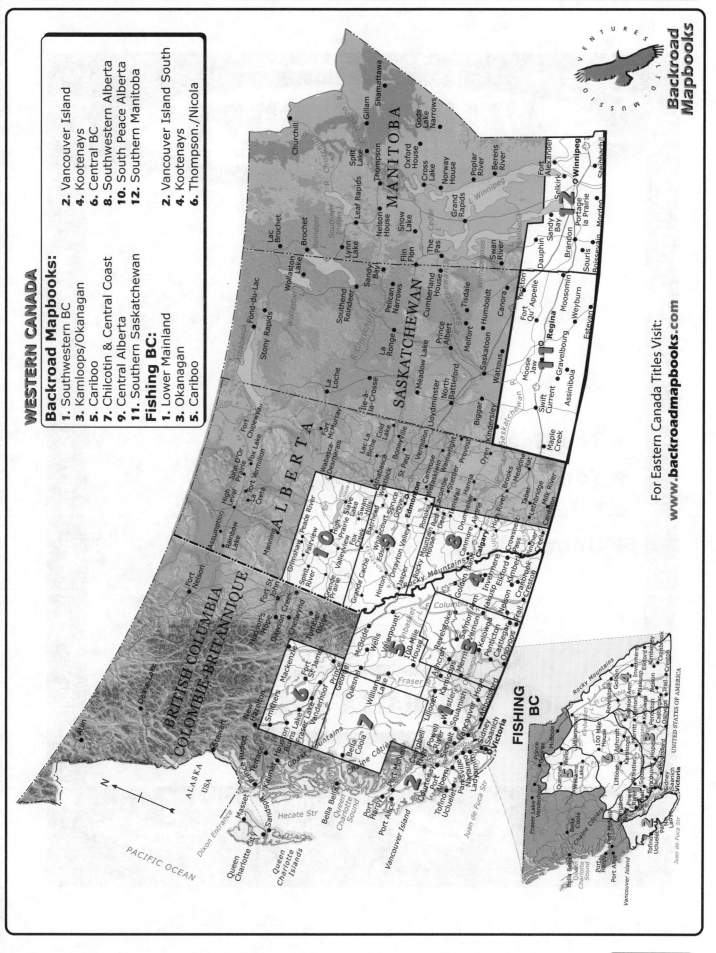

WESTERN CANADA

Backroad Mapbooks:
1. Southwestern BC
2. Vancouver Island
3. Kamloops/Okanagan
4. Kootenays
5. Cariboo
6. Central BC
7. Chilcotin & Central Coast
8. Southwestern Alberta
9. Central Alberta
10. South Peace Alberta
11. Southern Saskatchewan
12. Southern Manitoba

Fishing BC:
1. Lower Mainland
2. Vancouver Island South
3. Okanagan
4. Kootenays
5. Cariboo
6. Thompson./Nicola

For Eastern Canada Titles Visit:
www.backroadmapbooks.com

Backroad Mapbooks

VENTURES LTD. MISSION

Kootenay Mapkey

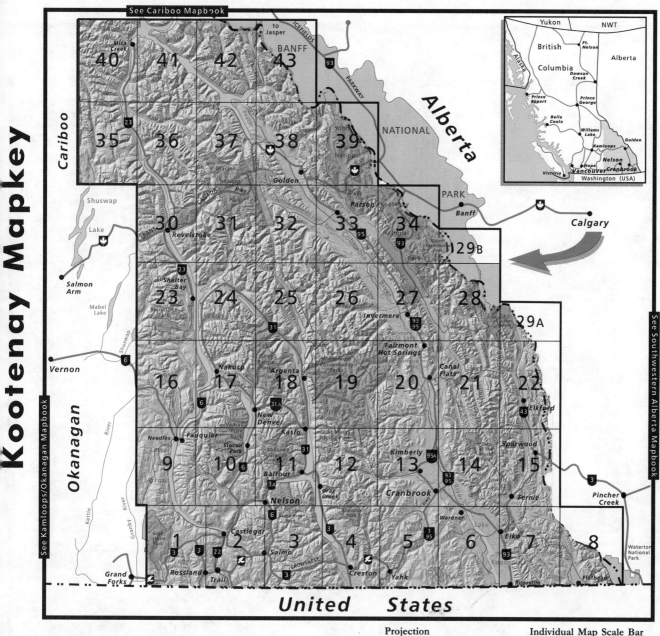

See Cariboo Mapbook

to Jasper

BANFF

NATIONAL

Alberta

PARK

Banff

Calgary

Yukon | NWT

British Columbia | Alberta

Ft. Nelson

Dawson Creek

Prince Rupert

Bella Coola

Prince George

Williams Lake

Golden

Kamloops

Nelson

Hope

Victoria | Vancouver | Cranbrook

Washington (USA)

Cariboo

Okanagan

Shuswap

Lake

Mabel Lake

Salmon Arm

Vernon

Mica Creek

Revelstoke

Golden

Parson

Shelter Bay

Invermere

Fairmont Hot Springs

Canal Flats

Nakusp

Argenta

New Denver

Kaslo

Kimberly

Sparwood

Elkford

Needles

Fauquier

Slocan Park

Balfour

Gray Creek

Cranbrook

Fernie

Nelson

Castlegar

Salmo

Creston

Yahk

Wardner

Elko

Pincher Creek

Grand Forks

Rossland

Trail

Roosville

Flathead

Waterton National Park

See Kamloops/Okanagan Mapbook

See Southwestern Alberta Mapbook

United States

Legend for the Maps

Projection
North American Datum 1983
Transverse Morcator Projection
Coordinate Conversion NAD83
(WGS84)

Individual Map Scale Bar
Scale 1:200,000 or 1cm = 2km
2km   0km   4km
1 km = 0.6214 mi.

Recreational Activities:

Anchorage
Boat Launch
Beach
Campsite / Limited Facilities
Campsite / Trailer Park
Campsite (trail / water access only)
Canoe Access Put-in / Take-out
Cross Country Skiing
Diving
Downhill Skiing
Fishing
Golf Course
Hang-gliding
Hiking
Horseback Riding
Mountain Biking
Motorbiking / ATV
Paddling (canoe-kayak)
Picnic Site
Portage
Rock Climbing
Snowmobiling
Snowshoeing
Wildlife Viewing

Miscellaneous:

Airport / Airstrip
Beacon
Cabin / Lodge / Resort
Fishing BC Lake
Float Plane Landing
Forestry Lookout (abandoned)
Gate
Highways
   Trans-Canada
   Secondary Highway
Interchange
Lighthouse
Marsh
Microwave Tower
Mine Site (abandoned)
Parking
Pictograph Site
Point of Interest
Portage (metres)
Ranger Station
Town Village, etc
Travel Information
Viewpoint
Waterfalls

Line Definition:

Highways
Paved Secondary Roads
Paved City Roads
Forest Service / Main Roads
Active Logging Roads (2wd)
Logging Roads (2wd / 4wd)
Unclassified / 4wd Roads
Deactivated Roads
Trail / Old Roads
Routes (Undeveloped Trails)
Long Distance Trail
Snowmobile Trails
Paddling Routes
Powerlines
Pipelines
Railways
Wildlife Management Units

Provincial Park

Recreation Area/ Ecological Area

City

Restricted Area / Private Property

Glaciers/ Swamps

Indian Reserve

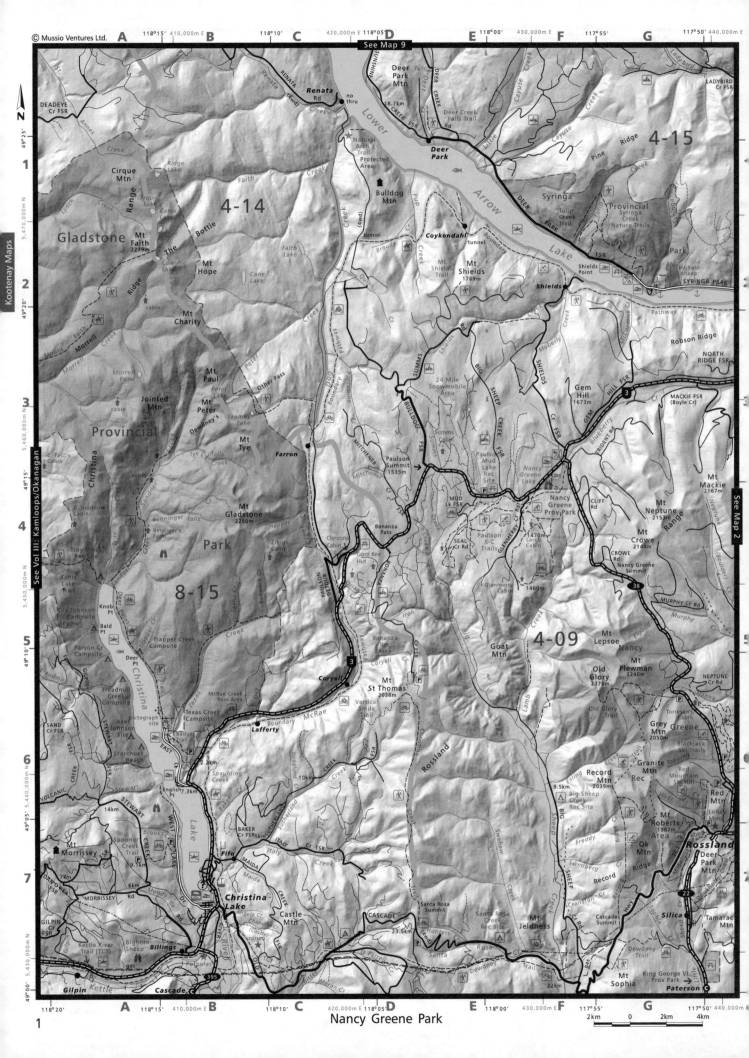

Kootenay Maps

See Vol III: Kamloops/Okanagan

N

Map labels (selected):

DEADEYE Cr FSR

Cirque Mtn

Gladstone Range

4-14

Mt Faith 2279m

The

Mt Hope

Mt Charity

Mt Paul

Mt Peter

Mt Tye

Provincial

Jointed Mtn

Christina

Park

8-15

Mt Gladstone 2250m

Farron

Renata (4wd) Rd

Renata

no thru

Deer Park Mtn

Deer Creek Falls Trail

18.7km

Deer Park

Natural Arch Trail Protected Area

Bulldog Mtn

Lower

Arrow Lake

Coykendahl

tunnel

Mt Shields Trail

Mt Shields 1789m

Shields

Shields Point

4-15

Syringa

Provincial Syringa Creek Nature Trails

SYRINGA PARK

bighorn sheep

Robson Ridge

NORTH RIDGE FSR

24 Mile Snowmobile Area

Summs Cabin

Gem Hill 1673m

MACKIE FSR (Boyle Cr)

Paulson Summit 1535m

Paulson Mud Lake Rec Site

Nancy Greene Lake

Nancy Greene Prov Park

Blueberry

Mt Mackie 2167m

Christina Cabin

Bonanza Pass

Gord Keir Hut

MUD Lk FSR

SEAL Cr Rd

Paulson X-C Trails

1470m Larch Cabin

CLIFF Rd

Mt Neptune 2153m

Mt Crowe 2144m

Glenmerry Cabin

1460m

Nancy Greene Summit

38

MURPHY Cr Rd

Bonanza Back Area

Goat Mtn

4-09

Mt Lepsoe

Old Glory 2376m

Mt Plewman 2240m

Mt St Thomas 2038m

Vertical Smile Trail

Coryell

Lafferty

Boundary Trail

McRae Creek Rest Area

Texas Creek Campsite

Rossland

Old Glory Trail

Grey Mtn 2050m

Greene

Blackjack Ski Trails

Record Mtn 2039m

Big Sheep Creek Rec Site

Granite Mtn

Red Mountain Ski Hill

Red Mtn

9.5km

Spaulding Creek

10km

Mt Roberts 1987m Area

LeRoi Mine

Rossland

Deer Park Mtn

Spooner Creek Trail

Mt Morrissey

Fife

MAIDA

Christina Lake

Castle Mtn

CASCADE

23.5km

Santa Rosa Summit

Santa Rosa Creek Rec Site

Mt Jeldness

Record

Cascade Summit

Silica

Tamarac Mtn

Kettle River Trail (TCT)

Bighorn Sheep

Billings

Potholes

gas

Gilpin

Cascade

395

Mt Sophia

King George VI Prov Park

Paterson

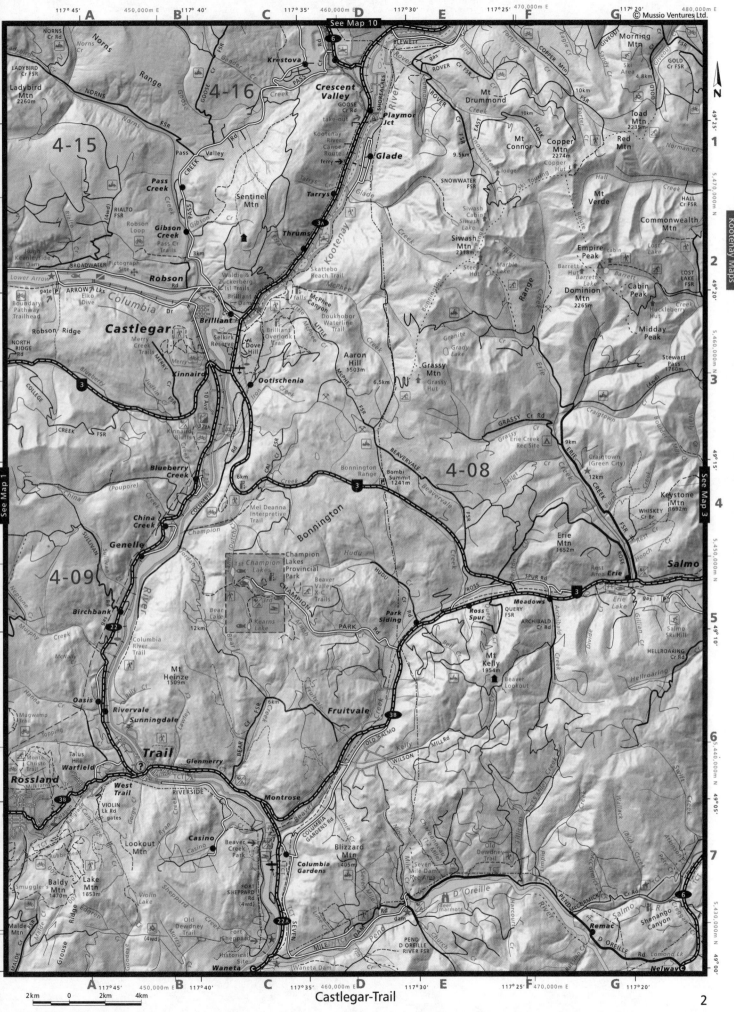

See Map 10

See Map 1

See Map 3

4-15

4-16

4-08

4-09

Castlegar

Trail

Rossland

Salmo

Crescent Valley

Glade

Tarrys

Thrums

Robson

Brilliant

Kinnaird

Ootischenia

Blueberry Creek

China Creek

Genelle

Birchbank

Oasis

Rivervale

Sunningdale

Warfield

West Trail

Glenmerry

Montrose

Casino

Columbia Gardens

Fruitvale

Park Siding

Ross Spur

Meadows

Erie

Remac

Nelway

Waneta

Krestova

Pass Creek

Gibson Creek

Playmor Jct

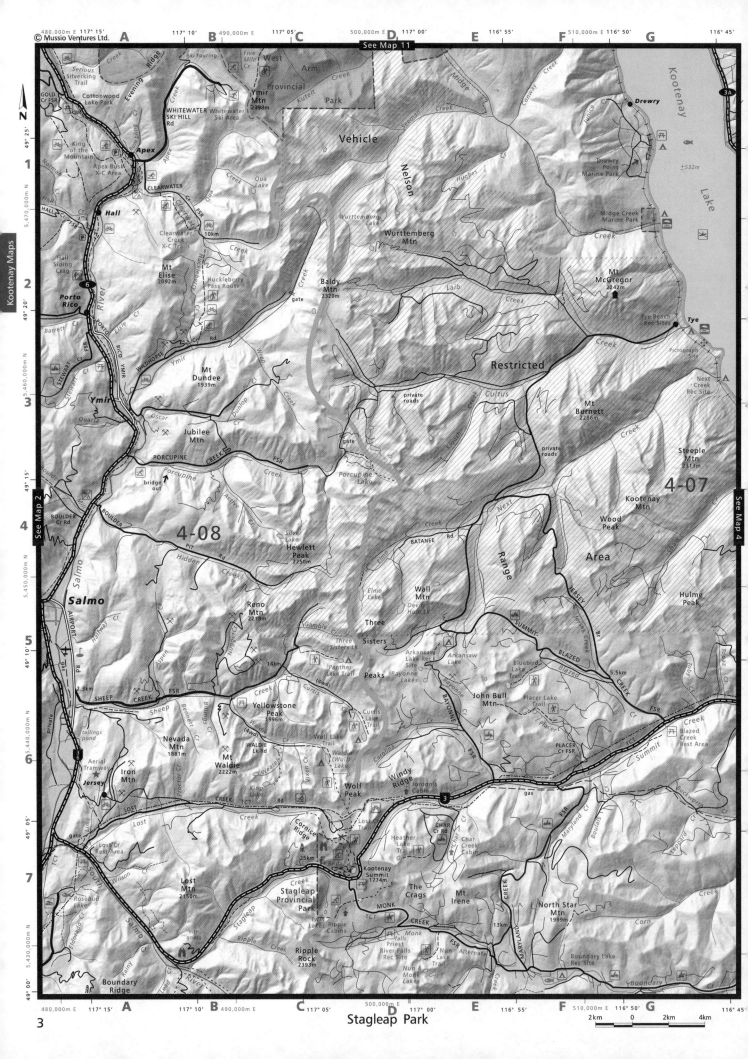

Kootenay Maps

See Map 2

See Map 4

Stagleap Park

3

2km 0 2km 4km

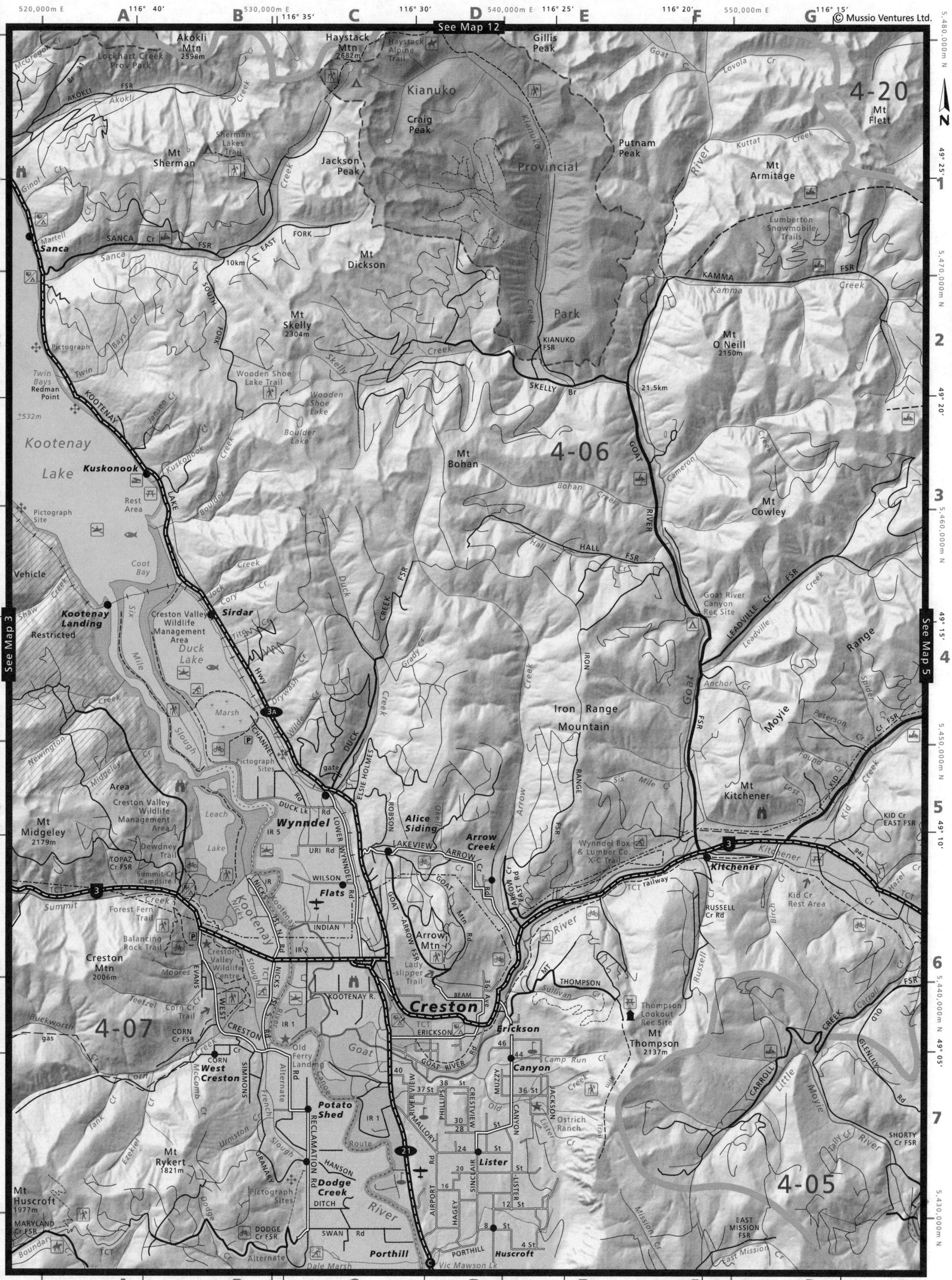

4-20

N

520,000m E 116° 40' 530,000m E 116° 35' 116° 30' 540,000m E 116° 25' 116° 20' 550,000m E 116° 15'

A B C D E F G

See Map 12

Akokli Mtn 2598m

Lockhart Creek Prov Park

Haystack Mtn 2682m

Haystack Alpine Trail

Gillis Peak

Kianuko

Craig Peak

Mt Flett

Mt Sherman

Sherman Lakes Trail

Jackson Peak

Putnam Peak

Mt Armitage

Provincial

Lumberton Snowmobile Trails

Sanca

SANCA FSR

Martell

EAST FORK

Mt Dickson

Park

KAMMA

Kamma Creek

10km

Mt Skelly 2304m

KIANUKO FSR

Mt O Neill 2150m

Pictograph

Redman Point

Twin Bays

Wooden Shoe Lake Trail

SKELLY Br

21.5km

±532m

Wooden Shoe Lake

Boulder Lake

4-06

Kootenay Lake

Kuskonook

Mt Bohan

Bohan Creek

Mt Cowley

Rest Area

Pictograph Site

Coot Bay

Goat River Canyon Rec Site

Mt Kitchener

Vehicle

HALL FSR

Creston Valley Wildlife Management Area

Sirdar

Iron Range Mountain

Moyie Range

Kootenay Landing

Duck Lake

IRON RANGE

Restricted

3A

Mt Midgeley 2179m

Marsh

Wynndel

Alice Siding

Arrow Creek

Wynndel Box & Lumber Co X-C Trail

Kitchener

Leach Lake

LAKEVIEW

Kid Cr Rest Area

Summit Cr Campsite

Flats

INDIAN 1

Arrow Mtn

Kid Cr EAST FSR

Forest Fern Trail

WILSON

Lady Slipper Trail

RUSSELL Cr Rd

Balancing Rock Trail

Creston Mtn 2006m

Creston Valley Wildlife Centre

KOOTENAY R.

Creston

THOMPSON

Thompson Lookout Rec Site

4-07

Corn Cr Trail

Erickson

Mt Thompson 2137m

Camp Run Cr

gas

West Creston

Old Ferry Landing

Canyon

Ostrich Ranch

Potato Shed

Lister

4-05

Mt Rykert 1821m

Dodge Creek

DITCH

Porthill

Huscroft

Mt Huscroft 1977m

MARYLAND Cr FSR

DODGE Cr FSR

SWAN Rd

Vic Mawson Lk

EAST MISSION FSR

2km 0 2km 4km

Creston

4

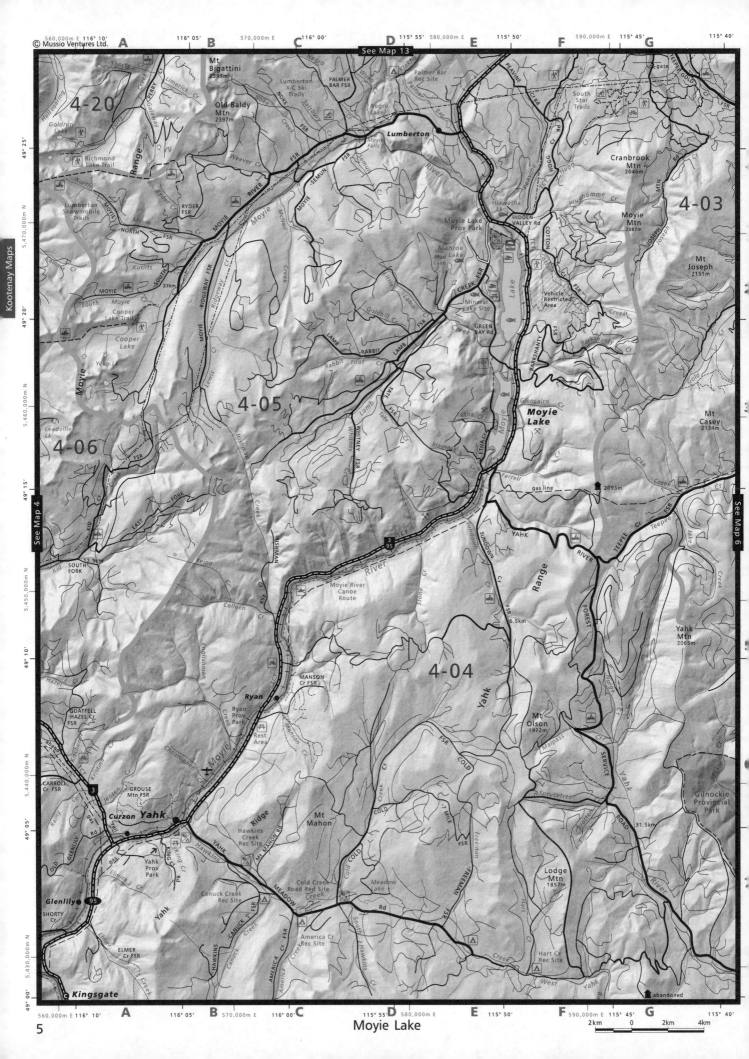

Moyie Lake

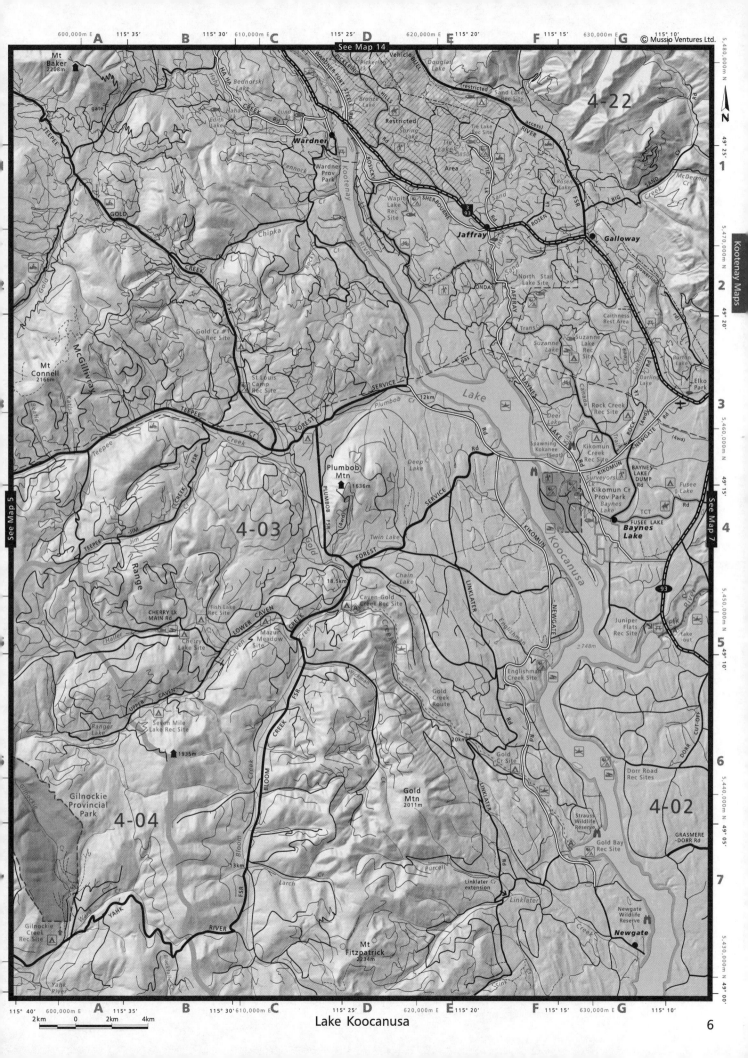

Lake Koocanusa

© Mussio Ventures Ltd.

6

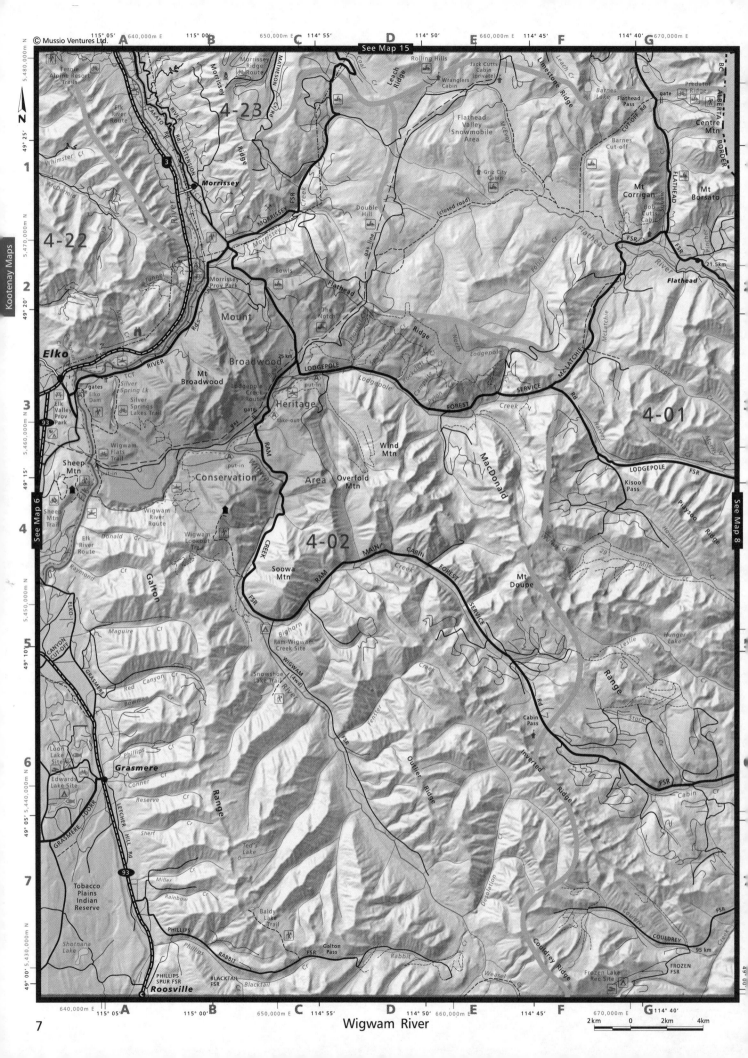

© Mussio Ventures Ltd.

Kootenay Maps

See Map 6

See Map 8

4-23

4-22

4-01

4-02

Elko

Morrissey

Mount

Broadwood

Heritage

Flathead

Flathead

Mt Corrigan

Mt Borsato

Centre Mtn

Grasmere

Roosville

Tobacco Plains Indian Reserve

7

2km 0 2km 4km

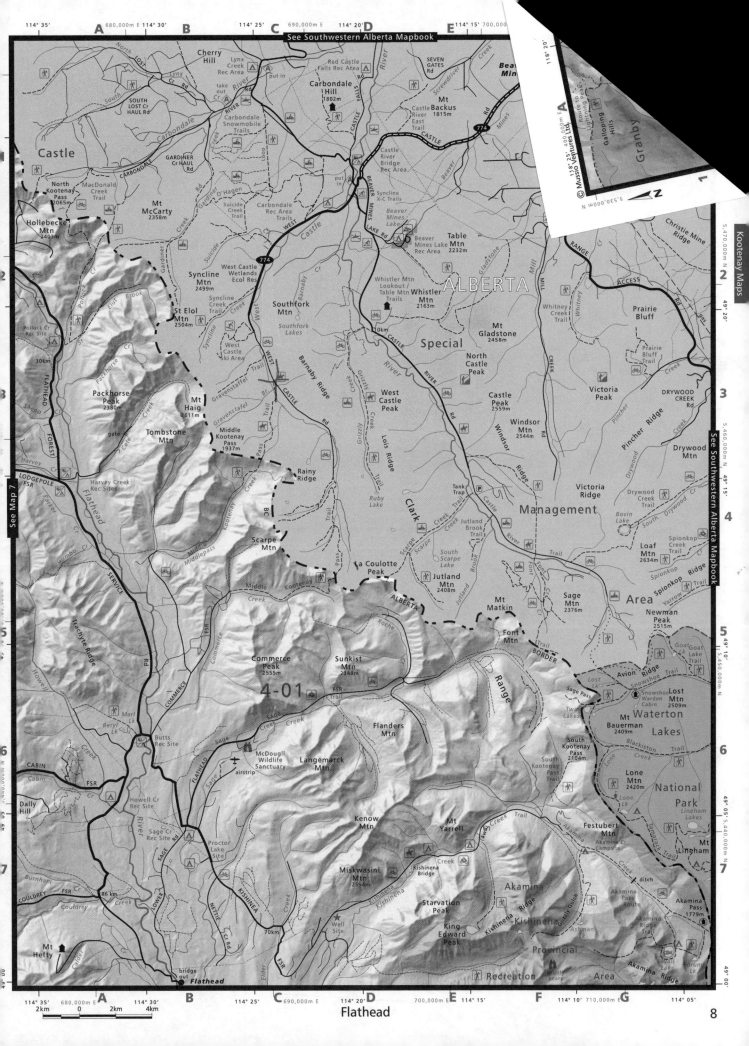

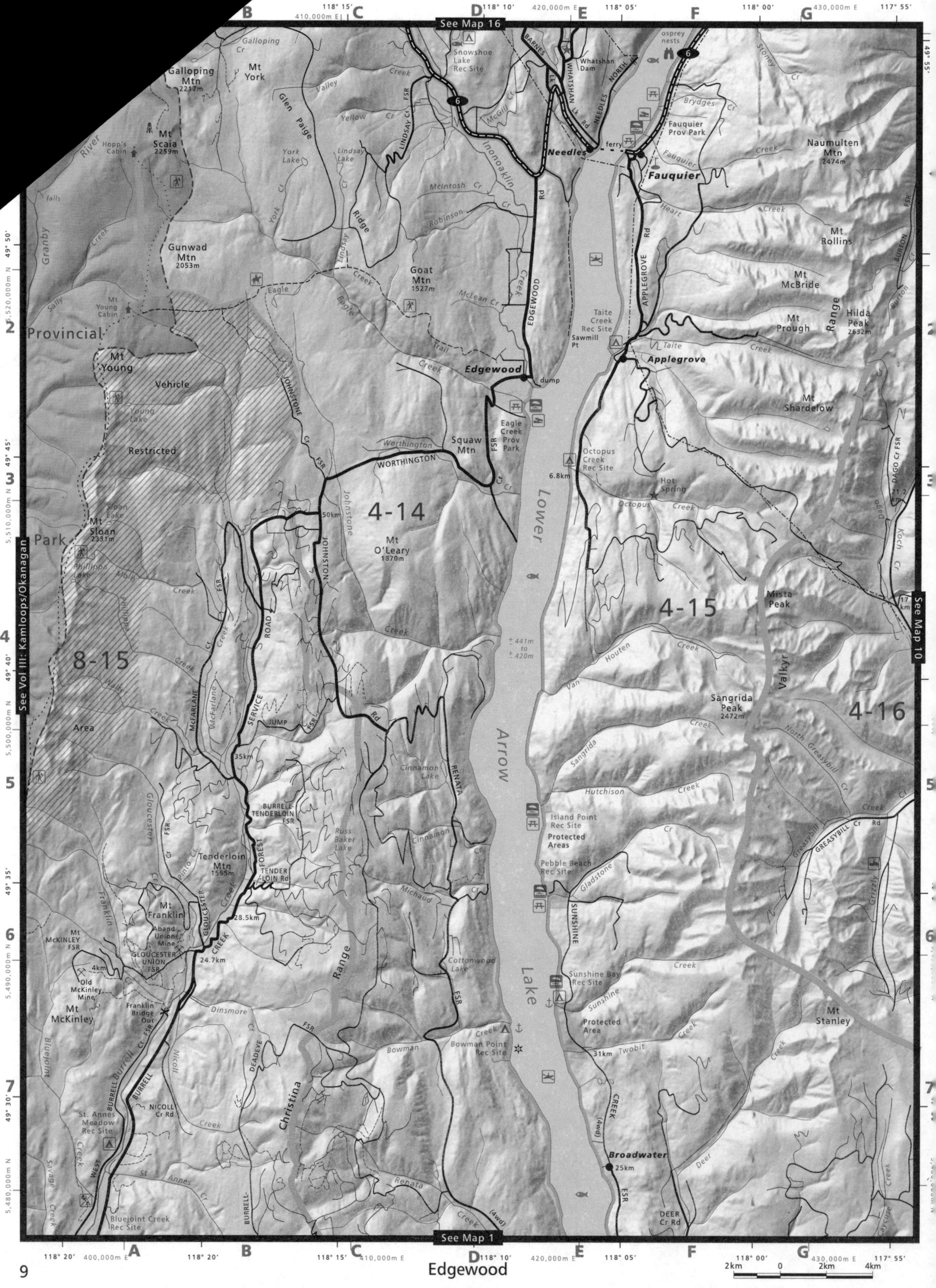

See Vol III: Kamloops/Okanagan

A B C D E F G

118° 20' 118° 15' 118° 10' 118° 05' 118° 00' 117° 55'
400,000m E 410,000m E 420,000m E 430,000m E

49° 55'
49° 50'
49° 45'
49° 40'
49° 35'
49° 30'

5,520,000m N
5,510,000m N
5,500,000m N
5,490,000m N
5,480,000m N

Galloping Cr
Mt York
Mt Scaia 2259m
Galloping Mtn 2231m
Hopp's Cabin
Granby River
falls
Gunwad Mtn 2053m
Mt Young Cabin
Mt Young
Provincial
Vehicle
Restricted
Park
Mt Sloan 2331m
Sloan Lake
Phillipa Lake
Young Lake
Area
8-15

Glen Paige
York Lake
Yellow Cr
Lindsay Lake
Ridge
McIntosh Cr
Robinson Cr
Eagle Trail
Goat Mtn 1527m
McLean Cr
Johnstone Creek
Worthington
WORTHINGTON
Squaw Mtn
4-14
Mt O'Leary 1870m
50km
JOHNSTON FSR
SERVICE ROAD
JUMP
35km
McFarlane Creek
Gloucester Cr FSR
Tenderloin Mtn 1565m
TENDERLOIN Rd
BURRELL TENDERLOIN FSR
FOREST
Mt Franklin
aband Unionet Mine
GLOUCESTER UNION FSR
4km
Old McKinley Mine
Mt McKinley
Franklin Bridge Out
28.5km
24.7km
Mt McKINLEY FSR
Pinto Cr
Franklin Cr
Bluejoint
Burrell Cr FSR
BURRELL
NICOLL Cr Rd
St. Annes Meadow Rec Site
Dinsmore
Savage Creek
St Annes Creek
BURRELL
Bluejoint Creek Rec Site
West Cr

LINDSAY Cr FSR
Inonoaklin Rd
6
BARNES Cr
WHATSHAN Lk Rd
NEEDLES NORTH Rd
Whatshan Dam
Snowshoe Lake Rec Site
osprey nests
6
McGill Cr
Needles
ferry
Fauquier
Fauquier Prov Park
Bridges Cr
Naumulten Mtn 2474m
BURTON FSR
EDGEWOOD Rd
EDGEWOOD Creek
Edgewood
dump
Eagle Creek Prov Park
Taite Creek Rec Site
Sawmill Pt
APPLEGROVE Rd
Applegrove
Taite Creek
Heart Cr
Fauquier Cr
Mt Rollins
Mt McBride
Mt Prough
Hilda Peak 2632m
Range
Mt Shardelow
DAGO Cr FSR
Octopus Creek Rec Site
6.8km
Hot Spring
Octopus Creek
Lower
Arrow
Lake
±441m to ±420m
4-15
Mista Peak
Valkyr
4-16
Houten Creek
Van Creek
Sangrida Peak 2472m
Sangrida Creek
Hutchison Cr
Cinnamon Lake
RENATA Rd
Russ Baker Lake
Cinnamon Cr
Michaud Cr
Cottonwood Lake
Bowman Cr
FSR
Christina Range
Island Point Rec Site
Protected Areas
Pebble Beach Rec Site
Gladstone Cr
SUNSHINE
Sunshine Bay Rec Site
Sunshine Cr
Protected Area
Twobit Cr
31km
Bowman Point Rec Site
Broadwater
25km
CREEK (4wd)
DEER Cr Rd
Deer Cr
North Greasybill
Greasybill Cr
GREASYBILL Cr Rd
Grizzly Cr
Mt Stanley
Koch Cr
Stoney Cr
DEER Cr FSR

9

Edgewood

2km 0 2km 4km

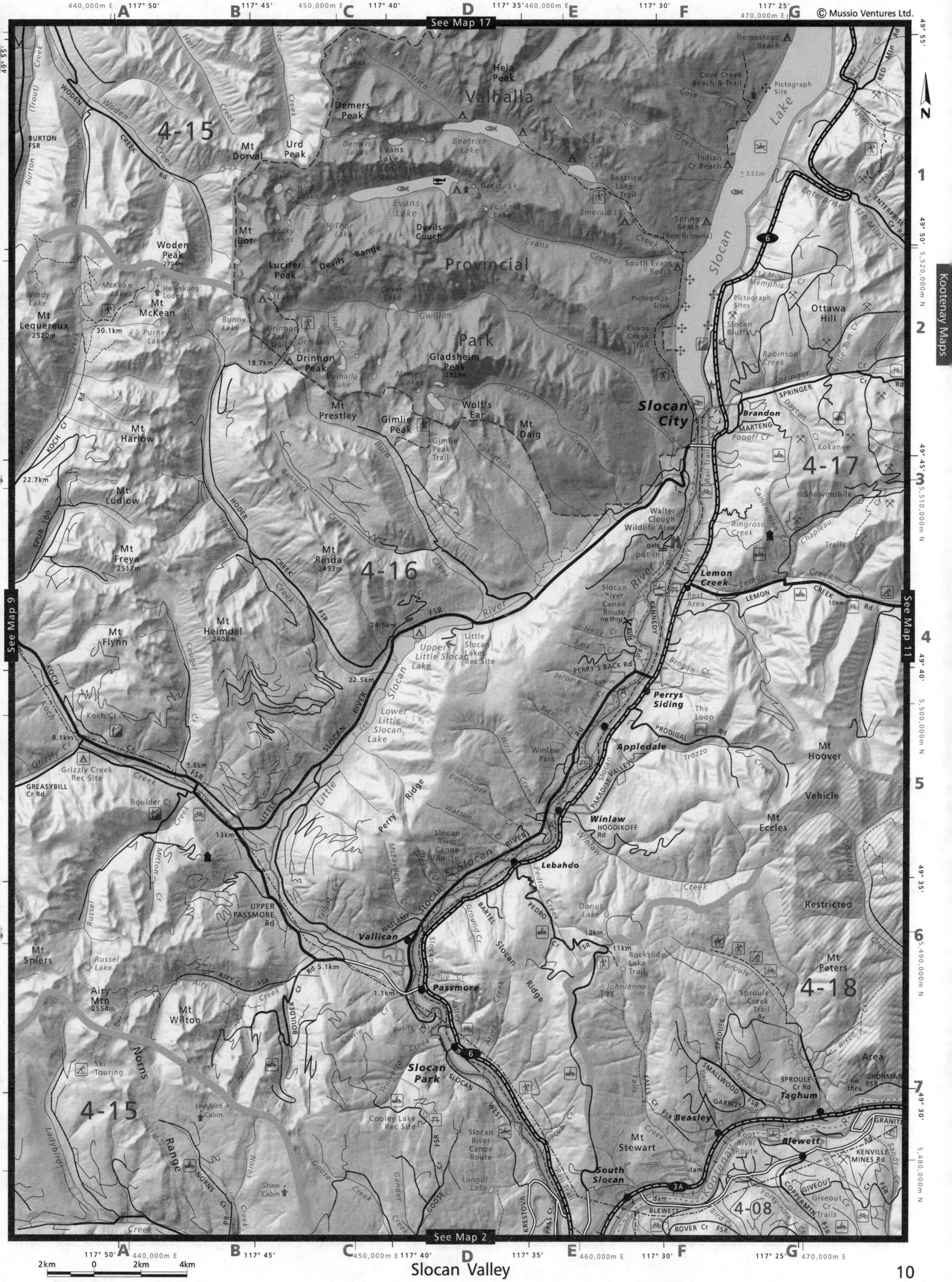

Kootenay Maps

440,000 E 117° 50' 117° 45' 450,000m E 117° 40' 117° 35' 460,000m E 117° 30' 117° 25' 470,000m E

49° 55' 49° 50' 5,520,000m N 49° 45' 5,510,000m N 49° 40' 49° 35' 5,490,000m N 49° 30' 5,480,000m N

A B C D E F G

N

See Map 9

See Map 11

Valhalla

Provincial

Park

4-15

4-16

4-17

4-18

Woden Peak 2704m
Mt Lequereux 2520m
Mt Harlow
Mt Ludlow
Mt Freya 2517m
Mt Flynn
Mt Heimdal 2408m
Mt Rinda 2493m
Mt McKean
Mt Dorval
Mt Bor
Urd Peak
Demers Peak
Hela Peak
Lucifer Peak
Drinnon Peak
Gladsheim Peak 2821m
Mt Prestley
Gimlie Peak
Wolf's Ear
Mt Daig
Devils Couch
Devils Range

Beatrice Lake
Evans Lake
Cadil Lake
Emerald Lk
Indian Cr Beach
Cove Creek Beach & Trail
Homestead Beach
Pictograph Site
Slocan Lake
Spring Beach (Ben Brown's)
South Evans Beach
Pictograph Sites
Slocan Bluffs
Ottawa Hill
Robinson Creek
Springer

Slocan City
Brandon
Marteng
Popoff Cr
Kokanee
Walter Clough Wildlife Area
Ringrose Creek
Chapleau Trails
Snowmobile

Lemon Creek
LEMON CREEK Rd
Rest Area
Slocan River Canoe Route
Perry's Back Rd
Perrys Siding
The Loop
PRODIGAL Rd
Appledale
Winlaw Park
Winlaw
HOODIKOFF Rd
Lebahdo
Donut Lake
Mt Hoover
Mt Eccles
Mt Peters
Vehicle Restricted Area

Little Slocan Lakes Rec Site
Upper Little Slocan Lake
Lower Little Slocan Lake
Perry Ridge
Slocan River Canoe Route

Mt Spiers
Russel Lake
Airy Mtn 2554m
Mt Wilton
Mt Stewart
Vallican
Passmore
UPPER PASSMORE Rd
Ski Touring
Ladybird Cabin
Norns Range
Staw Cabin
Slocan Park
Cooley Lake Rec Site
Slocan River Canoe Route
Langill Lake
South Slocan
Mt Stewart
Beasley
SMALLWOOD Rd
SPROULE Cr Rd
Sproule Creek Trail Br
Taghum
GARRITY
Kootenay River Route
Blewett
KENVILLE MINES Rd
GIVEOUT
COPPERMINE
4-08

Burton FSR
Greasybill Cr Rd
Grizzly Creek Rec Site
Koch Cr
Boulder Cr
Koch Creek
Koch Cr FSR
9.1km 3.8km 13km
Little Slocan FSR
22.5km 24.5km
30.1km 18.7km 22.7km
5.1km 1.1km
10km 11km 1.0km
Rockslide Lake Trail
Sproule Creek

2km 0 2km 4km

Slocan Valley

10

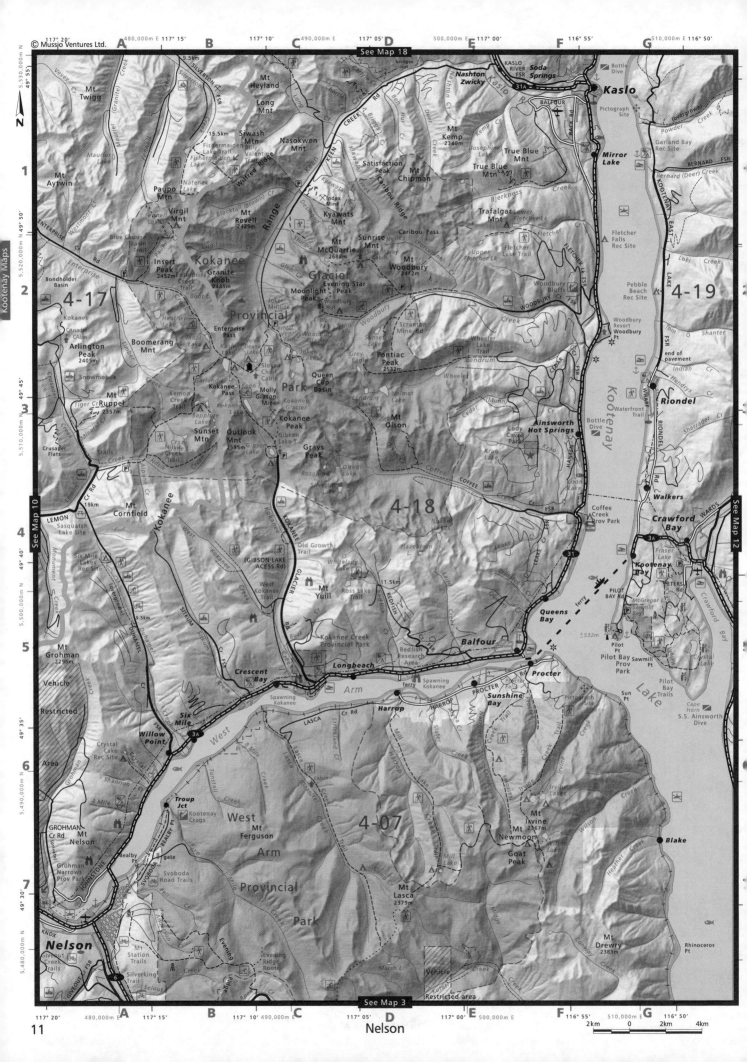

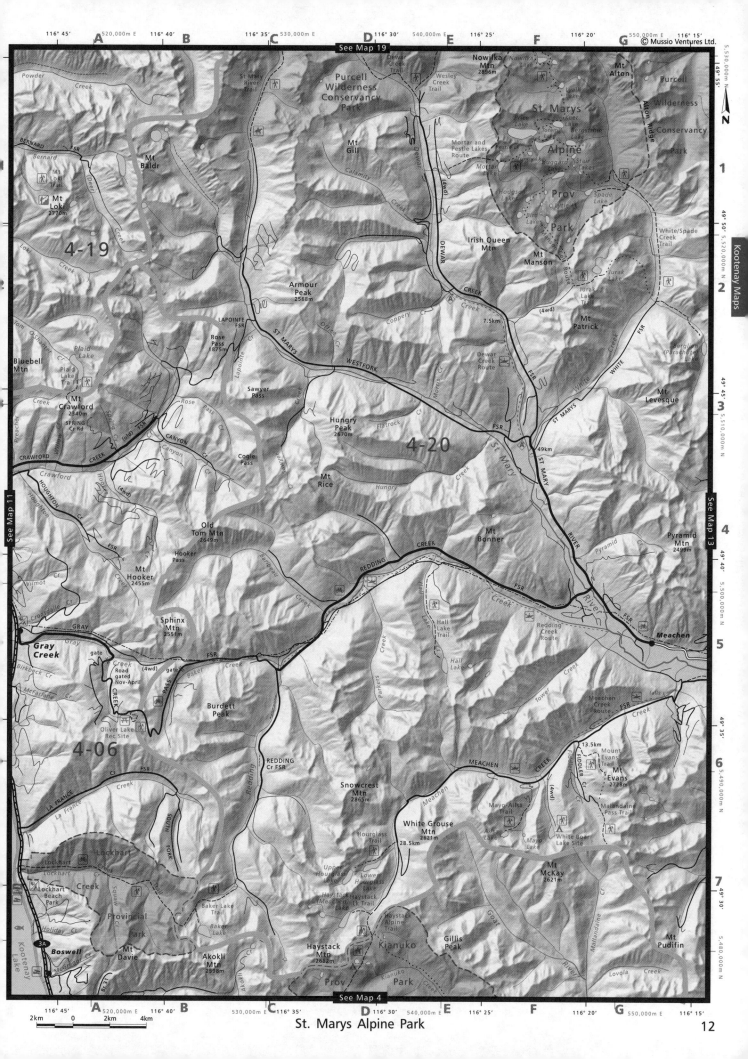

© Mussio Ventures Ltd.

Kootenay Maps

N

1

2

3

4

5

6

7

116° 45'   520,000m E   116° 40'   116° 35'   530,000m E   116° 30'   540,000m E   116° 25'   116° 20'   550,000m E   116° 15'

A   B   C   D   E   F   G

Powder   Creek

BERNARD   FSR

Bernard   Creek

Mt Loki Trail

Mt Loki 2770m

Mt Baldr

4-19

Loki   Creek

Tom O'Shanter   Cr

Plaid Lake

Bluebell Mtn

Plaid Lake Trail

Mt Crawford 2340m

SPRING Cr Rd

Spring Cr

CRAWFORD

Crawford   Creek

HOUGHTON   Houghton   Cr

Rose Pass 1875m

LAPOINTE FSR

Lapointe   Cr

Rose   Pass

CANYON   Canyon   Cr

Sawyer Pass

Cogle Pass

ST MARYS   Creek

Armour Peak 2568m

Olive Cr

Calamity   Creek

WESTFORK

Hungry Peak 2670m

Flatrock

Mt Rice

Hungry   Creek

Barbeau   Creek

Old Tom Mtn 2649m

Hooker Pass

Mt Hooker 2455m

Wilmot   Cr

Crossdale   Cr

GRAY   Gray   Cr

Gray Creek

gate

Creek Road gated Nov-April

(4wd)

PASS

CREEK

Oliver Lake Rec Site

4-06

Baker   Creek

BAKER

Sphinx Mtn 2551m

Burdett Peak

FSR

Birkbeck Cr

MeFarlane   Cr

LA FRANCE   La France   Cr

Lockhart   Cr

Lockhart

Lockhart Beach Park

Squaw   Cr

Holiday Cr

Boswell

Kootenay   Lake

3A

Br 31

McGregor   Cr

Mt Davie

SOUTH   FORK

Akokli   Cr

Akokli Mtn 2598m

Provincial   Park

Baker Lake Trail

Baker Lake

REDDING Cr FSR

Redding   Cr

Snowcrest Mtn 2865m

Hourglass Trail

Upper Hourglass Lake

Lower Hourglass Lake

Haystack (Meachen) Lake

Haystack Lk Trail

White Grouse Mtn 2621m 28.5km

Haystack Mtn 2682m

Kianuko

Prov   Park

Haystack Alpine Trail

Kianuko   Creek

Gillis Peak

REDDING   CREEK

Hall   Creek

Hall Lake Trail

Hall Lake

Parkers   Creek

Meachen   Creek

Tower   Cr

4-20

Mt Bonner

REDDING   FSR

Redding Creek Route

Pyramid   Cr

Pyramid Mtn 2499m

Meachen Creek Route

FSR

Fiddler   Cr

MEACHEN   CREEK

(4wd)

13.5km

Mount Evans Trail

Mt Evans 2728m

Malandaine Pass Trail

White Boar Lake Site

Mayo-Ailsa Trail

Ailsa Lake

Mayo Lake

Mt McKay 2621m

Mt Pudifin

Goat   Creek

Mallandaine

Lovola   Creek

Meachen   Creek

Falls

Meachen

5,530,000m N   49° 55'

49° 50'   5,520,000m N

49° 45'   5,510,000m N

49° 40'   5,500,000m N

49° 35'

5,490,000m N   49° 30'

5,480,000m N

Purcell Wilderness Conservancy Park

Mt Gill

St Mary River Trail

DEWAR   CREEK

Dewar   Creek

(4wd)

Dewar Creek Trail

Wesley Creek Trail

Nowilka Mtn 2896m

Nowilka Trail

Irish Queen Mtn

Coppery   Cr

Coppery   Creek

Morris   Cr

7.5km

(4wd)

Dewar Creek Route

Mortar and Pestle Lakes Route

St Marys Alpine

Price Lake

Totem Lake

Keer Lake

Bergstrom Lake

Huggard Lakes

Stair Lakes

Spade Lake

Hodgson Lakes

Bird Lake

Bottle Lk

Mt Manson

Mortar Lake

Mt Patrick

ST MARYS FSR

St Mary   River

49km

Mt Alton

Alton Ridge

Purcell Wilderness Conservancy Park

White/Spade Creek Trail

Jurak Lake

Jurak Lake Trail

Mt Levesque

WHITE   FSR

White   Creek

Berglten (Parachute) Lake

Meachen

St Mary   River

2km   0   2km   4km

116° 45'   520,000m E   116° 40'   530,000m E   116° 35'   116° 30'   540,000m E   116° 25'   116° 20'   550,000m E   116° 15'

A   B   C   D   E   F   G

St. Marys Alpine Park

12

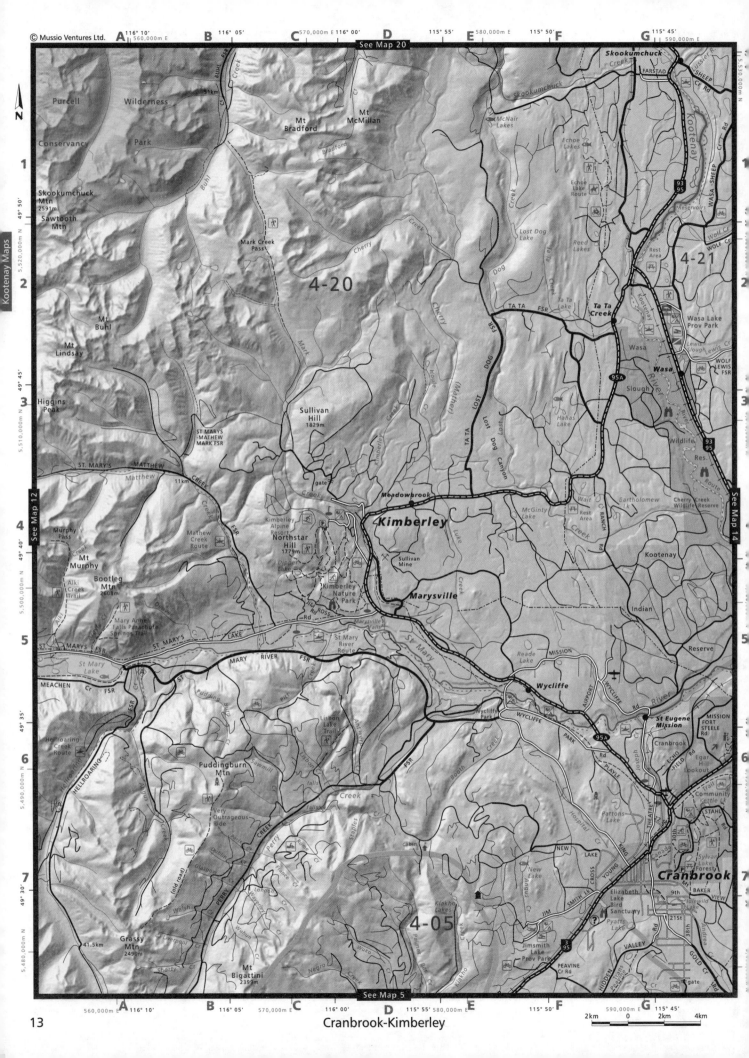

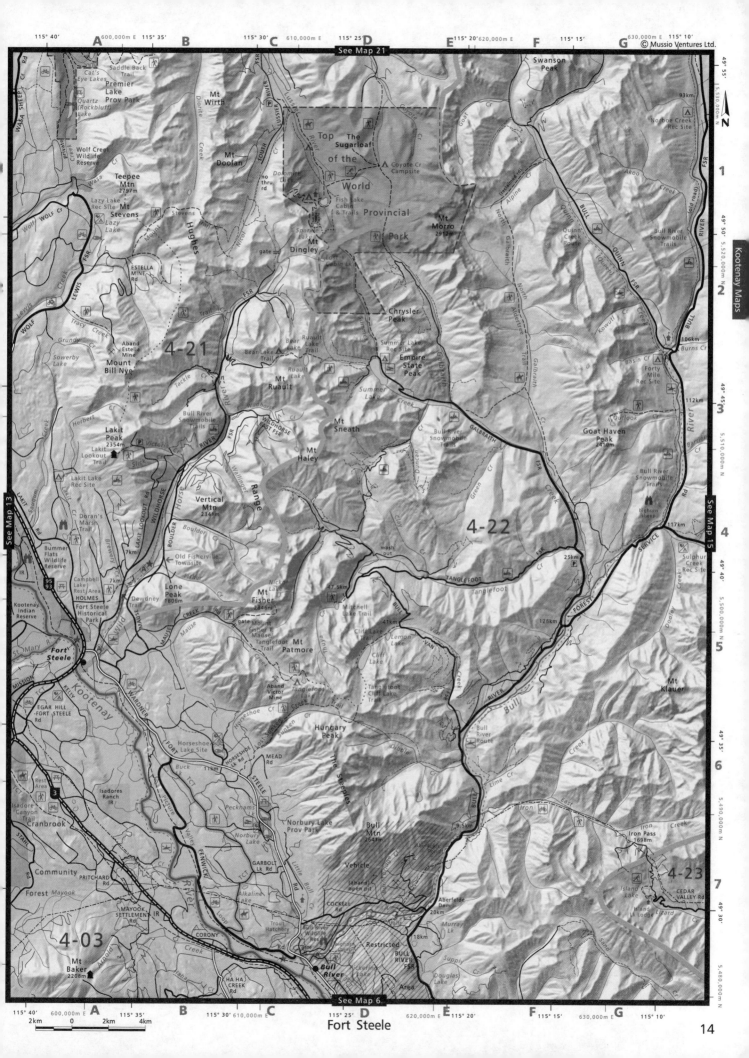

© Mussio Ventures Ltd.

See Map 21

See Map 13

See Map 15

See Map 6

Fort Steele

14

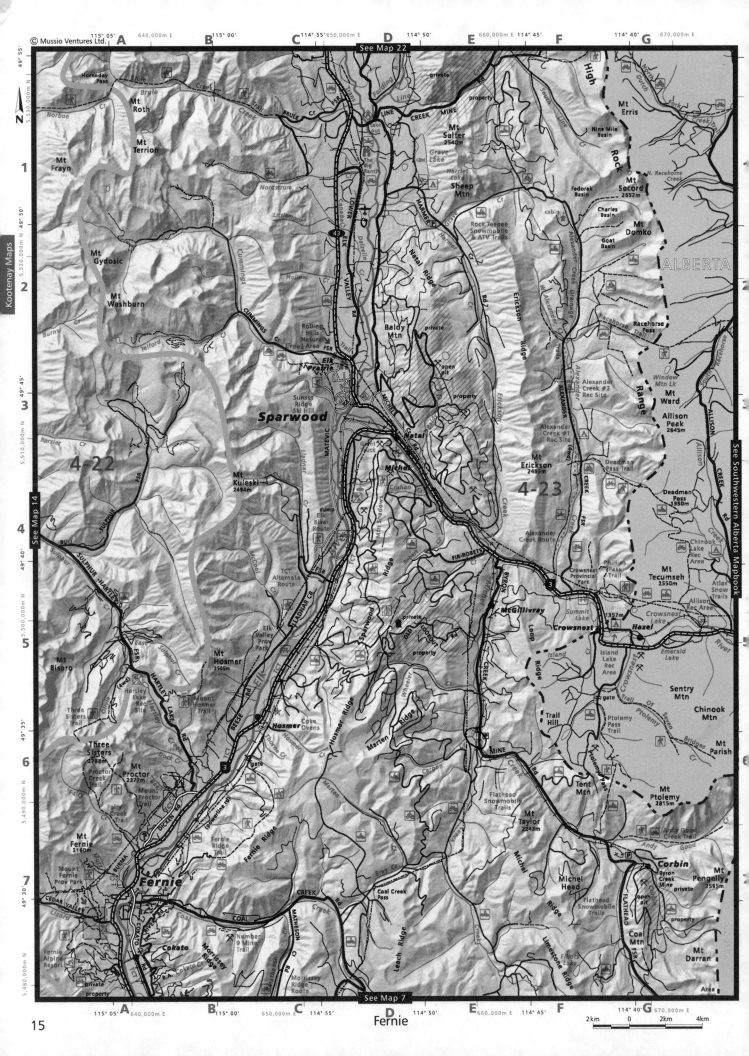

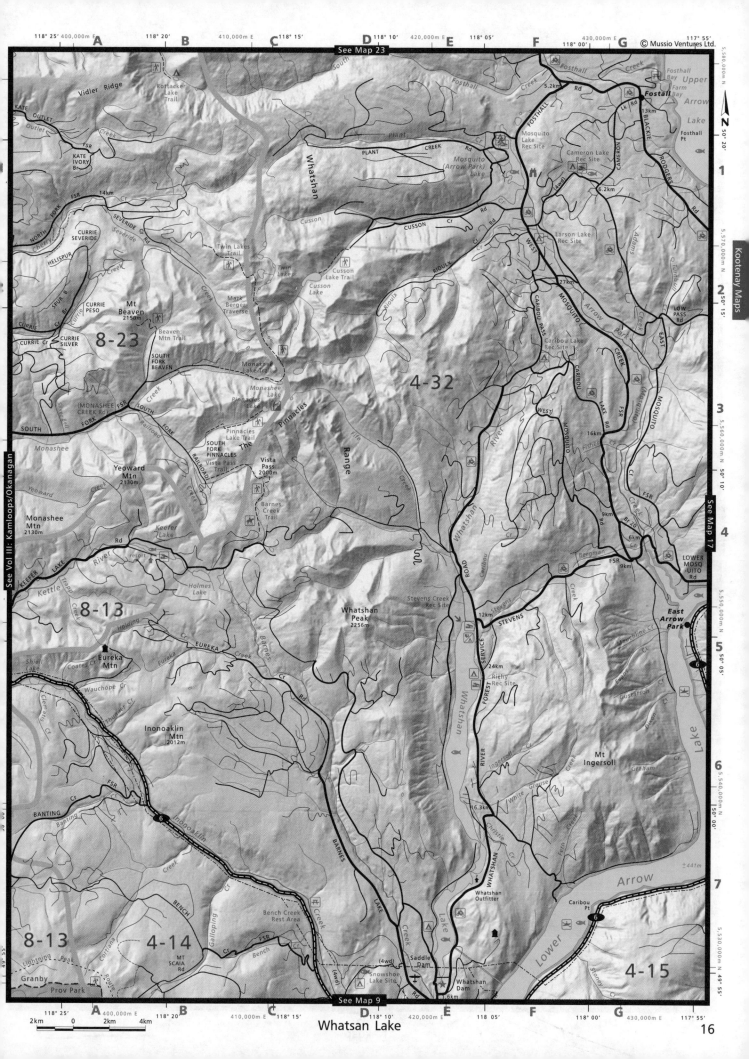

© Mussio Ventures Ltd.

See Vol III: Kamloops/Okanagan

8-23

4-32

8-13

See Map 17

8-13

4-14

See Map 9

4-15

Whatsan Lake

16

Vidler Ridge

Rottacker Lake Trail

KATE OUTLET

Kate Outlet Creek

KATE IVORY Br

NORTH FORK Cherry

FSR 14km

SEVERIDE CURRIE SEVERIDE

Severide Cr Rd

HELISPUR

SPUR B

CURRIE PESO

Mt Beaven 2150m

Beaven Mtn Trail

CURRIE SILVER

CURRIE Cr

SOUTH FORK BEAVEN

SOUTH FORK

(MONASHEE CREEK Rd)

FSR

SOUTH FORK

Monashee Lake Trail

Monashee Lake

Pinnacles Lake

Twin Lakes Trail

Twin Lakes

Cusson Lake Trail

Cusson Lake

Mark Berger Traverse

Whatshan

PLANT CREEK

Cusson

CUSSON Cr

Plant

South

Fosthall Creek

Fosthall Rd 5.2km

Fosthall Bay Upper

Fostall

Farm Bay

Fosthall Pt 13km

BLACKIE

RODGERS Rd

Arrow Lake

Mosquito Lake Rec Site

Cameron Lake Rec Site

6.2km

CAMERON

Larson Lake Rec Site

WEST

27km

Adams

LOW PASS Rd

Mosquito Arrow Park Lake

RIOULX

Rioulx

Rioulx Cr

CARIBOU PASS

MOSQUITO

Caribou Lake Rec Site

CARIBOU LAKE Rd

16km

9km Br 20

6km

East Mosquito

FSR

EAST

Park Creek

Fishtl

Yeoward Mtn 2130m

Yeoward Creek

Monashee Mtn 2130m

SOUTH FORK PINNACLES

Pinnacles Lake Trail

Vista Pass Trail

The Pinnacles Range

Vista Pass 2000m

Barnes Creek Trail

Fife Creek

West Creek

WEST

Whatshan River

9km FSR

Bergman FSR

LOWER MOSQ-UITO Rd

KEEFER LAKE

Keefer Lake

Rd

resort

Holmes Lake

Kettle River

Tranp Creek

8-13

Shiel Lake

Coates Cr

Eureka Mtn

Wauchope Cr

Clematis Ct

Thunder Ct

Holding Cr

EUREKA

Eureka Creek

Barnes Cr Rd

Whatshan Peak 2256m

Stevens Creek Rec Site

Whatshan RIVER

Caribou Creek

SERVICE

STEVENS

Stevens Creek

12km

24km

Richy Rec Site

East Arrow Park

6

Maschline Cr

Gusofson

Inonoaklin Mtn 2012m

BANTING

Banting Cr

FSR

6

Inonoaklin Creek

BENCH

Geologlog Creek

Cortiana Cr

BARNES LAKE CREEK

ROAD

FOREST

Ingersoll Cr

Whatshan RIVER

Mt Ingersoll

White Grouse Creek

Graham

16.3km

Christie Creek

Fern Creek

±441m

Arrow

Lower

Lightning Peak route

Granby Prov Park

4-14

MT SCAIA Rd

Bench Creek Rest Area

Bench Creek

Bench FSR

Snowshoe Lake Site

Saddle Dam

(4wd)

Whatshan Dam

1.6km

Whatshan Outfitter

Caribou Pt

6

Stoney Cr

Lake

Lower

2km 0 2km 4km

118° 25' 400,000m E
118° 20'
410,000m E
118° 15'
118° 10'
420,000m E
118° 05'
118° 00'
430,000m E
117° 55'

5,580,000m N
5,570,000m N
5,560,000m N
5,550,000m N
5,540,000m N
5,530,000m N

50° 20'
50° 15'
50° 10'
50° 05'
50° 00'
49° 55'

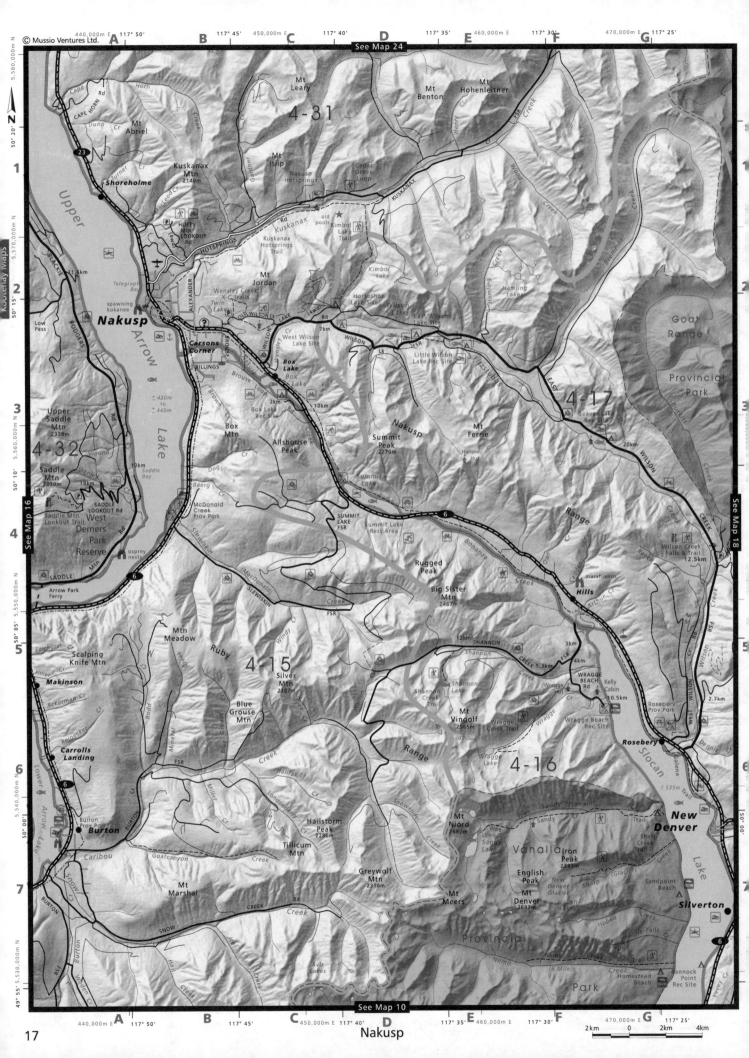

© Mussio Ventures Ltd.

See Map 25

See Map 17

See Map 19

4-27
4-28 songbirds
4-29
4-30
4-19
4-17
4-18

Spyglass Mtn
Poplar Icefield
Poplar Creek
Mt Emmens
Marion Lakes Trail
Marion Lakes
Cascade Mtn
Goat Range
Mt Marion 2966m
Blue Lake
Meadow Creek
Deception Cr
Howser Glay Rec Site
Howser
±577m
12km
Lardeau River Route
Duncan
Lower
Duncan River
GLACIER FSR
MacBeth Icefield Trail
Creek bridge out
Cirque Peak
Glacier Creek Rec Sites
LAVINA Mtn FSR
Mt Lavina
Grey Pass
Comb Mtn
Purcell Wilderness Conservancy (West) Provincial Park
Meadow Mtn 2550m
Meadow Mtn Trail
John (Williams) Creek
MEADOW (4wd)
McKIan
Spawning Kokanee (Sept)
Meadow Creek
Duncan Dam
Cable Car Crossings
Clint Creek
Mt Cooper 3089m
Mt Stubbs
Spokane Glacier
McKIAN Cr FSR
(Stony)
Cooper Creek
Cooper Creek
Lardeau-Duncan Flats Wildlife Reserve
Argenta Marsh Wildlife Reserve
Davis Creek Trail
Argenta
Argenta Cr
Mt Willet
Goat Provincial Park
Mt McHardy
Mt Dolly Varden 2570m
Marten Mtn
Alps Alturas Trail
Inverness Mtn
Marten Creek Dolly-Varden Trail
Mt Dryden
Mt Davis 2577m
Lardeau
Davis Creek Marine Park
Davis Creek
Kootenay
Bulmer Creek
Tooth Ridge
Salisbury
KOOTENAY JOE RIDGE Rd
10.3km Dennis Creek Trail
Whitewater Mtn
London Ridge
London Ridge Trail
Whitewater Creek Trail
Giegerich
Mt Brennan
Lyle Creek Trail
Eureka Mtns
Ledge Cr
Lost Ledge Marine Park
Johnson's Landing
±530m
Fry Pt
falls
Fry Creek Canyon Provincial Rec Area
4-17
KANE Cr FSR
Rest Area
Watson
Retallack
31A
Fish Lake
Bear Lake
Zincton
beaver ponds
Rambler
LYLE FSR
Mt Schroeder
Mt Jardine 2438m
Blue Creek
Schroeder
Schroeder Point
Birchdale
Clute Lakes Cr
Clute Creek
Three Forks 8km
Alamo
RAMBLER Rd
Jackson Basin Trail
Seaton
McGuigan
Payne Bluffs
Old Eureka Mine
Kaslo River Trailway
Milford Lake Rec Site
Milford Peak
Clute Lake Trail
Murphy Creek
Mt Carpenter
Parapet
Galena Trail
SANDON
K&S Railway
Mt Payne
Reco Mtn 2518m
Blaylock
10 MILE Cr Rd
BLUE RIDGE FSR
Campbell Bay M. Park Camp
Idaho Peak T
Idaho Peak 2280m
IDAHO LOOKOUT Rd
7km
Historical Site
Cody
Keen
12 MILE FSR
KASLO Ridge
Kemball Cr
31
Verandah Pt
Leviathan Lake
Waketield Trail
Silver
Selkirk Peak
Sandon Peak
Mt Cody
Noble Five Mine Trail
Paddy Peak 2487m
Texas Peak
Mt Holmes
4-18
Kaslo River Trailway
BUCHANAN LOOKOUT Rd
9km
Buchanan Lookout
Mount Buchanan 1909m
Shutty Bench
Leviathan Lake Trail
4.6km
9.5km
Bartloff
Emily
SILVERTON
ROAD 300
ROAD 500
Mt Twigg
Mt Heyland
Mt Carlyle 2648m
Carlyle Cr
Flint Lakes
Long Creek
Keen Cr
7 Mile FSR
Nashton Zwicky
Soda Springs
Kaslo
Bottle Dive

50° 20'
50° 15'
50° 10'
50° 05'
50° 00'
49° 55'

117° 20'
117° 15'
117° 10'
117° 05'
117° 00'
116° 55'
116° 50'

480,000m E
490,000m E
500,000m E
510,000m E

5,570,000m N
5,560,000m N
5,550,000m N
5,540,000m N
5,530,000m N

N

2km 0 2km 4km

Argenta

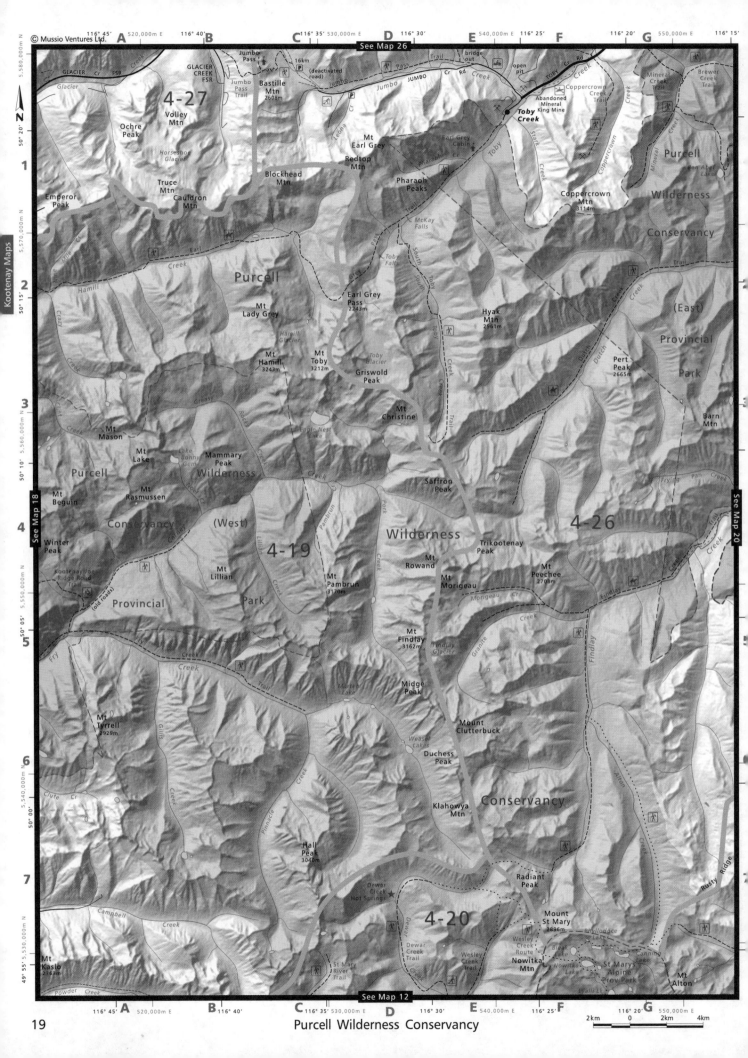

Kootenay Maps

116° 45' 520,000m E A 116° 40' B 116° 35' 530,000m E C D 116° 30' E 540,000m E 116° 25' F 116° 20' 550,000m E G 116° 15'

N

50° 20'

50° 15'

50° 10'

50° 05'

50° 00'

49° 55'

5,580,000m N
5,570,000m N
5,560,000m N
5,550,000m N
5,540,000m N
5,530,000m N

See Map 18
See Map 20

GLACIER Cr FSR

Glacier Cr

Glacier Creek

GLACIER CREEK FSR

4-27

Ochre Peak

Volley Mtn

Horseshoe Glacier

Emperor Peak

Truce Mtn

Cauldron Mtn

Jumbo Pass Trail

Jumbo Pass

Bastille Mtn 2608m

Blockhead Mtn

16km
P
(deactivated road)

P

Jumbo Cr

Jumbo Pass

JUMBO

Cr Rd

Toby Cr

Redtop Mtn

Mt Earl Grey

Pharaoh Peaks

Tegna Pass

open pit

bridge out

Abandoned Mineral King Mine

Toby Creek

Coppercrown Creek Trail

Mineral Creek Trail

Brewer Creek Trail

Purcell

den Abel Lake

Wilderness

Conservancy

Earl Grey Cabin

McKay Falls

Coppercrown Mtn 3114m

Stark Creek

Mineral Creek

Earl Mile Creek

Earl Creek

Purcell

Hamill Creek

Crazy Creek

Clint Creek

Greasy Creek

Mt Lady Grey

Hamill Glacier

Mt Hamill 3243m

Mt Toby 3212m

Toby Glacier

Griswold Peak

Earl Grey Pass 2243m

Toby Falls

South Toby

South Toby Creek

Toby Creek

Hyak Mtn 2961m

Dutch Creek

Dutch

(East)

Provincial

Park

Pert Peak 2665m

Barn Mtn

Mt Mason

Mt Lake

Mammary Peak

Lake Bonny Gem

Eagle Nest Lake

Mt Christine

Saffron Peak

Frying Pan Creek

Purcell

Mt Beguin

Mt Rasmussen

Wilderness

(West)

Conservancy

Winter Peak

Kootenay Joe Ridge Road Trail

(old roads)

Provincial

Mt Lillian

4-19

Park

Lillian Creek

Pork Creek

Pambrun Creek

Mt Pambrun 3170m

Wilderness

Mt Rowand

Mt Morigeau

Trikootenay Peak

Mt Peechee 2708m

4-26

Morigeau Cr

Findlay Cr

Fry Creek

Gilliss Creek

Hall Creek

Mt Tyrrell 2929m

Marten Lake

Weasel Lake

Mt Findlay 3162m

Midge Peak

Mount Clutterbuck

Duchess Peak

Klahowya Mtn

Findlay Glacier

Granite Creek

Findlay Creek

Conservancy

Alton Creek

Rusty Ridge

Clute Cr

Pinnacle Creek

Hall Peak 3040m

Dewar Creek Hot Springs

Radiant Peak

Mount St Mary 2896m

4-20

Mt Kaslo 2363m

Campbell Creek

Powder Creek

St Mary River Trail

Dewar Creek Trail

Wesley Creek Trail

Wesley Creek Route

Nowitka Mtn

Phillodace Creek

St Marys Alpine Prov Park

Canning Lake

Nowitka Lake

Mt Alton

116° 45' A 520,000m E B 116° 40' 116° 35' 530,000m E C D 116° 30' E 540,000m E 116° 25' F 116° 20' 550,000m E G

Purcell Wilderness Conservancy

2km 0 2km 4km

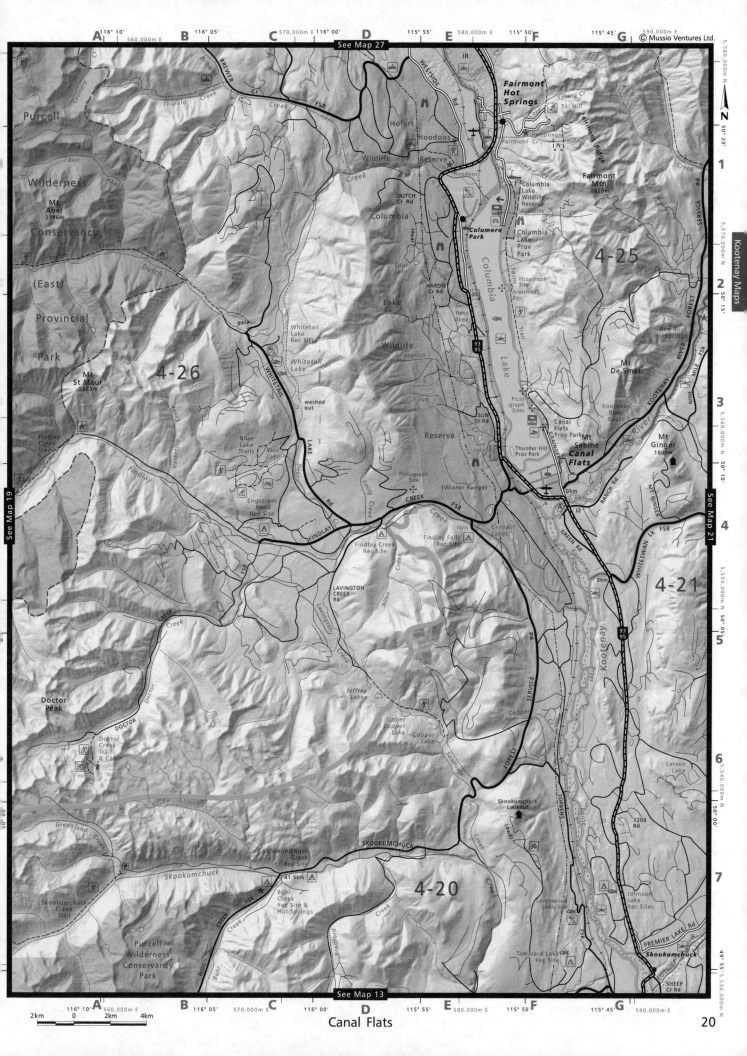

© Mussio Ventures Ltd.

See Map 27

See Map 19

See Map 21

See Map 13

Canal Flats

Purcell

Wilderness

Mt
Abel
2746m

Conservancy

(East)

Provincial

Park

Mt
St Maur
2863m

4-26

4-25

Findlay
Creek
Trail

Doctor
Peak

DOCTOR

Doctor
Creek
Trail
& Cabin

Greenland

Skookumchuck
Creek
Trail

Purcell
Wilderness
Conservancy
Park

Skookumchuck

Buhl
Creek
Rec Site &
Hot Springs

41.5km

Skookumchuck
Creek
Rec Site

SKOOKUMCHUCK

4-20

Whitetail Lake
Rec Site

Whitetail
Lake

washed
out

Blue
Lake
Trails

Blue
Lake

Engstrom
Pond
Rec Site

Findlay Creek
Rec Site

LAVINGTON
CREEK
Rd

Jeffrey
Lakes

Upper
Copper
Lake

Copper
Lake

Fairmont
Hot
Springs

Hofert

Hoodoos

Wildlife

DUTCH
Cr Rd

Columbia

Lake

Wildlife

HARDJE
Cr Rd

Spur
Lake

Reserve

Rest
Area

Marion

Sun

Reserve

(Winter Range)

Pictograph
Site

SUN
Cr Rd

Sun
Lake

Thunder Hill
Prov Park

Findlay Falls
Rec Site

falls

Centaur
Lakes

Skookumchuck
Lookout
(4wd)

IR

Fairmont
Hot Springs
Ski Hill

Spring Cr

Fairmont
Mtn
2620m

Columbia
Lake
Wildlife
Reserve
Warspite

Columbia
Lake
Prov Park

Fairmont Ridge

Pictograph
Site
Armstrong
Bay

Picto-
graph
Sites

Canal
Flats
Prov Park

Canal
Flats

Mt
Sabine

Mt
De Smet

Red Rock
Springs

Kootenay
River
Route

Mt
Ginger
1805m

4-21

4-20

Larsen
Lake

3200
Rd

Johnson
Lake Rec Sites

Tamarack Lake
Rec Site

Larchwood
Lake Site

Skookumchuck

SHEEP
Cr Rd

Doctor

Columbia Lake

Findlay

Valentine Creek

Deep

CREEK

Emily Creek

Allen Creek

Lavington

Creek

Sandown

Copper

Creek

Bradford

Creek

GREEN

GRANGER

RANCH Rd

Kootenay

River

FOREST

SERVICE

TORRENT

PREMIER LAKE Rd

WHITESWAN Lk FSR

NINE MILE FSR

KOOTENAY RIVER FSR

8km

0km

J2

93
95

93
95

WESTSIDE Rd

BREWER Cr FSR

WHITETAIL LAKE Rd

FINDLAY Cr

FSR

CREEK

BUHL CREEK FSR

2km   0   2km   4km

116° 10'   116° 05'   570,000m E   116° 00'   115° 55'   580,000m E   115° 50'   115° 45'   590,000m E

50° 20'
50° 15'
50° 10'
50° 05'
50° 00'
49° 55'

5,580,000m N
5,570,000m N
5,560,000m N
5,550,000m N
5,540,000m N
5,530,000m N

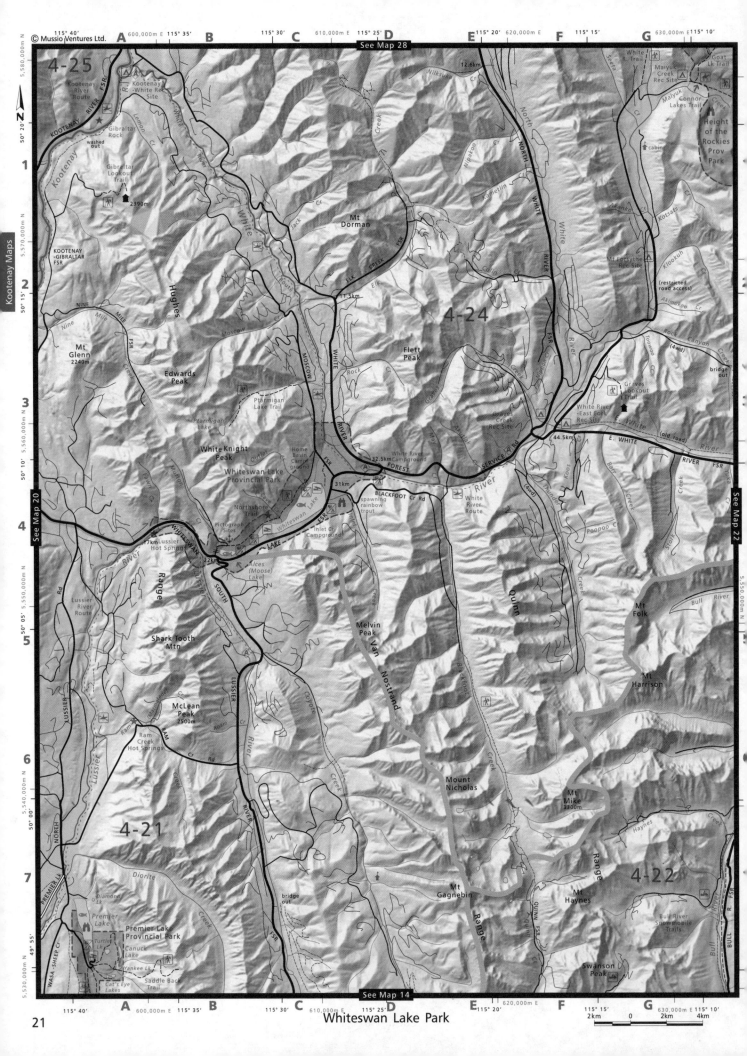

4-25

See Map 20

See Map 22

Kootenay River Route
Kootenay-White Rec Site
Gibraltar Rock
washed out
Gibraltar Lookout Trail
2390m
KOOTENAY-GIBRALTAR FSR

Mt Glenn 2240m
NINE MILE FSR
Nine Mile Creek
Hughes
Edwards Peak

Mt Dorman

4-24

12.6km
Nilksik Cr
White River
White R. Trail
Maiyuk Creek Rec Site
Malyuk Lakes Trail
Goat Lk Trail
cabin
Height of the Rockies Prov Park
Mt Forsythe Rec Site
(restricted road access)

Ptarmigan Lake Trail
Ptarmigan Lake
White Knight Peak
Whiteswan Lake Provincial Park
Home Basin Campground
Northshore Trail
Pictograph Sites

Flett Peak

Graves Creek Rec Site
Graves Lookout Trail
White River-East Fork Rec Site
44.5km
E. WHITE RIVER FSR
(old road)
bridge out

White River Campground
32.5km
31km
BLACKFOOT Cr Rd
spawning rainbow trout
White River Route
FOREST
River
SERVICE RD

17km Lussier Hot Springs
22km
Inlet Cr Campground
Alces (Moose) Lake

Lussier River Route
Range
Shark Tooth Mtn
LUSSIER
McLean Peak 2500m
Ram Creek Hot Springs
Ram Cr Rd

Melvin Peak
Van Nostrand

Quinn
Mt Folk
Mt Harrison

Bull River

LUSSIER Rd
NORTH
4-21
Diorite
bridge out
FSR

Mount Nicholas
Blackfoot Creek

Mt Mike 3300m
Haynes Range
4-22

PREMIER Lk
Premier Lake Provincial Park
Diamond Lk
Turtle Lk
Canuck Lake
Yankee Lk
Cat's Eye Lakes
Saddle Back Trail
WASA-SHEEP Cr

Mt Gagnebin
Mt Haynes
QUINN FSR
Bull River Snowmobile Trails
Swanson Peak

Whiteswan Lake Park

2km 0 2km 4km

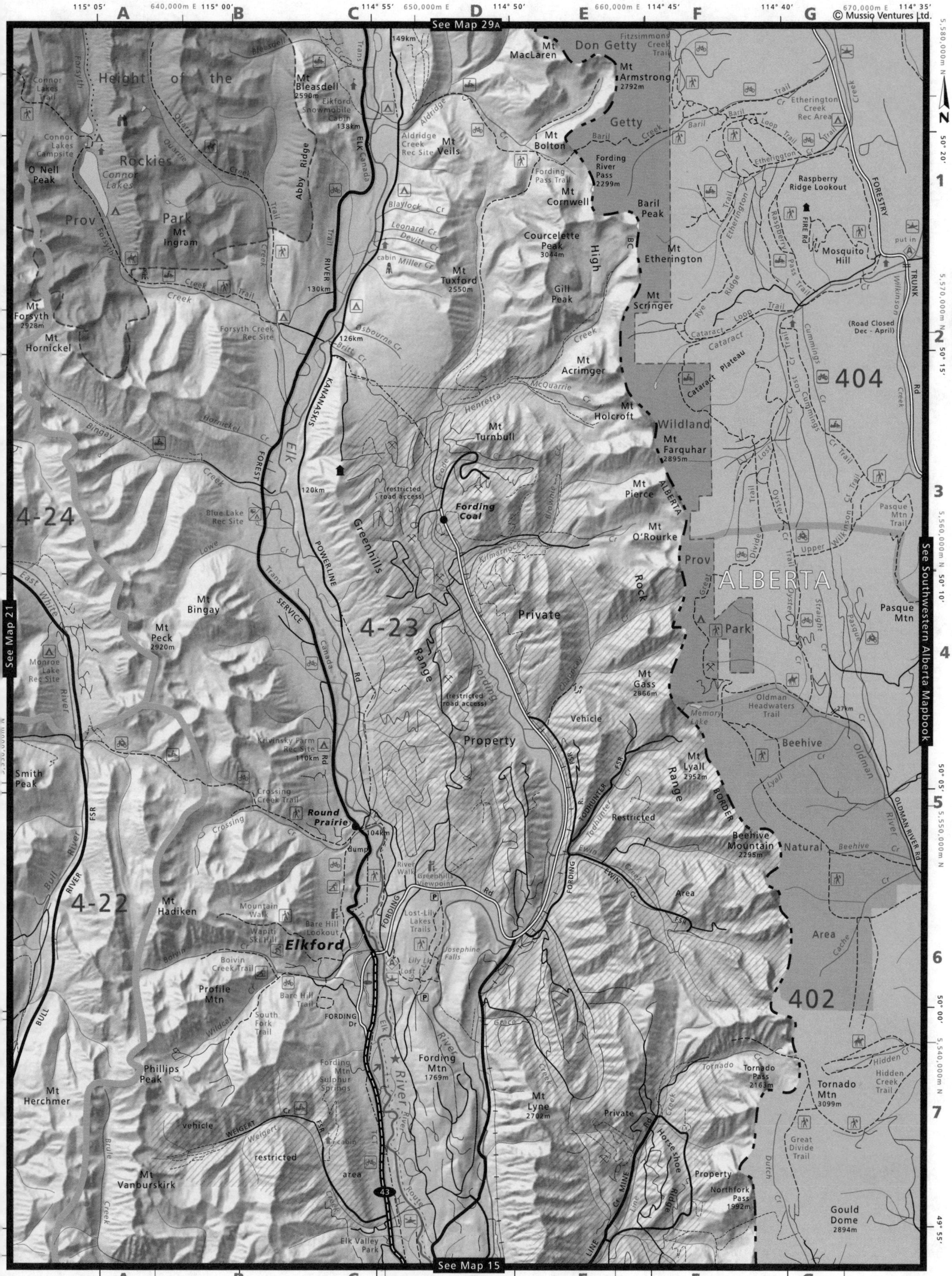

© Mussio Ventures Ltd.

Grid/coordinate labels (top): 115° 05', 640,000m E, 115° 00', 114° 55', 650,000m E, 114° 50', 660,000m E, 114° 45', 114° 40', 670,000m E, 114° 35'

Column letters: A B C D E F G

Side labels (right): N, 5,580,000m N, 50° 20', 5,570,000m N, 50° 15', 5,560,000m N, 50° 10', 5,550,000m N, 50° 05', 5,540,000m N, 50° 00', 49° 55'

Row numbers: 1 2 3 4 5 6 7

See Map 29A
See Map 21
See Map 15
See Southwestern Alberta Mapbook

Height of the Rockies

Connor Lakes Trail
Connor Lakes Campsite
O Nell Peak
Connor Lakes
Prov
Park
Rockies
Mt Ingram
Mt Forsyth 2928m
Mt Hornickel
4-24
Forsyth Creek
Forsyth Creek Rec Site
Bingay Creek
Hornickel Cr
Lowe Cr
Blue Lake Rec Site
East White
See Map 21
Monroe Lake Rec Site
Smith Peak
Bull River
4-22
Mt Hadiken
Mt Peck 2920m
Mt Bingay
Mountain Walk
Wapiti Ski Hill
Bare Hill Lookout
Elkford
Profile Mtn
Boivin Creek Trail
Bare Hill Trail
South Fork Trail
FORDING Dr
Phillips Peak
Mt Herchmer
Mt Vanburskirk
vehicle
restricted area
Weigert Cr
WEIGERT
Brule Creek
Wildkat Cr
Boivin Cr

Mt Bleasdell 2590m
Abby Ridge
Elk Snowmobile Cabin 138km
149km
Trans
Aldridge Creek Rec Site
Aldridge Cr
Mt Veils
Blaylock Cr
Leonard Cr
Devitt Cr
cabin
Miller Cr
Mt Tuxford 2550m
ELK RIVER
130km
126km
Osbourne Cr
Britt Cr
120km
KANANASKIS
FOREST
ELK
POWERLINE
TRANS
SERVICE
CANADA Rd
Greenhills
Range
restricted road access
Fording Coal
Fording
4-23
restricted road access
Property
Vehicle
Private
Kilmarnock Cr
Brownie Cr
Henretta
McQuarrie
Kiuinsky Farm Rec Site 110km
Crossing Creek Trail
Crossing Cr
Round Prairie
104km
Bump
River Wall
Greenhills Viewpoint
Lost-Lily Lakes Trails
Josephine Falls
Lily Lk
Lost Lk
FORDING
Grace Cr
Fording Mtn Sulphur Springs
Fording Mtn 1769m
cabin
Elk Valley Park
43
Elk River

MacLaren
Mt MacLaren
Don Getty
Fitzsimmons Creek Trail
Mt Armstrong 2792m
Getty
Mt Bolton
Fording Pass Trail
Mt Cornwell
Fording River Pass 2299m
Courcelette Peak 3044m
High
Gill Peak
Baril Peak
Baril Creek
Baril
Mt Etherington
Rye Ridge
Mt Scringer
Cataract
Cataract Plateau
Loop Trail
Raspberry Ridge Lookout
FIRE RD
Etherington Creek Rec Area
Etherington Cr
Raspberry pass Trail
put in
Mosquito Hill
FORESTRY TRUNK Rd
Wilkinson Cr
(Road Closed Dec - April)
404
Mt Acrimger
Mt Holcroft
Mt Turnbull
Wildland
Mt Farquhar 2895m
ALBERTA
Mt Pierce
BC
Mt O'Rourke
O'Rourke Cr
Lost Cr
Cummings Cr
Oyster Cr
Upper Wilkinson Cr
Straight Cr
Pasque Mtn Trail
ALBERTA
Prov
Rock
Park
Pasque Mtn
Mt Gass 2866m
Range
Oldman Headwaters Trail
Beehive Cr
Beehive
Oldman River
Oldman River
Memory Lake
Mt Lyall Range 2952m
Restricted
Tobermory Cr
Tobermory R.
FORDING Rd
FSR
EWIN
Fording R.
Natural
Beehive Mountain 2295m
Lyall Cr
Beehive Cr
Cache Cr
402
Area
Area
Mt Lyne 2702m
Private
Property
MINE LINE
Horse Shoe Ridge
Tornado Cr
Tornado Pass 2163m
Tornado Mtn 3099m
Hidden Cr
Hidden Creek Trail
Northfork Pass 1992m
Dutch Cr
Great Divide Trail
Gould Dome 2894m
BORDER

Scale: 2km 0 2km 4km

Elkford

22

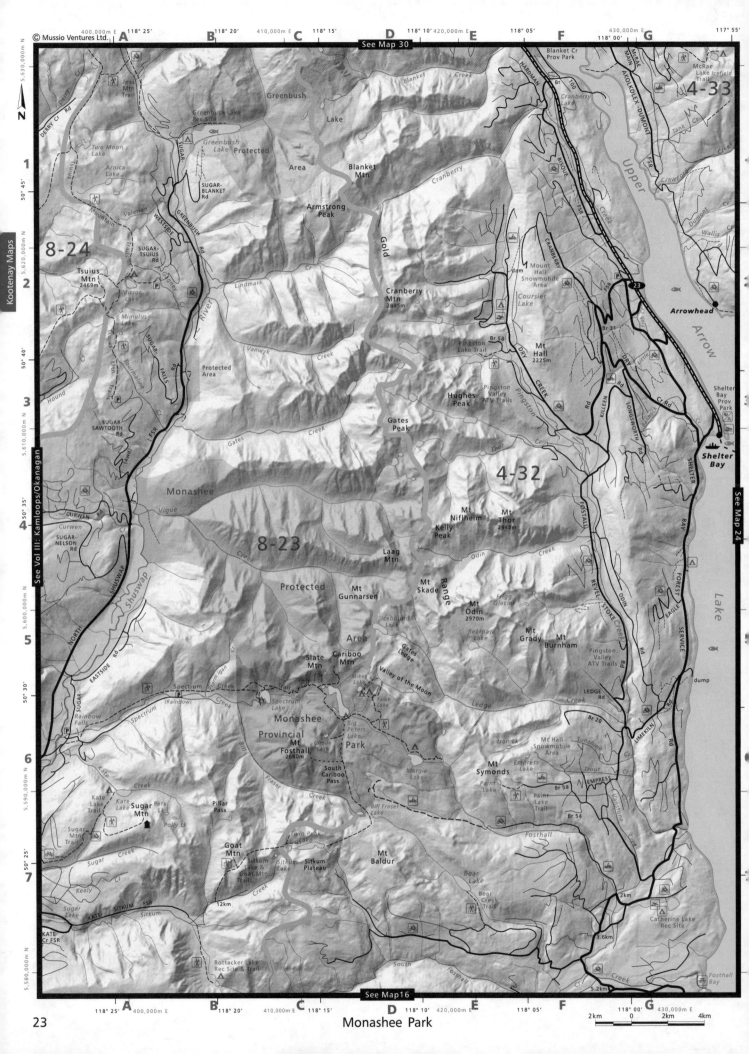

Kootenay Maps

See Vol III: Kamloops/Okanagan

8-24

8-23

8-23

4-32

4-33

Monashee Provincial Park

Monashee Park

See Map 24

23

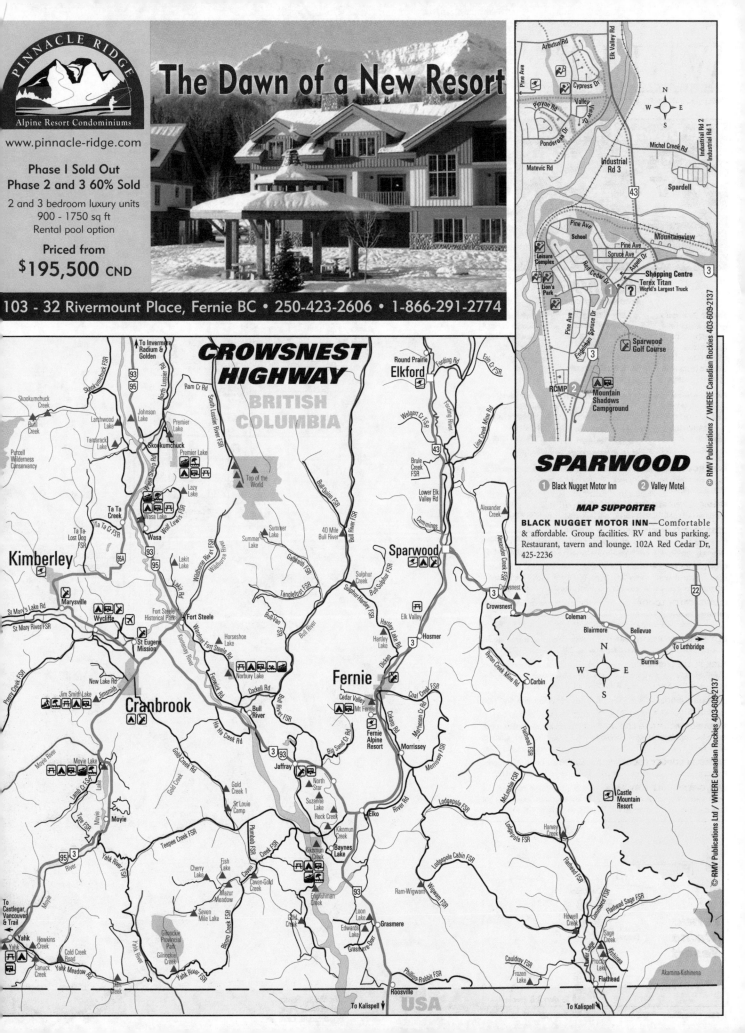

CROWSNEST HIGHWAY

BRITISH COLUMBIA

To Invermere
Radium &
Golden

Round Prairie

Elkford

Sparwood

KIMBERLEY

Top of the World

Fernie

Cranbrook

SPARWOOD

1 Black Nugget Motor Inn   2 Valley Motel

MAP SUPPORTER

Shopping Centre
Terex Titan
World's Largest Truck

Sparwood
Golf Course

Mountain
Shadows
Campground

RCMP

Coleman
Blairmore   Bellevue
To Lethbridge
Burmis

Crowsnest

Corbin

Castle
Mountain
Resort

To Castlegar,
Vancouver
& Trail

Yahk

USA
To Kalispell   To Kalispell

Roosville

© RMV Publications Ltd / WHERE Canadian Rockies 403-609-2137

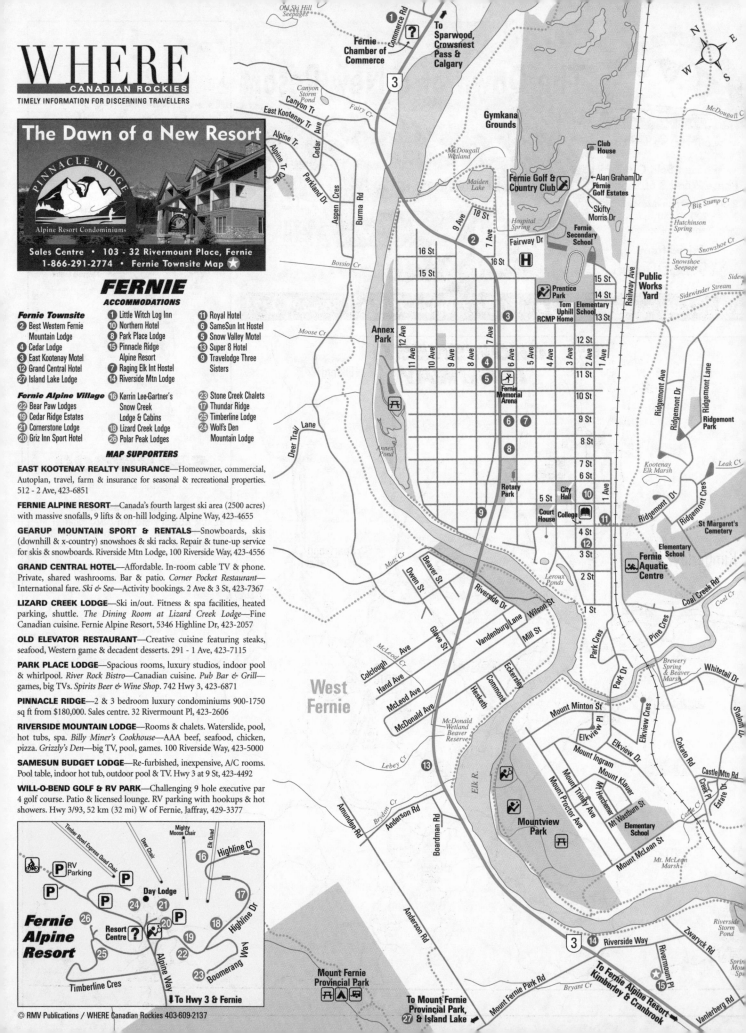

WHERE
CANADIAN ROCKIES
TIMELY INFORMATION FOR DISCERNING TRAVELLERS

FERNIE
ACCOMMODATIONS

Fernie Townsite
- 2 Best Western Fernie Mountain Lodge
- 4 Cedar Lodge
- 3 East Kootenay Motel
- 12 Grand Central Hotel
- 27 Island Lake Lodge

Fernie Alpine Village
- 22 Bear Paw Lodges
- 19 Cedar Ridge Estates
- 21 Cornerstone Lodge
- 20 Griz Inn Sport Hotel

- 1 Little Witch Log Inn
- 10 Northern Hotel
- 8 Park Place Lodge
- 15 Pinnacle Ridge Alpine Resort
- 7 Raging Elk Int Hostel
- 14 Riverside Mtn Lodge
- 16 Kerrin Lee-Gartner's Snow Creek Lodge & Cabins
- 18 Lizard Creek Lodge
- 26 Polar Peak Lodges

- 11 Royal Hotel
- 6 SameSun Int Hostel
- 5 Snow Valley Motel
- 13 Super 8 Hotel
- 9 Travelodge Three Sisters
- 23 Stone Creek Chalets
- 17 Thundar Ridge
- 25 Timberline Lodge
- 24 Wolf's Den Mountain Lodge

MAP SUPPORTERS

EAST KOOTENAY REALTY INSURANCE—Homeowner, commercial, Autoplan, travel, farm & insurance for seasonal & recreational properties. 512 - 2 Ave, 423-6851

FERNIE ALPINE RESORT—Canada's fourth largest ski area (2500 acres) with massive snowfalls, 9 lifts & on-hill lodging. Alpine Way, 423-4655

GEARUP MOUNTAIN SPORT & RENTALS—Snowboards, skis (downhill & x-country) snowshoes & ski racks. Repair & tune-up service for skis & snowboards. Riverside Mtn Lodge, 100 Riverside Way, 423-4556

GRAND CENTRAL HOTEL—Affordable. In-room cable TV & phone. Private, shared washrooms. Bar & patio. *Corner Pocket Restaurant*—International fare. *Ski & See*—Activity bookings. 2 Ave & 3 St, 423-7367

LIZARD CREEK LODGE—Ski in/out. Fitness & spa facilities, heated parking, shuttle. *The Dining Room at Lizard Creek Lodge*—Fine Canadian cuisine. Fernie Alpine Resort, 5346 Highline Dr, 423-2057

OLD ELEVATOR RESTAURANT—Creative cuisine featuring steaks, seafood, Western game & decadent desserts. 291 - 1 Ave, 423-7115

PARK PLACE LODGE—Spacious rooms, luxury studios, indoor pool & whirlpool. *River Rock Bistro*—Canadian cuisine. *Pub Bar & Grill*—games, big TVs. *Spirits Beer & Wine Shop.* 742 Hwy 3, 423-6871

PINNACLE RIDGE—2 & 3 bedroom luxury condominiums 900-1750 sq ft from $180,000. Sales centre. 32 Rivermount Pl, 423-2606

RIVERSIDE MOUNTAIN LODGE—Rooms & chalets. Waterslide, pool, hot tubs, spa. *Billy Miner's Cookhouse*—AAA beef, seafood, chicken, pizza. *Grizzly's Den*—big TV, pool, games. 100 Riverside Way, 423-5000

SAMESUN BUDGET LODGE—Re-furbished, inexpensive, A/C rooms. Pool table, indoor hot tub, outdoor pool & TV. Hwy 3 at 9 St, 423-4492

WILL-O-BEND GOLF & RV PARK—Challenging 9 hole executive par 4 golf course. Patio & licensed lounge. RV parking with hookups & hot showers. Hwy 3/93, 52 km (32 mi) W of Fernie, Jaffray, 429-3377

Fernie Alpine Resort

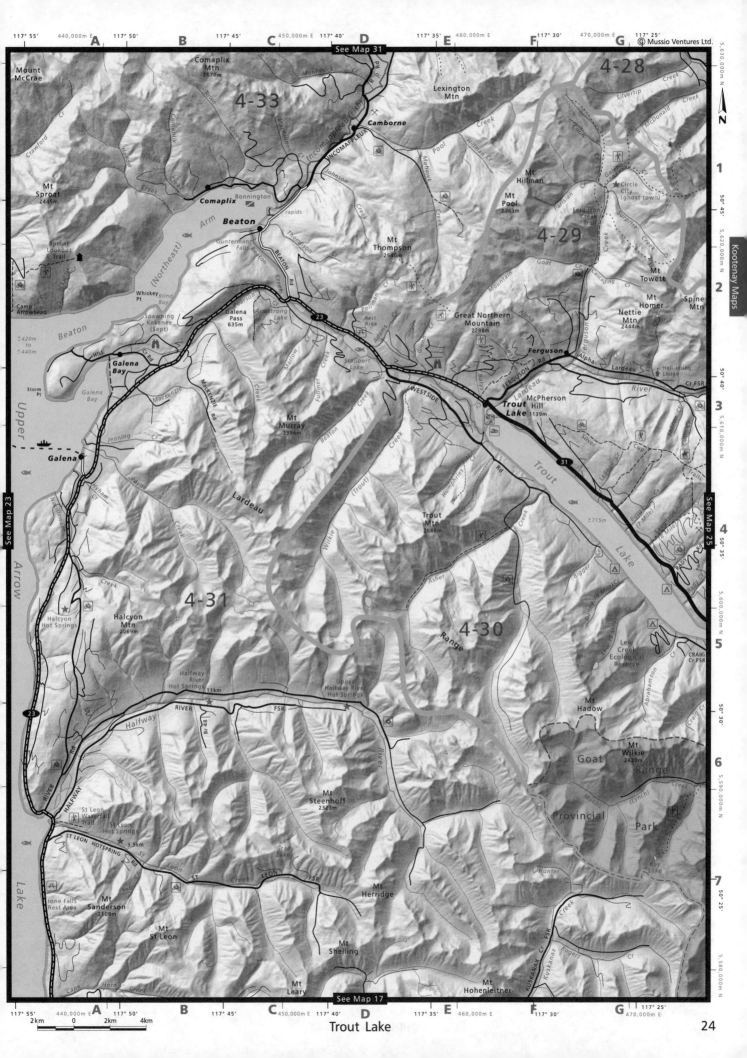

Kootenay Maps

See Map 31

See Map 23

See Map 25

See Map 17

4-28

4-33

4-29

4-31

4-30

Trout Lake

2km 0 2km 4km

24

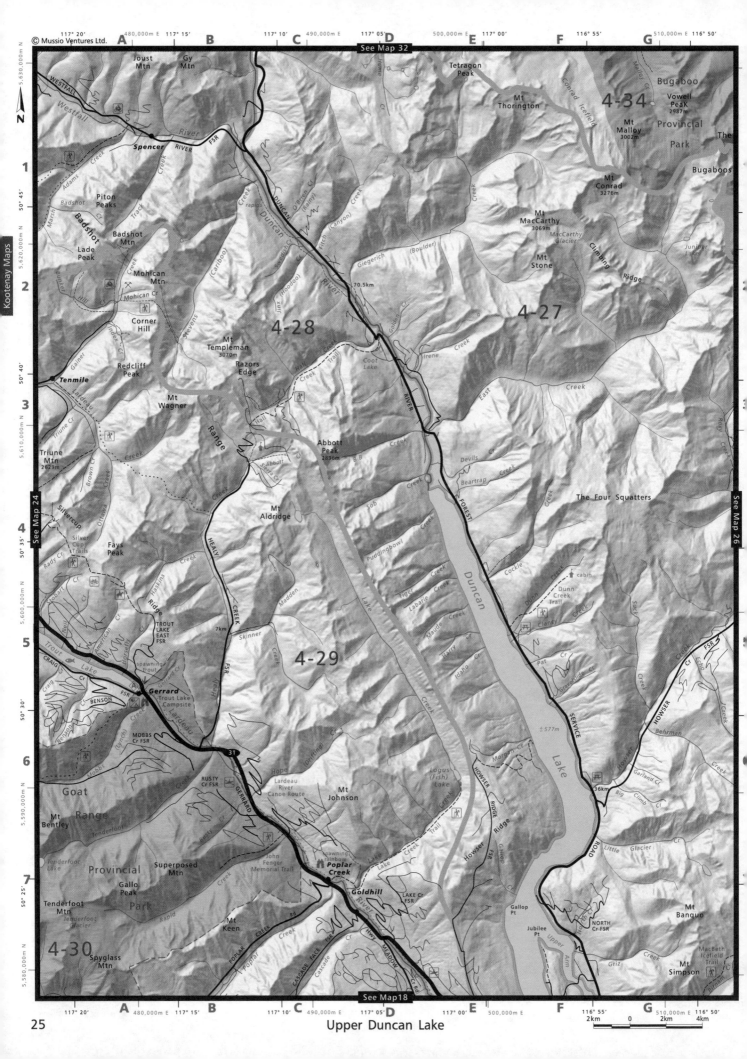

Upper Duncan Lake

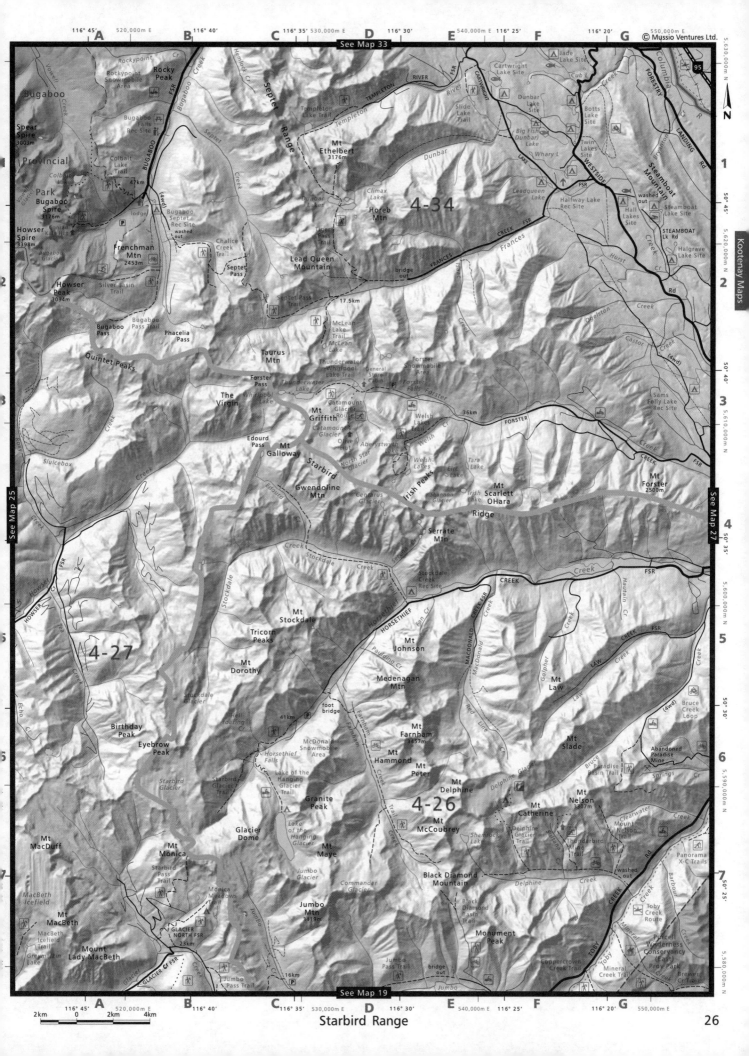

Kootenay Maps

See Map 25

See Map 27

Kootenay Maps

4-35

Kootenay

National

Park

4-34

4-25

4-26

Invermere

See Map 26

See Map 28

See Map 20

2km   0   2km   4km

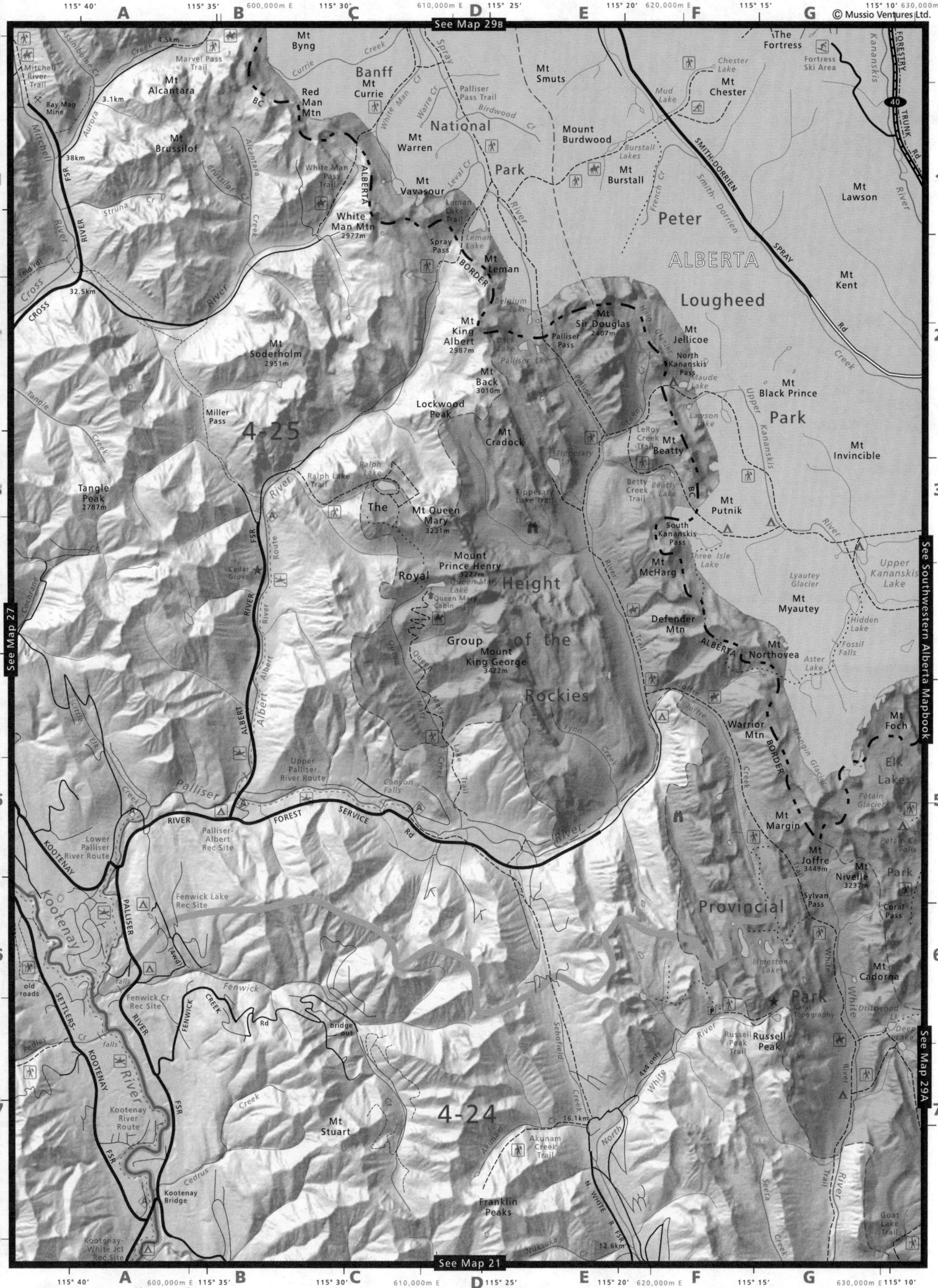

Kootenay Maps

See Map 29B

115° 40' A 115° 35' B 600,000mE 115° 30' C 610,000mE D 115° 25' 115° 20' E 620,000mF 115° 15' G 115° 10' 630,000mE

N
40

Mitchell River Trail
Assiniboine Cr
Marvel Pass Trail
4.5km
Mt Byng
Currie Creek
Mt Currie
Banff
Mt Smuts
The Fortress
Chester Lake
Fortress Ski Area
Kananaskis River
FORESTRY TRUNK Rd

Mt Alcantara
Bay Mag Mine
3.1km
Red Man Mtn
White Man Cr
Warre Cr
Palliser Pass Trail
Birdwood Cr
Mt Warren
National
Mount Burdwood
Mud Lake
Mt Chester
1

Mt Brussilof
38km
BC
Alcantara Creek
White Man Pass Trail
Mt Vavasour
Leval Cr
Park
Mt Burstall
Burstall Lakes
French Cr
Peter
Mt Lawson

Cross Fd tr
CROSS
32.5km
Mitchell River
Struma Cr
Brussilof Cr
ALBERTA
White Man Pass Trail
White Man Mtn 2977m
Spray Pass
Leman Lake Trail
Leman Lake
BORDER
Mt Leman
Belgium Lake
Smith-Dorrien Cr
Smith-Dorrien
SMITH-DORRIEN
ALBERTA
Lougheed
SPRAY
Mt Kent
50° 45'
5,620,000mN

FSR
Mt Soderholm 2951m
Miller Pass
Mt King Albert 2987m
Mt Back 3010m
Palliser Pass
Palliser Lk
Mt Sir Douglas 2407m
Mt Jellicoe
North Kananaskis Pass
Maude Lake
High Glacier
Mt Black Prince
50° 45'
2

Tangle Creek
4-25
RIVER
Ralph Lake Trail
Ralph Lake
Lockwood Peak
Mt Cradock
Tipperary Lk
Lawson Lake
LeRoy Creek Trail
Mt Beatty
Upper Kananaskis
Park
Mt Invincible
5,610,000mN
3

Tangle Peak 2787m
River Route
Cedar Grove
The
Mt Queen Mary 3231m
Tipperary Lake Trail
Betty Creek Trail
Betty Lake
BC
Mt Putnik
River
50° 40'
See Southwestern Alberta Mapbook

ALBERT
FSR
ALBERT
Mount Prince Henry 3227m
Royal
Queen Mary Lake
Height
of
the
South Kananaskis Pass
Three Isle Lake
Lyautey Glacier
Upper Kananaskis Lake
4

RIVER
River
Queen Mary Cabin
Group
Mount King George 3422m
Rockies
Mt McHarg
ALBERTA
Mt Northovea
Aster Lake
Hidden Lake
Fossil Falls
Mt Myautey
50° 35'

See Map 27
Upper Palliser River Route
Queen Mary Lake Trail
Canyon Falls
Fynn Cr
River
Defender Mtn
BORDER
Warrior Mtn
Joffre Cr
Mt Foch
Elk Lakes

Palliser Creek
RIVER
FOREST
SERVICE
Rd
Joffre Creek
Mt Margin
Mangin Glacier
Petain Glacier
Mt Joffre 3449m
Petain Cr Falls
50° 30'
5,600,000mN
5

Lower Palliser River Route
Palliser-Albert Rec Site
Fenwick Lake Rec Site
Mt Nivelle 3237m
Sylvan Pass
Park
Coral Pass

KOOTENAY
PALLISER
RIVER
falls
Fenwick Cr Rec Site
Fenwick
Schofield Cr
Provincial
limestone Lakes
6

old roads
SETTLERS Cr
Pedley falls
KOOTENAY
Fenwick Cr Rec Site
Fenwick
Creek
bridge out
Rd
Park
Russell Peak Trail
Russell Peak
Mt Cadorna
Driftwood Cr
See Map 29A

RIVER
FSR
Creek
4-24
16.1km
Akunam Cr
White River
North White River
Russell Peak
North White
Sesia Creek
White River
50° 25'
5,590,000mN
7

Kootenay River Route
Cedrus Cr
Mt Stuart
Akunam Creek Trail
N WHITE R FSR
12.6km
Niksuka Cr
Goat Lake Trail

Kootenay Bridge
Kootenay-White Jct Rec Site
Franklin Peaks

See Map 21

2km 0 2km 4km

115° 40' A 600,000mE B 115° 35' 115° 30' C 610,000mE D 115° 25' E 115° 20' 620,000mE F 115° 15' G 630,000mE 115° 10'

Palliser River

28

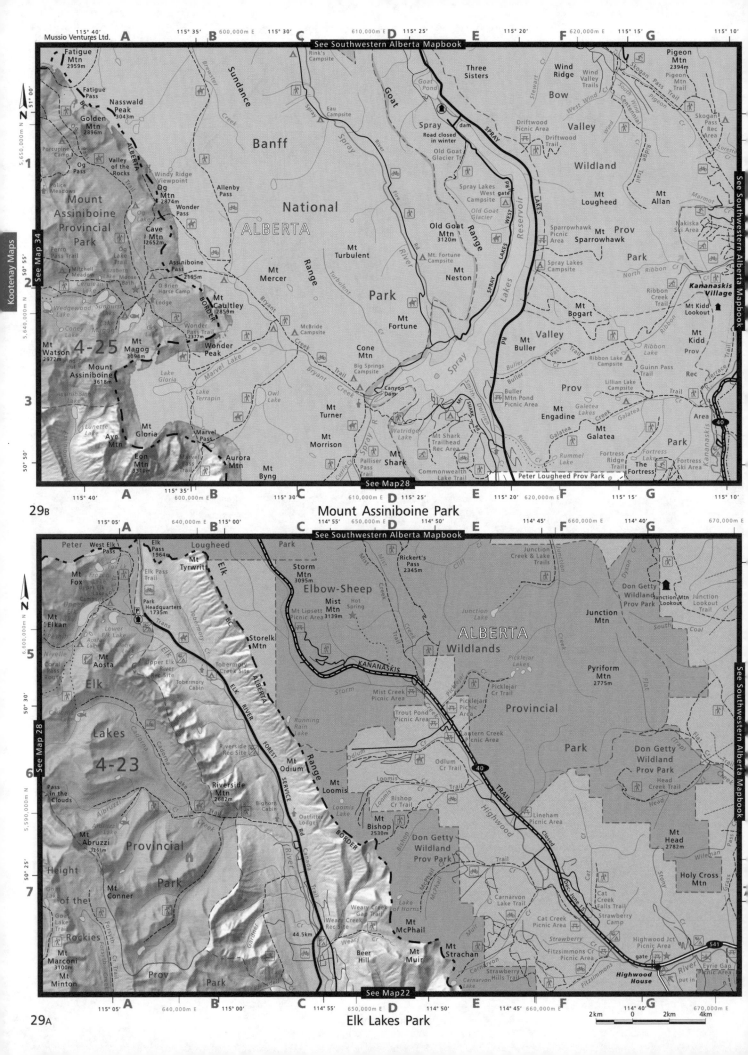

Kootenay Maps

See Map 34

ALBERTA

Banff

National

Park

4-25

Mount
Assiniboine
Provincial
Park

Mount
Assiniboine
3618m

Spray

Lakes
Reservoir

Wildland

Kananaskis
Village

Prov

Park

Valley

Prov

Rec

Park

See Map28

Mount Assiniboine Park

29B

Peter Lougheed Park

Elbow-Sheep

ALBERTA

Wildlands

Don Getty
Wildland
Prov Park

See Map 28

4-23

Elk

Lakes

Provincial

Park

Kananaskis

TRAIL

Highwood

40

Provincial

Park

Don Getty
Wildland
Prov Park

Height

of the

Rockies

Prov

Park

Don Getty
Wildland
Prov Park

Highwood
House

541

See Map22

Elk Lakes Park

29A

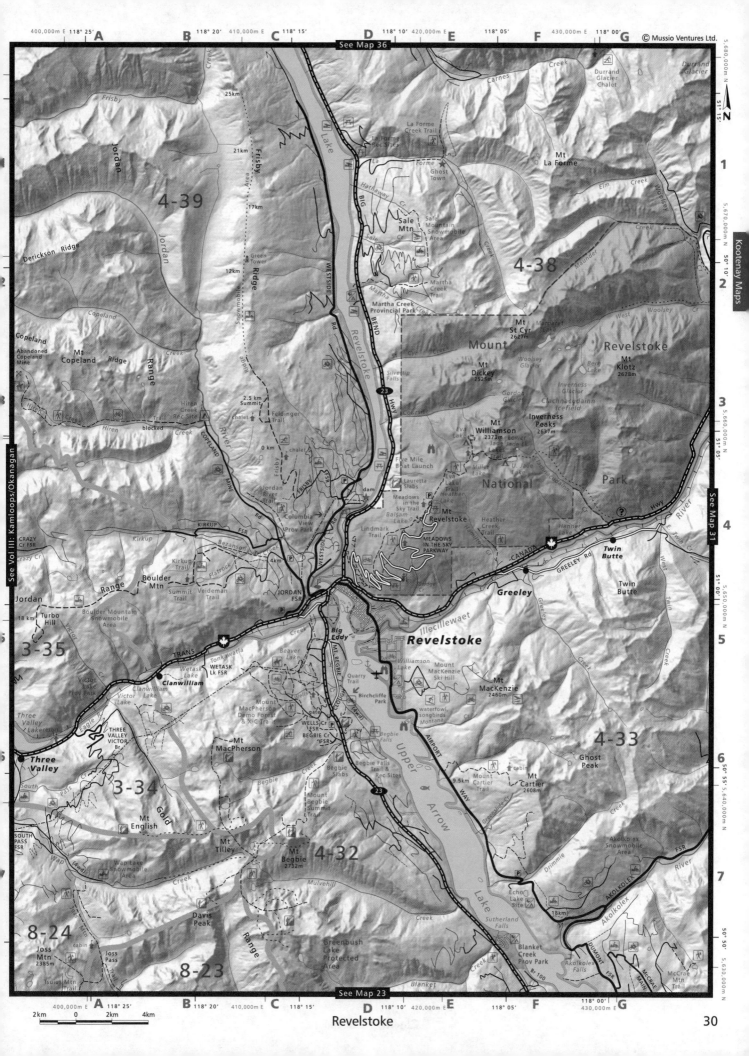

© Mussio Ventures Ltd.

Kootenay Maps

See Vol III: Kamloops/Okanagan

See Map 31

Revelstoke

2km   0   2km   4km

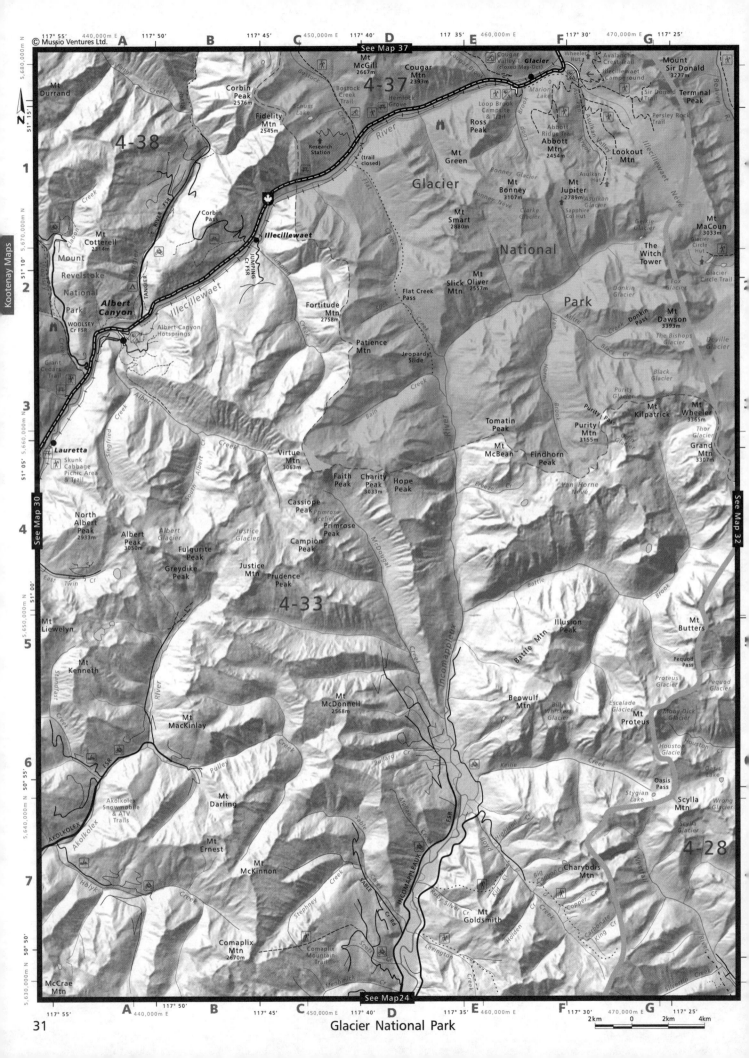

Kootenay Maps

See Map 30

See Map 32

4-38

4-37

4-33

4-28

Glacier

National

Park

Mt Durrand

Mt Cotterell 2314m

Mount Revelstoke National Park

Albert Canyon

WOOLSEY Cr FSR

Giant Cedars Trail

Lauretta

Skunk Cabbage Picnic Area & Trail

North Albert Peak 2933m

Albert Peak 3050m

Albert Glacier

Fulgurite Peak

Greydike Peak

Mt Liewelyn

Mt Kenneth

Mt MacKinlay

Mt Darling

Akolkolex Snowmobile & ATV Trails

Mt Ernest

Mt McKinnon

Comaplix Mtn 2670m

Comaplix Mountain Trail

McCrae Mtn

Corbin Peak 2576m

Fidelity Mtn 2545m

Corbin Pass

Illecillewaet

Research Station

(trail closed)

Schuss Lake

Bostock Creek Trail

JUMPING Cr FSR

Fortitude Mtn 2758m

Patience Mtn

Virtue Mtn 3063m

Faith Peak

Charity Peak 3033m

Hope Peak

Cassiope Peak

Primrose Icefield

Primrose Peak

Campion Peak

Justice Mtn

Justice Glacier

Prudence Peak

Mt McDonnell 2568m

Mt Goldsmith

Mt McGill 2667m

Cougar Mtn 2393m

Hemlock Grove

Mt Green

Ross Peak

Mt Smart 2880m

Flat Creek Pass

Jeopardy Slide

Slick Mtn

Mt Oliver 2557m

Tomatin Peak

Mt McBean

Findhorn Peak

Battle Mtn

Illusion Peak

Beowulf Mtn

Billy Whiskers Glacier

Charybdis Mtn

Cougar Valley Glacier (closed May–Oct)

Wheeler Hut

Avalanche Crest Trail

Illecillewaet Campground

Mount Sir Donald 3277m

Terminal Peak

Marion Lake

Loop Brook Campsite & Trail

Abbott Ridge Trail

Abbott Mtn 2454m

Sir Donald Trail

Persley Rock Trail

Lookout Mtn

Bonney Glacier

Mt Bonney 3107m

Bonney Névé

Mt Jupiter 2789m

Asulkan Hut

Asulkan Glacier

Sapphire Col Hut

Clarke Glacier

Mt MaCoun 3033m

The Witch Tower

Fox Glacier

Glacier Circle Hut

Glacier Circle Trail

Donkin Glacier

Donkin Pass

Mt Dawson 3393m

The Bishops Glacier

Doville Glacier

Black Glacier

Purity Glacier

Purity Pass

Purity Mtn 3155m

Mt Kilpatrick

Mt Wheeler 3365m

Thor Glacier

Grand Mtn 3307m

Van Horne Névé

Mt Butters

Pequod Pass

Proteus Glacier

Pequod Glacier

Escalade Glacier

Mt Proteus

Moby Dick Glacier

Houston Glacier

Oasis Lake

Oasis Pass

Stygian Lake

Scylla Mtn

Wrong Glacier

Scylla Glacier

Glacier National Park

2km 0 2km 4km

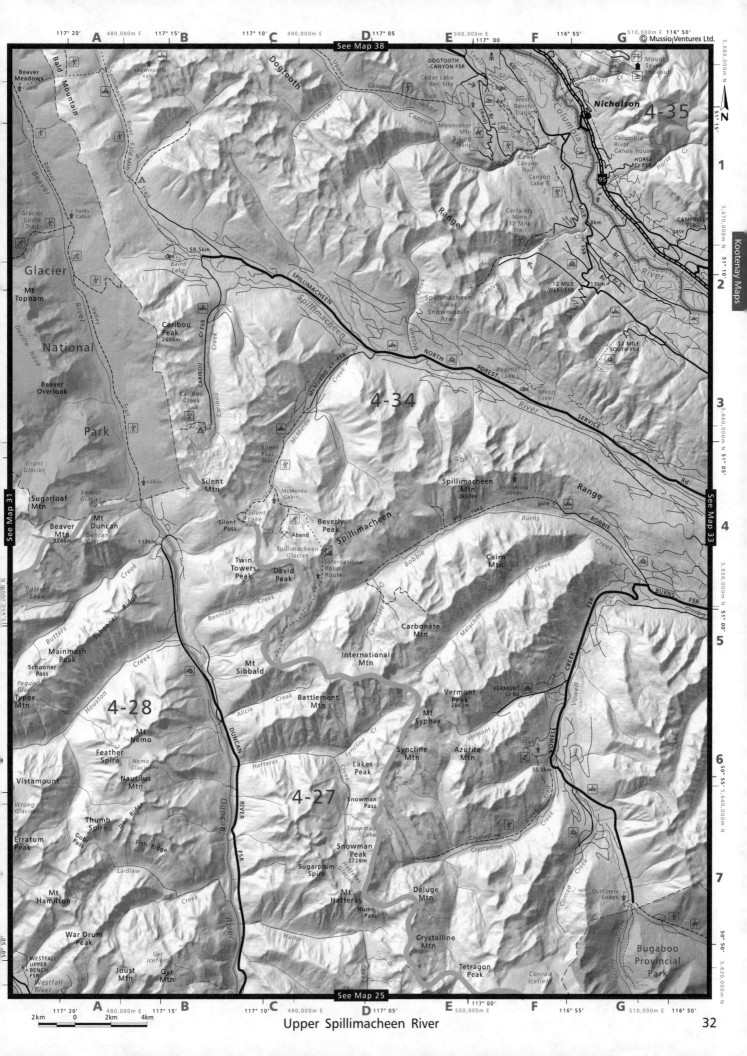

© Mussio Ventures Ltd.

4-35

4-34

4-28

4-27

Upper Spillimacheen River

32

See Map 38
See Map 31
See Map 33
See Map 25

2km 0 2km 4km

Kootenay Maps

See Map 32

See Map 34

Yoho

Mt Vaux
3320m

Hanbury
Peak
2911m

Kootenay

Mt Oke
2929m

Misko
Pass

Kapristo
Mtn
2722m

Chancellor
Peak
3280m

Garnet
Mtn
2315m

Sharp
Mtn
3049m

National

National

Aquila
Mtn

Mt
Goodsir
3562m

Helmet
Mtn
3138m

Clawson
Peak

Zinc
Mtn
2990m

Mt
Drysdale
2932m

Park

Buttress
Peak

Striped
Mtn

Coral
Mtn
2486m

Mt
Mollison

Vermilion

McMurdon

Tower
Peak

Ice River
Warden Cabin

Columbia

20.5km

Parson

Range

4-35

Loon Lake
Rec Site

Castle
Mtn
2530m

Marian
Lake
Site

Kootenay
Crossing
Rec Site

Spillimacheen

Rocky Point
Lake Site

Columbia Floodplain
Wildlife Reserve

2100m

39km

Summit
Lake

Rocky
Point Lake

Wilbur
Lake Site

Castledale

Harrogate
Pass Trail

Three Isl
Lake Rec Site

Bobbie

Burns

Lead
Mtn

Mitten
Lake

Harrogate

Range

Gavia
Lakes

Bittern
Lake Site

Mitten
Lake
Rec Site

Columbia River
Canoe Route

McLain
Lk Site

Nine
Bay Lk
Site

bridge
out

14 Mile
Lake

washed
out

Jubilee
Mtn

Jubilee
Lookout

4-34

Serpent
Lake

River

SPILLIMACHEEN

Spillimacheen

Kain Creek
Snowmobile
Area

28km

Moose
Lake

Jordan
Lake

SPILLIMACHEEN dam

FOREST

18.5km

Lower
Bugaboo
Falls Trail

Columbia National
Wildlife Area

Spillimacheen
Rest Area

Bugaboo

Prov

cabin

Rocky Point
Creek Trail

SERVICE

CleLand
Lang Lk Site

Topaz
Lake

Jade
Lake
Site

WESTSIDE
Rd

Park

Rocky
Point

Brisco

2km   0   2km   4km

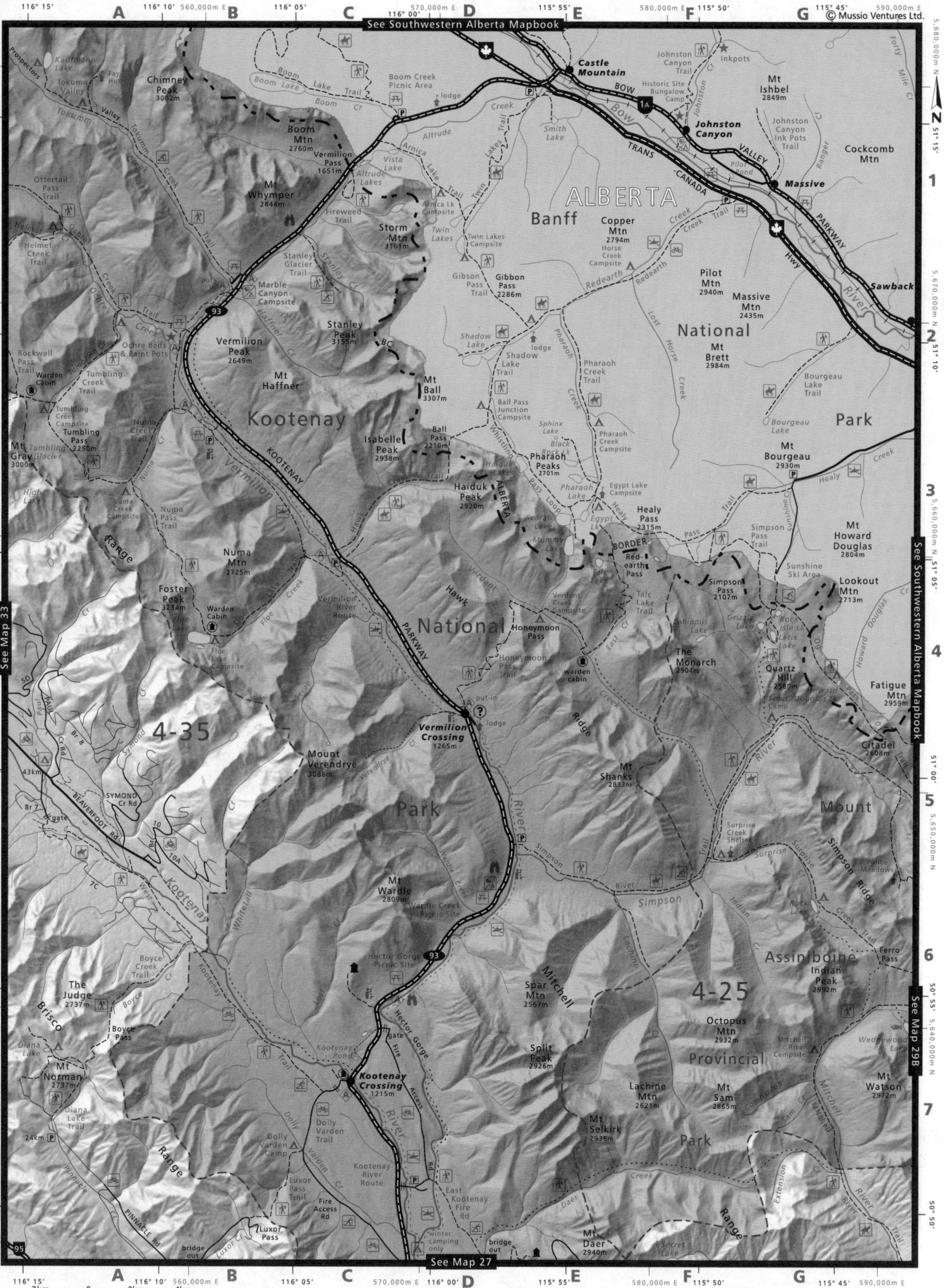

© Mussio Ventures Ltd.

ALBERTA

Banff

National

Park

Kootenay

National

Park

Peaks and Features:
- Kaufmann Lake
- Fay Hut
- Tokumm Valley
- Prospectors
- Chimney Peak 3002m
- Boom Mtn 2760m
- Boom Lake
- Boom Creek Picnic Area
- Castle Mountain
- Johnston Canyon Trail
- Inkpots
- Mt Ishbel 2849m
- Cockcomb Mtn
- Mt Whymper 2844m
- Vermilion Pass 1651m
- Storm Mtn 3161m
- Twin Lakes
- Johnston Canyon
- Massive
- Sawback
- Ottertail Pass Trail
- Helmet Creek Trail
- Stanley Glacier Trail
- Marble Canyon Campsite
- Vermilion Peak 2649m
- Mt Haffner
- Stanley Peak 3155m
- Gibson Pass Trail
- Gibbon Pass 2286m
- Shadow Lake
- Copper Mtn 2794m
- Horse Creek Campsite
- Pilot Mtn 2940m
- Massive Mtn 2435m
- Mt Brett 2984m
- Bourgeau Lake Trail
- Rockwall Pass Trail
- Warden Cabin
- Tumbling Creek Trail
- Tumbling Pass 2250m
- Mt Gray 3000m
- Gray Glacier
- Numa Pass Trail
- Mt Ball 3307m
- Isabelle Peak 2938m
- Ball Pass 2210m
- Haiduk Peak 2920m
- Pharaoh Peaks 2701m
- Egypt Lake Campsite
- Healy Pass 2315m
- Mt Bourgeau 2930m
- Mt Howard Douglas 2804m
- BORDER
- Redearth Pass
- Simpson Pass 2107m
- Sunshine Ski Area
- Lookout Mtn 2713m
- Numa Mtn 2725m
- Foster Peak 3234m
- Warden Cabin
- Floe Lake Campsite
- High Lake
- Numa Creek Campsite
- Honeymoon Pass
- Honeymoon Pass Trail
- The Monarch 2904m
- Quartz Hill 2580m
- Fatigue Mtn 2959m
- Vermilion Crossing 1265m
- Mount Verendrye 3086m
- Citadel 2608m
- Mt Shanks 2833m
- Mount Assiniboine Provincial Park
- 4-35
- 43km
- SYMOND Cr Rd
- BEAVERFOOT Rd
- Mt Wardle 2809m
- Wardle Creek Picnic Site
- Hector Gorge Picnic Site
- Spar Mtn 2567m
- Mitchell
- 4-25
- Surprise Creek Shelter
- Indian Peak 2992m
- Ferro Pass
- The Judge 2737m
- Boyce Creek Trail
- Boyce Pass
- Split Peak 2926m
- Octopus Mtn 2932m
- Mitchell River Campsite
- Wedgewood Lake
- Brisco Range
- Diana Lake
- Mt Norman 2737m
- Diana Lake Trail
- Kootenay Crossing 1215m
- Dolly Varden Trail
- Dolly Varden Camp
- Lachine Mtn 2621m
- Mt Sam 2865m
- Mt Selkirk 2938m
- Mt Watson 2972m
- Luxor Pass Trail
- Luxor Pass
- East Kootenay Fire Rd
- winter camping only
- bridge out
- Mt Daer 2940m
- Secret Lake
- Daer Range
- PINNACLE Rd

2km 0 2km 4km

See Map 27

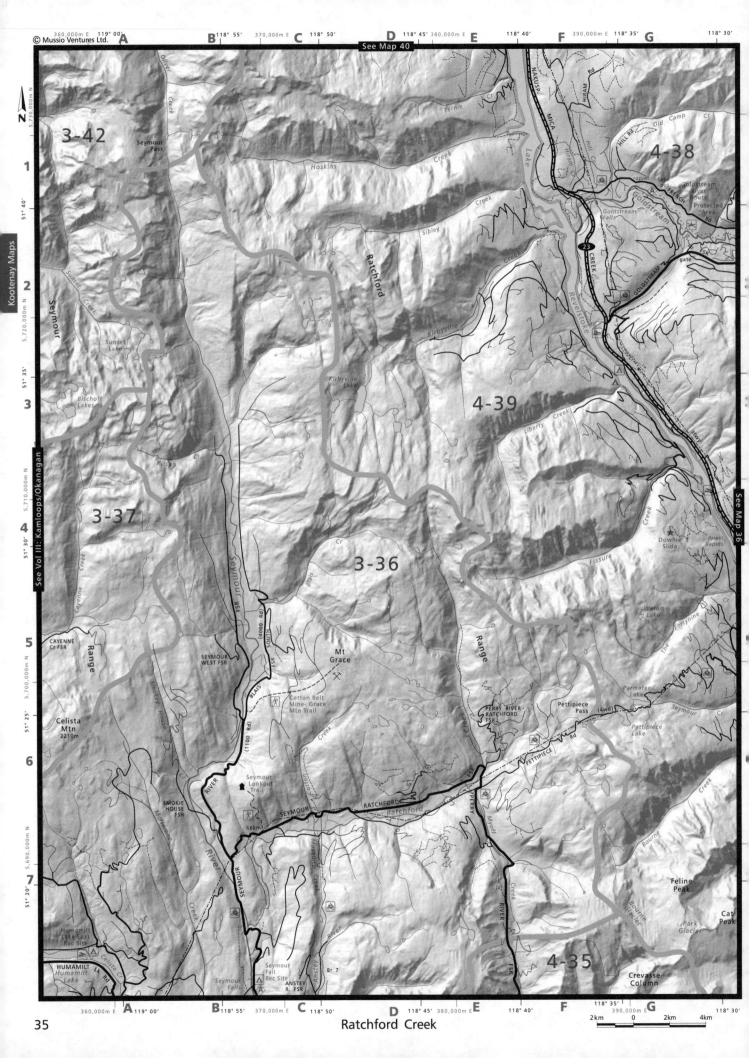

© Mussio Ventures Ltd.

Kootenay Maps

See Vol III: Kamloops/Okanagan

3-42

3-37

3-36

4-38

4-39

4-35

See Map 36

Seymour Pass

Oliver Creek

Hoskins Creek

Fernie Creek

Sibley Creek

Ratchford

Kirbyville Creek

Kirbyville Lake

Sunset Creek

Seymour

Sunset Lake

Bischoft Lakes

Kitson Cr

CAYENNE Cr FSR

Cayenne Creek

Range

Celista Mtn 2210m

Smokey House Creek

SMOKIE HOUSE FSR

McManus Creek

SEYMOUR RIVER

Seymour Falls

HUMAMILT Humamilt Lake

Humamilt Lake East Rec Site

Celista Cr

Lk Rd

Seymour Fall Rec Site

Anstey R. FSR

Br 7

Anstey River

Seymour RSR

SEYMOUR WEST FSR

BLAIS RSR

(4000 Rd)

(1100 Rd)

Blais Creek

Cr

Mt Grace

Cotton Belt Mine- Grace Mtn Trail

Seymour Lookout Trail

66km!

SEYMOUR

RATCHFORD

Ratchford

Uollio Creek

Mosquito Creek

Range

PERRY RIVER-RATCHFORD FSR

Perry Creek

PERRY FSR

Myoff Creek

RIVER

Pettipiece Pass

PETTIPIECE Rd

(4wd)

Pettipiece Lake

Parmater Lake

Watam Lake

The Fortynine

Seymour Cr

Liberty Creek

Downie Slide

Priest Rapids

Fissure

NAKUSP

MICA CREEK

23 CREEK

Lake Revelstoke

HIRAM Rd

HILL RD

Hiram Cr

Old Camp Cr

Goldstream

Goldstream Falls

Goldstream River Route Protected Area

FRENCH

lake out

gate

FSR

Bourne Glacier

Bourne Creek

Feline Peak

Park Glacier

Crevasse Column

Cat Peak

4-35

35

Ratchford Creek

2km 0 2km 4km

N

© Mussio Ventures Ltd.

Kootenay Maps

N

400,000m E · 118° 25' · 118° 20' · 410,000m E · 118° 15' · 118° 10' · 118° 05' · 430,000m E · 118° 00'

A B C D E F G

Old Camp Cr

Ground Hog Basin

McCulloch Cr

Goldstream River Route

abandoned

Gothics Lodge

gate

put-in

Goldstream Mine

GOLDSTREAM

Brewster Cr

French Creek

Graham Cr

Squawka Birch Cr

Norman Wood

Remillard Glacier

Remillard Peak

Wart Peak

Nadir Notch

Craw Peak

Hitchhiker Peak

Austerity Glacier

Redan Pass

Goldstream Mtn 2833m

Goldstream Néve

Triangle Mtn

Sir Sandford Pass

Moberly Pass

4-37

Goldstream FSR

River

Stitt Cr

Centurion Glacier

51° 40'
51° 35'
51° 30'
51° 25'
51° 20'
51° 15'

5,730,000m N
5,720,000m N
5,710,000m N
5,700,000m N
5,690,000m N
5,680,000m N

Boulder Peak

Downie Peak 2928m

Caribou Basin

Granite Cr

Boulder Cr

Long Cr

DOWNIE

CREEK

Pyrite Glacier

Caribou Cr

Downie Cr Prov Park

mountain caribou

See Map 35

NAKUSP

Downie Arm

RV Downie Resort

Sorcerer Cr

Mt Craib 2456m

Folly Peak

4-38

Downie FSR

See Map 37

Keystone Basin

KEY Rd

Keystone Peak 2373m

Keystone Creek

Standard Basin

Keystone Standard Cabin

Standard Cr

Murder Cr

Brown Cr

Pelkey Cr

Holway Cr

Tangier Pass

MICA

(4wd)

Keystone Cr

Keystone Snowmobile Area

P

Basin Trail

Mt Holway 3047m

Lake

Bourne Cr

NISSAN Rd

23

Mars Creek

Standard Peak 2311m

Belcher Ridge

Pass Peak 2458m

Pass Cr

Belcher Cr

Mt Sissons 2953m

Downie Lake

Mt Boat

CREEK

Park Cr

Eddy Cr

Cap Cr

Holdich Creek

Bridgland Peak

Abyss Glacier

Phogg Glacier

Carnes Glacier

Mt Moloch 3107m

Frenchman Cap 2897m

Revelstoke

Hwy

Kelly Burke Cr

Kelly-Burke Trail

Carnes Peak 3050m

Rosebury Mtn 2456m

Bridgland Pass

Tumbledown Cr

Dismal Glacier

Mt Levers

4-39

Hat Peak 2883m

Big Cr

Frisby Cr

Carnes Creek Rec Site

Carnes Cr

CARNES CREEK

Carnes FSR

Carnes Creek Trail

McKinnon Cr

Carnes Cr

Tumbledown Mtn 2717m

Durrand Glacier

Durrand Glacier Chalet

2km 0 2km 4km

400,000m E · 118° 25' · 118° 20' · 410,000m E · 118° 15' · 118° 10' · 118° 05' · 430,000m E · 118° 00'

A B C D E F G

Kootenay Maps

117° 55' 440,000m E   117° 50' A   117° 45' B   450,000m E C   117° 40' D   117° 35' E   460,000m E F   117° 30' 470,000m E G   117° 25'

Austerity Mtn
Adamant Mtn 3355m
Mt Wotan
Mt Stockmer 2830m

Kinbasket Lake

COLUMBIA WEST FSR

Gold River Camp ±755m to ±707m

52km
51
Br 37
Esplanade Bay Rec Site
Giant Cedars Rec Site & Trail
Chaperon Mtn
4-36

Silvertip Mtn
Redan Mtn
Azimuth Mtn
Palmer Creek
Trail
38.5km

COLUMBIA
Br 1
WEST
Br 17
FOREST
Br 35
Blackwater
Br 11
Help Lake & Pull Out Rec Sites
Aid Lake
Comfort Lake

Blackwater Mtn 2732m

Palisade Mtn
Ravelin Mtn
Guardsman Mtn
Great Cabin -Ben Ferris Hut
Mt Palmer
Sentry Mtn 2543m
Olafson
Br 9
Colpitti Cr
Blackwater Lake Rec Site

Mt Sir Stanford 3522m
Cornice Peak
Esplanade
Schlichting Cr
Br 8
1682m
Susan Lake

Citadel Mtn 2926m
43
Gold
ROAD
River
Spinster
Sunbeam Lake
Carrot
Mayvill
Cr
Br 7
Susan Lk Rd
Susan Lk Site

Sonata Mtn 3015m
Sonata Névé
BACHELOR
Cr
Cupola Mtn 2645m
Range
Br 6
Rd
BLACKWATER RIDGE

Argentine Glacier
Cherub Mtn 2968m
Br 31
Comedy Cr
Cupola
CUPOLA Rd
Br 4
resort
Beavermouth

Argentine Mtn 3045m
4-37
Seraph Mtn
Twilight Cr
Cupola Creek
CPR
Rogers
Br 8

Bachelor Pass
38
Bachelor
Benedict
Ventego Mtn
Ventego
Rd
Br 14

Br 41
7
ROAD
Cr
Creek
Mt Pearce 2861m
Heather Mtn 2405m

Br 40
Sorcerer Mtn 3168m
Sorcerer Glacier
Iconoclast Mtn 3251m
Ventego Lake
Mt McNicoll
Alder
Creek
TRANS
4-34

Tangier Pass
Mystic Mtn 2667m
Nordic Mtn 3002m
Creek
Sturdee
East Gate

Mt Anstey
Mountain
Glacier
Sturdee Cr
Beaver Picnic Site

Tangier
Creek
National
Mt Shaughnessy 2705m
Stoney Cr
Stoney Creek
Beaver Valley Trailhead

Mt Moloch 3107m
Moloch Cr
Mt Carson 2742m
Corson Cabin
Mt Rogers 3185m
Rogers Glacier
Hemit Mtn 3079m
Tupper Glacier
Mt Tupper 2804m
Bear Creek Falls
Beaver Falls Trail
Copperstain Trail

Mt Graham 2867m
4-38
River
Farm
Avalanche Cabin
Wolverine Ridge
Park
Mt Silton 2922m
Hermit Trail
Grizzly Mtn 2758m
Ursus Minor Mtn 2749m
Balu Pass Trail
Hermit
Mt MacDonald 2878m
Rogers Pass
Beaver Valley Trail

Dismal Glacier
Grey Fang
Fang Glacier
Farm Pass
Cassiday
Casualty Cr
Ursus
Ursus Major Mtn 2705m
Balu Hut
Connaught
?
Grizzly Mtn
Avalanche Crest Trail

Tumbledown Mtn 2717m
Fang Rock
Bostock Cr Trail
Hermit
Bagheera Mtn 2765m
Cougar
Cheops Mtn 2606m
Cougar Valley Trail
Avalanche Glacier
Uto Peak 2927m

117° 55' 440,000m E   117° 50' A   117° 45' B   450,000m E C   117° 40' D   117° 35' E   460,000m E F   117° 30' 470,000m E G   117° 25'

Rogers Pass

2km   0   2km   4km

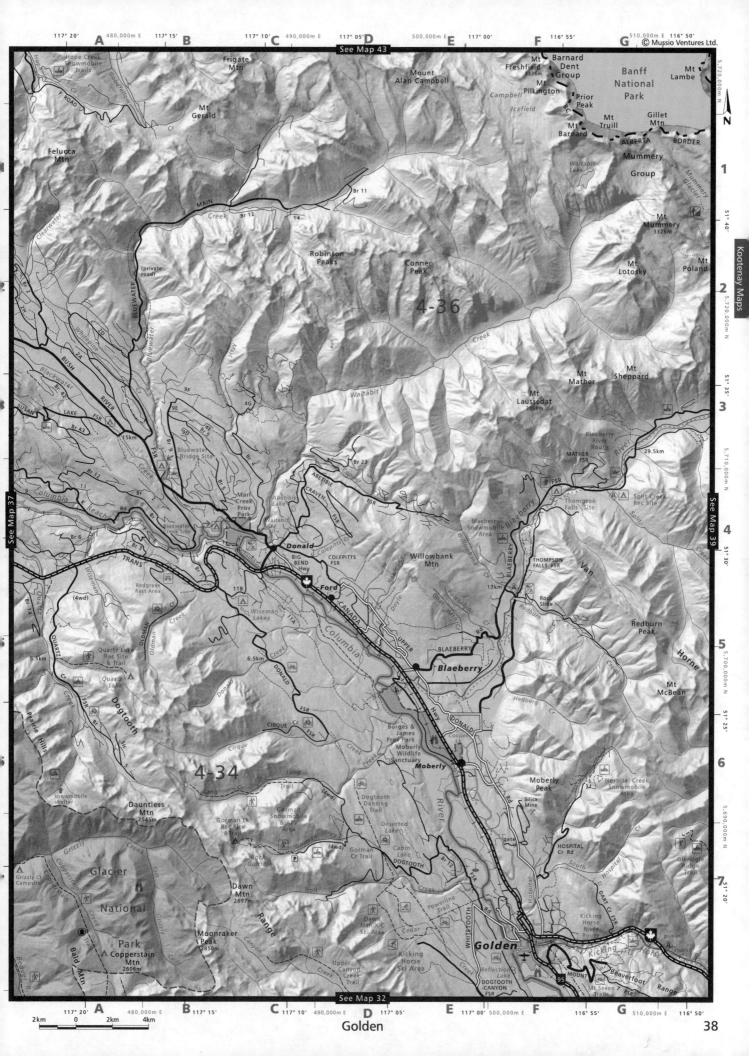

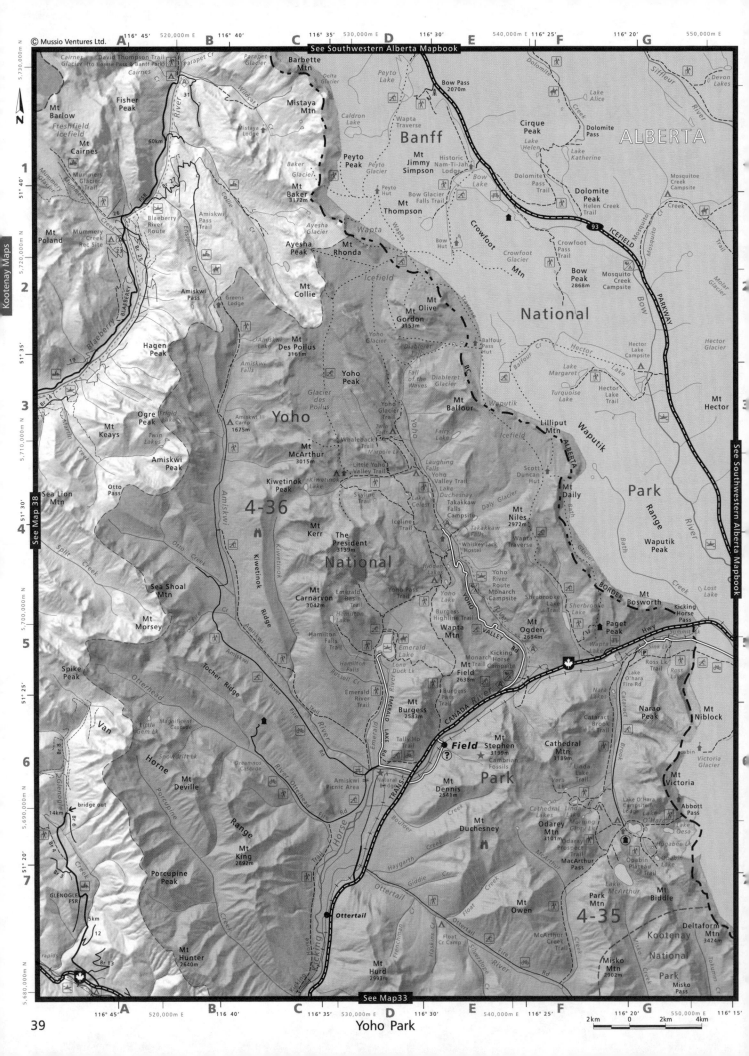

© Mussio Ventures Ltd.

Kootenay Maps

ALBERTA

Banff

National

Park

Yoho

National

Park

4-36

4-35

4-34

See Map 38

See Southwestern Alberta Mapbook

Yoho Park

2km 0   2km   4km

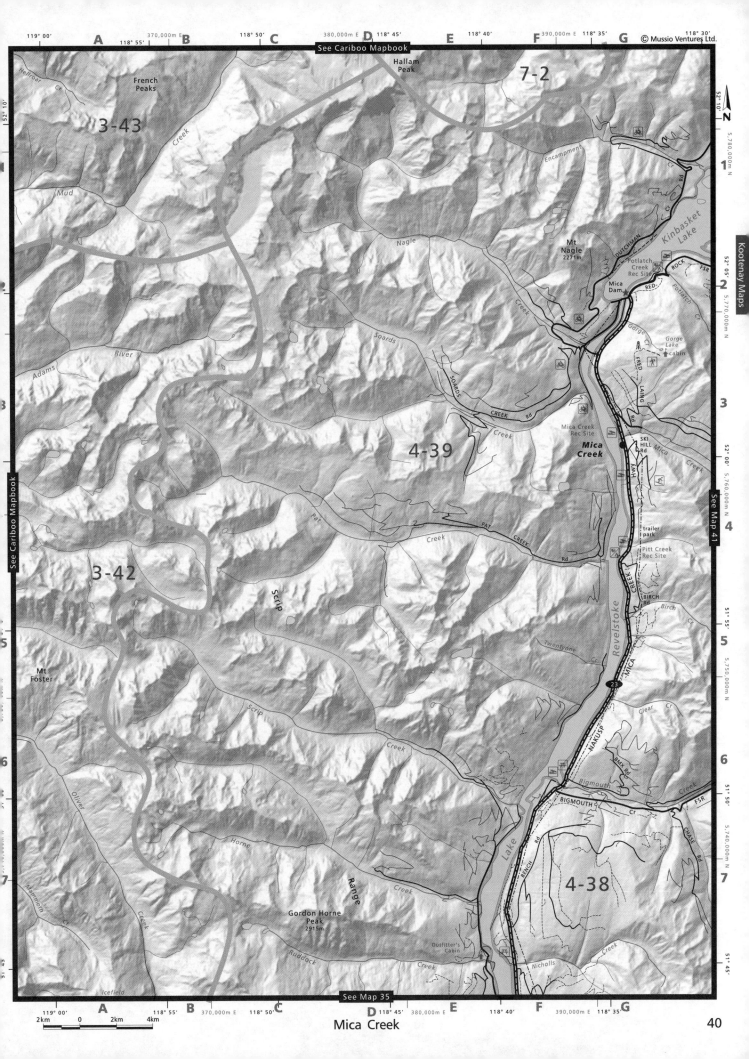

© Mussio Ventures Ltd.

Kootenay Maps

7-2

3-43

French
Peaks

Hallam
Peak

Helfroar
Cr

Mud

Nagle

Mt
Nagle
2271m

Kinbasket
Lake

Encampment

DUTCHMAN
Rd

Potlatch Creek
Rec Site

ROCK
FSR

Mica
Dam

RED

Potlatch
Cr

Adams

River

Soards

Soards
Creek Rd

SOARDS

Creek

Creek

Gorge
Lake
cabin

FRED

LAING
Rd

See Cariboo Mapbook

3-42

4-39

Scrip

Pat

Creek

Creek

PAT
CREEK

Rd

Mica Creek
Rec Site

Mica
Creek

SKI
HILL
Rd

Mica
Creek

trailer
park

Pitt Creek
Rec Site

BIRCH
Rd

Birch
Cr

Revelstoke

See Map 41

Mt
Foster

Scrip

Creek

Twentyone

23

MICA

Clear
Cr

NAKUSP

BMX Rd

Oliver

Horne

Range

Creek

Gordon Horne
Peak
2915m

Mammoth
Cr

Ruddack

Creek

Outfitter's
Cabin

Lake

BENCH
Rd

BIGMOUTH

Bigmouth

Cr

Creek

FSR

4-38

CHASE
Rd

Nicholls

2km 0 2km 4km

Mica Creek

40

Kootenay Maps

400,000m E
118° 25'
118° 20'
410,000m E
118° 15'
118° 10'
420,000m E
118° 05'
430,000m E
118° 00'

A   B   C   D   E   F   G

52° 10'
52° 05'
52° 00'
51° 55'
51° 50'
51° 45'

5,780,000m N
5,770,000m N
5,760,000m N
5,750,000m N
5,740,000m N

DAINARD FSR

Molson   Creek

Mt
Molson
2498m

Canoe Reach

Molson
Creek
Rec Site

Kinbasket
Lake

Garnet
Islands
Rec Site

Br 10
10A
WOOD
Br 9
WOOD-ARM
FSR

Wood

Arm

Br 11

RIVER
GOATBUSTER
CREEK Rd

Jumping
Jack Cr

Cummins

Cummins
Lakes

Mt
Shackleton

Cummins Glacier

Pic
Tordue

Stanley
Glacier

Mt
Livingstone

Br 18

FSR

Br 14

4-40

Lakes

Provincial

Park

± 754m
to
± 707m

Sprague Bay
Rec Site

RED

ROCK

Redrock
Harbour

YELLOW   CREEK

15km

FSR

Cummins
Lookout

Mt
Cummins
2586m

Cummins

Potlatch   Creek

Fred Laing Ridge

Warsaw
Mtn
2774m

Columbia

Goosegrass Ck

Goosegrass
Ecological
Reserve

1E

1E

Br 2

Br 1

Tsar
Camp

Br 3

1C

1B

Tsar Cr

Tsar

Kinbasket
Mtn
2470m

Kinbasket Bay
Rec Site

Reach

Kinbasket
Arm

Kinbasket

See Map 42

SULLIVAN FSR

Sullivan Arm

Mica   Creek

Anemone
Pass

Northeast
Mtn
3020m

See Map 40

Mud
Glacier

Lee   Creek

Louis   Creek

Birch Ck

Mt
Chapman
3075m

Trident
Glacier

Trident
Mtn
3091m

Neptune
Peak
3194m

Escarpment
Glacier

Stegosaur
Ridge

Range

Halia
Mtn

Misty
Glacier

Roseidon
Peak

Kyanite Cr

Trident Cr

Windy
Arm

Windy
Island
Rec Site

Adamant   Range

4-38

Bigmouth   FSR

BIGMOUTH FSR

Mt
Medea

Argonaut
Mtn
2974m

Argonaut   Creek

Mt
Hercules

Jason
Peak

Creek

Windy

Escarpment
Peak

Mermaid
Mtn

French   Glacier

Windy   Creek

Austerity   Creek

Ice Field

OK
Glacier

Mt
Ed. Falls

4-37

Granite
Glacier

CHASE
Rd

Argonaut
Pass

French   Creek

Norman Wood Cr

Mt
Onderdonk

Yard-Arm
Ridge

Ganner
Lake

Whiteface
Tower

Austerity
Mtn

400,000m E
118° 25'
118° 20'
410,000m E
118° 15'
118° 10'
420,000m E
118° 05'
430,000m E
118° 00'

A   B   C   D   E   F   G

Cummins Lakes Park

2km   0   2km   4km

Kootenay Maps

See Central Alberta Mapbook

ALBERTA

Jasper

National

Park

Clemenceau

Icefield

Shackleton
Glacier

Mt
Rhodes

Mt Ellis

Mt
Somervell

Apex Glacier

Wales
Glacier

Omega
Peak

Triad
Peak

Mt King
Edward
3475m

Mt
Columbia
3747m

Highest
Point
in Alberta

Columbia
Icefield

BC
ALBERTA
BORDER

Tsar
Mtn
3424m

Kinbasket

River

Br 12

Br 11

13

Lunatic
Creek

Bush

River

15 Rd

Br 14

4-40

River Rd

171.5km

Br 10

Br 12

(9 ROAD)

Prattle

4-36

Sullivan Bay
Rec Site

end
of FSR

Sullivan
River Camp

Sullivan

SULLIVAN

RIVER

Br 7

Br 8

Creek

Vertebrae

Stovepipe
Mtn

Br 5

5A

Garrett

Cr

Boulder

Creek

Br 4

Lid
Mtn

Sophist
Mtn

Poker
Mtn

Solitude
Mtn

Columbia

BUSH

Rd 14

Br 2

end of FSR

20

104km

67km

Br 8

Caribou
Creek
Rec Site

3B

Caribou
Cr

Nixon

Cr

River

Br

Cr

Br 1A

SULLIVAN

Game

Cr

Ridge

Chatter

Chatter Creek
Snowmobile
Area

51° 55'

5,750,000m N

72km

61km

Doubletop
Mtn

Double Eddy

Cr

Br 16

COLUMBIA

Reach

57.5km

Br 15

Br 1A

WEST

Br 12

Swan

Creek Trail

Smith Creek

Tabernacle

Cr

Tabernacle
Mtn
2548m

Little

Br

Fuster

Cr

20

FOREST

SERVICE

Rd

Bear
Island

Kinbasket
Lake

Succous
Arm

Bush
Harbour

Bush Arm
Rec Site

Robinson
Pt

BUSH

Hope Cr

Arm

Low water
short cut

FSR

F Road

Bush

RIVER

2

Granite
Glacier

4-37

Mt
Damon

Gothics
Glacier

See Map 37

See Map 41

See Map 43

0   2km   4km

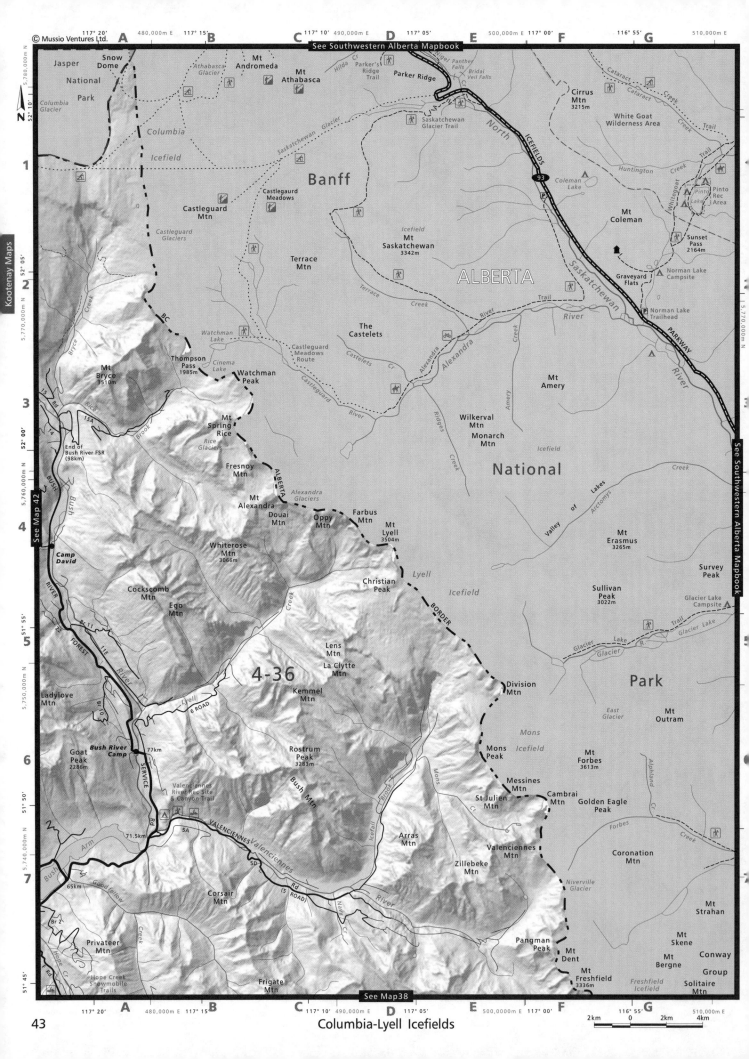

Kootenay Maps

A B C D E F G

See Southwestern Alberta Mapbook

Jasper

Snow
Dome

National

Park

*Columbia
Glacier*

Banff

ALBERTA

Cirrus
Mtn
3215m

White Goat
Wilderness Area

Pinto
Rec
Area

Columbia

Icefield

*Athabasca
Glacier*

Mt
Andromeda

Mt
Athabasca

Parker Ridge

Panther
Falls

Bridal
Veil Falls

Coleman
Lake

93

Mt
Coleman

Sunset
Pass
2164m

Norman Lake
Campsite

Graveyard
Flats

Norman Lake
Trailhead

Castleguard
Mtn

*Castlegaurd
Glaciers*

Castleguard
Meadows

Saskatchewan Glacier

Saskatchewan
Glacier Trail

Mt
Saskatchewan
3342m

Icefield

Terrace
Mtn

Terrace

Creek

The Castelets

Castelets Cr

Alexandra River

Mt
Amery

Watchman
Lake

Castleguard
Meadows
Route

Castleguard River

Mt
Bryce
3510m

Thompson
Pass
1985m

Watchman
Peak

*Cinema
Lake*

Mt
Spring
Rice

Rice Glaciers

ALBERTA

BC

End of
Bush River FSR
(98km)

Bush Brook

Fresnoy
Mtn

Mt
Alexandra

*Alexandra
Glaciers*

Douai
Mtn

Oppy
Mtn

Farbus
Mtn

Mt
Lyell
3504m

Christian
Peak

Whiterose
Mtn
3066m

Wilkerval
Mtn

Monarch
Mtn

Icefield

National

Mt
Erasmus
3265m

Survey
Peak

Camp
David

BUSH RIVER

Cockscomb
Mtn

Ego
Mtn

Lyell Creek

Lyell Icefield

Valley of Lakes

Arctomys

Sullivan
Peak
3022m

Glacier Lake
Campsite

Glacier Lake

FOREST

4-36

Lens
Mtn

La Clytte
Mtn

Division
Mtn

Park

Ladylove
Mtn

6 ROAD

Kemmel
Mtn

Mons Icefield

East
Glacier

Mt
Outram

SERVICE

Bush River Camp

77km

Goat
Peak
2286m

Rostrum
Peak
3283m

Bush Mtn

Mons
Peak

Messines
Mtn

Cambrai
Mtn

Mt
Forbes
3613m

Mons Brook

Alphland Cr

Valenciennes
River Rec Site
& Canyon Trail

71.5km

VALENCIENNES

5A

St Julien
Mtn

Golden Eagle
Peak

Coronation
Mtn

Forbes Creek

65km

Goodfellow Creek

Corsair
Mtn

5D

Valenciennes

Rd

(5 ROAD)

Navy Creek

Arras
Mtn

Zillebeke
Mtn

Valenciennes
Mtn

*Niverville
Glacier*

Bush Arm

Hope Cr

Privateer
Mtn

Icefall Brook

Valenciennes River

Pangman
Peak

Mt
Dent

Mt
Freshfield
3336m

Mt
Strahan

Mt
Skene

Mt
Bergne

Conway
Group

Solitaire
Mtn

*Freshfield
Icefield*

Br 2

Hope Creek
Snowmobile
Trails

Frigate
Mtn

See Map38

Columbia-Lyell Icefields

2km 0 2km 4km

Service Providers

Accommodations / Tours & Guides

Birch Meadows Lodge B&B

Fish, ski, bike, hike!

Log chalets with mountain views.

Hearty breakfasts, gazebo hot tub.

4485 Highway 3 South
Fernie, B.C. V0B 1M1

1-250-423-4236

www.birchmeadowslodge.com

CASA BLANCA B & B
and VACATION RENTALS

Nelson, BC

1-888-354-4431

Warm, Friendly, Comfortable and Classy.
Close to All Amenities and Activities. Boating,
Fishing, Hiking, Biking, Skiing

Shopping and Hot Springs

casa.bb@netidea.com
www.casablancanelson.com

Christmas Island Bed & Breakfast

Box 1284

523 West Third Street

Revelstoke, B.C. V0E 2S0

Toll Free **1-888-826-5555**

Phone 250-837-3262

Fax 250-837-2944

CREEKSIDE BED & BREAKFAST

16 Elkview Cres.

Fernie, B.C. V0B 1M3

Phone (250) 423-7394

www.elkvalley.net/pfeifersb&b

Email: pfeifersb&b@elkvalley.net

Dayspring Lodge

On Kootenay Lake near Kaslo

Spectacular location between the Purcells,
Selkirk & Goat Ranges - luxury waterfront
rooms or suite - world's largest Gerrard
Rainbows - all-inclusive Hiking Weeks
- Mountain Bike trails, 4WD & ATV mountain
roads

Dayspringlodge@hotmail.com
250-353-2810

Deere Ridge Luxury Cabins- B&B

Deluxe Rustic honeymoon, family, group log
cabins. Hot-Tub, fireplaces, decks, BBQ, kitch-
enettes, breakfast avail, non-smoking. Nearby,
Hot Springs, beaches, hiking, golfing. Dogs on
advanced approval.

Invermere, BC (Call for directions)

250-341-3477

www.deereridge.com

Elkford Lion's Campground
Downtown Elkford B.C. on Hwy 43

Gateway to the Elk Lakes
65 Well treed Sites, Firepits, Tables, Free-show-
ers, Flush Toilets & Firewood

www.tourismelkford.ca

or PO Box 108, Elkford, BC V0B 1M0

Fax 250-865-2652

Fernie Chamber of Commerce/
Visitor Information Centre

For all of your tourism, recreational, business
and community service needs, call

**1-877-4-FERNIE
or (250) 423-6868**

102 Commerce Road, Fernie, B.C.

info@ferniechamber.com

www.ferniechamber.com

Fort Steele Resort
& R.V. Park

200 sites, Pull-thrus, Tenting,
Log Cabin for rent, 30/50 amp Heated Pool,
Big Rig Friendly.

Located across from
Ft Steele Heritage Town

1-250-489-4268

www.fortsteele.com

Glacier House Resort
Outdoor Adventure Resort in Revelstoke BC.

ATV & Seadoo Tours, (heli) Hiking, Canoeing,
Wildlife viewing. BC's finest backcountry

Snowmobile Tours & Rentals

679 Westside Road / Box 250

Revelstoke, BC V0E 2S0

1-877-837-9594
www.glacierhouse.com

Kapristo Lodge

Nestled in the mountains overlooking the
Columbia Valley and River, located 10 mins
south of Golden. In addition to our First Class
Lodging our guests can enjoy skiing, dog
sledding, snow shoeing, horseback riding,
mountain biking and hiking.

Phone: 250-344-6048
Email: kapristolodge@redshift.bc.ca
www.kapristolodge.com

Kicking Horse Canyon Bed &
Breakfast

Jeannie and Jerry Cook

644 Lapp Road, Box 56

Golden, BC V0A 1H0

Phone/Fax :1-250-344-6848

Email: kicking_cook@hotmail.com

www.kickinghorsecanyonbb.com

Kokanee Springs Golf Resort

In the Gray Creek/ East Shore area pamper
yourself. With a relaxing stay at the luxurious
Kokanee Springs Gold Resort.
Show your Backroad Mapbook and receive a
25% discount off of our non package room rate.

1-800-979-7999

Crawford Bay, B.C. on the shores of
Kootenay Lake

Kokanee Chalets,
RV Park & Campground

Amid majestic cedar trees
By Kootenay Lake, Crawford Creek
& fantastic Gray Creek Pass
biking/ hiking/ fishing

15981 Hwy 3A
Crawford Bay, BC, V0B 1E0

1-800-448-9292
www.kokaneechalets.com

IMPORTANT NUMBERS

General
Alpine Club of Canada.............................(403) 678-3200
BC Hydro ....www.bchydro.bc.ca/environment
Discover BC 1-800-663-6000
....www.hellobc.com
Enquiry BC 1-800-663-7867
Ferry Information
   Galena Bay ....(250) 837-8416
   Kootenay Lake ....(250) 229-4215
   Needles ....(250) 269-7222
Highway Reports 1-800-550-4997
www.th.gov.bc.ca/bchighways/roadreports/roadreports.htm
To Report Forest Fires...........................1-800-663-5555
....*5555 (cellular phones)
Updates ....http://www.backroadmapbooks.com

BC Forest Service (Road & Trail Conditions)
Ministry of Forests ....http://www.gov.bc.ca/for/
   Arrow Forest District ....(250) 365-8600
   Columbia Forest District.....................(250) 837-7611
   Kootenay Lake Forest District.............(250) 825-1100

   Rocky Mountain Forest District ....(250) 426-1700
   Southern Interior Forest Region..........(250) 828-4131

Fish & Wildlife
BC Wildlife Federation..............................(604) 533-2293
....http://www.bcwf.bc.ca/
Fish and Wildlife Conservation 1-800-663-9453
....http://www.sportfishing.bc.ca

Parks
BC Parks ...http://wlapwww.gov.bc.ca/bcparks/index.htm
   Cranbrook Regional Office.................(250) 489-8570
   Nelson Sub-regional Office ....(250) 354-6333
   Park Reservations... (604)689-9025 / 1-800-689-9025
....www.discovercamping.ca

National Parks....................http://www.parkscanada.ca/
   Banff National Park ....(403) 762-1550
   Glacier & Revelstoke National Park....(250) 837-7500
   Kootenay National Park ....(250) 347-9615
   Yoho National Park ....(250) 343-6783

Index

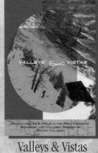